DOMINATION OF EASTERN EUROPE
Native Nobilities and Foreign Absolutism, 1500–1715

OREST SUBTELNY

DOMINATION OF EASTERN EUROPE
Native Nobilities and
Foreign Absolutism, 1500–1715

McGill-Queen's University Press
Kingston and Montreal

Alan Sutton
Gloucester

© McGill-Queen's University Press 1986
ISBN 0-7735-0438-9
Legal deposit first quarter 1986
Bibliothèque nationale du Québec

Printed in Canada

Published in Great Britain in 1986 by
Alan Sutton Publishing Company Limited
30 Brunswick Road
Gloucester GLI IJJ
ISBN 0-86299-237-0

This book has been published with the help of a grant from the
Social Science Federation of Canada, using funds provided by the
Social Sciences and Humanities Research Council of Canada.

Canadian Cataloguing in Publication Data

Subtelny, Orest.
   Domination of Eastern Europe
Bibliography: p.
Includes index.
ISBN 0-7735-0438-9
1. Europe, Eastern – Politics and government.
2. Europe, Eastern – Nobility. 3. Despotism.
I. Title.
DJK47.S87 1986   947   c85-098997-3

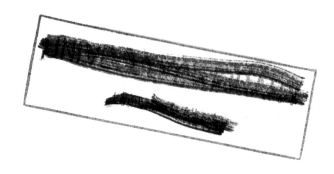

To Maria

Contents

Illustrations

Preface

One of the most important features of the political history of Eastern Europe is the domination of the region by foreign powers. To appreciate this point one need only recall that Eastern Europe has experienced throughout the ages the vast and repeated impact of such varied empires as the Roman, Hunnic, Mongol, Byzantine, Ottoman, Habsburg, and Russian. Nor has the twentieth century lacked for examples of foreign domination. In fact, from the early modern period onwards the political fate of the area has more frequently been controlled by others than by the inhabitants themselves. It is the goal of this study to examine the causes and forms of this condition as it was manifested in the early modern period and particularly in the late seventeenth and early eighteenth centuries.

A striking congruence of events dictated the choice of this time-frame: it was in the final years of the seventeenth century and in the first decade of the eighteenth that five extraregional, absolutist powers – the Habsburgs, Ottomans, Romanovs, Swedish Vasas, and Saxon Wettins – made their decisive efforts to expand their holds on Hungary, Moldavia, Ukraine, Livonia, and Poland-Lithuania respectively. The East Europeans resisted, and in the crucial series of confrontations that followed we find unusually graphic examples of the inability of the societies in the region to withstand foreign encroachment.

While foreign absolutism triumphed in the region, we cannot fully understand its victory without considering the nature of its main opponents (and later allies) – the native nobilities. Therefore, this study also surveys the socio-economic and political circumstances which led to the rise and pre-eminence of the Polish, Hungarian, Livonian, Moldavian, and Ukrainian elites. In so doing it views the struggle for political dominance in early modern Eastern Europe in terms which are quite familiar to students of West European history, that is, essentially as a conflict between monarchical absolutism and noble privilege. However, stress is laid on the East European variant of this widespread confrontation, on the success that the nobilities of the East had in stemming the rise of absolutism in their midst and on their subsequent vulnerability to absolutism from abroad.

We obviously assume that early modern Eastern Europe, which for the purposes of this study is defined as the area between Russia and the Germanies, can be treated as a whole. This assumption rests on an identification of basic economic, social, and political characteristics which the societies of the region shared to a greater or lesser degree and which were far less pronounced or completely absent in the case of their extraregional neighbours. Some of the most important of these characteristic traits are the region's "detour into agrarianism," the inordinately powerful position of its nobilities, and the aforementioned vulnerability to foreign encroachment.

The scope of the study is necessarily broad. Both the nature of the issues raised and the regional context in which they are treated demand it. By casting our nets so wide, we touch upon many aspects of East European history which have already been thoroughly studied, although this has generally been done from a national point of view rather than in an all–East European context. Our approach, therefore, is to synthesize these rarely connected segments of national histories into a coherent regional whole. By identifying the basic similarities among the East European societies, we hope to make a particularly complex aspect of the area's past more comprehensible to students of West European as well as of East European history.

Chapter 1 of the study surveys the economic development of early modern Eastern Europe. It focuses on the crucial differences which evolved between it and the West, differences which must be taken into account in any explanation of the particularities of the region's socio-political structure. In doing so the section also identifies the economic factors that encouraged the rise of the nobilities of the region and the expansion of their prerogatives.

Five East European nobilities – the Polish, Hungarian, Livonian, Moldavian, and Ukrainian – are discussed in chapter 2. The choice of these particular elites was predicated upon the fact that they retained their sovereignty or autonomy the longest and were the last in the region to mount resistance to foreign absolutism. The chapter deals with the institutionalization of the dominance of the nobilities in their respective societies, notes the conditions which made it difficult, if not impossible, for strong monarchical rule to evolve *within* their societies, and identifies the common characteristics shared by these nobilities.

The penetration of foreign absolutism into Eastern Europe is treated in chapter 3. It deals with how and why the Ottomans were able to move into Moldavia, the Habsburgs into Hungary, the Vasas into Livonia, the Romanovs into Ukraine, and the Wettins into Poland-Lithuania. The section also concentrates on the tactics which the foreign absolutist powers applied in attempting to expand their control over their East European holdings at the high point of the absolutist "offensive" in the late seventeenth and early eighteenth centuries.

Whereas previous sections deal with the structural elements of the confrontations between native nobilities and foreign absolutism, chapter 4 treats the conjuncture which brought these tensions to a head. It focuses on a series of decisive conflicts which occurred in the first decade of the eighteenth century between the Livonian, Polish, Ukrainian, Moldavian, and Hungarian elites and their respective Vasa, Wettin, Romanov, Ottoman, and Habsburg sovereigns. It argues that, in the political sense, this crucial decade was the East European equivalent of the "general crisis" which is so well known in West European historiography.

The final chapter examines another characteristically East European feature – political émigrés. It traces the attempts of the defeated leaders of the native nobilities – Ferenc Rákóczi of Hungary, Dimitrie Cantemir of Moldavia, Johann Reinhold von Patkul of Livonia, Ivan Mazepa and Pylyp Orlyk of Ukraine, and, with numerous qualifications, Stanisław Leszczynski of Poland – to continue their struggle from abroad against their absolutist enemies. In that context this first region-wide generation of émigrés emerges as the prototype of the many subsequent waves of East European refugees who fought and fled foreign domination of their homelands.

Work on this study began a decade ago, in 1974, when I taught a course at Harvard University on the nobilities of Eastern Europe. Thanks to the richness of the Widener Library I was able to research and develop ideas which evolved from the course. Subsequently, at Hamilton College I received frequent encouragement and assistance which enabled me to continue my research. A grant awarded by the National Endowment for the Humanities in 1977 as well as grants from York University in 1983 and 1984 were also most helpful. Among the individuals to whom I am grateful for assistance over the years are Ivan Marki of Hamilton College and Margaret Heibert of Harvard University, who aided me in dealing with Hungarian and Romanian-language materials respectively, and Perez Zagorin of the University of Rochester and Richard Hoffman of York University, who read the initial drafts. Susan Kent was a most discerning and meticulous editor in preparing the manuscript for publication by McGill-Queen's University Press. To my close friend, respected mentor, and colleague, the recently deceased Ivan L. Rudnytsky of the University of Alberta, I am especially indebted for his characteristically wise and insightful comments and suggestions. Most of all, I am grateful to my wife, Maria, an accomplished scholar, whose help went far beyond encouragement.

OREST SUBTELNY

DOMINATION OF EASTERN EUROPE

I

The Socio-economic Background

During the fifteenth and sixteenth centuries Eastern Europe experienced a remarkable socio-economic development. To be appreciated fully, this development should be viewed in conjunction with and in contrast to related processes in Western Europe. The importance of this development cannot be overstated.[1] It forms the socio-economic context not only for the period under discussion but for much of the subsequent history of Eastern Europe as well.

Recent research by East European economic historians has done much to elucidate the crucial turn that the economy of the area took in the early modern period.[2] It indicates that in about 1350 the differences between the eastern and western parts of the continent were, in socio-economic terms, essentially of a quantitative rather than of a qualitative nature. Nevertheless, these differences were striking, especially from the demographic point of view. For example, at this time the population densities of France and Italy were 36 and 30 per square kilometre respectively, while those of Poland and Lithuania were calculated at about 6–7 and 2–4 per square kilometre. In 1450 only one East European city – Prague – could be counted among the continent's fourteen largest cities. Of Europe's forty cities whose populations ranged between twenty and forty thousand, only Cracow, Toruń, and Wrocław lay in the East.[3] The differences were just as glaring in volume of trade, early industrial activity, and agricultural productivity.

But between 1350 and 1500, approximately, signs of multi-faceted growth became increasingly evident in Eastern Europe. In Poland, for instance, in part as a result of the heavy influx of Germans and Jews whom its kings had invited, the urban population rose from 15 per cent of the total population in the fourteenth century to 25 per cent in the sixteenth century. Of Europe's roughly 400 towns with a population of four to eight thousand, about 120 were located in the East.[4] A strong inducement for the formation of these new towns was the

East European monarchs' generosity in granting them Magdeburg law, a legal code that was based on German models and allowed towns to exercise wide-ranging autonomy. To be sure, most of these towns were semi-rural in nature; nevertheless, these growing population clusters exerted a marked effect on the local economies. In the process of providing food for the townsmen, peasants were drawn into the market economy. As money came to be used more widely, money rents slowly replaced rents in kind and in obligations, adding fluidity and expansiveness to the economy. Social differentiation, agricultural specialization, and rising productivity became increasingly apparent in the villages of the region. The mining of silver and gold developed rapidly in Hungary, Slovakia, and Transylvania near the end of the fourteenth century, when the Ottomans blocked the import of precious metals from Africa and American gold had not yet begun to flow. Meanwhile, Poland's salt mines grew to be among the largest on the continent. In view of these and similar developments, economic historians have come to the widely shared conclusion that, until roughly 1500, Eastern Europe's economic growth, while still lagging behind that of the West, was certainly following a path of development which was quite similar to that of its western neighbours.

But such widespread developments should not lead one to the conclusion that Eastern Europe's economy was uniform. Naturally, important regional variations did exist. Marian Małowist delineates three major zones whose economic structure and growth rates were quite distinct.[5] The first and most dynamic in the fourteenth century stretched between Bohemia and the Carpathians and included northern Silesia, southeastern Poland, southern Slovakia, and parts of Hungary and Transylvania; the second, which in the sixteenth century was to move to the forefront of economic development, consisted of the lands which bordered on the Baltic Sea; the third encompassed the lands of central Poland, Lithuania, Ukraine, and parts of Russia. Nor do we mean to imply that the boundary between Eastern and Western Europe was all that distinct. Parts of Bohemia, for instance, were so advanced in their socio-economic growth that they straddled the dividing line between East and West. Yet, although Eastern Europe did not represent a single economic unit, it did possess many common basic features.

During the sixteenth century almost the entire continent was booming. Expanding trade, overseas exploration, bustling cities, and plentiful capital had Europe humming with heightened activity. What is especially important for our study is that agriculture, which had long been dormant, again became a profitable undertaking. This was primarily the result of a dramatic rise in population. Not until 1500 did Europe recover from the demographic disasters it had experienced as a result of the Plague in the mid-fourteenth century, disasters which, according to reliable estimates, carried off 25 to 30 per cent of the total population. In the sixteenth and early seventeenth centuries Europe's population grew by leaps and bounds: in 1350 its population was about 51 million; in 1500, 69 million; in 1600, 89 million; and in 1700, 115 million. How were these burgeoning masses to be fed? The problem of food became acute in the more densely populated West. Countries such as Castile, Granada, Andalusia, and even Sicily, the traditional granary, which had formerly exported grain, now began to import it. As a consequence the price of food began to rise. By 1700 the price of grain in Western Europe was almost seven times as high as it had been in 1500.[6] Thus, what had begun as a steady rise in food prices in the early part of the sixteenth century became a veritable price explosion by the turn of that century. American bullion, which appeared in large quantities during the second part of the sixteenth century, was the other major contributing factor in what has come to be known as the Price Revolution of 1550 to 1650. As gold and silver poured into Europe, the value of currencies fell and prices rose dramatically, especially in the case of food. During the sixteenth century wheat prices in Spain increased sixfold, and in France they went up ten times. Some places fared even worse. Between 1529 and 1620 the German town of Speyer experienced a fifteenfold rise in the price of rye and a thirteenfold increase in that of wheat. Rises in the prices of meat and dairy products were not far behind. Meanwhile, increases in real wages and in the price of manufactured products crept up much more slowly. For example, in England during the period between 1475 and 1620, builders' wages increased by 200 per cent and the price of industrial products by 265 per cent, but food prices shot up by 555 per cent. In France the situation was even worse: builders' wages rose by 268 per cent, the price of industrial products by 335 per cent, and food prices by approximately 730 per cent.[7]

It is difficult to overestimate the impact of the Price Revolution on Eastern Europe.[8] To put it simply, the dramatic rise in the price of food had a decisive economic and, eventually, social and political effect on the eastern part of the continent. It thus marks the point at which the essentially quantitative difference between Eastern and Western Europe began to change into a qualitative one. Or, as Immanuel Wallerstein puts it, this development led "the slight edge [of the West] of the fifteenth century to become the great disparity of the seventeenth and the monumental difference of the nineteenth."[9]

As the crowded cities of the West, particularly those of Spain, Portugal, and Italy, clamoured for more food, Eastern landlords began to respond. But why should the East be so responsive, so ready, even eager, to accept the role of Europe's bread-basket? It was, to begin with, more agrarian than the West. With fewer cities to feed, its surplus of food was relatively large. Moreover, there were still in the East, as there were no longer in the West, vast stretches of open, arable land available. While these factors predisposed the region to a food-producing function, it was the promise of quick and easy profits assured by the high food prices that led the landowners of the region to commit themselves so whole-heartedly to this endeavour.

The great East European grain rush began in the early sixteenth century. Noblemen and well-to-do peasants leapt at the opportunity to sell their produce to well-paying agents of Western buyers. Soon, an ever-increasing stream of wheat, corn, barley, cattle, wood, and especially rye flowed westwards. Its main artery was the Baltic–North Atlantic sea route. Greatly improved ship-building techniques made this route the most efficient way of reaching the grain-fields of Poland-Lithuania, which were the largest and richest in all of Eastern Europe. A glance at the tax registers of Gdansk indicates how quickly the grain trade was growing: in the 1460s the city exported about 2,500 *lasts* of rye; in the 1490s the figure was between 6,000 and 10,000; in the 1560s it reached the 40,000 level; and in the 1620s a high point of 75,000 *lasts* was achieved.[10] In the sixteenth century about 35 per cent of Poland's rye went for export; in the seventeenth century the figure was 60 per cent. Other products such as wood and the traditional staples of the area – furs and mead – were also exported in increasing quantities, so much so that by the early seventeenth century the Baltic waterway was the most heavily travelled commercial route in all of Europe.

Baltic cities such as Riga, Reval, and Königsberg benefited greatly from the booming trade, but none as much as the city of Gdansk (Danzig), the unrivalled emporium of the north and the largest staging area for the produce of the East. Situated at the mouth of the Vistula, Gdansk had at its disposal a far-ranging system of waterways which enabled it to reach deep into Poland, Lithuania, and even Ukraine for grain and other products. Moreover, the city won for itself broad autonomy within the Polish-Lithuanian Commonwealth, and this allowed it to regulate the Vistula commerce to its own advantage. As a result, two-thirds to three-quarters of the Commonwealth's grain export passed through its port. In some years, the proportion was as high as nine-tenths. In addition, between 80 and 90 per cent of the important wood export went through Gdansk.[11] But while the merchants of that city dominated the purchase of grain and wood in the hinterland, they did not control the transit trade to the Atlantic ports. This extremely lucrative prize fell to the continent's middlemen par excellence, the Dutch.

Undoubtedly, the formidable commercial and seafaring capabilities of the Dutch accounted largely for their success. But fortune was also on their side. Shortly before the appearance of these new opportunities in the Baltic, the

Hansa, former mistress of the northern sea routes, entered into a protracted and irreversible decline. Another potential rival, England, was as yet too weak to offer serious competition. And the merchants of Gdansk, who initially posed a serious threat to the Dutch shipping monopoly, eventually preferred to concentrate their attention on the handsome profits to be made from the procurement of grain in their hinterlands. Thus, the Dutch soon controlled 70 to 80 per cent of the Baltic grain trade, and Amsterdam became the western terminus of the Baltic route. However, the Dutch needed only about one-quarter of the grain they imported for their own use. The rest was re-exported, usually to Spain and Portugal, sometimes to Italy.[12] In any case, through the intermediary of the Dutch, an important segment of the East European economy was being integrated into that of the West.

Not only sea routes but also land routes bound Eastern producers to Western markets. Shipping grain overland was not a very efficient operation, and it was done on a relatively minor scale. However, land routes were the most practical way of transporting cattle, Eastern Europe's other great food product, to the West. By the early sixteenth century about 10,000 head of cattle, mostly originating from Moldavia and Ukraine, were passing through Lviv and Cracow and moving on to Silesia, Austria, and especially to Nürnberg in southern Germany. By the latter part of the century the number of exported cattle rose to 40,000 per year. Some of this traffic also moved by way of a northerly route from Poznan to Leipzig and then on to central Germany. However, the main cattle breeder and exporter was not Moldavia or Ukraine but Hungary.

Hungary figured as the main exporter of cattle first because the famous *puszta* (plain) was well suited to cattle breeding. Furthermore, the Ottoman invasions had depopulated the land so drastically that labour-intensive work such as large-scale agriculture was not practical. Finally, the land did not have an adequate system of waterways that would provide for economical transportation of grain to far-away markets. For the Hungarians, therefore, cattle breeding and export appeared to be the most feasible way to profit from the new opportunities.

Hungarian and Croatian noblemen, burghers, and peasants plunged into the commerce with cattle with an abandon similar to that of their Polish neighbours' plunge into the grain trade. Between 1548 and 1558 over 550,000 head of Hungarian livestock were sold on Western markets. Later in the century there were instances where 100,000 and even 200,000 head of cattle were driven west in a single year. For most of the sixteenth century livestock constituted approximately 85 to 90 per cent of Hungary's total exports.[13] Most of the cattle were driven to Vienna and from there to such south German cities as Nürnberg and Augsburg. Some of the livestock was also sold in Venice and in other north Italian cities. Thus, Eastern European food products appeared on almost all of the major markets of the West.

It would be useful to pause in our discussion of these dynamic and prosperous times in Eastern Europe to consider the socio-economic and political ramifications of the windfall profits that were being reaped so enthusiastically east of the Elbe. The long-term effects of this boom were not as rosy as might be expected. Recent research by Polish, Hungarian, and Czech economic historians suggests quite strongly that, at best, the sixteenth-century boom was a mixed blessing for the region and that eventually it led to a detour and even a regression in the socio-economic development of the area. The main reason for such a development is to be found in the growing world market that was being created at this time. Instead of producing to meet the relatively limited needs of Cracow, Wrocław, or Prague, East Europeans oriented themselves to the much larger and more profitable trade with far-off Amsterdam, Vienna, or Venice. The seemingly insatiable demand of the West, the high prices it was willing to pay, and the favourable conditions for agriculture in the East encouraged the Easterners to concentrate almost exclusively on the production of food, to the detriment of other sectors of the economy. Why invest in the manufacture of textiles or in mining when grain or cattle brought in much higher profits, especially when English wool, Dutch linen, German metal products, herring, and salt could be had in exchange for Eastern produce?

Gradually there emerged what became a familiar pattern in world trade: the West imported raw materials and food from Eastern Europe and exported to it its finished products and luxury goods. The far-reaching implications of this relationship were lost on the East European nobles who exported the grain. They felt that all the trading advantages were on their side. For example, one of the leading tribunes of the Polish nobility in the sixteenth century, Mikołaj Rey, stated, "There are many lands and kingdoms who work daily for us, like peasants ... and we Poles enjoy by means of little effort and work the fruits of their valuable works."[14] Little did the East European noblemen know that a semi-colonial relationship was in the making, in which their part of the continent was gradually becoming ever more dependent on the West. The historical significance of this relationship has been neatly summarized by a modern Hungarian scholar who maintains that "Western European capitalism grew up on the East European market; with the profits the West made in the East, it could afford to expand all over the world."[15]

If the emerging continental divergence had developed more symmetrically – that is, if agriculture had declined in the West as did mining and manufacture in the East – then the mutual dependence of the two areas might have been roughly equal. But agriculture continued to be a major component of the Western economy, providing it with a balance and resilience that contrasted sharply with the emerging economic one-sidedness and vulnerability of the East. Like a mastodon that over-adapts, Eastern Europe was becoming ever more vulnerable to sudden shifts in her economic and political environment. No longer could the differences between Eastern and Western European socio-economic conditions be explained simply in terms of time-lag. A parting of the ways was taking place, with the West moving on to capitalism while the East retreated deeper into agrarianism.[16]

For the nobility of Eastern Europe the long-term effects of the grain boom were of little interest. Their main concern was to take advantage of it. Specifically, they sought to utilize their lands in the most profitable manner possible. The profit motive caught hold of the nobility and in the late sixteenth and early seventeenth centuries led to a crucial transformation of the forms and conditions of land ownership. Previously, noblemen had let out their lands to peasants in return for money rents and dues in kind. But in times of rising prices and growing fortunes, incomes such as these were too static. Rents were difficult to raise because there were limits on the amount of money a peasant could obtain by selling his goods on the already saturated local markets. The existing technology set limits on the amount of surplus peasants could produce and pass on to their lords. The noblemen, therefore, took matters into their own hands. They consolidated and took over the management of their estates, which were now organized specifically for the large-scale production of grain for foreign and, to a lesser extent, local markets. Land jumped in value. Large and medium-sized latifundia, established by means of colonization, consolidation, or expropriation of peasants, appeared everywhere. Estimates put the percentage of arable land which became demesne east of the Elbe at 30 to 50 per cent. The transition from what the Germans call the *grundherrschaft* to the *gutsherrschaft* was well on its way.[17]

The problem which immediately confronted the aspiring agrarian entrepreneurs was that of labour. Always a thorny issue, it did have, from the noblemen's point of view, one positive aspect: in the economic undertaking, labour was the one variable which landowners could control. In the early phases of the transition, hired labour was often used. But it soon became apparent that the most effective means of maximizing profits was to cut the cost of labour. Using medieval precedents, noblemen began to demand labour services from their peasants in return for access to the land. Initially this was done to avoid paying cash, which was in short supply in Eastern Europe, for the peasant's labour. Gradually, as the political influence of the nobility grew, noblemen realized that they could raise their demands with impunity. For example, in

Hungary in 1500 the usual corvée was one day per week; by the middle of the century it had risen to two days, and in the early seventeenth century it was four, five, and even six days per week. In Poland, in the crown lands of the Cracow palatinate, peasant plots, which averaged sixteen hectares per family, constituted 70.3 per cent of the arable land in 1564. By 1660 the percentage had sunk to 43.5 per cent. In the period between 1600 and 1725 the buying power of the nobility in Poland rose by 180 per cent, while that of the peasantry fell by 400 per cent.[18] Thus, the renewed enserfment of the peasants in Eastern Europe – which Engels called "the second edition of serfdom" – moved inexorably ahead.

There were numerous variations in the timing, extent, and circumstances which accompanied the formation of the East European demesne. Our sketch is clearly of an ideal type. Many East European noblemen organized their estates not in strict accordance with this model but rather by combinations of old rents and dues and new corvée labour. The direct impulse for the formation of the demesne also varied widely. In the Baltic, where the *gutsherrschaft* appeared earliest and in its purest form, foreign markets provided the strongest impetus for its formation. The same was true of Poland-Lithuania, although there the demesne based on corvée labour was weakly developed on the eastern fringes of the kingdom, in Byelorussia, Ruthenia, and Ukraine proper, which were far from the Baltic ports. In Hungary, by contrast, the internal markets – specifically, the need to feed the troops on the Ottoman border – encouraged large-scale grain production. Moreover, this was not the major economic undertaking of the Hungarians, at least not in the sixteenth century. Both in Hungary and in Moldavia the demesne was often associated with acquiring control of pasturage, and corvée was often utilized for work in wine-fields, not in grain-fields. In Bohemia and Moravia grain production was also not the initial primary interest of noblemen. Their predominant commercial activity involved the cultivation of fish-ponds. Only after the Thirty Years' War and the influx of foreign estate owners did the typical grain-producing demesne develop here. One could go on indefinitely pointing out the variations in the forms and development of the demesne east of the Elbe. Yet, while it is necessary to keep these variations in mind, they might lead one to miss the overall pattern. The basic fact remains that in the late sixteenth and early seventeenth centuries a new and eventually predominant form of economic production – the demesne based on corvée labour – appeared throughout Eastern Europe. And its complete control was in the hands of the nobility.

Not only the peasants but also the towns were hard hit by the development of the demesne economy. Noblemen were quick to realize that costs could be cut by avoiding the towns' middlemen. In selling their grain or oxen they tried to deal with foreign buyers directly, encouraging them to come to the demesnes to do business and preventing local merchants from acting as commercial middlemen. Further, the falling buying power of the peasantry meant that those internal and local markets were also drying up. Quite consciously the nobility was undermining the integrity of the towns.

Coinciding with the rise of the demesne was a series of measures passed by noble-controlled parliaments and openly aimed against the towns. In 1565 the Polish *sejm* (parliament) forbad merchants to travel abroad for goods, thus inviting foreign merchants to come to Poland. In 1608 in Hungary, the nobles succeeded in limiting the number of royal towns that could be established to the number that had existed in 1514. In Livonia, the struggle between the nobility and the towns often led to open confrontations. Matters had gone so far that in Poland the *sejm* could dictate to the towns the prices they had to pay for foodstuffs, which, quite predictably, were relatively high, and also the prices they could charge for their finished products, which, just as predictably, were relatively low.[19] In Hungary and Poland-Lithuania noblemen could live in towns without being subject to town laws or taxes. Moreoever, they could engage in trade without losing their noble status. It was not without reason that townsmen often referred to the nobles as "parasites."

Unable to withstand the pressure from the countryside, many townsmen decided to join it. Rich burghers invested their capital in demesne, obtained patents of nobility, and married their daughters into noble families. Craftsmen, unable to bear the high cost of living in the towns, often moved their shops to the manors of the nobles. An indication of how far the countryside had encroached upon the towns was the rise of vegetable gardens, small fields, and mills in the towns. For instance, in Košice in 1480 there were only 17 mills and no acreage; by 1633, with roughly the same population, the town had 464 mills, many vegetable gardens, and even produced 2,225 *scheffel* of grain.[20] In a word, the towns of Eastern Europe were being re-agrarianized.

But there were exceptions. A Polish economic historian has noted that, while many old towns degenerated, new ones, often founded by wealthy magnates, did appear.[21] And it is necessary to differentiate between the plight of the small and medium towns, which were especially vulnerable to the pressure of the nobility, and the large towns like Gdansk or Cracow, which not only succeeded in protecting their own interests but even managed to prosper. Nor was the decline of many of the towns due exclusively to external factors. The conservatism of the guilds and the opportunism of the patricians contributed much to the decline. The final blow came in the mid-seventeenth and early eighteenth centuries, when wars and epidemics mercilessly devastated the towns of the region.

During this period the general outlines of the socio-economic situation east of the Elbe were well established. The nobility was dominant economically, socially, and politically. The peasantry was subjugated, and the towns were isolated and weak. The region's economic development had taken a sharp, initially favourable but eventually disastrous detour. Instead of moving ahead towards urbanization, proto-industrialization, and economic integration as did the West, Eastern Europe veered further away into agrarianism, urban underdevelopment, and technological stagnation. Many factors served to create this situation, but for our purposes the one which deserves special consideration is the role of the demesne. It was the building-block on which the region's economic system rested. But its significance went beyond economics – the demesne was the microcosm of society.

If one word can epitomize the impact of the demesne on society as a whole, it is *atomization*. The demesne severed the links of the countryside with the towns and with foreign lands; it raised the tensions between noblemen and peasants to an irreconcilable level; and it elevated one estate far above the others. Regionalism and parochialism flourished during the period of the demesne economy. Ultimately the institution performed both an economic and a symbolic function; on the one hand it provided noblemen with the means by which to establish their grip on society, and on the other it served as a model for the role the nobility aspired to play in society as a whole.

II

Five East European Elites

Since Eastern Europe of the sixteenth and seventeenth centuries was rapidly becoming ever more agrarian, a few initial remarks about some of the general characteristics of agrarian societies might well be in order. Social scientists have noted that one of the most striking features of this generic type of society, especially when compared to its horticultural predecessors and industrial successors, is its marked proclivity for sharp social inequalities.[1] It appears that this feature is a function of one of agrarian society's most notable achievements – the ability to produce a relatively steady and sizeable surplus. The existence of this surplus produces an effect which, for our purposes, is especially noteworthy: it allows a stratum of military specialists to develop and encourages some technological innovations, primarily of a military nature. With specialized skills and sophisticated weapons exclusively at their disposal, military men become much more capable of providing their societies with effective protection. But the added security comes at a heavy price: the military specialists – whether they be knights, boyars, or samurai – eventually find themselves in a position which allows them to exploit society's surplus at will and to demand positions of privilege in that society. Thus, a gap develops between the producers of the surplus and those who control it, a gap so great that, in some cases, it leads the military elite or nobility to view itself as being of a different race from that to which the mass of the population belongs.

Another related and striking feature of agrarian societies is their high incidence of warfare. According to the extensive computations of Pitirim Sorokin, the median percentage of years that eleven European societies spent at war from the medieval and early modern period to 1925 was 46 per cent.[2] During the period which is of interest to us, war was even more frequent. For example, in the two-hundred-year period between 1500 and 1700 Russia spent 136 years at war, Austria 149, and the Ottoman empire 170.[3] With war such a pervasive activity, it is understandable why warlords, that is, the later monarchs, rose to prominence. As kingships and nobilities evolved, they became the two primary centres of power and privilege. It might be added here that, because of this division of powers in medieval Europe, law, which regulated the relationship between these two seats of power, was of paramount importance in the feudal societies of Western and, in some cases, Eastern Europe.

As might be expected, the relationship between European monarchs and the feudal nobilities generally was characterized by tension, marked by protracted periods of mutual suspicion and struggle, yet studded by moments of co-operation. As Gerhard Lenski puts it, "The outward form of these struggles was highly variable, but their basic character was essentially the same: each party constantly fought to maximize its own rights and privileges."[4] In these widespread, recurrent conflicts the ruler's basic goal was to make the nobility's privileged position dependent upon the performance of various services to the monarch, services usually of a military and administrative nature. Meanwhile, the nobility was most intent on obtaining a secure, hereditary hold on its privileges and properties and on reducing the ruler to the status of primus inter pares, or at least to that of a distant overlord who did not have the right or capacity to interfere in the affairs of the nobility. In these contests the nobles had a great advantage, for, as long as the kings did not develop other options, they were totally dependent on the nobility in so far as the conduct of war and the administration of the land were concerned. Clearly conscious of their strengths, the nobles were often able not only to ensure their rights and privileges but to encroach deeply on those of their sovereigns. This was especially true if they had the advantage of an economic windfall. This power of the nobility was demonstrated most notably in Eastern Europe. And it is to an overview of the leading political and socio-economic elites of this part of Europe that we will now turn.

THE POLISH *SZLACHTA*

Rooted in the medieval arrangement whereby, in return for the military service of knights, kings provided lands and privileges, the Polish *szlachta* was similar in its origins to the other European nobilities. What made the *szlachta* unique, however, was its unmatched ability to subvert these original compacts, to its own uncompromising advantage.[5] Economic developments certainly worked in its favour. With the spacious lands of Poland under its control, the nobility was able to profit immensely, both in economic and in political terms, from the great grain boom of the sixteenth century. But important as it was, the grain boom alone is not sufficient to explain the *szlachta*'s eventual dominance. Even before it occurred, the Polish nobility had demonstrated a remarkable ability for wringing concessions from its monarchs. This was facilitated by the presence of certain peculiarities in the formative process of the *szlachta*.

If there is one feature of the *szlachta* which historians invariably emphasize, that feature is its vast size. While in Western Europe there were on the average one to two nobles per hundred in the population at large, in Poland the proportion was about one in ten, and in some older, more settled Polish lands such as Mazowia it reached as high as one in five. What were the reasons for the *szlachta*'s great numbers? Although Polish historiography is surprisingly vague on this important question, at least part of the answer seems to lie in the enduring survival of clan and local solidarity.[6] Strong clan ties, evident as late as the fifteenth century, led clansmen to help each other in attaining and maintaining privileged status. Reinforcing these organic bonds were artificial ones. When heraldic devices were introduced in the twelfth and thirteenth centuries, the clientele of the great magnates, often consisting of poorer relations and indigent clansmen, tended to adopt the devices and mottos of their leaders. In the process, extended "heraldic families" were formed which included diverse elements of the nascent nobility. These communalist tendencies in the formation of the Polish nobility were reflected in the term *szlachta*, which was derived from the German *geschlecht* (family, lineage), in the ceremony of the "adoption" of newly created noblemen into heraldic families, and in the practice of referring to these as "brothers." While clan solidarity in Poland survived much longer than it did in the West, legal distinctions between nobles and non-nobles were introduced only in the fourteenth to fifteenth centuries, about a century later than in most of Europe. Thus, with more candidates having a longer time to achieve the privileged status accorded by the *ius militare* (military law), the numbers and the political weight of the *szlachta* were bound to grow.

Another striking feature in the evolution of the *szlachta* is the speed with which it managed to gain allodial or hereditary rights to its landholdings. This was the result in part of the political situation which obtained during the feudal fragmentation of the twelfth to thirteenth centuries, when powerful regional magnates threatened to undermine the Piast dynasty and to impose their will on the local *rycerzy* (knights). In order to gain the support of the knights against the magnates, the Piast princes began to grant them lands with hereditary rights of ownership in both the male and female lines. Furthermore, noblemen who colonized and developed empty lands also established hereditary claims to them. Thus, in one way or another, control over the land gradually passed out of the hands of the princes and into those of the rising knights.[7]

Related to these developments was the absence in Poland of a feudal hierarchy of counts, dukes, and princes, an absence which resulted from the political process of the unification of Piast lands in the fourteenth century. Twelfth-century Poland was the domain of an entire dynasty of Piast princes, not of a single ruler. It was to these princes that the *rycerzy* owed their allegiance. However, when Lokietek (died 1333) and his son, Casimir (died 1370), managed to remove their Piast rivals and consolidate their lands, the knights transferred their allegiance to them as the only remaining rulers of the dynasty. Since it was in the interests of neither the king (Lokietek assumed the royal title in 1320) nor the nobility to have the recently defeated princes and magnates serve as feudal intermediaries, the relationship of the evolving nobility with the king became a direct one.[8] It was the theoretically equidistant position of all members of the nobility to the monarch, regardless of their socio-economic condition, which prevented a legal distinction between magnates and noblemen from arising and which discouraged the introduction of such distinguishing titles as count, duke, or prince. Hence the foundation was laid for the treasured concept, if not the reality, of the equality of all members of the *szlachta*.

During the fourteenth to sixteenth centuries the *szlachta* managed to transform its initial advantages into a privileged and predominant position in society. Initially the *szlachta* concentrated on obtaining the best possible terms in its relationship with the kings; it then evolved a representative system which allowed it not only to participate in the highest levels of government but actually to control government. In the process it managed to limit the prerogatives and advantages of its two major rivals, the king and the magnates.

A fortuitous circumstance greatly facilitated the achievement of the *szlachta*'s goals. In 1370 the native Piast dynasty became extinct. Henceforth many of Poland's kings would be foreigners, and as such they were most insecure about their own and their children's claims to the Polish crown. This in turn led them to barter far-ranging concessions in return for the support of the *szlachta*. Thus, between 1370 and 1433, during the reigns of Louis of Anjou and the Lithuanian Jagiello and their children, the nobility won a number of concessions, including the commutation of dues and obligations except for the nominal payment of 2 *groszen* per *lan* (one "small" *lan* = 25 hectares or 62 acres); guarantees of inviolability of person and property except when sanctioned by court rulings; exclusive rights to high secular (and later) ecclesiastical offices; guarantees of military service only within the homeland's boundaries, or of special payment if nobles were required to fight abroad; and the right to be consulted about the raising of a general levee. Especially noteworthy were the limitations on military service, for they signalled basic changes which were taking place in the nature of the *szlachta*. As the economic boom got under way, the Polish nobility transferred its attention from making war to making money. Or, as Polish historians put it, the *rycerz* became a *zemianin* (demesne owner). Not surprisingly, therefore, the next series of concessions wrested from the king at the end of the fifteenth century was economic in nature and stipulated that nobles could buy salt at lower prices; have access to lumber from crown lands; prohibit burghers from owning land; tie peasants to the land and exercise judicial jurisdiction over them; and pay no taxes on exports and personal imports. With political and economic prerogatives such as these, the Polish nobles were now ready and able to assume a predominant position in their society.

With privilege came exclusivity. During the fifteenth century the question of who was and who was not a *szlachcic* was finally defined. As the *szlachta* fought less, the military deeds of its ancestors increased in value. Only if one could prove that three generations of forebears had been under the *ius militare* could he be accepted as a nobleman. Eventually, only the *sejm* had the power to name a nobleman, and from the fifteenth century to 1795 only 1,400 new noblemen were created. Moreover, the privilege could be lost by a nobleman only if he engaged in trade.[9] Entry into the privileged estate was quickly becoming closed.

From the growing influence of the *szlachta* in general, and the increasing need of the kings to consult it in particular, there arose the further need for a representative body of the nobility. Previously, if the *szlachta* had any grievances, the most common way it had of airing them was to form a confederation – an alliance of one or more estates which disbanded once the specific goals of the alliance were achieved. But neither the confederations nor the tumultuous, haphazard local gatherings of the *szlachta* could take the place of a more structured, institutionalized forum for the expression of the views of the entire estate. This need was met by the *sejm*, which evolved from two basic elements: the senate or the former council of the king, which was usually the domain of magnates; and the assembly of noble representatives, who were elected by their local assemblies (*sejmiki*). Eventually a two-chamber institution emerged which gave the nobility as a whole direct influence on the conduct of government.[10] Since no limits were set on the prerogatives of the *sejm*, its influence increased rapidly, as did that of the *szlachta*. This was especially true after 1505 and the passage of the famous *nihil novi* law, which forbade the king to legislate on matters concerning the nobility or to introduce innovations without the concurrence of the nobility. The period which Polish historians call "*szlachta* democracy" was now well under way.

It would be naïve to imagine that the *szlachta* had won these concessions easily. It had to face stiff competition from both the king and the magnates. Despite equality before the law, shared heraldic devices, and common participation in the *sejm*s and *sejmiki*, there was a vast gap between the average, isolated *szlachcic*, with his one to three *lan*s of land, and the magnate, who often controlled hundreds of thousands of acres and had easy access to the court which allowed him to attain high office which, in turn, provided him with even more lands. The Jagiellonian dynasty was also a power to contend with. It presided over the unification of the land, one-sixth of which it controlled, and waged successful wars against the German knights (as a result of which Polish nobles gained access to the Baltic ports), Muscovy, and the Ottomans. Moreover, in the 1490s it created a Jagiellonian dynastic conglomerate which briefly consisted of Poland, Hungary, and Bohemia. When, therefore, in the first half of the sixteenth century, the crown and the magnates united against the *szlachta*, the latter was faced with a mortal threat.

The battle was joined primarily over the issue of the seventy-five major government offices and of the lands connected with them. Realizing that the distribution of high offices was the means by which the crown won its adherents and magnates enriched themselves, the *szlachta* insisted on limiting this practice. In 1537 it gathered en masse and for the first time declared a *rokosz*, an act of open opposition to the king, and threatened civil war. Surprised by this show of determination, King Sigismund I and his supporters retreated. Growing increasingly confident, in subsequent years the *szlachta* initiated a movement called *egzekucja praw*, or, in loose English translation, "execution-of-the-laws"(so named because the *szlachta* came to the far-reaching conclusion that the entire problem had arisen because the "good old laws" had been ignored), which forced many magnates to return to the treasury lands they had held illegally. Moreover, it forbade any individual from holding more than one office lest he accumulate too much land. However, because the execution-of-the-laws movement was never fully implemented, it hurt but did not permanently cripple the magnates.

Much more serious were the setbacks suffered by the Polish kings. Again it was a dynastic crisis – the Achilles' heel of royal rule – that caused the greatest damage. Unable to beget an heir, Sigismund August, the last male of Jagiellonian line, died in 1572. Even before his death both the *szlachta* and the magnates had been jockeying to take advantage of the interregnum. In the end, at the cost of royal prerogatives, both realized their goals, but with the magnates enjoying a clear advantage. After much infighting, Henry of Valois was chosen king. But he was not overjoyed by the honour, for the terms on which he was chosen were demeaning for one used to Western absolutist principles. Henry was required to agree, for himself and his successors, that henceforth every king would be elected freely by direct vote of the nobles (*viritim*), every nobleman having the right to participate in the election. Furthermore, the king was to conclude a bilateral agreement with the nobility (*pacta conventa*) as to the specific terms under which he was to rule; and should the king ever in future not adhere to these terms, the nobility had the right to withhold its obedience (this was a clear echo of the medieval right of resistance). Within a year of signing these terms, Henry surreptitiously returned to France. But the Henrician articles remained to serve as a revered acquisition of the *szlachta* and as a permanent handicap to its kings.

Despite the political struggles, the sixteenth and early seventeenth centuries were Poland's golden age. Economic prosperity was at its height. The momentous union between Poland and Lithuania in 1569 more than doubled the territory of what was now called the Commonwealth (*Rzeczpospolita*), making it one of the largest polities in Europe. In sharp contrast to the West, wars, especially of the religious variety, were avoided, while cultural activity flourished. Little wonder that the Polish *szlachcic* had become convinced that the society in which he lived was the best of all possible worlds.

For the Polish nobleman, the preservation of what he came to call his "golden freedoms" now became his paramount concern. For him these freedoms did not possess abstract value; rather, they represented a concrete patrimony passed on to him by his ancestors, and he nervously sought to protect them in an increasingly unstable world. Clearly, the way in which he could best do this was to preserve the status quo. Since the guardian of the status quo was the law, it came to be endowed with sovereign authority. This entailed a modification of the role of the king. According to the tribunes of the nobility, the king was primarily to be a military man who protected his subjects and cared for their interests, in particular for those of the *szlachta*. He was to adhere meticulously to the law and to rule not by means of power but with humanity and generosity. The nobleman-citizen (*obywatel*), however, always had to be ready to fight for his rights and his land himself. This, to his way of thinking, obviated the need for a strong army and heavy taxes. Furthermore, through his interest in political affairs and participation in the *sejm* and *sejmiki*, the nobleman was always to be on his guard against innovation, which was considered, ipso facto, to be harmful.

Since the old ways were increasingly considered to be the best ways, traditionalism became the supreme political and cultural value of the *szlachta*. This view was buttressed by the spreading Counter-Reformation in the seventeenth century and by the way of life of the nobleman-*zemianin*. There was, however, an essential conflict between the roles of citizen and estate owner, which the nobleman had sought to combine. In contrast to the idealized nobleman-citizen, with his activism in public affairs, the actual nobleman-*zemianin* wished primarily to lead a quiet, mundane life, enjoying the fruits of his estate (*folwark*). Geographically isolated and immersed in domestic matters, the noble landowner developed a suspicion of everything foreign, an attitude common among agriculturalists. At the same time, his social isolation from the peasant and the townsman increased, leading him to see himself and his colleagues as belonging to a class apart and as a separate race marked by its own distinct origins, customs, privileges, and dress. These aspects of the developing culture of the *szlachta* provided the basis for the Sarmatian myth, which became the embodiment of the nobility's view of itself.[11]

During the seventeenth century there emerged among the *szlachta*, with the aid of its chroniclers, the conviction that it was descended from the ancient Sarmatians, who at some time in the past had conquered the lands between the Vistula and the Dnieper and enslaved the inhabitants. In time this myth developed into a virtual ideology, providing as it did a rationale for the belief that the rights and privileges of the nobility were inviolable and that the nobility always had and always would dominate society. Its adherents also cultivated the xenophobic belief that since other nobilities had betrayed the ideals of knightly freedom, the Commonwealth must cut itself off from a Europe diseased with the absolutist tyranny. By extension, the myth eventually took on messianic tendencies: it encouraged the nobility to view itself as chosen by God to protect Christianity's frontiers against the Muslim threat, to believe as well that a true noble had to be a Catholic. Whether the Sarmatian myth was a cause or an effect of the *szlachta*'s increasing complacency and self-delusion is difficult to say, but it is clear that it clouded the nobility's vision and its political instincts precisely at a time when these were needed most.

In 1648 the storm struck with unexpected fury. The entire Ukraine burst forth in a violent Cossack-led uprising which expelled the Polish *szlachta* and magnates from their lands. Just as the Commonwealth was recovering from this devastating blow and preparing to retake the land, the Ukrainians, placing themselves under the tsar's protection, drew Muscovy into the conflict, which, with only two brief intermissions, lasted until 1667. In the midst of this war, Sweden, desirous of gaining the Baltic ports, launched an invasion (1655–60) together with the Transylvanians, Brandenburgians, and Ukrainians. The Commonwealth was plunged into the "Deluge." After a brief respite the Lubomirski *rokosz* (1665–6) sparked a civil war. Six years later the Ottomans invaded and conquered Polish Podolia, initiating a conflict that lasted from 1672 to 1676 and from 1683 to 1699. It was a wonder that the Commonwealth survived the strain of all these events. To a large extent this was due to the solidarity of the *szlachta*, which held the Polish, Lithuanian, and Ukrainian (Ruthenian) components of the Commonwealth together.

But survival came at a tremendous cost. As a result of the wars and the ensuing famine, pestilence, and territorial losses, the Commonwealth lost over 20 per cent of its territory and almost 50 per cent of its population by 1667. Moreover, the basis of the economy, the grain export, dropped by 80 per cent by 1690. These catastrophic demographic and economic losses had vast political ramifications: the rise of the magnates, evident since 1569, when the vast magnate-owned lands of Lithuania and Ukraine were incorporated into the Commonwealth, rapidly accelerated and became irreversible.[12] It was difficult for the *szlachcic*, who for generations had boasted of his equality with the magnates and watched carefully that the wealthy clique in his midst did not usurp power, to accept the magnates' growing dominance. But he had no choice; it was dictated by economic necessity. The formerly well-to-do *szlachcic* who owned less than one hundred *lans* did not possess the resources to rebuild his devastated and depopulated estate. Nor was he capable, in view of the weakness of the central government, to protect himself from rebellious peasants and growing anarchy. His only option was to sell out to the magnates, who were much more capable of absorbing the losses brought about by the Deluge. As his money dwindled as a result of the raging inflation, the *szlachcic* more often than not entered the magnate's service. Although the magnates were careful to espouse continually the slogans of *szlachta* equality and freedom for their own political purposes, behind the rhetoric it was clear that the *szlachta* was fast losing its economic and political independence.

The magnates were not a legally or formally defined group with its own institutions. In fact, it served their interests to emphasize constantly that they were a part of the "*szlachta* nation." And modern Polish scholars are still unclear on the precise definition of the magnate stratum. In general some of the characteristic features of the magnates were vast estates (over twenty thousand acres), incumbency, especially over several generations, in the senate or senate-level offices, the resultant access to crown lands, and the external signs of prestige and power such as large private militias and courts. Although not originally a hereditary group, in time, especially in the eighteenth century, such leading magnate families as the Lubomirski, Opalinski, Potocki, Jablonowski, and Sieniawski in Poland and the Radziwill, Pac, and Sapieha in Lithuania tended to intermarry with increasing frequency.[13]

The magnates, less than one hundred families in number, preferred to remain on their vast eastern latifundia. Amid hundreds of thousands, even millions of acres, thousands of villages, and dozens of towns, they built up vast administrative staffs, militias numbering in the thousands, and splendid courts. The term *kinglets*, which is often applied to them, was apt, for with the king helpless to control them and the *szlachta* dependent on them, the magnates were practically sovereign. They even conducted their own foreign policies, concluded agreements with foreign powers, and kept their residents at foreign courts. The one institution that might have claimed sovereignty over them – the *sejm* – they emasculated. In 1652 Władysław Sicinski, a *szlachta* delegate at the *sejm*, backed by a group of magnates, invoked for the first time the notorious *liberum veto*, the right of a single delegate to break off the deliberations and dissolve the *sejm* by invoking the principle of unanimity. Thereafter, up to 1794 only a minority of *sejm*s concluded without interruption. It was clear that the *sejm* was no longer a viable instrument of government. As a result the centre of political activity shifted to the sixty-four *sejmiki*, which were completely controlled by the magnates. As the magnate oligarchy took hold, sovereignty became totally fragmented. Indeed, central government, not to speak of statehood, had practically ceased to exist.

POLAND-LITHUANIA: SELECTED STATISTICS[14]

Population and area circa 1700

Population: approximately 8 million (about 50% non-Polish)
Area: 727,000 square kilometres: 415,000 crown (Poland); 312,000 Lithuania
Population density: 15 per square kilometre in Poland; 5 in Lithuania

Social structure

Nobles: approximately 10%
Townsmen (13% burghers, 7% Jews): 20%
Peasants: 70%

Landholdings

Crown: 19% of all cultivated land
Church: 17%
Nobles: 63%
Magnates with 500 *lan* or more held 30% of all cultivated land (about a dozen magnate families owned 25% of all cultivated land).
The nobles of the Commonwealth owned in sum about 80,000 entire estates and about 70,000 parts of estates. They controlled 66% of the peasants and about 50% of the urban population.

The army of the Commonwealth

Peacetime: 12,000–15,000; wartime: 30,000–40,000
About 90% of the Commonwealth's budget went to maintain the army.

THE HUNGARIAN NOBILITY

Of all the nobilities of Europe, the Hungarian most closely resembled that of Poland. Indeed, up to 1526 its internal development was almost identical with that of the Polish nobility. Both benefited greatly from the economic boom of the fifteenth and sixteenth centuries, during which time they were successful in limiting their monarchs and magnates, in pushing the towns into economic and political regression, and in maintaining the peasants in abject bondage. In fact, the members of the two nobilities frequently acknowledged each other as equals without equal in the defence of nobles' rights and on those grounds laid the foundations of the traditional Polish-Hungarian friendship.[15]

But there were also important differences between the two nobilities, some of degree and others of a qualitative nature. The towns were never quite as powerless in Hungary as they were in Poland; the kings were more assertive; and Hungarian magnates, at least under the Habsburgs, did not become the semi-sovereigns they did in the north. The qualitative differences were largely the result of external pressures – specifically, of the Ottoman wars, which left two-thirds of Hungary under foreign domination for over 150 years. It will suffice to say at this point that the Ottoman presence in Hungary led to an almost constant state of war, which forced the Hungarian nobles to choose as their kings members of a strong dynasty. This meant that their royal competitors for power were much more dangerous than any of those the Poles ever had. Finally, religious differences between the Hungarian nobility and the Habsburg sovereigns added a dimension to internal politics that was absent in Poland.

There was yet another difference between the Hungarians and the Poles, one having to do with the question of origins. While the Polish *szlachta* had had to invent the myth of its descent from ancient Sarmatian conquerors, the Magyars, about 400,000 in number, actually had come out of the East as a conquering nomadic horde. Like the Lombards in Italy, the Franks in Gaul, the Varangians in Rus' (Kievan Russia), and the Normans in England, the Hungarian nobility had originally defined itself through an act of conquest.

During the tenth to eleventh centuries, as the Hungarians gradually adopted sedentary ways, the major structures of their new ruling establishment began to emerge. The Arpad dynasty, chosen from among the tribal leaders, defined and mastered the functions of kingship. It provided the society with military and political leadership, took responsibility for its security, and, by establishing a royal council and assembly of elders, organized the rudiments of non-tribal government.[16] Meanwhile, the younger members of the dynasty and magnates, some of whom were descendants of tribal elites, others of whom had achieved their status by serving as royal officials, thereby gained practically independent control of vast parts of the land. As a group they were strong enough to overthrow or, if legitimacy demanded it, replace one Arpad with another if he threatened their interests. The only real check on their power was their mutual

feuding, which allowed more astute princes to apply a policy of divide et impera. With the introduction of Christianity in the tenth century, at which time
the Arpads received the kingly title, the ranks of the magnates were augmented
by ecclesiastical lords, who, growing rich and powerful on the tithe and other
donations, actively competed for power with their secular counterparts.[17]

The formation of a large class of military servitors (*servientes regis*), which was
to constitute one of the major sources of the Hungarian nobility, was largely
the work of the kings. Needing men to garrison their extensive system of seventy
castles, which, up to the thirteenth century, were all in their hands, the kings
offered land in reward for military service. It was a typical feudal arrangement,
except that, by comparison with the West, it was delayed by several centuries.
Because the semi-free military servitors were directly dependent on the kings,
sub-infeudation was not as widespread as in Western Europe, marking another
feature which Hungarian nobles shared with Polish nobles.

In reaction to the king's growing military capacity the magnates began to
recruit their own military servitors and tried to gain control over those in royal
service. During the thirteenth century this led to the evolution of the institution of *familiares*.[18] Because many of the military servitors held lands in areas
where the magnates were all-powerful, they were forced to join the retinues
of the magnates while still nominally serving the king. In return they were
offered protection and, a departure from Western vassalage, sustenance by their
overlords. As the king's forces diminished, those of the magnates grew, but so
did the numbers and dissatisfaction of the more stringently exploited military
servitors. This set the stage for the proclamation of the Golden Bull (1222) by
Andrew II, the first, although very tenuous basis for the nascent nobility's constitutional rights.

Unlike the Magna Carta, to which it is often compared, the Golden Bull
was not primarily a response to the grievances of the magnates against the king,
but rather to those of the military servitors against the magnates. After
threatening revolt, the military servitors and other fighting men, appearing
as a body for the first time and now referred to as *miles* and *nobiles*, won three
important concessions: the right to be judged by the king and not by the
magnates; payment for participating in foreign military campaigns; and the
right to dispose of their lands more freely. If the lowly military servitors could
obtain such concessions, so could the magnates. Therefore, the Golden Bull
also acquiesced to the magnates' demands that no foreigners be allowed to hold
office or own lands, and it acknowledged, with heavy consequences, the *ius
resistendi*, the right to resist the king legally if he did not adhere to the conditions of his rule. Actually, despite its later fame, the Golden Bull was often
ignored by subsequent kings, and it was not until 1351 that the Hungarian nobility succeeded in having it confirmed and implemented.[19]

Despite these periodic agreements, Hungary experienced extreme vacillation between the rule of the magnate oligarchs and that of strong monarchs during the fourteenth and fifteenth centuries. Inevitably, the extinction of dynasties such as the Arpad in 1301 and the Anjou in 1382 ushered in periods of anarchy when rival magnate factions looked for a king "whose plaits they could hold in their hands." The dominance of the magnates during such periods was graphically illustrated by the changes in landholding patterns. For example, at the death of the strong King Louis I in 1382, about 15 per cent of Hungary's 21,000 to 22,000 towns and villages belonged to the crown, 12 per cent to the church, 53 per cent to the nobles, and 20 per cent to the sixty leading magnate families. However, after the death of Sigismund, the last king of the weak Luxemburg dynasty, in 1437, the crown's share of these properties sank to 5 per cent; the church's remained the same; the nobles' dropped to 43 per cent, while the magnates' portion doubled, to 40 per cent.[20] None the less, in contrast to their counterparts in Poland, the Hungarian magnates never succeeded in permanently crippling the kingship with burdensome limitations, either because they miscalculated by installing a king who not only outmanoeuvred them militarily and politically but also extirpated most of them, as in the case of Charles of Anjou, or because a "national" king was forced upon them who had a powerful domestic base of support, as in the case of János Hunyadi.[21]

Meanwhile, while playing a subsidiary role in "high politics," usually as allies of the kings, the Hungarian nobility consolidated its position. Its grip on the land became firmer as the result of a royal ruling which allowed noblemen dying intestate to pass their land on to consanguine relations or to sell it to neighbouring noblemen rather than return it to the crown. Their relationship to their dependents was regularized by a royal decree that ordered peasants to pay one-ninth of their income to their lords. However, the greatest strides forward were made on the institutional level. Control of the approximately seventy *komitats*, administrative units which the kings had established in the thirteenth century around their castles, was slowly passing into the hands of the nobles. Although the highest administrative office in the *komitat* – that of *iszpan* – went to a magnate who was nominated by the king, this became little more than an honorific position because of magnate absenteeism. The real power in the *komitats* fell to the vice-*iszpans* and judicial officials, usually wealthier nobles who controlled ten to forty villages (*bene possessienti*) and who were elected by the assemblies of local nobles. The kings often encouraged the transformation of a royal administrative unit into an institution of noble self-rule because it helped to counterbalance the influence of the magnates in the provinces. In any case, by the fifteenth century the *komitats* had become the stronghold of noble influence and the nobles' institutional springboard to greater power.

From the mid-fifteenth century onwards the influence of the nobility began to reach the all-kingdom level. The process was accelerated by the growing importance of the parliament, which, growing out of the royal assizes, was dominated by the nobles who had originally attended it individually.[23] As cooperation increased between the pliant Jagiellonian kings and the nobility, regular meetings of the parliament were instituted in which magnates, prelates, and elected representatives of the lower clergy, the towns, and the nobility (the latter having the plurality) took part. Aside from their regular functions, such as voting taxes, the parliaments on the one hand provided the nobles with an uncommon opportunity to apply pressure to the magnates and, on the other, gave the kings a chance to counterbalance magnate influence in the upper levels of government. By means of the parliament the nobility managed to gain control of the high court, obtaining sixteen seats while only two went to the prelates and two to the magnates. This had unprecedented results: by pushing through a law that decreed that half the noble judges on the high court were to participate in the royal council, the nobles finally reached the inner sanctum of the decision-making establishment.

The nobility's institutional and political gains were buttressed with metaphysical and juridical supports. Of the former the most famous was the mystical concept of the Holy Crown. Subscribed to with nearly religious devotion by the *komitat* nobility, the doctrine argued that Hungary's political essence resided in the mystical Holy Crown – symbolized by the physical crown, the crown of St Stephan – of which the king was the head and the nobility the body. Each member was incomplete without the other, and yet the two were complementary, for the king was the fount of nobility, and the nobles, by virtue of the right to elect the king, were the fount of kingship.[24]

In 1514 the nobility received a juridical basis for its expanding power. In that year Istvan Werböczi presented to the parliament the so-called *Opus Tripartitum*, a codification of Hungary's customary laws and the nobility's privileges.[25] A salient feature of this work was its insistence on the legal fiction that all nobles were equal because all enjoyed the same rights. Written under the immediate impact of the traumatic peasant uprising of 1514, the *Opus Tripartitum* also dealt, in a most vengeful manner, with the status of the peasants: as punishment for their uprising, all peasants were consigned to complete subjugation by their lords in perpetuity. Thus, as the sixteenth century began, a curious combination of mysticism and legalism characterized the nobility's pre-eminent influence in Hungary.

The conflict between the nobles and the magnates was still undecided when, in 1526, the Ottomans attacked. Louis II, the young Jagiellonian king, and his hastily gathered army were annihilated at Móhacs, and the Ottomans invaded

Hungary. Because of Ottoman over-extension and stiffening Hungarian resistance, not all of the land fell to the Ottomans. But the long frontier between the warring Muslim and Christian worlds that ran through the width of Hungary exposed it to recurrent warfare that was to last for generations.

The demographic losses from these wars, especially the exhausting Fifteen Years' War of 1590–1604, were staggering. In 1450 Hungary's population was about four million; in 1600 it was only about three million. Comparatively speaking, in 1490 the inhabitants of Hungary constituted 6 per cent of Europe's population, while in 1600 they made up only 3.3 per cent of the total.[26] Material losses were even greater. In many of the western *komitat*s about 40 per cent of the dwellings were destroyed, while in the eastern *komitat*s destruction rates of 60 per cent and even 80 per cent were common. Obviously, the resources of the land were drastically reduced. For example, the war tax of one florin per household yielded 240,000 florins in 1590, 190,000 florins in 1598, and only 65,000 in 1604.[27] To make matters worse, at the turn of the century the price of corn and later of livestock plummeted by 50 per cent, catastrophically undermining the once-flourishing trade with Europe.

Finally, to complete the list of misfortunes, Hungary was completely dismembered as a result of the Ottoman wars. The largest but not the most populous part, centred on the Great Plain, was incorporated into the Ottoman administrative system. The fate of the remaining lands was more complicated. After a long struggle between Ferdinand of Habsburg and János Zapolyai, the Habsburg was finally acknowledged king of a thin, elongated but populous crescent of land in the west and north which came to be called Royal Hungary. Undoubtedly, the Hungarians who supported him, and many did not, hoped that he would be able to tap the rich resources of his dynasty for the struggle against the Turk. A third part of Hungary, originally called the Eastern Kingdom and later the principality of Transylvania, was, with the aid of Polish and French intervention, granted to Zapolyai by the sultan on the terms of vassalage. The formation of the Transylvanian principality, which in the early seventeenth century would become a major power in Eastern Europe, was to play a crucial role in the political history of the Hungarian nobility.[28] Once the elective princes of Transylvania had established a strong, centralized rule in their own land, for the Hungarian nobles in Royal Hungary (whose fate Transylvanians always considered as their own) Transylvania would serve as a bastion of the nobility's struggle against Habsburg absolutism and as a driving force for the reunification of Hungary.

While the Ottoman wars were an unmitigated disaster to the peasants and the townsmen, their impact on the two major components of the Hungarian elite varied greatly. For the nobility, the wars brought a sharp halt to their burgeoning influence; the magnates, however, experienced a relative rise in power. As was the case in Poland, the major reason for this was the magnates' greater ability to absorb losses and thus survive a general catastrophe. While thousands of noblemen lost their plots to the invader, the magnates and prelates, with much of their land concentrated in the west (in the lesser Alföld they owned 58 per cent of the estates, while the nobles had only 9 per cent), often preserved their holdings intact.[29] Because they had the wherewithal, the magnates played the leading role in the defence of the land, constructing, together with the Habsburgs, an extensive network of castles and organizing semi-private armies. The cost was not cheap. Only about ten of the old families survived into the eighteenth century. The places of the others were quickly filled by families of military and political entrepreneurs, such as the Nádasdy, Batthyány, Dobó, Forgách, Pálffy, and Rákóczi. A clear indication of the magnates' regained predominance over the nobles was the rebirth of the medieval institution of *familiares*, occasioned by thousands of ruined noblemen taking service in the castles, entourages, and military forces of the magnates.

Although the relationship of the magnates to the new dynasty was generally a positive one, it was leavened with some ambiguity. For co-operating with the Habsburgs in the defence of the land, the magnates received the usual prizes a sovereign had to offer – prestigious and profitable offices. They also received some unprecedented signs of royal favour: under the Habsburgs, formal distinctions were drawn between the magnates and noblemen as reflected in the creation in parliament of an upper house for the former and a lower house for the latter, and in the granting of aristocratic titles. As a sign of their loyalty to the dynasty, most magnates remained Catholic, while the majority of the nobility converted to Protestantism. But some aspects of Habsburg rule grated heavily on the magnates. Specifically, they resented the appointments of foreign *condottieri* to military commands, the growing dominance of Vienna-backed Austrian capitalists in Hungarian trade, and, in particular, the disquieting disregard of the Habsburgs for traditional forms and principles of Hungarian government.[30]

Fate was less kind to the lower and middle nobility. Already in the mid-sixteenth century poor noblemen had become liable to taxation. By the seventeenth century between 50 and 60 per cent of them either had no land or only a single plot. Their status was further threatened by the increasing numbers of *hayduk*s, an intermediate class between free peasants and nobles, who performed military service but who did not have noble privileges, a fact that made them a source of chronic discontent. In some of the eastern *komitat*s nobles and semi-nobles constituted 20 to 30 per cent of the population, while in the magnate-dominated western *komitat*s nobles were no more than 2 to 3 per cent. Caught between the *hayduk*s and the ever more numerous Habsburg mercenaries, many noblemen were squeezed out of military service.[31]

The scope of their political activity also narrowed. Under the pretext of war the Habsburgs called parliaments less often and, after 1662, not at all. With access to "national" politics shut off, nobles made the insular world of the *komitat*s their sole concern. They immersed themselves in the rehabilitation of their estates, in the struggle for *komitat* offices, in the administration of justice to their serfs, in innumerable lawsuits, and in all the intricacies of custom and law that spread their fame as a "nation of lawyers." Alongside and in sharp contrast to this legalistic tendency, Hungarian noblemen also developed an exaggerated, self-glorifying notion of themselves as Christianity's bulwark against the heathen Turk. The emphasis which noblemen placed on this myth was both curious and understandable. Precisely at a time when they were defending the land less and less, they chose to emphasize the struggle against the Turk and the privileges which they had "won with blood" more and more. Yet beneath the bluster and the myths, the typical insecurities, anxieties, and symptoms of a class fearful of becoming déclassé were clearly visible. Moreover, these frustrations could just as easily be turned against the German Habsburgs as against the Ottomans.

HUNGARY: SELECTED STATISTICS[32]

Population and area

Total population in 1604: about 3 million

Area: Royal Hungary (1–1.2 million): 92,000 square kilometres; Transylvania (about 750,000): 85,000–90,000 square kilometres; Ottoman Hungary (800,000–900,000): 110,000–120,000 square kilometres

Total population and area in 1720: 4 million (about 50% non-Hungarian); 280,000 square kilometres

Population density in early eighteenth century: approximately 9 per square kilometre

Social structure (late seventeenth century)

Nobles: 4-5% (about 70–100 magnate families and 25,000 noble families; total number about 150,000)

Townsmen: 2–2.4%

Peasants: 90%

Others: 3–4%

Landholdings (sixteenth-century Royal Hungary)

Crown: 7%
Church: 12%
Nobles: 79%
Towns: 2%

Nobles with fewer than 5 *portea* represented 55% of noble landholdings; with 5-10 *portea*; 18%; with more than 10 *portea*, 27%; 50–60% were landless or held single plots.

Magnates held 45% of all cultivated land.

The army (seventeenth century)

Royal Hungary: cavalry 7,775; infantry 5,840
Transylvania: levee, about 5,000

THE LIVONIAN *RITTERSCHAFT*

A classic embodiment of a feudal nobility in Eastern Europe was the Livonian *ritterschaft.*[33] In view of the fact that the ancestors of the "Baltic barons" came from Germany at a time when feudalism had reached its highest stage of development there, this is not surprising. Nevertheless, it is striking to observe the speed and thoroughness with which the *ritterschaft*, one of the smallest but most cohesive and durable nobilities in Europe, established itself. The achievements of this ethnically isolated elite of two to three hundred families in Baltic society are all the more noteworthy because, after 1562, they were accomplished under powerful sovereigns and in one of the most war-torn and famine-ridden areas of the continent. The *ritterschaft* not only survived the many catastrophes of the sixteenth to eighteenth centuries but even managed to profit from them. In so doing it manifested, for better or worse, a remarkable self-confidence and sense of direction. Whether viewing its historical role, as did German polemicists of the nineteenth century, in terms of a *kulturträger* of Western civilization in the eastern Baltic or, as did the Latvian historian Ian Zutis, as a fortuitously preserved anachronism, "a museum containing feudal antiquities," one is hard put to find a European nobility which preserved its rights and privileges more completely and for a longer period of time (after an existence of almost seven hundred years it was dissolved in 1920) than did the Livonian *ritterschaft.*

A combination of the *Drang nach Osten* and the crusading spirit brought the Germans to Livonia in the final decade of the twelfth century. The moving forces in this enterprise were the three most dynamic elements in medieval German society – the church, the merchants, and the knights (*ritter*). Responding to the invitations of German merchants who traded in the eastern Baltic, Albert, "Germany's last great proselytizing bishop," set out in the footsteps of two of his predecessors to bring Christianity to the heathen Livs, Letts, and Ests. With Pope Innocent III's call for a crusade against the heathen Balts mobilizing support, in 1220 Albert sailed to Livonia with twenty-three ships. Before his death in 1229, he made fourteen such voyages, establishing in the process an ecclesiastically dominated German colony which eventually consisted of the archbishopric of newly founded Riga and the bishoprics of Dorpat, Kurland, and Oesel.

Because the resistance of the Balts was fierce and the flow of crusaders undependable, the churchmen needed a more permanent source of military support. For this purpose they organized the Order of the Sword. But this fledgling crusading fraternity was decimated by the Lithuanians in 1236, and in 1237 its place was taken by the well-established Teutonic Order or, as its eastern Baltic branch was sometimes called, the Livonian Order. For its services the Livonian Order received one-third of all the conquered land and two-thirds of the land yet to be conquered. Eventually, this arrangement gave the order control of most of Livonia (51,000 square kilometres), while the archbishoprics of Riga (18,400 square kilometres) and Kurland (4,500 square kilometres) constituted the rest. In addition, self-governed Riga possessed 750 square kilometres. Thus, during the thirteenth century a loose confederation emerged which acknowledged the distant sovereignty of the Holy Roman Empire and the Pope and in which the local overlords, the order, the archbishop, and the bishops competed for power.[34]

As tension between the order and the bishops grew, the latter sought to recruit a dependable military force of their own. Therefore, the bishops and, to a much lesser extent, the order itself began encouraging the immigration of fighting men from Germany. Coming almost exclusively from Lower Saxony and Westphalia, the homeland of Albert, these fighting men were given liberal portions of land on terms of vassalage as codified by Saxon law (*sachsenspiegel*). With three to five hundred knights of its own, the order could be somewhat less generous. Unlike the churchmen and the Livonian knights, who were celibate and often returned to Germany after completing their terms of service, the vassals settled on the land and, together with a growing number of townsmen, constituted a permanent German presence in Livonia. Contrary to popular opinion, it was the vassals and not the members of the Livonian Order who were the ancestors of the Livonian *ritterschaft*.[35]

It was clearly to the advantage of the various groups of vassals or *ritterschaften*, as they were called from the sixteenth century onwards, that their overlords compete not only with each other but also for the loyalty of their vassals. This advantage became especially evident when a portion of the German vassals, about one hundred families in Harrien-Wierland (northern Livonia or Estland), came under the distant and very feeble overlordship of the Danish king. In 1259, hoping to securing the loyalty of his new vassals, the Danish king allowed them to form a corporate body (*universitas vassalorum*), to convene assemblies (*manntagen*), and generally to rule themselves. Moreover, the vassals of Harrien-Wierland obtained hereditary rights to their lands and judicial authority over their peasants.[36] Encouraged by the accomplishments of their colleagues, the vassals in the rest of Livonia pressed on to emulate them.

The expansion of vassal rights and privileges was blocked for a time by the growing power of the Livonian Order. With sixteen castles and a tight, centralized organization at its disposal, with, in addition, the leading role in the struggle against the Balts to its credit (in the fourteenth century, the order conducted about a hundred campaigns against the Lithuanians alone), the order was on the verge of establishing its primacy in the land. In 1330 Riga was forced for a time to recognize the order's overlordship; in 1394 the archbishopric of Riga was incorporated into the order; and in 1397 the Danes were expelled from Estland. The successes of the order did not bode well for the vassals, who considered the Livonian knights to be demanding overlords. However, just as the order was about to attain its goal, it suffered a series of disastrous setbacks, the most spectacular of which was its defeat at Grünwald in 1410. This was a signal for the knights' internal enemies to take advantage of the situation.

On the initiative of the weakened but not completely subordinated archbishop of Riga, the first all-Livonian *landtag* (parliament) met in 1419; after 1422, it was held annually. The purpose of the *landtag* was to serve as an assembly of overlords (the order and the bishops) and of estates (the vassals and townsmen) which met to discuss such issues as the relationship of the overlords to each other and to the estates, and matters relating to the peasants and to the conduct of war. The organization of the *landtag*, four curiae consisting of the order, the bishops, the vassals, and the townsmen, was especially advantageous to the vassals because only they managed to form a united front and thus apply pressure on their overlords.[37]

Soon one concession followed another. In 1435, after the order had suffered more defeats at the hands of the Lithuanians, it was forced to agree to make no more wars without the estates' consent and to confirm the latter's rights and privileges. Several decades later, in 1472, the order was even pressured to recognize the vassals' right of resistance should the order break the terms of its overlordship. Meanwhile, the vassals strengthened their hold on the peasants by concluding mutual agreements among themselves and their overlords, in 1482 and 1494, to return runaways and to increase their control over the peasants.[38]

Even with the increasing exploitation of the peasantry, the first half of the sixteenth century was a time of peace and plenty in Livonia, assured by the grain boom. As a result, military expenditures were cut; over 140 castles fell into disrepair, and fighting men neglected their training. All this made the on-coming catastrophe even more shattering: in 1558 Muscovite troops launched a sudden, brutal invasion of Livonia, plunging it into a war which would last for twenty-four years. Hoping to break through to the Baltic, Ivan IV committed almost all of his resources to the Livonian war. But as Livonian defences crumbled, Poland-Lithuania, Sweden, and Denmark moved in to thwart the tsar's ambitions and to share in the spoils. The long years of warfare brought tremendous suffering to the land. By the end of the war in 1582 many regions were depopulated by 70 to 75 per cent; in some areas 90 per cent of the cultivated land was unused; and in general Livonia lost close to 50 per cent of its populace. So great were the demographic losses that in 1583 a new colonizing effort had to be mounted.

Equally drastic was the political upheaval of the land. Unable to resist the invaders, the order and the bishops collapsed. In the end the Muscovites were totally repulsed; the *ritterschaft* of Estland accepted Swedish sovereignty; the island of Saarmaa went to the Danes; and the Polish king, Sigismund II August, received the bulk of the prize, the central and major part of old Livonia. Mean-while, Gotthard Kettler, the last master of the order, received Kurland as a vassal duchy of the Polish king.

Despite the devastation and the chaos, the war was not an unmitigated disaster for the Livonian nobility. With its former overlords swept away it now became the sole spokesman for the land (Riga preferred to act on its own). Although most of the Livonians preferred Swedish sovereignty if only because the Swedes were also Lutherans, circumstances forced the Livonians to accept the overlordship of Sigismund II August on 28 November 1562. In return for their submission the king granted them the famous *Privilegium Sigismundi Augusti*, which confirmed all their previous rights, added some new ones, and became a kind of Magna Carta for the *ritterschaft*.[39] Among its key stipulations were guarantees to the nobility of freedom of worship according to the Augsburg Confession, and of the high offices of the land; the recognition of the nobles' complete and hereditary ownership of their lands (never confirmed by the order) and of their complete jurisdiction over their peasants (a new privilege); limitations on the merchants' monopoly on the grain trade; and payment to the nobles for military service (a new privilege). Thus, the Livonian nobles emerged from the war with a stronger political and socio-economic position in the land than they had ever had before the conflict.

Despite the promising start, the *ritterschaft*'s time under Polish rule was neither long nor happy.[40] Soon after the war Stefan Batory, the aggressive successor of Sigismund August, made it clear that he had no intention of honouring his predecessor's promises. As Poland moved to the forefront of the Counter-Reformation, Catholicism came to be favoured by the Polish authorities in Livonia. Poles and Lithuanians were first given access to and then, in 1589, preference in appointments to the offices of the land. The Poles attempted to implement colonization projects which, though largely abortive, called for increased immigration of Catholic Polish peasants. Not surprisingly, therefore, when the Swedes invaded Livonia in 1601, most of the *ritterschaft* sided with the invaders, and many died for the Swedish cause. Although this invasion failed, another one, launched in 1617 by Gustav Adolphus, succeeded, and by 1621 most of Livonia was in Swedish hands.

For the *ritterschaft* the long-awaited advent of Swedish sovereignty was disappointing. Because Gustav Adolphus viewed Livonia as a conquered province, he did not find it necessary to confirm the rights and privileges of its elite immediately, despite that elite's strong pro-Swedish sympathies. The loss of the original of the *Privilegium Sigismundi Augusti* during the war, the precedent to which the *ritterschaft* constantly referred, only complicated matters. By now, deeply involved in the Thirty Years' War, the most Gustav Adolphus was willing to do was to grant the Livonians, in 1632, a provisional confirmation of their rights until such time as the entire issue could be studied more thoroughly. Equally disillusioning was the king's policy on land distribution. When the Polish crown estates, about 50 per cent of all cultivated land in Livonia, were taken over by the Swedish king, the *ritterschaft* expected some of these lands to come its way. Its disappointment was great when Gustav Adolphus awarded the lands almost entirely to Swedish aristocrats, generals, and ministers. By 1638, 47.75 per cent of all cultivated land in Livonia was held by sixteen aristocratic Swedish families. Not only had the Livonian nobility been deprived of rich pickings, but it had now to accept a new, foreign element in its midst.[41]

But happier times were soon to follow for the Livonians. As Sweden's involvement in the war deepened and the Livonians' contacts with the Swedish establishment grew – Livonia's aristocratic and largely absentee Swedish landholders came to be of great service in this area – the *ritterschaft* again managed to extract important concessions from its sovereigns. In 1634 it was allowed to elect a *landmarschall*, or representative of the corporate body; in 1637 a corporate treasury, designed to collect the taxes imposed by the diet, which had long since become the exclusive domain of the nobles, was established; in 1643 a six-member *landrat*, or council, whose members bore the imposing title of *patres patriae et defensores iustitiae*, was formed to monitor the Swedish officials so that they did not break the laws of the land (in 1648 it was expanded to twelve members); and in 1662 a compendium was compiled of the *ritterschaft*'s rights and privileges.[42] In short, as the seventeenth century came to an end, the Livonian elite had acquired all of the institutional accoutrements necessary to govern itself and to dominate the rest of Livonian society.

LIVONIA: SELECTED STATISTICS[43]

Population and area

Population circa 1700: about 300,000. German: about 7%; Latvian: about 43%; Estonian: about 50%

Area: about 50,000 square kilometres

Population density: about 6 per square kilometre

Social structure

Nobles: about 2,000 (.7%)

Townsmen: about 18,000 (6%)

Peasants: about 270,000 (90%)

Others: about 10,000 (3.3%)

Landholdings

Total cultivated land in 1680s: 6,317 *haken* (537 estates, 41 pastorates, 12,272 peasant households)

Crown: 1.25%

Pastorate: 1.32%

Nobles: 93%

Towns: 2.16%

Others: 2.27%

The Swedish aristocracy held 45.87% of all cultivated land (2,869 *haken*); the Swedish ennobled gentry, 12.23% (773 *haken*); and the Livonian *ritterschaft*, 34.90% (2,206 *haken*).

Army of the ritterschaft

None

THE MOLDAVIAN BOYARS

A feudal nobility emerged belatedly and evolved somewhat irregularly in Moldavia. This was due in part to the long-delayed establishment of sophisticated forms of political organization in the area, with their concomitant socio-economic, political, and military hierarchies. The fact that animal husbandry rather than agriculture long remained a primary occupation among the Vlachs, as the Romanians were called in the medieval period, also helps to explain the extended presence of clan or communal rather than feudal relationships among them. When, in the fourteenth and fifteenth centuries, the conditions for the evolution of a feudal nobility did appear, the gradually expanding impact of the Ottomans imbued this development with a number of sharply distinctive traits.

The thorny question of the ethnogenesis of the Vlachs, generally considered one of the great unsolved mysteries of the medieval period, need not be treated here. It is commonly accepted, however, that after the chaos of the Great Migration of Peoples, the Vlachs descended from the Carpathian and Balkan highlands and settled on the northern banks of the lower Danube and in large parts of Transylvania. For centuries thereafter they were ruled by Kievan Rus', Galicia-Volhynia, the Golden Horde, and, in the late thirteenth and early fourteenth centuries, by Hungary. As Tatar power declined and the extinction of the Arpad dynasty plunged Hungary into anarchy, the Vlachs cast off the suzerainty of the Hungarian king and established their own principalities, first in Wallachia (1330) and then in Moldavia (1359).[44]

Bogdan, *voievode* of Maramarosh, the leader of the anti-Hungarian uprising of 1359, became the first *voievode* of Moldavia (the title of *hospodar* was introduced about fifty years later). To him and his successors went all the attributes of sovereignty: the *hospodar* held titular ownership of all the land, possessed the highest political, military, and judicial authority, and made appointments to the high offices of the land, which evolved from his household. His vast income, made up of peasant dues, proceeds from newly founded mines, and taxes on townsmen and on the growing trade, constituted a major source of his power. Succession to the rank of *hospodar*, at least in the first several generations, was a combination of hereditary right and election – that is, the new *hospodar*s were elected by the elite from among the members of Bogdan's dynasty. But this newly acquired sovereignty carried its usual obligations, the most notable of which was responsibility for the defence and order of the land.[45]

In dealing with these responsibilities the *hospodar*s did not have to work in a vacuum. In the *knez*es, Vlach society already had a stratum of hereditary military leaders of the clans. However, the *knez*es' activities were usually limited to the clans, and their authority was modest, as reflected in the fact that the clansmen owed them only three to five days of service per year and gifts at Christmas and Easter. By giving the *knezes* as well as their own closest associates land on hereditary terms in return for their service in defence and administration, the *hospodars* laid the foundations both for an effective fighting force and for the Moldavian boyar oligarchy. As was the case elsewhere in Eastern Europe, the grants of land to boyars and to lesser military servitors, called *miles*, came directly from the sovereign, thus preventing a system of subinfeudation from developing.

As agriculture and town life evolved, the latter encouraged by the acquisition in the 1390s of the two important Black Sea ports of Bilhorod and Kilia, the boyars' desire and ability to extract more land from the *hospodars* increased. The means by which boyars exerted pressure on the *hospodars* were familiar.[46] On the one hand, boyar influence was institutionalized in the twenty- to thirty-member boyar council, which became the effective if not formal co-ruler of the land. On the other hand, the boyars were able to manipulate the system of succession to their own advantage. This was especially evident in the period between 1432 and 1457, when a series of weak *hospodars* was chosen who were then quickly deposed. Taking advantage of the *hospodars'* desire to win supporters, the boyars plied them with demands for more land. The following statistics show the extent of their success: between 1384 and 1432, under the rule of relatively strong *hospodars*, the records show 22 major land grants to the boyars; during the chaotic period between 1432 and 1457, however, as many as 110 grants were recorded.[47] During this period the wealthiest boyars owned about fifty villages, and feudal landholders held 81 per cent of all cultivated land. Within the elite the 45 largest landholders (ten or more villages) held 39 per cent of the land; 320 middle landholders (one to five villages) held 42 per cent; and 836 small landholders (no more than one village) held 19 per cent.[48] The church owned about 10 per cent, and the *hospodars'* domain shrank to 6 per cent of the land. However, their income from the towns and mines increased during this period.

The fortunes of the boyars in Moldavia, as in other lands of Eastern Europe, fluctuated sharply in the fifteenth century. During the reign of Stefan III (1457-1504), when Moldavia and its *hospodars* reached the peak of their power, the boyars suffered a severe setback. Stefan made the diminution of boyar power and wealth a central goal of his internal policy. He proceeded carefully, waiting to establish his hold on the throne and picking up support among the usual enemies of the magnates – that is, among the military servitors, the townsmen, and the peasants. How successful he was in strengthening the military servitors as a counterweight to the boyars may be seen from the figures in the table.

LAND GRANTS IN FIFTEENTH-CENTURY MOLDAVIA[49]

	1432 – 56	1457 – 72	1473 – 1504
Extant land grants	95	52	261
Less than 1 village	20%	30.7%	77.8%
1 – 5 villages	49.5%	52.1%	20.6%
More than 5 villages	30.5%	17.2%	1.6%

However, although Stefan III halted it for a time, he could not reverse the long-term trend. His efforts to develop a strong servitor class were hampered by the largesse of his predecessors: with most of the cultivated land in the hands of the large and middle landholders and with *hospodar*'s domain severely depleted, land was simply not available for further distribution among the *kurtiany* and *karalashi*, as the various types of servitors were called. Later *hospodars* attempted to bypass this problem by quartering their servitors on the boyars' hereditary lands. However, the servitors, in addition to performing military service, also had to pay rents to the boyars. This arrangement often strained the resources of the servitors to such an extent that they preferred to become simple peasants.

The inability of the servitors to retain the use of land and their higher socio-economic positions explains to a large extent why no juridical distinctions developed between them and the free peasants. Even functional divisions based on military service were blurred between the two strata because, while the servitors fought in the "small army," of about ten thousand men, in times of emergency the *hospodars* called up the "great army," of about forty thousand men, which included peasants and townsmen. Thus, despite Stefan III's efforts, the relatively small servitor class – about two thousand in the mid-fifteenth century and about five thousand in 1591 – was unable to acquire the prerogatives which lesser nobility enjoyed elsewhere in Eastern Europe. For example, while a general assembly did exist, it was rarely called, because of the servitors' weakness.[50]

Insecurity also plagued the highest levels of the Moldavian elite. The *nemesh*, or middle-range hereditary landholders, were the principality's closest analogy to the *szlachta*-gentry. However, even they were taxable. And when, in the sixteenth century, under Ottoman pressure, rising taxes outpaced incomes from their estates, this stratum faced ruin. During this period, as there was no law of primogeniture in Moldavia, a large number of old boyar families also experienced a sharp decline because of the constant subdivision of their estates. The breakup of the large estates was evident in the fact that, while in the fifteenth century small landholdings constituted 19 per cent of noble lands, in the sixteenth century they rose to 55 per cent.

Downward and, of course, upward mobility was common to all nobilities, but the relatively new, only vaguely defined elite of Moldavia suffered from a surfeit of it. This situation was aggravated when, in the sixteenth century, the inescapable Ottoman presence began to be felt increasingly in the land. Unlike Hungary and neighbouring Wallachia, Moldavia was not subjected to a sudden, overpowering Ottoman conquest. There were no disastrous defeats such as that of Louis II at Mohács. Indeed, Stefan III even won several signal victories over the Turks. Yet it soon became clear that this was merely a postponement of the inevitable and that eventually the Moldavians would have to reach a modus vivendi with their mighty southern neighbour.

In 1456 Petru Aron came to an understanding with the Porte, but it was abrogated by Stefan III, only to be reinstituted again in 1487. Initially, the agreement seemed fairly harmless. The Porte demanded that the *hospodar*s recognize the sultan's suzerainty, symbolized by the payment of token tribute, and agreed to allow the Moldavians to conduct their own affairs with practically no interference. But gradually the demands for tribute began to rise: in 1456 it was 2,000 gold pieces; in 1487, 4,000; in 1514, 8,000; in the 1520s, 10,000; in 1541, 12,000; in 1563, 65,000; and in the seventeenth century the last figure was tripled and then quadrupled.[51] In addition, other onerous economic and military duties were imposed. When *hospodar*s would not or could not meet these demands, the Porte easily found candidates among the boyars who were willing to try. Suffice it to say that in the sixteenth and seventeenth centuries Ottoman extortion became so great that it seriously altered the socio-economic and political structure of Moldavian society.

This was particularly evident among the nobility in the accelerated decline of many old boyar and *nemesh* families. Caught between rising tribute payments and declining incomes from their estates – the peasants could not yield more because Ottoman tribute already bled them dry – many *nemeshi* and poorer boyars became déclassé, forming a category called *mazyl*s. However, as Ottoman extortion directly or indirectly ruined many of the old elite, others, both from within the elite and beyond it, learned to profit from this situation. As taxes and duties were piled on each piece of land – in seventeenth century one plot could have as many as seventy different taxes – the more adaptable boyars realized that land, in and of itself, was no longer a means to power and wealth, although it did remain an attribute of it.[52] Indeed, the value of land dropped sharply. This was a key reason why the *gutsherrschaft* or *folwark,* so dominant elsewhere in Eastern Europe, never fully developed in Moldavia.

If land no longer paved the way to wealth and power, then what did? High offices, especially those which allowed the holder to skim off a part, usually about 10 per cent of the Ottoman tribute, now assured high political and economic status. There appeared the so-called new boyars, families such as the Ureche, Rossetti, Costin, and Cantacuzine, which were both of Moldavian and of non-Moldavian origin but well connected at the Porte.[53] They were about seventy-five in number, and all owed their rise to their ability to gain the lucrative high offices of the land. Because they profited from these offices, they became strong advocates of the authority of the holders of high office while they simultaneously tried to limit the prerogatives or, more concretely, the "take" of the *hospodar*. They also opposed the granting of immunities and other exemptions to the lower levels of the elite lest these undermine the taxation base. It was this peculiar "centralist" tendency of the boyars that distinguished them from other East European magnates.

The impact of this exploitative system on Moldavian society was disastrous, leading, in the late seventeenth century, to a steep decline in the population and in the productivity of the land.[54] In the 1690s, the taxpaying population declined to the size it had been in 1591 – that is, to about 45,000 families. The number of houses in Jassy dropped from twelve to four thousand. An important factor in explaining the decline in productivity was the Porte's insistence that Moldavians sell their grain in Istanbul at an artificially set low price. This was one of the factors which caused many Moldavian peasants to flee to Transylvania. Finally, the reverberations of the economic decline in Western Europe led to a 50 per cent drop in the price of livestock, Moldavia's main export to Poland and the West. As the boyars' income was reduced, their demands on the peasants increased, and this further accelerated the downward spiral in population and productivity.

The deteriorating situation was also reflected in a general negativism and lack of self-confidence which came to characterize the attitudes of the elite. Where fifteenth-century chroniclers extolled Moldavians for being brave, constant, and tough fighting men, the chronicles of the seventeenth century, written mostly by the boyars themselves, criticized the Moldavians for their propensity for "treachery and cowardice" and for "always being ready to pillage and flee." The one bright spot which some of the more thoughtful boyars found in their fallen self-image was Moldavia's role as a "bulwark of Christianity against the heathen tide." When members of the elite discussed ways in which the situation could be remedied and the "good old ways" brought back, they inevitably looked to their northern neighbour, Poland, and extolled the virtues of a system in which "nobody, not even the Polish king can fetter a nobleman, unless the law commands it."[55] Because some of the boyars were connected to Poles by marriage, owned lands in the Commonwealth, and were even acknowledged as members of the *szlachta*, it is little wonder that they knew the Polish model well and found it most appealing.[56] In fact, the Code of 1646, one of the first Moldavian documents to define the rights of the nobility, was clearly based on Polish models. There were even echoes of the Polish nobility's Sarmatian myth in Moldavia; for example, the enlightened Dimitrie Cantemir justified serfdom because, according to him, the serfs were descendants of the original and lowly inhabitants of the land, while the boyars stemmed from the racially superior Roman conquerors. Thus, benefiting from an oppressive system and simultaneously yearning for Polish-type freedoms, the Moldavian boyars anxiously sought to find a way out of their frustrating situation as the seventeenth century came to an end.

MOLDAVIA: SELECTED STATISTICS[57]

Population and area (seventeenth century)
Population: approximately 300,000
Area: approximately 50,000 square kilometres
Population density: approximately 6 per square kilometre

Social structure
Nobles (boyars and servitors): 3.5%
Townsmen: 13.5%
Peasants: 83%
Of approximately 10,000 nobles, 300 were adult male boyars; 4,983 were
    military servitors; while *nemeshi* and others accounted for the remaining 3,795

Landholdings (sixteenth century)
Hospodar: 5% of all arable land
Church: 10%
"Nobles": 81%
Others: 4%
Among the nobility, boyars held 26% of all cultivated land, and small holders,
    55%.

The army of the principality
Fifteenth century: "small" army: 10,000; "large" army: 40,000
Seventeenth century: total (including mercenaries): 6,000-8,000

THE UKRAINIAN COSSACK *STARSHYNA*

One of the most notable features of the vast, deep-rooted, and bloody Ukrainian revolt of 1648 was its success, rarely duplicated in early modern European history, in expelling its feudal elite, the Polish or polonized *szlachta*, from the land.[58] And herein lay a paradox, for it was from among the leaders of the anti-noble revolt that soon thereafter there arose another elite which, although Ukrainian, none the less modelled itself closely and consciously on the deposed Polish nobility, to the point where later in the eighteenth century it even referred to itself as *szlachta* (Ukrainian: *shliakhta*).

Viewed broadly, the appearance of this Ukrainian elite close on the heels of the expelled Polish one was a clear indication of the structural need for a nobility in a pre-modern agrarian society. More specifically, this development marked the appearance of what was perhaps the latest nobility to emerge in Eastern Europe. As such, the Ukrainian elite possessed all the typical characteristics of *homines novi*: it did not find easy acceptance from its peers, its subjects, or its sovereign; its institutions were incomplete or ill defined; and it was plagued by insecurity and instability. Nevertheless, by the end of the seventeenth century it had begun to master the essentials of its role. It monopolized the political and socio-economic heights of society of Left Bank Ukraine – that is, Ukraine on the left bank of the Dnieper – and learned to identify the interests of the land with its own. And the more it dominated its society, the more it was loath to share its power with anyone else, including far-off sovereigns. To appreciate fully the rapid evolution of the Ukrainian elite, it is necessary to review the historical context within which it developed.

A hallmark of Ukrainian history in the early modern period was the colonization of its vast, open lands. One of the major outgrowths of this century-long process was the emergence of the Ukrainian Cossacks, a class of frontiersmen and fighters from the steppes. Because the socio-economic system of the Polish-Lithuanian Commonwealth, of which Ukraine was then a part, had no place for a class that belonged neither to the elite nor to the downtrodden peasantry, the Cossacks were left to occupy a tenuous and ambiguous place in society. None the less, the numbers of Cossacks, fed by runaway peasants and impoverished burghers, continued to grow. Just the registered or legally recognized Cossacks numbered one thousand in 1578, three thousand in 1583, eight thousand in 1624, and in times of war the figure of registered and unregistered Cossacks was well over forty thousand. Eventually the ambiguity of their position created dangerous tensions which, in turn, were exacerbated by the changes taking place within the Polish *szlachta*.

As the *szlachta* in Ukraine obtained ever greater land grants from the king and as it concentrated its efforts on organizing its *folwarks* and exploiting its peasants, it began increasingly to neglect its original military functions. To a large extent these functions, especially those pertaining to anti-Tatar and anti-Ottoman warfare, were taken over by the Cossacks.[59] Thus, a dangerous contradiction arose: while one class enjoyed the rights of a military elite, another, devoid of those rights, did much of the actual fighting. When the Cossacks demanded some juridical recognition of their "knightly" functions, the *szlachta*, enraged by the audacity of "upstart peasants," adamantly refused to make any concessions. When to these roughly administered rebuffs were added the oppression of the Orthodox church brought on by the Polish Counter-Reformation, and the ever-increasing exploitation of the peasants, the result was a series of fierce, Cossack-led uprisings against the *szlachta*. All of these failed. However, in 1648 a catalyst appeared in the person of Bohdan Khmelnytsky, who united the diverse elements of Ukrainian dissatisfaction and led them in a successful revolt.

In the chaos that ensued, most of the *szlachta*, never very numerous in Ukraine (in 1640 in the Kiev palatinate, there were between 2,000 and 2,400 nobles in a total population of 350,000 to 420,000), the Jesuits, and the Jewish merchants and tax-farmers either were massacred or fled.[60] Rebellious peasants, many of whom had fought in Khmelnytsky's forces, cast off their obligations and declared themselves free men.[61] At their height the rebel forces numbered close to 200,000 peasant auxiliaries and 40,000 to 60,000 experienced Cossacks. The wealthier among them, who were able to outfit themselves properly, registered as Cossacks. Meanwhile, the hereditary or registered Cossacks, and their leaders in particular, were catapulted into positions of power and authority. It seemed that a radical restructuring of Ukrainian society was about to take place.

But while Khmelnytsky and the other leaders of the revolt, well-established Cossacks of position and property, had their personal and collective grievances against the status quo ante, a complete socio-economic revolution had by no means been their goal. Their demands centred on raising the Cossacks to a more privileged position in existing society and to a greater role in the government of Ukraine.[62] When negotiations with the Poles failed, it was in these areas that the Cossacks pushed ahead most resolutely.

With remarkable speed and effectiveness the Cossacks established a new polity in Ukraine. Its government was essentially an extension, over the entire land and most of the people, of the Cossack system of self-rule, which was based on their military organization. The larger towns, subject to Magdeburg law, were autonomous. In this system the highest military and political authority rested with the *hetman*, while his staff, or *heneralna starshyna*, carried out the functions of a cabinet and board of advisers. Local authority rested with the colonels (*polkovnyky*) of the territorially based regiments and their staffs and, on the lowest level, with the captains (*sotnyky*) of the companies and their associates. In line with the Cossack traditions of egalitarianism, all of the offices were elective and subject to the will of the general Cossack council, or *rada*, which met according to need. The formal name of this new political entity was the Zaporozhian Host.[63]

The political restructuring of Ukrainian society did not, however, take place in an atmosphere of complete victory, but rather in one of constant crisis. Mobilizing their main forces, the Poles counter-attacked, and the hard-pressed Cossacks were forced to seek foreign aid. For a time Khmelnytsky considered accepting the sovereignty – that is, the military aid and protection – of the Ottoman sultan, but, primarily for reasons of religious affinity, his choice finally rested upon the tsar of Muscovy. In 1654, at Pereiaslav, after long and difficult negotiations the Ukrainians accepted Tsar Aleksei Mikhailovich as their sovereign.[64]

Even with full Russian involvement the war with the Poles dragged on interminably, ending only in 1667, nine years after Khmelnytsky's death, with a compromise between the Poles and Russians, struck at the cost of the Ukrainians. As a result of the Treaty of Andrusovo, Right Bank Ukraine returned to rather precarious Polish control, while the Left Bank, consisting of ten of the original twenty regiments, remained in Cossack hands and under the sovereignty of the tsar. In subsequent years Cossack *hetman*s on both sides of the Dnieper made repeated and unsuccessful attempts at reuniting the land. In the process, which invariably involved the Poles, Russians, Ottomans, and Tatars, the Right Bank suffered complete devastation and was left almost uninhabited. This period in Ukrainian history is usually called the *Ruina* (the Ruin).

As this period of havoc and turbulence came to an end, the new Ukrainian elite began to emerge.[65] The obvious social stratum from which it could evolve was that of the *starshyna*, or Cossack officer corps. Members of this social group generally belonged to old, registered Cossack families for whom leadership had been a tradition within their own estate, and now, with the rise of the Zaporozhian Host, their influence expanded to include most of Ukrainian society. The *starshyna* was not the only element which constituted the new elite, however. In some areas, particularly in the northern Starodub region, the impact of the uprising had been relatively mild, and much of the local *szlachta*, especially those who were Orthodox, had survived. In 1654, 188 of these families swore allegiance to the tsar and recognized the Zaporozhian Host as its immediate overlord. In return they were accepted into the Cossack estate, allowed to keep their lands, and many obtained responsible positions in the Host.[66] Finally, the chaos created many opportunities for simple Cossacks, burghers, and even peasants to become officers. This was especially true in the 1650s to 1670s, when the mortality rate among Cossack leaders was extremely high and volatile political conditions made frequent changes of leadership commonplace.

Only during the *hetman*cies of Ivan Samoilovych (1672–87) and Ivan Mazepa (1687–1709), when relative stability was restored, did all these elements begin to coalesce into a hereditary elite.

As it evolved, the Ukrainian *starshyna*-nobility had to surmount several formidable barriers. One of these was the principle of election to all offices, a condition which, if maintained, would have prevented the rise of a hereditary caste of officers. During the first two decades after the uprising, when the masses were a factor of considerable political importance, the elective principle was maintained. However, as the situation stabilized, the inherent advantages of incumbency – that is, the extended opportunity, since there were no set terms of office, to amass wealth and influence – allowed *starshyna* families to monopolize various offices. By the end of the seventeenth century most elections had become mere formalities.

Another constraint on the evolving Cossack elite was the paucity of offices and the over-abundance of contenders: in 1700 the Zaporozhian Host had only about five hundred openings. Indeed, much of the murderous factionalism of the 1660s and 1670s was related to this intense competition for offices. However, as the Zaporozhian Host expanded to deal with its added administrative and judicial responsibilities, it also found a way to create more room in its upper echelons. The *hetman*s began to appoint "fellows of the standard" to deal with important ad hoc problems. The colonels (*polkovnyky*) followed suit, appointing "fellows of the banner" to meet various needs on the regimental level. Eventually an intermediate category, called the "fellows of the Host," was nominated by the general staff to aid it in its duties. By the early eighteenth century five to six hundred of these fellows or notables, most of them sons of *starshyna* members, formed a kind of reservoir from which a large part of the *starshyna* was chosen and to which those officers who lost their positions returned. Thus, by 1700 the Ukrainian elite consisted altogether of about 1,000 to 1,100 families divided almost evenly between members of the *starshyna* and the "notable military fellows" (*znatne viiskove tovarystvo*), as the above-mentioned categories of fellows were called. To simplify matters, both categories were referred to as *starshyna*.

It was the rewards which the *starshyna* received which drew a permanent distinction between it and the Cossack rank and file. Only the *starshyna* had the right, for the duration of office, to demand services from the peasants who inhabited the land that belonged to their office. As was the case with all other feudal elites, the crux of the problem was how to transform a conditional hold on the land and the peasants into a hereditary one. This was complicated by the fact that, in view of the recent revolt, the *starshyna* had to be careful in its dealings with Cossacks and peasants. Initially, the officers enlarged their private landholdings by buying out rank-and-file Cossacks and peasants with the incomes obtained from their rank-lands. Later, as it grew more secure, the *starshyna* applied various types of pressure to force its underlings to sell their lands at low or nominal prices, and there were frequent cases in which it simply drove peasants from their lands.

Another means for enlarging private landholdings was to obtain, with the aid of *starshyna* offices, grants of open steppe-land (*slobodas*) from the *hetman* or the tsar. By the end of the seventeenth century the elite had become so well established that it simply demanded and obtained outright grants of land and peasants from the *hetman* and the tsar. Moreover, this practice became quite widespread. During the course of his entire *hetman*cy Khmelnytsky had confirmed only twenty grants of land to the *starshyna*, with eighty going to the monasteries and fifty to the former *szlachta*. Incomplete records indicate, however, that during Mazepa's *hetman*cy, when the *starshyna* had come fully to the fore, at least one thousand land grants were made to Cossack officers. Furthermore, whereas Khmelnytsky's grants had usually consisted of one or two villages, Mazepa's often involved hundreds of peasants and vast stretches of land.

In juridical terms, the higher *starshyna* and notables obtained another right typical of a feudal nobility: they could be judged only by the highest judicial authority in the land, that is, by the *hetman*. In addition, the distinctions which the old Lithuanian Statute, which remained the basic law of the land, made between nobles and non-nobles were often applied in their cases, thus helping to accentuate the judicial inequality between the elite and the rest of society.

A most telling indicator of this increasing differentiation was the *starshyna*'s tightening monopoly on political influence. By definition the *starshyna* possessed greater political weight than simple Cossacks; but originally this had been true of its individual members, not of the *starshyna* collectively, and this only for the duration of their tenure in office. During the Khmelnytsky period and shortly thereafter, the collective political will of the Zaporozhian Host was expressed by the traditional Cossack general *rada*, which was often dominated by the rank and file and their spokesmen. The *rada* decided questions of war and peace, of relations with foreign rulers, and of elections of *hetmans* and general officers. However, as relative stability returned and Cossacks dispersed to their far-flung homes, the practical difficulties of attending these general councils reduced both their frequency and the numbers of their participants. Moreover, the *starshyna*'s growing grip on their offices made elections a mere formality. Finally, the later Russian practice of stationing troops near places where the councils were held, in order to influence their decisions, deprived this institution of any real significance.

As the general council declined, a council of the *starshyna* emerged to take over many of its functions. Because the *starshyna* was still formally elected, it seemed to be an assembly that continued to represent all Cossacks and had merely been reduced in size for practical reasons. In reality, however, the *starshyna* council, which met twice a year at the *hetman's* residence, excluded common Cossacks and peasants and allowed the representatives of the burghers and higher clergy only a limited voice. It thus became the assembly of the Ukrainian elite. Although its decisions were not binding on the *hetman* and its prerogatives were never clearly defined, its influence on the *hetman* and on general policy was often decisive. Like the Polish *sejmiki* and the Hungarian *komitats*, local councils of the *starshyna* were organized on the regimental level. Had it not been for a sharp increase in Russian interference, the Ukrainian elite would, it appears, have been well on its way to developing some sort of parliamentary system, most probably one modelled on the Polish type.

As the *starshyna* established its pre-eminence, it began to evolve a mythical pedigree for itself. Identifying themselves with Cossacks as a whole, the spokesmen of the elite stressed what was generally considered to be the ultimate argument for the legitimacy of a nobility's rights and privileges – the antiquity of these rights and their acquisition through military service. Even as early as 1621, Cossack leaders, with the aid of Kievan scholastics, argued that they were a "knightly order," descended from Kievan princes, which had earned its rights and privileges by spilling its blood in the defence of the Christian faith against the Muslim infidel. They argued that the privileged status they had earned had been formally confirmed by King Stefan Batory. However, in the late seventeenth and early eighteenth centuries, as the *starshyna* became a territorial elite and more receptive to the influences of Polish Sarmatism, the concept of the knightly order was modified. Now the apologists of the *starshyna* spoke of a "Cossack nation" which, like the "*szlachta* nation," was descended from the ancient lords of the land.[67] Thus, in the so-called Bender Constitution (1710), we read that the Cossacks had forebears similar to those of the Polish *szlachta*: "The courageous and ancient Cossack nation, previously called the Khozars, first arose due to its eternal glory, vast lands, and knightly bravery. And it was feared, on land and sea, by all the neighbouring peoples and even by the Eastern Empire [Byzantium]."[68] In addition to identifying themselves with the Khazars, the Cossacks were in other documents identified even with the more ancient Roxolanians.[69] This obvious imitation of the myth of Polish Sarmatism clearly indicates that the Ukrainian *starshyna* was intent on attaining the same position that the Polish *szlachta* enjoyed.

LEFT BANK UKRAINE: SELECTED STATISTICS[70]

Population and area

Population circa 1720: approximately 1.2 million

Area: approximately 90,000 square kilometres
Population density: about 13 per square kilometre

Social structure
Starshyna: about 6,000-6,600 family members (.5%)
Cossacks: about 480,000 (40%)
Burghers: about 50,000 (4%)
Peasants: about 640,000 (53%)
Others: about 34,000 (2.2%)

Landholdings (1729)
Zaporozhian Host: 11%
Church: 17.2%
Starshyna: 35.2% (hereditary lands)
Towns: 1%
Cossacks and peasants: 35.6%

The army of the Zaporozhian Host (1700)
Total: about 30,000

It is not an easy matter to draw general conclusions from the individual histories of these five East European elites, for, given their stubborn attachment to local tradition, an attachment which was inextricably connected with their privileged position, nobles in all lands and regions tended to be extremely particularistic. Yet, despite the infinite variety of their ways, several generalizations may be ventured.

Compared to their Western colleagues, the five nobilities emerged belatedly. The oldest among them, the Polish and Hungarian, appeared when Western nobles were already long established, and the most recent, the Ukrainian *starshyna*, evolved when nobility in the West was already in decline. As in so many other instances in Eastern Europe, much of the initial impetus for the formation of these five elites came from the top – that is, it was strongly encouraged by kings, *hospodars*, archbishops, and *hetmans*. Because of the direct relationship between the overlord and the nascent noble, the feudal ladder in Eastern Europe had only two stages and, formally at least, never developed the myriad intermediate lordships which were typical of the West – hence the much greater emphasis in the East on the equality and even the mystical brotherhood of all nobles, especially evident in Poland and Hungary. While this equality of all nobles was extolled much more in principle than in practice, it was, none the less, a characteristic shibboleth of the Eastern nobles. And because the feudal hierarchy was sparse and land relatively plentiful, the nobles' conditional hold on their lands was transformed into a permanent one much more rapidly than in the West. Thus, the impression that emerges is that, once stimulated, the East European nobles enjoyed a looser, less controlled or structured, and more expansive growth than did their counterparts in the West.

One of the crucial experiences which justifies treating these elites as a group is their common participation in the transformation of Eastern Europe into the granary of the West. This development, and especially the ability of the nobilities to capitalize on it, provided them with a distinct set of characteristics which, by the seventeenth century, they shared in varying degrees. They had by then in each of the societies that we have examined gained overwhelming control of the land, which, in Eastern Europe, became the sole means of production (the nobles of France, England, and Germany owned on the average only about 20 per cent of their homelands). They exercised total control over the peasants, and that control contributed to their stifling impact on the commerce of the towns. On their estates they had a monopoly over judicial and administrative affairs, which made each noble, within the limits of his estate, a law unto himself. They possessed the political power and constitutional means to muzzle royal authority, as in Poland, or to keep it at bay elsewhere, and they cultivated a mystical vision of themselves as a superior race, apart from the rest of society, whose privileged position was justified by their and their forefathers' defence of the fatherland and of Christianity. These features created a socio-economic and political elite the like of which was not to be found in the West.

It goes without saying that important differences existed among these five nobilities, the more obvious of which will be mentioned here. The differences in the size and political impact of the Polish and Hungarian nobilities on the one hand and those of Livonia, Moldavia, and Ukraine on the other were most striking. Because the former dominated sovereign societies, participating in the elections of their monarchs and in powerful parliaments, they had a share in this sovereignty. Therefore, their constitutional rights were well defined and their representative institutions of paramount importance. Meanwhile, neither Moldavia, Livonia, nor Ukraine were sovereign societies. Therefore, their nobles had to recognize the overlordship of foreign rulers, although in practice this sovereignty was quite limited during most of the seventeenth century (during this period, Hungary slipped from the first category to the second). Also, their relatively small size precluded armed resistance against their overlords based exclusively on their own resources, as was possible in Poland. The less favourable position of these three nobilities vis-à-vis their overlords, although they had always remained strong with respect to their own native leaders, explains why their constitutional rights and representative institutions were relatively underdeveloped. Obviously, the fact that the elites of Moldavia and Ukraine were more recent and had sovereigns who did not formally recognize contractual arrangements also contributed to this state of affairs. But even the much older Livonian *ritterschaft* completed all the institutions of its self-government only in the seventeenth century. Nevertheless, despite these and other distinctions, the East European nobles shared a basic set of common values, and this was most clearly demonstrated in their general admiration for their ideal – the Polish *szlachta* and its "golden freedoms."

If the France of Louis xɪv was the model of absolutism in the West, then Poland of the "*szlachta* democracy" was the epitome of a noble-dominated society in the East. Little wonder that most of Poland's expansion came not by way of conquest but through voluntary unions of territorial elites: in 1569 the Lithuanian and Ukrainian nobles voted in Lublin to unite with Poland; in 1595 Moldavian boyars accepted Polish sovereignty; in 1658 at Hadiach, just eight years after their revolt, the Ukrainian *starshyna* made the first of several attempts to rejoin the Commonwealth. If they were unable or unwilling to join the Commonwealth, the neighbouring nobles were certainly ready to recreate it in their own lands: in 1699 the Livonians, in 1707 the Hungarians, and in 1710 the Ukrainians formulated constitutional projects which were directly based on the Polish *pacta conventa*. Even the Russian boyars tried to copy the Polish system, first during the Time of Troubles and then again in 1730. Meanwhile, the Polish *szlachta* observed its neighbours with a mixture of pity, self-satisfaction, and foreboding, as its tribunes pointed to Bohemia and later, in the seventeenth century, to Hungary as examples of the evils which could befall a society if absolutism were allowed to triumph.

This is not to say that the *szlachta* democracy lacked critics. No less a personage than Piotr Skarga, the most important Polish political writer of the seventeenth century, fulminated against the unbridled growth of noble privilege and urged his countrymen to support an absolutist monarchy. The huge Ukrainian revolt of 1648 was itself first and foremost a violent rejection of the nobles' predominant position in society. Its leader, Bohdan Khmelnytsky, also argued that the only solution to the excesses of noble rule was a stronger monarchy; in the early stages of the rebellion he wrote to the Polish king, Jan Casimir, "We pray to God that you should become an autocrat [*samoderzhets*] like other kings are, and that you should no longer remain, as did Your Royal Highness' predecessors, a slave of the *szlachta*."[71] But neither Skarga's eloquence nor Khmelnytsky's violence persuaded the Polish nobility to admit the shortcomings of its political system. Indeed, they only strengthened the nobles' fanatical commitment to it.

Eastern Europe's sharp detour to agrarianism and the related upsurge of the nobility had political ramifications of epochal significance. With so much power in the hands of the nobles, native rulers in the region were unable to establish enduring bases of power. When they attempted to build strong standing armies, the nobles, fearful that these might be used against them, insisted that they themselves could defend their land (the more demanding offensive campaigns were generally frowned upon) and blocked the creation of such forces. Because standing armies were practically non-existent, the bureaucracies which would have been engendered by the need to support them did not develop. Without these two pillars of statehood, strong monarchies were impossible. Moreover, because of the debilitated towns the kings had no bourgeoisie with which to counterbalance the nobility, as was the case in the West. Thus, native rulers, already hamstrung by the elective principle, remained political weaklings. While Vienna, Stockholm, Moscow, and Istanbul loomed around Eastern Europe like towering boulders of power, the region stretched out like a pebble beach of petty, self-contained lordships.

This spatial distribution of power, concentric in absolutist monarchies and contiguous in noble-dominated ones, encouraged regionalism in the latter and further blocked the centralization of power. However, as we have noted, in Eastern Europe's heyday in the fifteenth and sixteenth centuries this contiguous, decentralized distribution of power encouraged unions of territorial elites such as those of Poland with Lithuania and Hungary with Croatia. Yet, while these unions, so typical of the region, in turn created larger polities, these were not necessarily stronger ones. In any case, decentralization made dismemberment that much easier. This was painfully underlined by the dissection of Livonia into three parts, Hungary into three parts, Ukraine into two parts, and by Poland-Lithuania's loss of 35 per cent of its territory. East European historians like to explain the Polish Deluge, the Ukrainian Ruin, the Ottoman invasion of Hungary, and the devastation of Livonia and Moldavia in terms of external factors akin to natural disasters. But it is clear that most of these catastrophes were brought on by structural weaknesses in East European societies, in particular by their inability to centralize power.

With weak rulers, minuscule armies, handfuls of officials, and complete decentralization, seventeenth-century Eastern Europe was in effect a region of stateless societies. The institutions of modern statehood which did exist, such as standing armies and bureaucracies, had been imposed upon the region from the outside, by Vienna, Stockholm, Istanbul, and Moscow. But during most of the century these institutions were too few and far between to serve as a basis for modern statehood in the region. How then is one to describe the political institutions by which the area was ruled? To call Hungary a kingdom, Poland-

Lithuania a commonwealth or republic with a monarchic head, Moldavia a principality, or Ukraine a *hetman*ate is not very enlightening. These terms serve a descriptive but not an analytical function. Yet to argue that these East European polities were states in the modern or, indeed, in any sense of the word is simply misleading. Nor does calling them weak states solve the problem, for that appellation assumes that power rested, albeit insecurely or incompletely, in a specific type of political organization which, as we have seen, was functionally non-existent in the region.

If the East European polities of the seventeenth century were not states in the strict sense of the word, what were the predominant political institutions in the region? The answer, in our view, is associations of nobles. The emphasis is on the word *association* – that is, a body of persons associated for a common purpose, a league, or fellowship. The purpose for which the nobles banded together was the protection of their interests. And the associations which they formed for this purpose imposed their will on society as a whole, distributing power according to their own, associative principles.

Only if East European politics and nobilities are examined from the point of view of associations, without such hackneyed labels as "noble republics," "oligarchies," or "feudal states," may we gain a deeper insight into the nobles' instinctive distrust of political hierarchies, their abhorrence of the use of force against their colleagues, their insistence on strict adherence to rules, their commitment to the elective principle, their rejection of outsiders, and their emphasis on fellowship and on myths of group exclusiveness. The crown, which elsewhere was the symbol of monarchy and, eventually, of statehood, was in Eastern Europe the symbol of the associated nobles of the land, among whom the king was only a leading member. By failing to recognize this specifically East European conception of the crown, many historians have fallen into a nominalist fallacy: because they saw crowns and kingdoms in the region, they assumed that states were the predominant mode of political organization. But prior to the eighteenth century it was not kings, standing armies, or bureaucracies which dominated the region and set the tone of its politics; rather, the predominant, defining political institutions of the area were associations of nobles, which, in Weberian terms, were the ideal form of government in Eastern Europe and the basic element of its political system.

III

The Absolutist Offensive in Eastern Europe

A glance at Eastern Europe as of 1700 from a geopolitical perspective reveals a number of striking features. No society within the region had its own, native sovereign; none was capable of concentrating political and military power or of defending the integrity of its lands. Power lay beyond the limits of Eastern Europe; it lay in the capitals of its sovereigns, in Vienna, Moscow, Istanbul, Stockholm, and Dresden. The dichotomy between the East European societies on the one hand and their powerful neighbours such as Russia, Sweden, Saxony, the Habsburg and Ottoman empires, and Brandenburg-Prussia on the other rested on the basic differences between their political systems. At the heart of the East European political system was, as we have argued above, the associative principle, whereas the major political trait that was common to such glaringly diverse societies as Russia, Sweden, Saxony, and the Habsburg and Ottoman empires was absolutism.

Obviously the provenance, forms, extent, and impact of this absolutism varied greatly. The Habsburg, Swedish, and Saxon regimes were clearly patterned on European models. The Russian system was a combination of traditional patrimonialism and of Western administrative techniques and principles. And the Ottomans were the direct inheritors of the Oriental and Mediterranean imperial traditions. Absolutism did not guarantee omnipotence. Although the Habsburgs, Vasas, and Wettins managed, sometimes only briefly, to dominate the elites in their "core" lands, they could not subjugate them completely. Theoretically, the Ottoman rulers enjoyed the greatest prerogatives. However, decentralization, inefficiency, and corruption in their government severely limited their actual power. Even the Romanovs, unusually powerful both in theory and in practice, were careful not to antagonize all of the nobility all of the time. Another difference among the absolutist regimes was the times at which they gained their footholds in Eastern Europe. As of

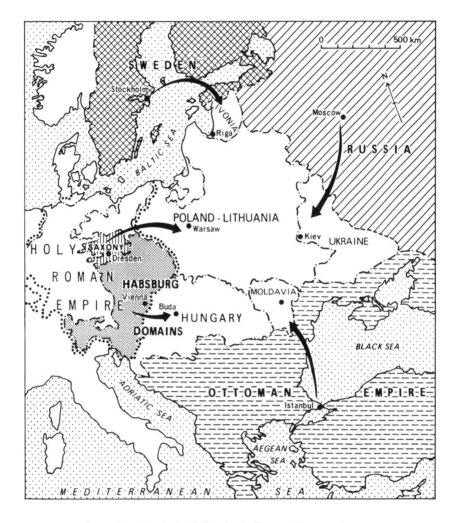

Map 1 The Absolutist Offensive in Eastern Europe circa 1700

1700 the Ottomans and Habsburgs had been there for centuries, the Vasas and Romanovs for decades, and the Wettins for only a few years. What is most noteworthy, however, is that although they gained sovereignty at vastly different times, the foreign sovereigns of East European lands commenced their absolutist offensive – that is, the implementation of absolutist, centralizing policies in the region – almost simultaneously, in the late seventeenth and early eighteenth centuries.

One explanation for this similarity in timing is that the sovereigns adopted or refurbished absolutism in their core lands at more or less the same time and therefore sought to extend it to their East European domains concurrently. Thus, the rise of Habsburg, Vasa, and Wettin absolutism dates from the end of the Thirty Years' War. Although the heyday of Ottoman absolutism, which peaked in the sixteenth century, was long past, the Köprülü revival of the late seventeenth century rejuvenated it briefly. And while Peter I's absolutist innovations in Russia came somewhat later, they quickly matched and surpassed those of other rulers.

One could dwell endlessly on the differences among the absolutist states and empires in Eastern Europe. This, however, would be tantamount to ignoring the forest for the trees. It is more important for our purposes to stress the features which the absolutist regimes had in common, so that we might elucidate more fully the nature of the confrontation between them and the nobilities of Eastern Europe.

To say that absolutism was the major feature shared by Eastern Europe's expansionist neighbours implies, first of all, that these societies accepted, to a greater or lesser degree, the principle that the power of their sovereigns was unlimited. Although the ruling dynasts often argued that their claim to unlimited power was a God-given right, in practice this claim depended primarily on the ruler's skill in political entrepreneurship. And political entrepreneurs were precisely what the Wettins of Saxony, the Vasas of Sweden, the Romanovs of Russia, the Habsburgs, the Ottomans, and the Hohenzollerns were, for their goal was always to monopolize power within their societies and to expand it at the cost of their neighbours.

Concomitant with its monopolization of power – indeed, interwoven with it – was the growth of absolutism's central institutions, such as the court, the standing army, and the bureaucracy. As dynasts accumulated power, their courts evolved from groups of personal servitors who looked after their monarch's household into imposing institutions which encompassed most of the major offices in the land. As the court placed all the major office-holders under the monarch's watchful eye, the standing army freed the ruler from his dependence on the levees of the elite, his most dangerous competitors for power.

And as standing armies grew, bureaucracies expanded, in order to cope with the complex logistical demands of modern warfare. Meanwhile, absolutism's proclivity for war provided the dynamic which constantly generated the need for strong leadership, powerful armies, and large, grasping bureaucracies. Thus, when we say that Eastern Europe's neighbours were absolutist, we are postulating basic structural similarities in their political systems, similarities among structures that were conspicuously absent in the East European polities.

Absolutist states resembled each other not only in terms of their basic structure but also in terms of their essential functions. Briefly, these functions consisted of the co-ordination and centralization of the governments of the various lands that constituted the absolutist ruler's domain; the extraction from subjects of the wherewithal needed to support the mainstays of the absolutist regime – that is, the standing army and bureaucracy; and the coercion of internal and external opponents of the ruler's policies. It was precisely these essential functions of the absolutist state that the East European polities sought to stifle in their midst and that they rejected most vehemently when efforts were made to impose them from without.

Perhaps the most simple and effective way of defining the quintessential differences between these two political systems is to state the opposition in the following terms: while the East European polities circa 1700 were based on an *associative* principle, the absolutist states which surrounded them functioned on an *organizational* principle. This distinction is useful because it stresses the fact that the absolutist state was basically an organization (as opposed to an association), which, like all formal organizations, was goal (power) oriented and possessed a hierarchy of authority and a rational system of rules and regulations which demanded efficiency and effectiveness in its operation. It thus stood in direct opposition to the East European association, with its stress on (theoretical) egalitarianism, particularism, mysticism, and with its goal of being a "welfare association" of the noble elite. The counterposing of these two terms may serve as a useful analytical tool that will help us to grasp the nature of the historical confrontation that was coming to a head in early eighteenth-century Eastern Europe.

In connection with the concept of organization, it would be appropriate at this point to touch on the question of statehood. It will have been apparent that, while referring to the absolutist powers as states, we have studiously refrained from applying this term to the polities of Eastern Europe. We use the term *state* selectively rather than in the usual sense – that is, as a catch-all term for all types of governing entities – to denote a specific type of political organization which usually first emerges when a ruler manages to establish relatively complete and effective control over his subjects. In Europe this type of power-producing and power-monopolizing organization appeared in roughly the sixteenth century and largely as a reaction to the inherent chaos of the feudal (associative) political system. The rise of royal absolutism and the formation of the first states in Europe thus perforce occurred simultaneously and interdependently. The prerequisites of royal absolutism – the institutions of the court, the standing army, and the bureaucracy – were also the sine qua non of emergent statehood. It follows, then, that polities that thwarted the rise of absolutism in their midst also prevented the evolution of the state. It is for this reason that the East European polities cannot be properly called states in the narrow sense. The dichotomy between these two political systems can be extended even further to that between the traditionalist noble estate-association and the modernizing absolutist state-organization.

Another striking aspect of Eastern Europe's absolutist neighbours is that the Russian, Swedish, Habsburg, Ottoman, and Saxon sovereigns all ruled multi-ethnic conglomerates. This may be explained by the fact that, in most cases, early state building was equivalent to empire building. In the pre-national age, before the concept of national sovereignty established itself, ethnic boundaries did not pose any meaningful limits to a ruler's expansionism. As the strength of a monarch's army and the effectiveness of his bureaucracy increased, so too did the size of his domains and the number of different peoples under his suzerainty. The absolutist state simply took on as much territory and as many people as it could handle and as foreign competition would allow. Because of the power vacuum which existed in Eastern Europe, a ruler who possessed a formidable military and administrative organization was naturally drawn into the region. From the sixteenth century onwards the area became a kind of open hunting-ground for the imperialistically inclined monarchies on the periphery of Eastern Europe, just as the Americas were the prime target for the colonial imperialism of the West European monarchies.

By 1700 each of Eastern Europe's absolutist neighbours had established a foothold in the area. Initially, however, these contacts did not take the form of direct takeovers, except in the case of the Ottoman invasion of Hungary. They were based instead on loose dynastic links, established under various circumstances, between the foreign sovereigns and their East European subjects. Thus, by 1512 the Moldavians had accepted Ottoman overlordship; in 1526 the Hungarians elected a Habsburg as their sovereign; in 1561 a part of Livonia negotiated the acceptance of Vasa suzerainty, and in 1621 the rest of Livonia became a part of the Vasa domains; in 1654 the Ukrainians voluntarily acknowledged the tsar's overlordship; and finally, in 1699 the Poles and Lithuanians elected August II of Saxony as their king. By and large the widespread presence of foreign sovereigns did not cause the individual East European peoples major alarm. It seemed to them that they were merely receiving, or had merely been forced to receive, new overlords, an event which they had experienced many times in the past. There was certainly little reason to believe that, with the new sovereigns, a new political system would be introduced. On the contrary, the new sovereigns invariably made the usual assurances that they would respect and preserve the traditional order, that is, of non-interference in internal (local) affairs.

At times it seemed that it was the East European polities which benefited the most from the new arrangements. With their election as kings of Hungary it was the Habsburgs and no longer the Hungarian nobles who were saddled with the costs and responsibilities of carrying on the war against the Ottomans. In Ukraine the Russians, forced to come to the aid of the Cossacks, involved themselves in a gruelling thirteen-year war with the Poles, in the course of which the Ukrainians rebelled several times against the tsar. No wonder that Athanasius Ordyn-Nashchokin, one of Moscow's leading statesmen, counselled the tsar to "give the Cossacks back to the Poles." In Poland-Lithuania one of August II's major election promises was that, at his own cost, he would regain for the Commonwealth its lost lands in Livonia and Moldavia. Of course, some of the new lands proved to be profitable to the new sovereigns. Livonia, for example, which comprised 12 per cent of the Vasas' domains, yielded 14 per cent of its income (although this only after three-quarters of a century of Swedish rule). In any case, in Hungary, Livonia, Moldavia, and Ukraine, the first few decades of rule by their new sovereigns did not bring about dramatic changes and led East Europeans to believe that their relations with them would be "business as usual."

After the initial period of the establishment of their sovereignty, during which the absolutist rulers generally respected their original compacts with their new subjects, came the inevitable tightening of their hold on their new lands. There were two basic factors that impelled them towards this goal. On the one hand, it seemed to them only logical to extend to their new lands the same system of government that obtained in their other holdings. Thus, if the Swedish crown imposed the *Reduktion* in Sweden in order to regain from the magnates the royal lands which they had amassed, why should it not extend the same measure to Livonia, where even more royal land had passed into the hands of the nobility? Or, if the Habsburgs found it easier to rule Bohemia by centralizing its administration in Vienna, why not do the same in Hungary? And if Peter I was willing to liquidate the *streltsy* (musketeers) in order to facilitate the modernization of his army, it was only natural that he should also consider reorganizing the Ukrainian Cossacks into regular army regiments. On the other hand, as the absolutist powers came into direct conflict with each other in Eastern Europe, they were faced with the necessity, and the opportunity, of tightening their control over their lands in the area. For example, the Swedish-Russian conflict of the early eighteenth century led to the stationing of more Swedish garrisons in Livonia and to a massive influx of Russian troops into Ukraine. August II's involvement in the Great Northern War gave him the excuse he needed to quarter his Saxon troops in Poland. The long wars of the Habsburgs with the Ottomans made their armies an almost permanent fixture in Hungary. Great-power conflicts thus provided absolutist monarchs with a useful cover and a telling argument for establishing the instruments of coercion, co-ordination, and, eventually, of exaction in East European lands.

But outright coercion was a costly alternative, to be used only as a last resort. A preferable if slower method of extending control was the manipulation of tensions within the resisting elites and of conflicts between them and the rest of society. It could also include the creation of a kind of fifth column interested in the extension of the sovereign's power; the gradual imposition of administrative and judicial changes; the cultural assimilation of the elite; judicious colonization, and so on. The goal of this approach was to manoeuvre the resisting elites into a position where they were left with no alternative but to acknowledge the unlimited power of their new sovereigns, or at least to admit the futility of resistance. It was this long-drawn-out, systematic approach, which Dimitrie Cantemir, *hospodar* of Moldavia, called "mechanica," that established the basis for the power of absolutist sovereigns in their East European lands. We will turn now to a case-by-case examination of the strategy and tactics employed by absolutist regimes in their encroachment on the politics of Eastern Europe.

THE OTTOMANS IN MOLDAVIA

It is not surprising that the Ottomans, the first of the absolutist powers to establish a magnificent court, a standing army, and a vast, specialized bureaucracy, were also the first to make great territorial gains in the Balkans and in Eastern Europe. As the immediate inheritors of the ancient Middle Eastern and Byzantine imperial, state-building traditions, the Ottomans were well aware of the principles and practices involved in the construction of an imperial system. How acutely aware their predecessors were of the precepts of imperial rule is evident from the example of Yusuf Khass Hajib of Balasagun, a scholar and statesman in the service of the Karakhanids, the first Islamic dynasty of Turkic empire builders, who in 1069 wrote: "To control the state requires a large army. To support the troops great wealth is needed. To obtain this wealth, the people must be prosperous. For the people to be prosperous,

Map 2 Moldavia in the Ottoman Empire circa 1700

the laws must be just. If one of these is neglected, the state will collapse."[1] About six hundred years later the Ottoman chronicler Mustafa Naima, in a tract entitled "The Cycle of Equity," repeated these same thoughts almost word for word. To these views may be added those of Tursun Bey, an Ottoman bureaucrat and historian of the fifteenth century: "Government based on reason alone is called *yasak*; government based on principles which ensure felicity in this world and the next is called divine policy or *şeriat* ... Only the authority of the sovereign can institute these policies ... God has granted this authority to one person, and that person, for the perpetuation of good order, requires absolute obedience."[2] Combined, these statements constitute not only a succinct expression of Ottoman political wisdom but also a cogent articulation of the concepts of sovereignty and divine-right absolutism, one that long predated the appearance of similar ideas in the West.

Even more elaborate and imposing than their ideas of rulership were the Ottomans' ruling institutions. In fact, throughout the sixteenth century the Ottoman standing army, bureaucracy, and court served as classic examples in Europe of how well such institutions could serve the cause of strong, effective government. A key to this effectiveness was the Ottoman *devişirme*, a recruitment system which was based on the old Middle Eastern idea, accepted by the Ottomans early in their empire-building career, that well-trained slaves made more loyal soldiers than did free men, since the latter tended to be less malleable and more inclined to place their own interests before those of their rulers. Elaborating on this idea, the Ottomans established a system in which only their personal slaves (*kuls*) were used in the standing army and in the bureaucracy. Their reasoning was simple: "he [the sultan] can elevate them [the slaves] or destroy them without any danger to himself."[3] Thus, every three to seven years, the Ottomans drafted promising Christian youths from the Balkans and brought about one to three thousand to Istanbul for training (the more privileged Muslims were excluded from the *devşirme*). There they were screened again and the more talented assigned to the palace for long and careful training that often led to the highest offices in the land, while the others were sent to the provinces for equally extensive and arduous training that eventually led to their assignment to the Janissaries, the standing army of the sultan. This system of recruitment had two distinct advantages: on the one hand it provided the sultan with well-trained, reliable soldiers and officials; on the other it allowed him to avoid any dependence on the Turkic landed aristocracy and on the Muslim urban population for military and administrative personnel. Advantages such as these were a long time coming to the monarchs of Western Europe.

At their peak in the mid-sixteenth century, the Janissaries represented an awesome force. Although they numbered only about 20,000 men, their unmatched training, discipline, and high morale made them the most effective fighting unit in the world. However, about a hundred years later, when the Ottomans were in decline, the Janissaries lost much of their effectiveness. This is evident from the fact that, while their numbers swelled to 70,000, largely because Muslims and the sons of Janissaries began to join in order to share in their privileges, only about 10,000 of the Janissaries were combat ready. In the late seventeenth century, as a result of badly needed reforms introduced by the Köprülü grand viziers, the Janissaries, trimmed in number to 34,000 combat-ready men, regained some of their former strength. If to this number is added the artillery and cavalry, the total number of men in the standing army in 1700 was about 60,000 to 70,000 men. In addition to these troops the Porte also had about 100,000 *sipahi*s, or feudal cavalry, and about 40,000 irregulars, mostly Crimean Tatars, at its disposal.[4] Thus, even in their declining years the Ottoman "men at the sword" represented a formidable force.

The size of the sultan's bureaucracy, or "men of the pen," as they were called, is more difficult to estimate, and its subdivisions are too many to enumerate here. Suffice it to say that late in the seventeenth century the central bureau of the treasury alone employed about 700 to 900 men.[5] To this figure may be added some of the approximately 4,000 *iç oğlans*, or trainees, who resided in the palace and performed some bureaucratic tasks as part of their training. As a measure of the degree of specialization of these bureaucrats and secretaries it might be noted that in 1527 the imperial council alone had eighteen secretaries, eleven of whom specialized in the preparation of political and administrative documents, the remaining seven of whom worked on financial decrees. Although it is hazardous to give estimates of the total number of Ottoman bureaucrats, the massive volume of documents which they produced is in itself ample evidence that the Ottoman bureaucracy was one of the largest in the world in the early modern period.

Finally, like a resplendent arch astride the two pillars of statehood, the Ottoman court provided a splendid setting for the sultan and the leading officials of the bureaucracy and commanders of the army. The vast size and richness of the Ottoman court is and was proverbial. Rough estimates of the total number of palace personnel range from 10,000 to 12,000. It would be erroneous, however, to assume that the function of the splendour of the palace was merely to cater to the personal whims of individual sultans. Like all absolutist courts, the Ottoman court also had a more pragmatic role to play. It was meant to suggest vast power and wealth, on the assumption that the suggestion would work to enhance the sultan's chances of claiming even greater power and wealth.

Such, in brief, were the forms and functions of the three main pillars of the political organization of the Ottoman empire. After it reached its peak in the sixteenth century, the Ottoman governmental system was in a steady state of decline. None the less, it remained an essentially absolutist form of organization and one which, during the reign of the Köprülü viziers (1656–1703), was still capable of some rejuvenation. In any case, even in the early eighteenth century the Ottoman empire was strong enough to thwart the separatism and limit the autonomy of its more recalcitrant provinces.

In terms of administration, the Ottoman lands fell into two categories. In the early seventeenth century approximately five-sixths of the empire was constituted by the fifty-six provinces which were ruled directly from Istanbul. The remaining sixth were vassal lands – Moldavia, Wallachia, Transylvania, and the Crimean Khanate – which served as buffers for the empire in areas of conflict with Christendom.[6] Although the terms of vassalage varied greatly, by and large vassal lands were obliged to pay the sultan a tribute and to provide military support when required. In return they were allowed to retain their traditional system of government. During the ascendancy of the empire, vassalage served as a preliminary stage to complete absorption, as was the case with Bulgaria, Bosnia, and Serbia. However, when the empire began to decline, the Ottomans viewed the vassal lands more as buffers against the Habsburg and Russian armies. By the seventeenth century total absorption of vassal lands was no longer seriously considered, although now and then the Porte threatened to turn recalcitrant vassals into regular Ottoman provinces. But this by no means meant that the Porte intended to loosen its control over these lands. On the contrary, it was prepared to do everything necessary, short of absorption, to maintain its influence and authority over its vassals.

Moldavia provides an excellent example of how Ottoman suzerainty was first established in the land and then extended and strengthened.[7] In 1455–6 *hospodar* Petru Rareş first made a symbolic payment of 2,000 *galben* to the Porte. This act established a precedent which, by 1538, led to the establishment of full and formal Ottoman sovereignty over Moldavia. The initial conditions which persuaded Stefan III to "plead for the divine protection of the Almighty Padişah" seemed quite innocuous. All that the Moldavians were obliged to do was to have the sultan confirm their choice of *hospodar*, pay a nominal "gift," and accept a token Ottoman garrison in some border fortresses. However, by the end of the sixteenth century the cost of the "gifts" and tribute to the Porte had become unbearable; the sultan was appointing *hospodar*s (and foreigners at that); Moldavian troops had to join the Ottomans in campaigns; and even Muslim mosques and fortresses were being constructed in the land.

Dimitrie Cantemir, the last of the native *hospodar*s, who ruled for a brief period at the beginning of the eighteenth century, analysed the "treacherous mechanica" of the Ottoman encroachment on Moldavia in his famous *History of the Ottoman Empire*. In his opinion it was not so much the brute force of the Ottomans as their systematic duplicity and bad faith that spun the web of economic and political entanglement which left Moldavia at the mercy of the Porte. He believed that the bait which had ensnared Moldavia into accepting the suzerainty of the sultan was its initial agreement to provide nominal "gifts" to the Porte: "For the Turks are most interested in enticing their enemy into paying some small sum of money, which they then readily called tribute. And once this is accomplished, there is nothing to prevent them from inventing various reasons for increasing the sum and transforming it into formal tribute. In this manner they completely subject to their rule lands which [originally] intended to accept only their protection."[8]

By this simple and obvious stratagem of constantly increasing the tribute, a measure which was enforced by nearby concentrations of Ottoman troops, the Porte systematically sapped the economy of Moldavia.[9] Thus, by 1593 the original gifts of 2,000 *galben* had risen to 65,000. Moreover, this was only part of the money extracted from the Moldavians. During the sixteenth century, a high point of Ottoman exploitation of the principalities, the Porte received about 250,000 *galben* from Moldavia. After the determined resistance which the Moldavians and Wallachians mounted in the early seventeenth century, Ottoman exactions in Moldavia were reduced by 50 per cent and in Wallachia by 80 per cent. However, by the 1690s the exactions began to creep upwards again and during this time averaged about 155,000 *galben* annually, one-third of which represented tribute while the remainder consisted of bribes, gifts, and other dues.[10]

An indirect but equally effective method of economic extortion in the principalities was the food monopoly. During the reign of Suleiman the Magnificent, the Ottomans reserved the right to purchase major exports such as cattle, grain, and honey for the needs of their troops and for the provisioning of Istanbul, a city of almost a million people in the seventeenth century. Later, the *hospodar*s had to guarantee the collection, shipment, and, what was most painful, the purchase of these foodstuffs at the lowest possible prices. Furthermore, foreign merchants, mostly Greeks and Turks, were given privileged status in this trade. Although the boyars managed to pass most of these burdens on to the peasants, the land as a whole was deprived of the means for capital accumulation; new investments were discouraged, and economic stagnation deepened.

A technique which produced both economic and political benefits for the Porte was the commercialization of the *hospodar*'s office. Theoretically, the *hospodar* was freely elected from among the boyar families, and the sultan only confirmed him in office. However, the Porte soon made it clear that confirmation would have to be bought. Between 1593 and 1595, when the two principalities were still relatively wealthy and the *hospodar*'s office had more prestige than it did later, the Ottomans realized a profit of 3,500,000 *galben* from the sale of the Moldavian and Wallachian *hospodar*ships. A century later the *hospodar*'s office sold for about 150,000 *galben*, an indication of the economic exhaustion of the principalities and of the decrease in the importance of the office of *hospodar*. Nevertheless, candidates for the *hospodar*ship still abounded, even though they had to pay interest at a rate as high as 20 per cent in order to raise the necessary funds.[11] Even with these tremendous costs many of the *hospodars* managed to profit from their investments during their increasingly brief tenures in office. Those who did not had their debts covered by their successors, as decreed by custom. In political terms, the practice of selling the office of *hospodar* meant that the office-holder had a vested interest in maintaining the status quo in order to realize a profit on his investment.

There were other political benefits for the Porte from the sale of the *hospodar*'s office. Since any man from one of the leading boyar families qualified for the *hospodar*ship, competition among the boyars was fierce. As a result the Moldavians broke up into warring factions which could easily be manipulated by the Porte. Moreover, the permanent existence of a pro-Ottoman party among the boyars, one which sought the Porte's support in order to attain or maintain power in the principality, became assured. Finally, in order to have one more check on the *hospodar*, the Porte demanded that he leave one of his sons as hostage in Istanbul.

Because it was financially profitable and politically preferable, the Porte frequently replaced *hospodars*. In the late seventeenth and early eighteenth centuries the average length of tenure was two and one-half years. Such a rapid turnover not only brought in more money to the sultan's coffers but also deprived the *hospodars* of the possibility of developing an independent power-base. Convinced that opposition was futile, most *hospodars* tended to behave more like tax-farmers than autonomous rulers. As this fiscal, Istanbul-oriented view of their own office began to prevail, the traditional role of the *hospodar* as one who ruled, administered justice, and cared for the needs of his subjects began to fade.

Although Moldavia's political and economic emasculation was directed from Istanbul, the Porte's policies could be effective only if the means for enforcing them were available in the principality itself. Therefore, the Ottomans sought to establish zones of direct control in and around the land. The initial step in this direction was the forced occupation in 1484 of Kilia and Bilhorod, two strategically important fortresses at the mouth of the Dniester. The fortresses and the surrounding area were detached from Moldavian administration and placed under the authority of local Ottoman commanders. Gradually, other Ottoman-administered territories were formed: in 1538 Bender, in 1595 Ismail, in 1622 Reni, and in 1711 Khotyn were converted into Ottoman strongholds. Since these strongholds stretched along the volatile Polish-Ukrainian border, the Porte argued, not without reason, that their purpose was to prevent foreign incursions. Yet it was also obvious that these fortresses could easily be used to crush any opposition to Ottoman influence in the principality. Moreover, since 1538 a Janissary guard of five hundred men had been assigned to the *hospodar*. Ostensibily, its function was to protect him, but in reality it represented just another means of controlling his actions.[12]

In the event that the fortresses and the Janissaries did not suffice, the Porte employed another of its favourite techniques of "political engineering," namely, that of the forced transfer of populations. Transferring troublesome nomads or rebellious townsmen to less vulnerable parts of the empire and bringing in more stable elements in their stead was an old Ottoman practice. It was applied to Moldavia in the following manner: in 1538 a large part of the territories on the west bank of the Dniester, in the vicinity of Kilia and Bilhorod, was removed from Moldavian jurisdiction, and the native population was forced to leave. In its place Nogai tribesmen, who had previously lived as nomads along the Black Sea littoral, were brought in. Eventually, the new inhabitants were called the Bilhorod Horde, and their land was referred to as the Bucak. At the first sign of Moldavian recalcitrance the Porte loosed the Nogais upon the principality to pillage, burn, and take captives. The mere threat of these raids constituted yet another check on any rebellious designs of the Moldavians. Finally, in the seventeenth century another foreign element appeared in Moldavia. Having accumulated vast fortunes in the grain and cattle trade as well as great influence in the Porte, the Levantine Greeks, or Phanariots, began to make heavy financial and political investments in the principalities. With the penetration of the Phanariots into the boyar class, the Porte was assured candidates for the *hospodar*ship who were more reliable than the native Moldavian elite.

In general, Ottoman policies towards Moldavia concentrated on two areas: extraction and coercion. The Porte's interest in co-ordinative policies, that is, in those that might lead to the principality's absorption into the Ottoman empire, while varying at times, was generally much less pronounced. There were several reasons for the Porte's underplaying of its co-ordinative tendencies. One was directly related to the changes which took place in Ottoman administrative practices during the sixteenth century. At the time the Ottoman administration changed from one that relied heavily on feudal warrior-administrators who received allotments of land (*timar*s) for their services to a specialized bureaucracy which was paid in cash by the central treasury. For this reason – in order to pay their bureaucrats – the Ottomans wanted cash from Moldavia and the other vassal states rather than tighter control over the land. Because it realized that the *hospodar*s, operating in their homelands, were able to extract much more wealth than could Ottoman governors, the Porte did not abolish the office or interfere in Moldavian internal affairs, although it did systematically replace *hospodar*s, thus undermining their political significance. Strategic considerations as well help to explain Ottoman respect for Moldavian autonomy. Since Moldavia, Wallachia, Transylvania, and the Crimea were meant to function as buffers – a role which increased in importance as the Ottoman empire grew weaker – the installation of the administrative system in areas which might fall to the enemy was avoided. This attitude changed somewhat in the late seventeenth century, when, during the Köprülü revival, the Ottomans again went on the offensive in Eastern Europe.[13] It was then that, much to the distress of the Moldavians, rumours began circulating to the effect that the Ottomans intended to transform the principality into an Ottoman province.

OTTOMAN EMPIRE: SELECTED STATISTICS[14]

Population and area circa 1700
Under direct imperial control: approximately 1,600,000 square kilometres
Under tributary control: approximately 160,000 square kilometres
Population: 12 million to 15 million

Standing army (mostly Janissaries and not including navy)
Peacetime army: approximately 70,000; wartime army (with Tatar auxiliaries): 180,000–200,000

Budget (late seventeenth century)
Military expenditures: 62.5%
Court expenditures: 29.5%
Expenditures for Divan (imperial council) officials: .7%
Other expenses: 7.5%

THE VASAS IN LIVONIA

In the Baltic area empire building always had a markedly commercial character. For almost a millennium *dominium maris Baltici* was synonymous with control of the shipping lanes, of the wealthy coastal ports, and of the resources of the vast hinterlands. In the seventeenth century Sweden succeeded in establishing her dominance over the region. Her venture into empire building was thoroughly modern in that it followed the latest dictates of European absolutism. It was, however, short lived. By 1709 it had become clear that Swedish mastery over the Baltic could not be maintained. For Sweden, a poor land of only about one and one-half million inhabitants in 1700, the gap between the means and the end had simply become too great. None the less, Sweden's venture into empire building had been a brilliant attempt which aroused fear among neighbouring countries and which was emulated by those who had their own imperial ambitions.

The groundwork for Sweden's brief burst of imperial glory was laid in the 1530s and 1540s, not long after the Swedes rose up against their Danish king, abrogated their dynastic union with Denmark, and elected, in 1523, Gustav Vasa as their king. During the reign of the first Vasa came the initial attempts to establish a regular bureaucracy, which at first consisted mainly of Germans, as well as the skeleton of a standing army and navy and a royal court. Not long afterwards, in 1561, Sweden made her first conquest overseas, wresting Estland from the invading Russians. By the 1580s the so-called Eastern Program for expansion in the Baltic had been established, and as Russia slipped into turmoil after the death of Ivan IV, the Swedes took over the Neva's outlet to the sea and much of the surrounding area. Sweden's attempt to secure *dominium maris Baltici* was well under way.

Initially, Swedish society reacted favourably to the growth of state institutions and to the external expansion. Most of the inhabitants of this vast, rugged, and sparsely populated land felt that they had more to gain than to lose from these developments. The nobility, which was quite small (only 320 titled and untitled noble families in the early seventeenth century) and not very wealthy, found employment in the army and in the bureaucracy. Moreover, many nobles received direct benefits from the foreign conquests, in the form of grants of land in the newly acquired provinces in return for their service. The tiny burgher class, which constituted only about 2 per cent of the population, also had much to gain. The heightened activity of the state and the foreign conquests placed many Baltic ports under Swedish control, injected a new vitality into iron mining, the land's oldest industry (about 4 per cent of the population was involved in this field), encouraged the budding arms-manufacturing industry, and led to a surge of urbanization. Thus, whereas in 1581 Sweden had only 33 towns and Stockholm had a meagre population of between 6,000 and 7,000, by the end of the seventeenth century 31 new towns had been established and

Map 3 Livonia in Sweden's Baltic Empire circa 1700

Stockholm's population had risen to between 42,000 and 43,000 inhabitants[15] The peasants, who were free and who formed a separate estate in the diet, saw in the growth of royal power a counterbalance to the nobility, with its tendency to exploit the peasantry. However, as Sweden's military, political, and socio-economic growth increased rapidly in the early seventeenth century, it began to create serious tensions within society.

The greatest problems arose from the attempt of the nobility, more specifically, of the approximately fifty titled aristocratic families, to monopolize the gains of Sweden's expansion. Strong kings like Gustav II Adolphus (1611-32) and Charles X (1654-60) raised enormous armies of 100,000 to 150,000 men and honed them to near invincibility; they rationalized Sweden's administration until it became a model for all of Europe; and they added Livonia, Ingria, Pomerania, and northern Germany to their empire, thereby raising Sweden to great-power status. In return for their contribution, the aristocrats who helped to lead these armies and to organize the empire demanded and received ever larger portions of the newly acquired lands. This granting of nominally royal lands was especially prevalent during the periods of regency, such as from 1632 to 1644, when five aristocrats, led by Axel Oxenstierna, constituted the Regents' Council and ruled the land. By 1654 almost 65 per cent of all arable land was in noble hands, although legally the nobles owned only 33 per cent of all the arable land. So great was the self-confidence of the aristocracy during the regency that in 1634 they passed the Form of Government Act, which assured them a predominant influence in government and gave rise to the so-called *monarchia mixta*, or half-royal and half-oligarchic rule. During the reign of Queen Christina (1644-54) the aristocrats and nobles continued to prosper, as attested by the rise, during the decade of the queen's rule, of the number of non-titled noble families from 300 to 600, while the number of titled families rose from 13 to 16.[16] But the demands of a well-run imperial state and the limitless self-interest of an oligarchy could not co-exist indefinitely. In the second half of the seventeenth century matters came to a head.

As the nobles, who were exempt from taxes, acquired more and more royal lands, the tax-base shrank. This meant that the taxpaying estates, the burghers, clergy, and peasants, had to shoulder the continually expanding financial burden of the aggressive and belligerent state (between 1600 and 1720, for example, Sweden spent seventy-five years at war). Beginning in 1650, the taxpaying estates and the poorer nobility began to demand that the alienated royal lands which had fallen into the hands of the aristocrats be returned to the treasury, or, as they put it, that a *Reduktion* be carried out. Finally, when in 1680 Charles XI turned to the diet after an unsuccessful war with Denmark with a request for more funds, the taxpaying estates and the lower nobility stated that they would meet this request only if all the alienated lands which yielded over 600 *talers* were returned to the crown (the 600-*taler* limit excluded the lower nobility from the measure, thereby winning its support). Realizing that this was a golden opportunity to undermine the power of his dangerous aristocratic rivals, the young king sided with the taxpaying estates and agreed to put the *Reduktion* into effect.

But the passage of the Great Reduction Act of 1680 was not enough for Charles XI. Taking advantage of the pro-royalist and anti-aristocratic mood of the diet, the king pushed through the abolition of the Act of Government of 1634, which had provided the regents with vast influence. In the coming years he continued to enlarge his powers, always using the threat of an aristocratic return to power as an excuse. Finally, in 1693 the estates were persuaded to pass the Declaration of Sovereignty, which formally recognized the king as a divinely ordained autocrat "responsible only to God for his actions." Absolutism had now become fully entrenched in Sweden.

It was in 1626, during the time of imperial expansion, of growing oligarchic influence, and before the sudden emergence of absolutism, that Sweden acquired Livonia.[17] Because the province soon came to serve as Sweden's granary and the source of its largest cash receipts, and because it contained Riga, the empire's busiest commercial centre, the relationship between the Livonians and the crown was a crucial one. Initially, it seemed that the *ritterschaft* and the Vasas were quite compatible. A common faith, Lutheranism, precluded the possibility of religious conflicts. Swedish aristocrats who received lands in Livonia were just as interested as was the *ritterschaft* in preserving the "good old ways." Moreover, since most of these aristocrats preferred to remain in Stockholm, there was no sudden influx of foreigners to irritate the Livonian elite. On the contrary, many of the poorer German nobles benefited by obtaining employment as administrators of Swedish-owned estates. Indeed, as long as Swedish magnates managed to control royal power, Livonian interests and, in particular, the cause of Livonian autonomy prospered. It was, after all, during the rule of Regents' Council that the Livonian *landesstaat* had reached its apogee. Little wonder, then, that in 1660 the Livonian *ritterschaft* petitioned the magnate-controlled Swedish diet for Livonia's incorporation "in perpetuum" into the Swedish empire as a "membra regni."

Because of legal complications, however, the question of the complete incorporation of Livonia into the empire was postponed for several years. Meanwhile, political developments in Sweden drastically dampened Livonian enthusiasm for the Swedish *reich* (empire). Talk of the *Reduktion* had been heard in the diet for decades before 1680. But, as it became increasingly evident that the measure would finally be put into effect, the Livonians, whose province contained many crown lands, became increasingly apprehensive about the effect of the reform. In 1678, before the final decision to implement the *Reduktion* had been made, a Livonian delegation was on the way to Stockholm to seek reassurances. It was instructed to obtain Charles xi's confirmation of the *ritterschaft's* "previous and ancient privileges, statutes, knightly rights, immunities, liberties, and legal and hereditary possessions." True to their reputation for pragmatism, the Livonians were ready to bargain: in exchange for the king's confirmation of their rights they offered to agree to the planned imposition of the *Reduktion* in Livonia. However, a crucial qualification was added – the *Reduktion* was to apply only to the recently acquired estates of the Swedish magnates in Livonia and not to those of the *ritterschaft*. Since the Swedish oligarchs were rapidly losing power, the German nobles sought to profit from their misfortune by bartering away their interests to the crown in return for a confirmation of Livonian rights. The manoeuvre was apparently successful. In 1678 Charles xi confirmed the rights and privileges of the *ritterschaft*, which, no doubt, breathed a collective sigh of relief.

This sense of relief was short lived. Only three years later, in 1681, the Livonian nobility was informed that the crown, although it had by means of the *Reduktion* in Sweden reclaimed 80 per cent of its alienated lands and reduced noble landholdings by 50 per cent, was still in financial trouble. The king, with all due respect for the legal forms, presented three recommendations to the Livonian diet: that the *Reduktion* apply to all crown land alienated since the days of the Livonian Order – in other words, that the *ritterschaft's* lands also submit to the revision; that new measurements of the land be made and that the obligations of the serfs be reviewed; and that serfdom be abolished. The Livonians were stunned. After a number of fiery speeches they voted to accept the second proposal but refused to consider the other two. Then the deputies counterattacked. By what right, the Livonians inquired, did the decisions of the Swedish diet apply to Livonia? Gustav Mengden, the *ritterschaft's* representative, composed a lengthy and emotional statement defending the nobility's privileges and sent it to the king. In it he openly referred to the bargain that had been struck in 1678 as well as to previous royal guarantees, and concluded with the audacious phrase: "Even the new king is bound by previous contracts." Among the agitated Livonians one angry question led to another until the basic issue was breached: what was the exact relationship of Livonia to Sweden? Had the province been completely incorporated into the Swedish kingdom after it had been wrested from the Poles in 1626, or was it, as the Livonians argued, merely a personal union that bound the two lands together?

Charles xi found the Livonian arguments and protestations not only irrelevant but insulting (to become insulted was the king's favourite way of reacting to anyone who dared to question his prerogatives). He responded cautiously, however. After waiting several years until after the furor had subsided, in 1686 he appointed a new governor-general. Unlike previous appointees, who had invariably been chosen from among the Swedish magnate families, the representative of the crown, Johann Jacob Hastfer, was a German noble from Estland who owed his rise solely to royal favour. With the help of this loyal, dedicated, and well-informed administrator Charles XI prepared to impose the *Reduktion* on his recalcitrant Livonian subjects. After issuing some legalistic rationalizations he ordered Hastfer to proceed, with the aid of Swedish troops, to impose the decision of the Swedish diet on the Livonian nobility.

The *Reduktion* hit Livonia hard.[18] Roughly five-sixths of the arable land was restored to the crown (5215 *haken* out of 6318). The land was then leased back to the noblemen, creating a windfall for the Swedish treasury: between 250,000 and 320,000 *talers* flowed into its coffers annually. In 1694 a high point of 415,000 *talers* was reached. The leases accounted for 33 to 40 per cent of all the income from the provinces.[19] Income from Livonia was the highest of all incomes from Sweden's overseas provinces. Thus, Sweden provided about 54.7 per cent of the imperial revenue in 1699, Finland 8.7 per cent, the three German holdings of Pomerania, Bremen-Verden, and Wismar 15.5 per cent, and the Baltic provinces of Livonia, Estland, and Ingria 21.1 per cent.

The furor over the *Reduktion* in Livonia brought an issue to the fore which Swedish statesmen had been debating throughout the seventeenth century, namely, what was Sweden's policy towards her overseas provinces? The representatives of the crown and of the bureaucracy viewed the question in terms of efficiency of administration. As early as 1630 Johann Skytte, the governor of Livonia, Ingria, and Karelia, had argued that the provinces should be completely incorporated into the empire, that their inhabitants should be absorbed into the Swedish estates, and that they should receive seats in the diet, become subject to Swedish law, and enjoy Swedish privileges. Skytte's proposals were opposed by the powerful chancellor, Axel Oxenstierna, and by the leading aristocrats. Oxenstierna believed that, if the Livonians became part of the estates of the realm, "in such matters as concern Livonia ... [they] will try to thwart me."[21] Thus, to the chancellor, incorporation of Livonia meant the diminution of central authority, and therefore he resisted this policy. The magnates, for their part, resisted the incorporation of the Baltic provinces into the Swedish crown lands on the one hand because they enjoyed the same broad privileges in the provinces as the local German nobility did, on the other because they did not want to share their influence in the Swedish diet and the Regents' Council with the German newcomers.

Until the 1680s and 1690s Swedish policy in the Baltic provinces wavered between these two positions. Once absolutism triumphed, however, the crown resolutely moved to eliminate provincial particularism. In 1690 Charles xi called for Livonian delegates to come to Stockholm to argue the case for their land's special rights. The dramatic and far-reaching confrontation which took place in the capital will be discussed later. In essence, however, the Livonian position was that a contractual arrangement had existed between the *ritterschaft* and the crown and that to alter this agreement was illegal. The Swedes countered with the argument that Livonia had entered the Swedish empire in 1626 by an act of conquest, not, as had Estland in 1561, on the basis of a contractual arrangement. Furthermore, the Swedes argued, the king's concessions to the Livonians were signs of favour and not binding commitments at all.

The uproar that this position of the crown evoked in Livonia convinced Charles xi that he had to act firmly. In 1694 the representative institutions of the Livonian nobility were disbanded. The Livonian autonomy ceased to exist. Moreover, a systematic policy of cultural assimilation was implemented in the Baltic provinces as a whole. It took the form, for example, of requiring candidates for bureaucratic office in Livonia and other Baltic lands to study for two years at Livonia's Dorpat University, where the language of instruction and most of the staff were Swedish. Whereas in the 1640s only seven of twenty-four professors at Dorpat had been Swedish, in the 1690s the proportion was twenty-four of twenty-eight.[22] In all bureaucratic appointments Swedes were given preference over local candidates. How this affected the ethnic composition of the imperial bureaucracy may be seen from the following: in 1640 Swedes constituted about 65 per cent of the higher civil servants, Finns 11 per cent, Germans 5 per cent, and Baltic Germans about 4 per cent. By 1700 the ethnic composition of the imperial bureaucracy was Swedes, 74 per cent; Finns, 15 per cent; Germans, 2.6 per cent; and Baltic Germans, only 1.5 per cent. The remainder of the bureaucrats were of unknown ethnic origin.[23] As well, positions in the pastorate were more often than not awarded to Swedish and Finnish candidates. And to make matters even worse for the *ritterschaft*, the galling question of serf reform was continually raised by the crown's representatives.

For the Livonian noblemen the Swedish reforms were not simply an attack on their "ancient" institutions, most of which dated back only to the 1630s. Nor was wounded German cultural pride a major issue. What worried the *ritterschaft* most was that these reforms implied an attack on the basis of the nobility's existence, its privileged position in society. Crucial decisions regarding Livonia were now made in Stockholm, thus stifling Livonian participation; Swedes were taking over the most influential offices in the land; even the noblemen's livelihood, their control over the peasants, was threatened. Therefore, it is not surprising that there were those among the *ritterschaft* who felt that more than legalistic arguments were needed to preserve what they had attained after generations of service to the Swedish crown.[24]

SWEDEN: SELECTED STATISTICS[25]

Population and area circa 1700
Sweden alone: approximately 1.4 million
Rest of empire: approximately 1 million (of which Livonia accounted for 300,000)
Area of empire: approximately 900,000 square kilometres

Social structure
Peasants: 90%
Burghers: 5%
Miners: 4%
Nobles: less than 1%

Landholdings (Sweden only)
Crown: 35.6%
Nobles: 32.9%
Peasant lands (taxable): 31.5%

Armed forces
Standing peacetime army: 40,000-60,000; wartime army: 110,000
Navy: 42 ships-of-the-line and 12 frigates (approximately 15,000 men)

THE HABSBURGS IN HUNGARY

If we accept the general rule that empire building also involved state building, then the Habsburg experience prior to the seventeenth century presented an exception. To a large extent the separation of these two related undertakings may be explained by the manner in which the Habsburg dynasty acquired its far-flung domains. The well-known Habsburg dictum, "Let others engage in war. You, fortunate Austria, marry!" openly acknowledged, even boasted of the dynasty's remarkable skill and luck in acquiring rich and important lands not by war but through marriage. One of the reasons it was able to arrange favourable marriages was the Habsburg accession to the leadership of the Holy Roman Empire, first in 1273 and them uninterrupted from 1438 onwards.

Originally, Rudolf I Habsburg had been elected to the prestigious although

Map 4 Hungary in the Habsburg Empire circa 1700

not particularly powerful position of Holy Roman Emperor because, with relatively modest landholdings in Austria and Switzerland, he posed no threat to the mighty territorial princes of the empire. Yet clever use of this position allowed the Habsburgs to conclude marriages which in 1477 brought in the rich Burgundian inheritance; in 1496 gave them title to Castile and Aragon; and in 1515–16, through a complicated matrimonial arrangement, allowed them to claim the crowns of Bohemia, Hungary, and Croatia. Even after the split in 1556 of this vast conglomerate of overlordships between the Spanish and Austrian lines of the dynasty, the latter still retained the imperial title and extensive holdings.

The Habsburg marriage policy had its drawbacks, however. Since military conquests played a relatively minor role in the dynasty's rise to prominence, the institutional by-products of war, the standing army and its supporting bureaucracy, remained relatively underdeveloped in the realm of the Austrian Habsburgs. Moreover, the three different roles that the Austrian Habsburgs played, as leaders of the ramshackle Holy Roman Empire, as the elective limited kings in the Eastern monarchies, and as the hereditary, relatively powerful overlords in their Austrian *erbländer*, made the formulation of a coherent policy, let alone centralization, a difficult matter. A concrete reflection of how underdeveloped the dynasty's central agencies were was the fact that, up to the sixteenth century, the entire court and chancellery could fit into the few wagons in which the Habsburgs made their frequent peregrinations to Prague, Pozsony, and back to Vienna. Thus, although they had long been associated and even infatuated with the imperial idea, the Habsburgs were far behind their competitors, the Bourbons and Ottomans, in developing the infrastructure of the state.

The great German historian Leopold von Ranke often argued that Habsburg Austria was not an "old power."[26] Tracing its rise from the medieval period, he concluded that the dynasty became an independent power of European significance only after the reconquest of Hungary in the late seventeenth century. The significance of this conquest lay not in the acquisition of a large and strategic territory that ensured the entry of the Habsburgs into the ranks of the superpowers. According to Ranke, territorial expansion was of only secondary importance. By explicitly connecting the establishment of the dynasty's power with the expulsion of the Ottomans from Hungary, a goal which took almost 150 years to achieve, Ranke wished to emphasize the relationship between the protracted period of war and the development of powerful Habsburg Austrian statehood.

To illustrate this point we need only note that the first permanent Habsburg military organization was created in 1552 with the establishment by Ferdinand

1 of a series of strong points on the Styrian-Croatian border to ward off the Ottomans. Within ten years this buffer zone, or *militärgrenze*, consisted of fifty-five strong points, about four thousand military colonists, and cost Vienna about 500,000 *gulden* annually. Although this buffer zone, which eventually extended along the entire Habsburg-Ottoman border, could not yet be equated with a standing army – it was established only in 1649 – it was certainly a major step towards the formation of a permanent military establishment. To provide a necessary administrative base for the struggle against the Ottomans, a mixed civilian-military body, the Vienna-based *Hofkriegsrat*, was established in 1566 to supervise the military affairs of the entire realm. Thus, these two institutions, designed specifically for the struggle with the Ottomans, were among the early building-blocks of Habsburg Austrian statehood.

An even more graphic illustration of the relationship between the Ottoman war and the growth of Habsburg state institutions was the policy and actions of the dynasty in Hungary.[27] During the Thirty Years' War the Hungarians had complained bitterly that the Habsburgs were neglecting the war against the Ottomans. Therefore, as soon as the European war ended, the Hungarian diet readily agreed, in January 1649, to let the Habsburgs take on full responsibility for the defence of the 150-mile Hungarian border with the Ottomans and for the maintenance of the eighty strong points along it. It was a crucial decision. So anxious were the Hungarians to rid themselves of the burdens of defence that they were slow to realize that, in so doing, they were giving Vienna the legal right to bring its troops into the kingdom. In 1652 there were already 4,000 Imperials – that is, Habsburg troops – in the land. By 1660 the number had reached 18,000. It was this development that gave the Habsburgs the solid power-base they had always wanted in Hungary.

There were, of course, other reasons for the growing Habsburg presence in Hungary. The Thirty Years' War had destroyed once and for all the dynasty's cherished dream of presiding over a European Christian empire. It had become evident that its future now lay in the East, in Austria, Bohemia, Hungary, and Croatia. But dynastic claims alone to overlordship in these lands were no guarantee of power. To profit politically and financially from these holdings, the Habsburgs had to control them more closely than they had in the past. In Austria the defence of the land against the Ottomans had provided Vienna with the opportunity to impose its bureaucratic controls. The Thirty Years' War had done the same in Bohemia. Moreover, the Bohemian Revolt of 1618 allowed the Habsburgs to set a precedent by brutally putting down the recalcitrant elite of the land. Hungary was clearly next. Both the political and military demands of the moment and the ideas on government then current in Vienna called for tighter control of the land. Almost all of the leading statesmen in Vienna, including men like Wenzel Lobkowitz, Johann Paul Hocher, Johann Becher, and Raimundo Montecucolli, were dedicated adherents of the absolutist and mercantilist ideas that were sweeping the continent at the time, and they avidly urged the Habsburg ruler, Leopold I, to implement these ideas in Hungary.

Becher, a classic mercantilist, for example, felt that, with the subjugation of Bohemia, Hungary's "special status," that is, its right to maintain its traditional form of government, did not make economic sense. He argued that if a realm was large enough, economic self-sufficiency could best be achieved if it was united by a single language, currency, religion, and system of government. This emerging perception of the Habsburg lands as constituting a single economic unit led Vienna to establish companies in Hungary which monopolized the Hungarian cattle export and which were designed to guarantee Vienna with sufficient quantities of meat while at the same time funnelling the profits into the dynasty's coffers. Similar monopolies were established in 1690 in silver mining and in the salt trade. This was a clear indication that, although the Habsburgs still recognized the constitutional and political individuality of Hungary, they had already begun to view it as part of a larger economic whole which included all the lands under their control. Indeed, it appeared that Hungary had already been assigned a specific role in this economic conglomerate, that of providing raw materials for the more advanced economies of Austria and Bohemia.

Mercantilist motives alone did not lead Viennese statesmen to view Hungary in terms of centralization. Hocher, the talented son of German burghers, who was one of the organizers of the nascent Habsburg bureaucracy, had a deeply ingrained, almost reflex aversion to the particularistic Hungarian system of government and, by extension, to the Hungarian people in general. At every opportunity he argued for the elimination of this system. Even more antagonistic towards the Hungarians was Montecucolli, a Habsburg field marshal and one of Europe's foremost military strategists. In 1670, with characteristic military directness, he proposed that the most effective way of dealing with the attachment of the Hungarians to the "antiquated" laws was to apply force. Only in this manner would the spirit of insubordination which was so typical of this "nation of rebels, robbers, and restless men" be quelled.[28] Emperor Leopold I, however, was loath to act on the advice of his ministers. Ethnic, cultural, and political heterogeneity had always been a characteristic feature of the Habsburg domains, and he could not be easily persuaded that that diversity had to be done away with. Ironically, it was not so much the advice of his ministers as the actions of the Hungarians themselves that finally convinced Leopold I that reforms were necessary in Hungary.

In 1666–7 a group of Hungarian and Croatian magnates, led by such illustrious men as Ferenc Wesselényi, Péter Zrinyi, Ferenc Nadasdy, Ferenc Frangipán, and Ferenc Rákóczi I, concluded a secret pact to organize a revolt against the Habsburgs. Preparations included overtures, which proved to be fruitless, to the French and Ottomans, as well as agitation among the lower nobility and even the peasants. Since it had uncovered the plot, the Viennese court was ready for the revolt when it broke out in March 1670, and thus crushed it easily. Seeing that all was lost, several of the magnates voluntarily and rather self-confidently went to Vienna to ask for pardon. However, the days were over when the Hungarian elite could resist its sovereigns almost as a matter of course and at little risk.

Although initially Leopold I had been inclined to pardon the magnates, the strident protestations of his ministers changed his mind. Essentially, the ministers stressed two lines of argument. On the one hand they cited historical precedents, such as the failure of the Spanish Habsburgs to deal resolutely with the Dutch, which resulted in their loss of the Netherlands, and the Bohemian Revolt of 1618, which was a frightening example of how conflicts between the sovereign and the estates could explode into international wars of uncontrollable proportions. On the other hand they found legalistic and theological justifications to support a hard line on Hungary, especially since the Catholic church had little sympathy for the predominantly Protestant Hungarian nobility. Specialists in civil and canon law assured the emperor that any nation which rebelled against its rightful sovereign forfeited its rights and privileges. This theory of "forfeiture by rebellion" became a long-standing favourite of the Habsburgs in dealing with rebellious, particularistically inclined subjects. Convinced by the arguments of his ministers, Leopold I agreed "to use this opportunity to arrange things differently in Hungary."[29]

To begin with, severe punishment was meted out to the rebels. After a brief trial, Zrinyi, Frangipán, Nádasdy, Bónis, and Tattenbach, an Austrian co-conspirator, were beheaded in Vienna. Rákóczi saved himself only by raising 400,000 *forints* for a pardon. The executions sent shock waves through the Hungarian elite. The whole affair had been particularly painful because, despite Hungarian protestations, the magnates had not been judged in Hungary according to Hungarian laws. In addition, over two thousand Hungarian and Croatian noblemen were interrogated, and of these about three hundred were deprived of their estates for allegedly collaborating with the rebels.

The Habsburgs' new severity did not spare the masses. On 21 March 1671 Leopold I issued an edict which ordered the *komitats* to pay for the support of Habsburg troops on their territory. To meet these expenses, the *komitats* had to level an extraordinary tax on the peasants which came to sixty *forints*, almost ten times the normal annual tax. The outbreaks of popular discontent that followed the promulgation of this edict were dealt with harshly and effectively.

On the heels of these measures came more far-reaching attempts to reform the Hungarian form of government. In order to liquidate the pillars of the traditional system, the office of palatine was abolished in 1671, and from 1672 the Hungarian diet was no longer called. A committee consisting of a president, the Master of the Teutonic Order, Johann Gasper Amperignen, and four German and four Hungarian advisers was established on 27 February 1673. The committee was designed to act as the highest administrative institution in Hungary; although it never functioned effectively, its very establishment was a clear indication of the bureaucratic, centralizing trend in Habsburg thinking.

To make matters worse, Vienna allowed the Counter-Reformation to sweep over Hungary. On 5 March 1674 about 730 Protestant ministers were brought to the court and forced to accept Catholicism. Those who refused were sold as galley slaves, despite the great hue and cry raised throughout Europe. Meanwhile, Archbishop György Szelepcsény boasted that he alone converted almost sixty thousand Protestants to Catholicism.[30]

It soon became evident, however, that these initial, hastily conceived reforms had gone too far too fast. In 1678 a dangerous *kuruc* uprising took place. The *kuruc* ("crusaders") were Hungarians of various classes who had fled to Transylvania and other eastern borderlands in order to escape Habsburg rule. Their uprising was led by Imre Thököly, an ambitious young magnate who had managed to survive the 1670 uprising. In 1680 Thököly, supported by the Ottomans, gained control of thirteen eastern *komitats* and proclaimed himself their lord. The Ottomans offered him a royal title, which he, however, refused. Faced by the growing threat from the Ottomans, the Habsburgs had no choice but to back away from their ambitious plans for reform. On 28 April 1681 Leopold I again convened the Hungarian diet. When the estates assembled at Sopron, the king allowed them to elect a palatine. He also declared the equality of all religions, abolished the governing committee, and offered amnesty to the rebels. Thus, the first attempts at reform in Hungary came to a rather ignominious end.

One aspect of Habsburg rule that could not be removed from Hungary was the imperial army. The constant wars with the Ottomans and with Thököly's followers demanded its presence. During the last third of the seventeenth century the number of Imperials in Hungary was at times as high as 64,000. However, on average the figure was closer to 24,000. Since almost all of Hungary was a war zone during this period, it was ruled largely by military administration. For the Imperials, who were for the most part mercenaries drawn from all parts of Europe, Hungary was a foreign land. When pay was late, as it invariably was, or when the indigenous population refused to co-operate, as it often did, the Imperials sought redress by ransacking Hungarian villages and manors in a way which made the Ottomans appear mild. The Hungarians in turn regarded these troops as little better than the enemy. As a result, constant friction between the two sides became endemic in the land.

Ill feelings notwithstanding, the spectacular defeat of the Ottomans at Vienna in 1683 and their rapid retreat from Hungary profoundly affected the relationship between Leopold I and his Hungarian subjects. Since it was the imperial armies and not the noble levees of the Hungarians that had triumphed in the age-old struggle against the Turk, Leopold I could represent himself as the liberator of the land. This allowed him to place certain demands on his grateful subjects. Thus, in 1687, one year after the capture of Buda from the Turks, he convened the famous Diet of Pozsony. After persistent cajoling the Hungarian estates were persuaded to make crucial changes in their constitution as a "token of gratitude" for their liberation from the Ottomans. They agreed to accept the male line of the Habsburgs as hereditary kings of Hungary. Only if the Habsburgs had no male issue would the Hungarians again have the right to elect their own monarch. Even though the dynasty had been on the throne for over 150 years, the formal recognition of its hereditary right to the crown of St Stephan was a great victory. Moreover, the famous Article Thirty-one of the Golden Bull of 1222, which gave the Hungarian nobles the right to resist their king if he acted illegally, was removed from the constitution. In order to calm and reassure the suspicious Hungarians, Leopold I solemnly promised to respect all their privileges, even though, as he pointedly reminded the estates, he did not have to do so in most of Hungary because it had come to him by right of conquest.

As a result of the diet's resolutions the Viennese authorities were now on much more solid ground vis-à-vis the Hungarians. Their rekindled confidence was manifested in a new series of reforms that they prepared to impose on Hungary. In 1688 the *Neoacquisitica commissio* was formed. Its purpose was to take over all the reconquered territories and to administer them according to the law of conquest, not according to the traditional Hungarian *komitat* laws. If a Hungarian nobleman wished to claim that land in the newly won lands had once belonged to his family, the commission demanded that he produce solid documentary evidence to that effect. In the rare cases where such documents were available, the claimant was expected to pay a sizeable fee (10 per cent of the value of the property) to the treasury before he could claim the land. With these conditions it is not surprising that most of the newly acquired territories remained in the hands of the Vienna government instead of reverting to Hungarian noblemen.

Long years of war and pillage had depopulated much of the reconquered territories. Colonization was clearly a necessity, but the authorities in Vienna did not wish to hand lands over to Hungarians for fear of a re-establishment of the *komitat* system. Therefore, orderly and industrious peasants from various German lands of the empire (in Hungary these peasants were called "Schwaben" because many of them were from Swabia) were invited to colonize the empty lands. The government's rationale for these invitations was "that the kingdom, or at least large parts of it, might [thereby] slowly become more Germanized and the Hungarian race, which is inclined to revolution and unrest, become more tempered by the Germans, thereby arousing in it a constant love and loyalty to its natural and hereditary king and lord."[31] Not only Germans but also Slovaks, Wallachians, and Serbs, who were relocating from Ottoman lands, were given lands in Hungary. Meanwhile, eight thousand Hungarians who served as garrisons in the fortresses along the borders were disbanded for "unreliability" and replaced by German troops.

At the same time that it encouraged ethnic diffusion, Vienna strove to impose religious uniformity. Again an attempt was made to undermine Protestantism. In order to circumvent the guarantees made by Leopold I at Pozsony regarding the equality of religions, the Austrian ministers argued that Protestant services could only be held in those lands which had belonged to the Habsburgs before 1681, that is, before the reconquest of most of Hungary. Protestantism was thus prevented from becoming firmly entrenched in the reconquered territories.

The statesmen in Vienna were quick to realize that if they could dictate the reorganization of the reconquered lands, they could do the same with all of Hungary. Convinced that a basic restructuring of the Hungarian legal, administrative, financial, and ecclesiastical institutions had finally become feasible, in 1689 Leopold I established the *Einrichtungswerk des Königreichs Ungarn* (Regulations of the Kingdom of Hungary). Cardinal Count Leopold Kollonich, a Hungarian prelate, eventually became the moving force behind this commission. After careful analysis the commission submitted a lengthy series of recommendations, the most important of which proposed the complete reorganization of the Hungarian chancery; the codification of Hungarian laws which favoured the nobility; the establishment of a standing army of twenty-four thousand men, half of whom would be Hungarians and the other half Germans; a policy of judicious colonization which would intermingle Germans and Hungarians; and strong measures to support the Catholic church. Although the commission's recommendations were never implemented as a whole for fear of antagonizing the Hungarian elite, a number of them were put into effect separately in subsequent years.

Several years later the sensitive issue of taxes was tackled. Hungary had never been a profitable enterprise for the Habsburgs. During the reconquest it had cost them 500,000 *gulden* annually to maintain their troops and to administer the country, while their income from the land amounted to only 60,000 *gulden*. Since only the peasants and burghers were liable to taxation and since it was these classes that had suffered most during the reconquest, they obviously could not bear a heavier financial burden. The solution was to extend taxation to the privileged classes, the magnates, nobles, and clergy. As a justification for these plans the Viennese ministers pointed out that the Hungarian nobility no longer rendered the military service for which it had originally been excused from taxation. Therefore, in 1693 indirect taxation of the nobility was slowly and cautiously introduced.

Between 1694 and 1697 Habsburg officials assessed Hungary at 2 million *forints* (Bohemia, which was smaller, was to pay 1.5 million *forints*). Despite the fact that the Hungarians considered this amount excessive, it was increased to 4 million *forints* in 1698. The apportionment of these taxes was revealing: 1/16th, or 250,000 *forints*, was to be paid by the towns – a clear indication of their economic weakness; another 5/16ths, or 1.25 million *forints*, by the nobility and clergy; and the remaining 10/16ths, or 2.5 million *forints*, by the peasants. The nobles furiously insisted that they could pay only 50,000 *forints*. As a result of the bargaining which ensued, the nobility finally agreed to pay 250,000 *forints*. This represented a victory of sorts for Vienna, for it did not have to lower its original assessment. It simply raised the peasants' share from 2.5 million to 3.5 million *forints*.[32]

These measures soon dissipated the goodwill which Leopold's victories over the Ottomans had won for him, and the long-standing antagonism of the Hungarians towards "the Germans" rose to a new pitch. Yet, as the Hungarian elite again considered resistance, its chances for potential success suffered a serious setback. In the final decades of the seventeenth century Transylvania, which had been the traditional base for anti-Habsburg revolts, fell under Vienna's control. This was a major achievement for the Habsburg cause, for, from its very establishment as a principality in 1541, Transylvania had been an obstacle to the dynasty's attempts to subjugate Hungary. The sovereignty which the Ottomans exercised over the principality had been so loose that its princes were able to pursue their dominant political objective – the expulsion of the Habsburgs and the reunification of Hungary – relatively freely. In the early seventeenth century, when such talented princes as Gàbor Bethlen and György Rákóczi I raised Transylvania to the level of a major power in central and Eastern Europe, it seemed that this goal was well within reach. But the reckless policies of György Rákóczi II (1648–60) led to a series of military and political catastrophes which permanently undermined Transylvania's strength. Taking advantage of its weakness, in the second half of the seventeenth century the Ottoman Porte tightened its hold on the principality by applying its tried tactics of control: by manipulating the ambitions of the Transylvanian magnates the Porte was able to involve them in a destructive competition for the princely title. Between 1660 and 1662, for example, the title changed hands seven times. As had been the case in Moldavia, this competition sapped the resources of the land and made it a mere plaything in the hands of the Ottomans and the Habsburgs.

After the Ottoman defeats in Hungary, it became apparent that a Habsburg occupation of Transylvania was inevitable. In 1687 Mihaly Apafi, the reigning prince, signed an agreement with Vienna which led to the military occupation of the land three years later. For their co-operation Apafi and his son were guaranteed the princely title, but only as vassals of the Habsburgs. Thereafter, princes would be chosen by means of a free election by the Transylvanian estates. However, after Apafi's death in 1690, Transylvania was brought under the direct rule of Vienna. While guaranteeing the social and political order of the land, Leopold I did not allow the younger Apafi to claim the princely title, and thus, in effect, brought the semi-independent existence of Transylvania to an end.[33] It now appeared that Vienna had all the Hungarian lands under its own complete control.

THE HABSBURG EMPIRE: SELECTED STATISTICS[34]

Population and area circa 1700
Area: approximately 430,000 square kilometres
Population: approximately 7,500,000
Bohemia: 3,400,000
Austria: 2,100,000
Hungary: 2,000,000

Imperial budget
Total in 1683: 6,400,000 florins. Bohemia contributed 1,170,000 florins; Hungary contributed nothing.
Total in 1699: 16,460,000 florins. Bohemia contributed 2,280,000; Hungary contributed 4,000,000.

Army
Peacetime army (1690): approximately 60,000; wartime army (1703): approximately 130,000

THE ROMANOVS IN UKRAINE

Muscovite autocracy pre-dated Russian statehood. If one were to compare the tsars' monopolization of power with that of Western absolute rulers and Ottoman sultans, it would be evident that the latter achieved their uncontested dominance primarily with the aid of powerful standing armies and large, efficient bureaucracies, of which pre-Petrine Muscovy could not boast. Although the tsars could raise armies of more than 100,000 men, these consisted largely of *dvoriane*, or gentry levees, and lost as many battles as they won; moreover, they were disbanded after every campaign. Consisting of only about one to two thousand officials and scribes and based for the most part in Moscow, the Muscovite proto-bureaucracy of the seventeenth century exerted little direct impact on the tsars' eight to nine million subjects. An example of this bureaucratic underdevelopment was the important bureau of the *tainyi prikaz* (secret chancellery), which consisted of a single official and ten scribes. Despite the great expanse of the tsars' realm and the number of their subjects, Russian society was notorious for its social, economic, military, and cultural backwardness. None the less, the achievements of the Muscovite autocrats were remarkable.[35]

From less than 47,000 square kilometres in the early fourteenth century Muscovy grew to encompass an estimated 15,280,000 square kilometres by 1688. Expanding for hundreds of years at the rate of 80 square kilometres per day, it assimilated such strong, individualistic polities as Novgorod and Tver in the late fifteenth century and, in the mid-sixteenth, launched a new stage in its expansion by the conquest of the Tatar khanates of Kazan and Astrakhan, its first non-Russian acquisitions. Perhaps the most impressive achievement of the tsars, specifically of Ivan IV, was their crushing victory over the boyar oligarchy. During the *Oprichnina* (1565–72) Ivan IV succeeded first in isolating the boyars politically and then in systematically liquidating them. Of some three hundred boyar families only a handful escaped unscathed. After this bloodbath the Russian nobility never again seriously challenged its rulers.

Yet, despite the rather unimpressive military and bureaucratic apparatus at their disposal, Muscovite rulers were extraordinarily successful in concentrating power in their own hands. A plausible explanation of their success is that Russian society, constantly under attack during its evolution in the exposed Eurasian plain, simply could not afford the luxury of political pluralism. Survival demanded that power be vested in a single strong ruler. Moreover, the impressive Mongol and Byzantine models encouraged such thinking. Thus, unlike in the West, where absolutism evolved as a result of military and institutional innovations and social change, in Muscovy autocracy

Map 5 Ukraine in the Russian Empire circa 1700

became a long-standing response to the grievous threats that surrounded the society and its rulers. In other words, in terms of the monopolization of power, Muscovite rulers always knew what they wanted to accomplish, even though their means were deficient, while Western absolutist monarchs realized what they could accomplish only after they had acquired the means.

That is not to say, however, that Muscovite rulers were entirely without resources. The very size of their lands and the huge populace under their control were great advantages. Even their geopolitical location, despite its drawbacks during times of Tatar supremacy, had its positive aspects, for it allowed Moscow to use borrowed Western technology against its eastern enemies (as was the case when Ivan IV used German gunners and artillery against Kazan) and yet to impose on its subjects in the western borderlands conditions that only Eastern potentates could think of (such as the use of the term *kholop*, or slave, to designate a subject). But the Muscovite rulers' greatest asset was the uncanny political skills which they developed under Mongol rule. These were demonstrated by a masterpiece of political manipulation: after enlisting the aid of their Mongol overlords in their struggle against rival Russian principalities, they cajoled the latter into helping them to overthrow the Mongols themselves. During the centuries of tortuous manoeuvring and intrigue Moscow learned that political skill was as useful as military power and that undermining the enemy was often as effective as overwhelming it. As a result Moscow tended to concentrate on destroying real or potential centres of power rather than building up strong institutions of its own. It became especially adept at spotting the internal weaknesses of its opponents and at manipulating these in such a way that, as was the case with Novgorod, Tver, and Kazan, the opponents disintegrated once military pressure was applied. Moscow would make great use of such skills when the time came to deal with the thorny problem of Ukraine.[36]

At the outset of Khmelnytsky's Uprising of 1648 Tsar Aleksei Mikhailovich neither expected nor desired to take Ukraine "under his high hand." Although the vast and rich land must certainly have been a tempting prize, the cost of securing it seemed prohibitive. If the tsar took the rebellious Ukrainians under his aegis, war with the Commonwealth would be inevitable. With the memory of Polish intervention during the Time of Troubles and of the defeats at the hands of the Poles during the Smolensk War (1632-4) still very much alive, Moscow continued to regard the Commonwealth as a powerful enough opponent to wish to avoid conflicts with it. However, the Commonwealth's inability to quell the uprising attested to the sharp decline that had occurred in its military capacity. Meanwhile, Khmelnytsky's impatience with the tsar's reticence had led him to begin openly to negotiate with the Ottomans about the question of overlordship. Therefore, in 1653, five years after the beginning of the uprising, Tsar Aleksei Mikhailovich, urged on by the *zemskii sobor* (assembly of the land), cautiously decided to accept the Ukrainians under his sovereignty "for the sake of the Holy Orthodox Faith."

Khmelnytsky and the Ukrainians formally recognized the tsar's overlordship at Pereiaslav in January 1654.[37] The agreement represented a kind of compromise between the form of Muscovite autocracy and the content of feudal vassalage. Using terminology reminiscent of Moscow's imposition of its sovereignty over Novgorod, Tver, and other acquisitions, the tsar declared that he was willing to accede to the "pleas" of the Ukrainians and to accept them "under his high hand." As a special sign of favour, in March 1654 he conferred on his new subjects the privileges they had requested. These rights were unprecedented in their scope and, more importantly, in their implications. Among the more important commitments made by the tsar were his pledges to respect the customs and traditions of Ukraine; to allow the Zaporozhian Host to elect its own officials, who would be confirmed by him; to permit the Ukrainians to judge themselves according to their own laws, without interference from the tsar's representatives; and, a rare concession, to allow the *hetman*s to receive foreign envoys, except from such enemy countries as Poland and the Ottoman empire. These rights, in effect, gave the Ukrainians self-rule.

Not unexpectedly, Ukraine proved to be a valuable, albeit troublesome acquisition. It increased the number of the tsar's subjects by about 15 per cent and added about 200,000 square kilometres to his domains. But it also involved Muscovy in thirteen years of almost continuous warfare with the Poles, from 1654 to 1667, and in five years of brutal fighting with the Ottomans, from 1676 to 1681. In addition, Moscow soon realized that the Ukrainians, and their *starshyna* in particular, were just as apt to create vexatious difficulties for their new Orthodox overlords as they had for their former Catholic sovereigns. Convinced that Moscow was infringing on Ukrainian rights, every *hetman* up until 1708 engaged in "seditious" behaviour, or revolted against the tsars, or both. It is little wonder that the leading Muscovite statesman and diplomat of the time, Athanasius Ordyn-Nashchokin, advised the tsar to return "the undependable Cherkassy" (as the Muscovites called the Ukrainians) to the Poles and that Muscovite officials openly grumbled that "all the *hetman*s ... were traitors."[38] Yet, despite these tribulations, Moscow doggedly continued to tighten its hold on Ukraine.

What were the means by which it exercised its authority in Ukraine and to what extent could it count on having its orders obeyed in the land? The agency that maintained contact between the tsar and the *hetman*ate was the *malorossiiski prikaz* (Little Russian chancellery). From its establishment in 1663 until its liquidation in 1717 the *prikaz* had a staff of about twenty, including officials, scribes, translators, and guards, all of whom were based in Moscow. In its dealings with the Ukrainians it carried out three basic functions: it conducted the tsar's correspondence with his Ukrainian subjects and gathered information about conditions in the *hetman*ate; it supervised and supplied the Russian garrisons in the Ukrainian towns; and it regulated travel and settled jurisdictional disputes between the two lands. However, while it assured the tsar continual contact with Ukraine, the *prikaz* obviously could not guarantee that his orders would be carried out in it. To this end, the tsar had to be able to deploy adequate force.

At first glance it would seem that Moscow had a direct and effective coercive capacity in Ukraine. Five Ukrainian towns – Kiev, Chernihiv, Pereiaslav, Nizhyn, and Oster – had Russian garrisons. Yet the total number of these troops fluctuated greatly during the latter part of the seventeenth century. In the mid-1660s it reached as high as 12,000, but it later fell to a low of 1,900. The coercive impact of these garrisons was limited by their relatively low numbers. Even at peak strength their ratio to combat-ready Cossacks was one to four, and at times the ratio sank to one to twenty. Thus, since the discipline and military technology of the Ukrainian and Russian troops was roughly equal, the tsars and their representatives in Ukraine could not count on force to execute their orders. For example, in 1668 Ukrainian townsmen and Cossacks, angered by the exactions of the tsarist officials, attacked and expelled the Muscovites from the Ukrainian towns with relative ease. Even a full-scale army could not cow the Ukrainians. In 1659 Tsar Aleksei Mikhailovich raised over 100,000 men to crush the rebellious *hetman* Ivan Vyhovsky, who in June 1659, with his Tatar allies, decimated a greater part of the Muscovite force at Konotop. The traditional Muscovite cavalry formations never recovered from this blow, and Moscow fell into a panic for fear of an invasion.

Unable to control the Ukrainians by means of either military force or bureaucratic institutions, Moscow utilized a policy of divide et impera, to pit the *starshyna* against the rank-and-file Cossacks and peasants on the one hand and to create tensions between the *starshyna* and *hetman*s on the other. In both cases the tsars played the role of arbiters, and herein lay the real basis of their influence in Ukraine. But to ensure the success of such a policy, Moscow had to prevent the election of powerful *hetman*s.

There was little that Moscow could do about Khmelnytsky. Confident of his own tremendous personal prestige, the *hetman* interpreted his relationship with the tsar as a loose form of overlordship and acted accordingly. For example, in 1656, when Cossack and Muscovite troops occupied Byelorussia and an intense rivalry broke out for control of the area, Cossack commanders refused to surrender the towns they had captured to the Muscovites. In some cases they even expelled the tsar's garrisons from towns which they considered to be within their jurisdiction. The Cossack commander, Ivan Zolotarenko, went so far as to dissuade the local populace from swearing loyalty to the tsar, and urged it to take on oath to Khmelnytsky and the Zaporozhian Host instead.

What infuriated the tsar even more was Khmelnytsky's independence in foreign affairs. While dutifully informing Moscow about foreign contacts of secondary importance, the *hetman* proceeded to join a grand coalition, which included György II Rákóczi of Transylvania and Charles IX of Sweden, the avowed purpose of which was the partition of the Commonwealth. Since the Poles had signed an armistice with the tsar at the same time that war broke out between Sweden and Moscow, the coalition directly harmed the tsar's interests. None the less, when Aleksei Mikhailovich admonished Khmelnytsky, the *hetman* not only refused to mend his ways but took the opportunity to express his own grievances against the tsar:

I will never break with the Swedish king, for there has always been a long-lasting friendship and co-operation between us. It has existed for more than six years, even before we came under the high hand of the tsar. Moreover, the Swedes are an honest people; when they pledge friendship and alliance, they honour their word. However, the tsar, by establishing an armistice with the Poles and by wishing to return us to them, has behaved most heartlessly with us.[40]

In fact, shortly before his death Khmelnytsky's irritation with Moscow became so great that he seriously considered exchanging the overlordship of the tsar for that of the sultan. It was probably with a sigh of relief that Moscow learned of his death on 6 August 1657.

Not surprisingly, when Khmelnytsky's elitist successor, Ivan Vyhovsky, became *hetman*, Muscovite politicians carefully searched for a way to weaken his position. They discreetly sided with the rank-and-file Cossacks, who rose up against the newly elected *hetman* and the *starshyna*. Vyhovsky reciprocated by renouncing the tsar's overlordship, negotiating a reunion with the Commonwealth by means of the Hadiach Treaty of 1658, and, as noted earlier, defeating the Muscovites at Konotop. Internal dissension among the Cossacks continued, however, and Vyhovsky was forced to resign.

The next *hetman* was Khmelnytsky's young son, Iuras. Since it was customary to renegotiate the Pereiaslav Treaty at the election of a new *hetman*, the tsar's representatives used the occasion to force a doctored version of the original treaty on the inexperienced Iuras. This version allowed more tsarist officials in Ukraine, categorically forbade unauthorized foreign contacts, and called for the Cossacks to abandon their positions in Byelorussia "so that confrontations between Cossacks and the tsar's men might be avoided."[41] But the Muscovite representatives had pushed too hard. Like his predecessor, Iuras promptly joined the Poles and Tatars, and in 1660 at Chudniv helped them to inflict another crushing defeat on the Muscovites. Thereafter, Ukraine was plunged into the fratricidal *Ruina*, which led to the election of rival *hetmans* on both the right and left banks of the Dnieper. In 1663, in the midst of the chaos, Ivan Briukhovetsky, the champion of the rank-and-file Cossacks and a protégé of Moscow, was elected *hetman* of Left Bank Ukraine. With his election Moscow finally obtained what it had desired – a servile *hetman*.

Convinced that without Muscovite support he would be unable to maintain himself as *hetman*, Briukhovetsky made abject subservience to the tsar the keystone of his policy. Shortly after his confirmation he declared openly that "it is not the *hetman*, but the tsar that is master of Ukraine."[42] He introduced Muscovite terminology into his titulature, calling himself the tsar's *kholop*, and he was the first *hetman* to journey to Moscow, where he received the rank of boyar and was given a Muscovite wife; the *starshyna* who accompanied him were granted the rank of *dvoriane* and were also encouraged to marry Muscovite women.

During his stay in Moscow in 1665 Briukhovetsky made one concession after another. Agreeing with the boyars that his predecessors' betrayals had been brought on primarily by the possibility of foreign contacts, he ostentatiously renounced all claims to such contacts. Open diplomacy, a right which Khmelnytsky had staunchly insisted upon, now became a thing of the past for Left Bank *hetmans*. On the question of tsarist officials, or *voevodas*, Briukhovetsky's concessions surprised even the Muscovites. He accepted the appointment of *voevodas* in thirteen Ukrainian towns and agreed to raise the number of Muscovite garrisons in Ukraine from three thousand to almost twelve thousand. Taking advantage of Briukhovetsky's malleability, Moscow made two new demands: that Ukrainians contribute to the support of Muscovite garrisons, and that they agree to a census. Again Briukhovetsky consented.

As Muscovite *voevodas* and troops poured into Ukrainian towns, as their officials began "with great joy" to collect contributions from the people, as the tsar's prying census-takers criss-crossed the country, and as word of the *hetman's* concessions spread among the Cossacks, popular reaction against the Muscovites increased. Sensing the dangerous mood of the country, Briukhovetsky urged the *voevodas* to "give the Little Russians time to become accustomed to payments in cash."[43]

In 1667 Ukrainian resentment turned to rage. In January of that year, ignoring the protests of the *hetman*, Moscow signed the Treaty of Andrusovo with the Poles. At the cost of renouncing all claims to Right Bank Ukraine and, within two years, to Kiev, the tsar finally brought to an end the exhausting conflict with the Commonwealth. For the Ukrainians, however, who were not even consulted in the renunciation of their capital and half of their territory to the hated Poles, these terms were tantamount to the tsar's betrayal of his duty to protect their land. Bitterly they predicted that the next step would be Moscow's renunciation of Left Bank Ukraine, which would leave them in the same predicament they had been in before 1648.

Even for Briukhovetsky, Andrusovo was too much. Secretly he established contact with Petro Doroshenko, *hetman* of the Right Bank Cossacks, and together with him sought the protection of the Ottoman Porte. Meanwhile, he placed himself at the head of an anti-Muscovite uprising that was already brewing. In February 1668 one Ukrainian town after another rose against the *voevodas* and the garrisons. Only two of thirteen garrisons managed to withstand the attacks; the others were either massacred, taken prisoner, or sent back to Moscow. Within weeks the entire Russian administrative presence in Ukraine was in shambles. As for Briukhovetsky, he was torn limb from limb by a furious mob of Cossacks who could not forgive him for his concessions to Moscow.

After the revolt of 1668 the situation stabilized. The Muscovite presence in Ukraine dropped to two thousand troops, while the *hetmans* appeared to be cured of their tendency to seek foreign aid whenever they had a grievance against the tsar. For the Ukrainian political elite the main issue became the smouldering conflict between the *hetmans* and the *starshyna*. The former, in particular men like Damian Mnohohrishny and Ivan Samoilovych, sought to strengthen their positions by making their office hereditary, at times even with a distinctly monarchical flavour, while the latter, fearful of overly powerful *hetmans*, resisted these attempts. Taking advantage of this conflict, Moscow again proceeded to chip away at Ukrainian autonomy. In 1686 it subordinated the metropolitan of Kiev to the patriarch of Moscow, thereby, in effect, giving the tsar control of the Ukrainian church. This was too much for Samoilovych, who protested vehemently against the measure. His criticism of the Muscovite regime continued on the issue of the disastrous Crimean campaign of 1687, which he had advised against. It had become clear to Moscow that he would have to be removed.

On 23 July 1687, in the midst of the Crimean campaign, Samoilovych was arrested at the Cossack camp near the Kolomak River on the basis of a denunciation submitted by the *starshyna*. He was charged with treasonous contacts with the Crimean khan and was sent first to Russia and then to Siberia. His arrest provoked unexpected turbulence in the Cossack camp. Disgruntled by the conduct of the campaign and dissatisfied with the *starshyna*'s growing exactions at home, the rank-and-file Cossacks mutinied and killed some of their officers. This placed the *starshyna* in a precarious position: confronted by their rebellious men, they turned for support to Prince Vasilii Golitsyn, the empress's favourite and the commander of the Russian troops. But Golitsyn was only willing to provide help on his own terms. One of these was the election of his friend and Samoilovych's former chancellor, Ivan Mazepa, as *hetman*. Thus, on 25 July, at a hastily called and poorly attended council, the election of Mazepa as *hetman* of the Zaporozhian Host took place.

Golitsyn, however, was still not satisfied, and he demanded a renegotiation of the Pereiaslav pacts. As was to be expected, the so-called Kolomak Articles, which Mazepa and the *starshyna* were forced to accept, reflected a further diminution of Ukrainian autonomy. The Ukrainian request for the original right to maintain contacts with neighbouring monarchs was flatly rejected. Russian garrisons in Ukraine were to be enlarged, and the *hetman* and *starshyna* were now obliged "to unite by all means possible the Little Russian and Great Russian people ... and bring them into tight, indissoluble agreement ... so that no one might dare to say that Little Russia was under the *hetman*'s rule ... [but that] all in unison could say that the *hetman* and the *starshyna* and the Little Russian and Great Russian people were under His Tsarist Majesty's autocratic rule."[44]

For the almost two decades of the *hetman*cy of the wily and sophisticated Mazepa, relations between Moscow and Ukraine appeared to be mutually satisfactory. The tsar's overlordship became a well-established fact of political life in Ukraine, while the Russian presence in the land was kept to a minimum. After Peter I came to power in 1689, Mazepa adroitly developed a close personal relationship with the young tsar. Meanwhile, in Ukraine, Mazepa consolidated his position by encouraging the economic development of the land, patronizing the church, and continuing to distribute lands among the *starshyna*. In the process he became the richest man in the land, with over 100,000 dependent peasants. However, the era of goodwill between Ukraine and Moscow rapidly came to an end with the outbreak of the Great Northern War.

The war and, more specifically, the early defeats at the hands of the Swedes precipitated the famous Petrine reforms. The tsar realized that if he wished to compete with the Swedes, he would have to imitate them. He would have to reorganize along Western lines not only his army but also the entire society that supported it. This made the war doubly painful for his subjects: its demands totally exhausted them (during the twenty-one-year war, the population loss in Russia was close to 25 per cent), and the radical reforms left them confused and insecure.

The burdens of the war were particularly resented in Ukraine. Compared with the rest of the tsar's lands, Ukraine bore a disproportionately high share of the war's human and material losses. In 1700, with a population of about one million, it put nearly 35,000 troops into the field, while Russia, with over twelve million, had an army of 112,000. Moreover, for the first time Ukrainians had been asked to fight in a distant war that had little to do with their interests. Complaints related to the war poured in from every segment of Ukrainian society. Between 1705 and 1708 both the *hetman* and the tsar received a constant stream of complaints about how Russian troops stationed in Ukraine beat and insulted Ukrainians, raped their wives and daughters, destroyed their homes, and in some cases even killed them. "From everywhere," wrote Mazepa to Moscow, "I receive complaints about the wilfulness of the Great Russian troops."[45]

Civilian discontent was only matched by that of the Cossacks on campaign. For the latter the war brought a series of painful novelties. It soon became clear that the Cossacks were no match for the regular Swedish regiments, and Peter 1's German and Russian commanders treated them accordingly by using them as auxiliaries and even as cannon fodder. This did little for Cossack pride and even less for their chances of survival. Year after year Cossack regiments returned from the north with casualty rates as high as 60 and even 70 per cent. As if that were not enough, when they arrived home, they were often forced to work under bullying Russian supervisors on the construction of fortresses. What irritated the Cossacks, and especially their *starshyna*, the most were the recurrent rumours that the tsar planned to reorganize them. A Cossack commander in Peter 1's camp informed Mazepa that the tsar intended to send the Ukrainians to Prussia for training as dragoons. Another of the *hetman*'s officers claimed that the order had already been signed and that only the exigencies of war had led to its cancellation. The *starshyna*'s sensitivity on the issue is understandable when we recall that the military organization of the Cossacks corresponded to their socio-economic structure; to alter the former was tantamount to challenging the latter.

The *starshyna*'s nervousness about Russian plans for Ukraine turned to near panic when Mazepa informed it that the tsar and his advisers were indeed plotting to undermine the Ukrainian elite. In 1706 he recounted to his officers how the tsar's favourite, Prince Aleksander Menshikov, had praised him for his loyalty to Peter 1 but stated that, as far as the *starshyna* was concerned, "it was time to rid the tsar of these enemies."[46] Later the *hetman* reported that "the tsar and his ministers want to destroy the *starshyna* and bring the towns under their own control by installing more *voevoda*s. If we resist, they will force us across the Volga and settle Ukraine with their own people."[47] After several such reports, which were exaggerated somewhat by Mazepa for his own purposes, a distraught Cossack colonel cried out to the *hetman*: "Just as we always prayed to God for the soul of Khmelnytsky and blessed his name for freeing Ukraine from the Polish yoke, so we and our children will forever curse your soul and bones if, as a result of your *hetman*cy, you leave us in this [Russian] slavery."[48] Clearly, the tsar's actual and projected reforms had pushed the *hetman* and the *starshyna* to the point where they felt that an onslaught against their traditional order was imminent. They therefore began to consider ways of extricating themselves from the menacing situation.

THE RUSSIAN EMPIRE: SELECTED STATISTICS[49]

Population and area circa 1700
Population: approximately 15 million
Area: approximately 15,280,000 square kilometres

Landholdings
Dvoriane (nobles – approximately 15,000 family heads): owned 360,000–380,000
   peasant households (61%)
Church: 130,000–140,000 (21%)
Dynasty: 100,000 (17%)

Army
Peacetime army: approximately 60,000; wartime army circa 1725: 363,000,
   made up of 220,000 regular army (120,000 field army); 5,000 artillery; 26,000
   navy; and 112,000 irregulars

THE WETTINS IN POLAND-LITHUANIA

To understand the Saxon attempt to establish a *gross-staat* in Eastern Europe, we must glance once more at the geopolitical map of the region. By the end of the seventeenth century Poland-Lithuania was the only indigenous polity that had retained its sovereignty in the region. Meanwhile, there was on the periphery only one relatively strong state inclined towards absolutism which had not yet gained a foothold in Eastern Europe – Saxony. Thus, although con- temporaries expressed surprise when in 1697 August 1 Friedrich, the twenty- four-year-old elector of Saxony, declared his candidacy for the vacant Polish throne, there was, from the perspective of absolutist expansionism, a definite situational logic to his move.

Obviously, there were also more concrete and specific reasons for August's

Map 6 Dynastic Union of Saxony and Poland-Lithuania circa 1700

Polish venture. The six-hundred-year old Wettin dynasty of Saxony had long considered itself a competitor of the Austrian Habsburgs and the Hohenzollerns of Brandenburg for predominance in the Germanies. As the seventeenth century came to a close it was evident that the Wettins had fallen behind their rivals. One of the indications of this widening gap was the fact that, while the Habsburgs and Hohenzollerns extended their realms in the East, the Wettins had failed to do so. A galling reminder of this failure came in 1693, when the news arrived in Dresden that Friedrich, elector of Brandenburg, was planning to crown himself king in Prussia. Clearly, Saxony had no choice but to expand.

Several fanciful schemes to acquire new lands were proposed to the impetuous and extremely ambitious Saxon elector. They included plans to establish his dynasty in Naples, in present-day Belgium, and even in Istanbul (the Saxon ruler was enamoured of the legend that predicted that Istanbul would soon be conquered by a second Augustus).Yet even the reckless August had to admit that these schemes were too far-fetched. However, the death in 1696 of the Polish king, Jan Sobieski, created an unexpected opportunity for him to gain a royal title.

Traditionally, the prevailing opinion among Polish and German historians has been that August sought the Polish crown primarily to satisfy his personal ambitions and to raise the prestige of his dynasty. "My ambition," he wrote to a confidant, "is glory, and I will seek it to my dying day."[50] A man of unbridled energy, August was what the Germans call a *kraftmensch*. Power fascinated him, and his desire for it was only heightened by the successes of his rivals. While seeking power and glory, however, he had also to take into consideration the impact of a union with the Commonwealth on his hereditary Saxon lands, the very basis of his power. Several recent studies have shown that Saxon raison d'état played an influential role in August's thinking. This was most evident in the mercantilist terms in which he and his advisers, most notably his chief minister, Jacob Heinrich von Flemming, discussed the merits of the Polish undertaking. Just before the election Flemming wrote enthusiastically of how the manufacturers of Saxony, one of the most industrialized lands in Europe, would benefit from open access to the vast supplies of raw materials in Poland-Lithuania and of how the commerce of Leipzig would "flower once again because of the traffic with Poland."[51] Furthermore, the possibility of joint Polish-Saxon ventures into overseas trade and North American colonization was discussed, and much was made of Saxony and Poland-Lithuania's potential for controlling Europe's trade with Persia and the Far East. In all of these projects the implication was that the Commonwealth would function as a province of the Saxon heartland and that the union of the two societies would pave the way for transforming Saxony into a first-rate power.[52]

The projected venture was remarkably audacious. It presumed nothing less than the establishment of a strong, even absolutist kingship in the Commonwealth, which was the very embodiment of a noble-dominated society. True, in contemplating this undertaking, August could count on advantages that previous kings of Poland had not enjoyed. Most important, he had a strong power-base in Saxony. This is not to say, however, that his prerogatives in his own land were as extensive as those of the Habsburgs or Hohenzollerns. Saxon absolutism had never managed to remove the estates completely from political influence. For example, during August's reign the estates still had the right to assess the amount of the land tax that they paid and to meet in the diet. None the less, while the Saxon estates and their representative institutions were highly developed and influential, the office of elector and its institutions were even more so.

The elector was responsible to the estates only in matters of taxation. In many other areas, especially war and foreign affairs, he could pursue an almost unlimited policy. Moreover, the bureaucratic institutions at his disposal were impressive. As early as 1547, under the rule of the illustrious Duke Moritz, Saxony had reorganized its governing institutions along collegial, bureaucratic lines so successfully that, until the Thirty Years' War, its government served as a model for other German states. Numbers alone indicate how highly developed the Saxon bureaucracy was: in the mid-eighteenth century it consisted of over six thousand officials, about one bureaucrat per 250 inhabitants (in Prussia the ratio was one to 500).[53] The Saxon army, however, while one of the most advanced and best equipped in Europe, was relatively small when compared to the armies of other absolutist states. A standing army was organized in the electorate only in 1682, and initially it numbered 10,000 men. By 1700 the peacetime strength of the army was 12,000, while its wartime strength ranged between 25,000 and 30,000 men. Because Saxony was not a first-rate military power, its rulers tried to enhance their image by creating one of the most magnificent courts of late seventeenth- and early eighteenth-century Europe. During the reign of August in particular, vast sums of money were spent on the court and on the beautification of Dresden.

The ability of the Saxon electors to finance and develop these expensive components of statehood rested to a great extent on the economic wealth of the country. Although, like the rest of the Germanies, it had suffered terrible devastation during the Thirty Years' War, losing about 30 to 40 per cent of its population, by the end of the seventeenth century the economy was well on its way to recovery. With its superb geographical location (it bordered on thirteen countries) the electorate straddled many major east-west and north-south trade routes. Its commercial importance is evident from the important trade fairs which were held in Leipzig, a bustling city of eighteen thousand. Industry and handicrafts were also highly developed, a condition that was closely related to the unusually high population density (over forty people per one square kilometre) and extensive urbanization. About 33 per cent of the population lived in the electorate's ninety-eight cities. In 1694 an astoundingly high percentage of the work force, about 10 per cent, or 152,000, was employed in the non-agrarian sector.[54] Thus, with the considerable economic resources of this extensively developed land at his disposal, August had good reason to believe that he could be successful in his Polish undertaking.

August's first hurdle was to win the Polish crown. With eight other candidates – the two sons of Sobieski, Jakub and Constantine; Prince Conti, a cousin of Louis XIV; Prince Ludwig of Bavaria; Prince Karl von Neuberg; Duke Leopold of Lorraine; Prince Ludwig of Baden; Don Livio Odescalchi, a nephew of Pope Innocent VII – vying for the same title, this was not an easy matter. At the outset it seemed that Conti, the French candidate would have no trouble winning the crown. However, when Austria and Russia threatened to intervene if he were elected, his fortunes declined rapidly. This cleared the way for August, whose strategy was simply to outbid the other candidates. To raise the necessary cash he sold or leased some of his choicest properties, took out huge loans, and sold his jewellery to the Jesuits of Prague. All in all, within a few hectic months he had raised about 2.6 million *gulden* and 970,000 *talers*. (We might derive an idea of the sum that represented by noting that the average annual yield from all of Saxony's taxes from 1723 to 1735 was 1.9 million *talers*.) This money was then sent to Flemming in Poland, who distributed it in the following manner: bribes for leading magnates and prelates, 615,000 *gulden* and 161,000 *talers*; subsidy for the Polish army, 333,333 *talers*; subsidy for the Lithuanian army, 166,666 *talers*. This, however, did not satisfy the Poles, and informed observers reported that by Christmas of 1697 August had spent about 5 million *talers* in the Commonwealth.[55]

In addition to the huge bribes August also courted the Poles in another way. In a secret ceremony which took place during the summer of 1697, this scion of one of Germany's leading Protestant dynasties converted to Catholicism. He justified his action with the casual remark, "Warsaw is worth a Mass." If need be, the elector was also ready to apply pressure to the Poles. Near the end of the summer he stationed about ten thousand Saxon troops on Poland's borders as a pointed reminder to the *szlachta* of his determination. Soon afterwards, on 15 September 1697, after a splendid entry into Cracow and despite rumblings of discontent from some of the leading magnates, the Saxon elector was crowned August II, King of Poland and Grand Duke of Lithuania.

As had been the case with previous kings, the *pacta conventa*, or terms of election which August signed, severely limited his prerogatives. Among the most important of the thirty-seven conditions which he accepted were his acquiescence to the principle of free elections; the renunciation of any attempt to convert the crown into a hereditary one; the promise not to bring into the Commonwealth any foreign – that is, Saxon – troops without the permission of the *sejm*; and the commitment to regain the Commonwealth's lost provinces in Livonia and Ukraine at his own cost. Thus, with the coronation of August a personal union of Saxony and Poland-Lithuania, two sharply dissimilar societies, was effected. Standing at the head of this ostensibly imposing conglomerate, August was suddenly catapulted into the forefront of European politics.

At the outset of his reign, all seemed possible, and the new king had a clear idea of what he wanted to achieve in the Commonwealth. To make his heavy financial investment in the Polish crown worthwhile, August planned to make his royal title hereditary.[56] He then hoped to loosen the constitutional restraints on the kingship and to curtail the prerogatives of the *sejm*s and *sejmiki*. Clearly, the power of the magnates would have to be broken. In addition to these high-priority goals there was a series of secondary objectives. Among these was the acquisition of a common border between Saxony and the Commonwealth, the alignment of the Commonwealth's institutions with those of Saxony, the easing of restrictions on Saxon noblemen's rights to obtain lands and offices in Poland-Lithuania, and the partial dismantling of the Commonwealth's army, with the resulting surplus going to support Saxon troops that would then be stationed in Poland and Lithuania. The formulation of these ambitious goals was one thing; their implementation would be an infinitely more difficult matter.

But fortune seemed to smile on August II. An opportunity to achieve some of his objectives in Lithuania appeared in 1698, when the Lithuanian *szlachta* rose up in arms against the oppressive dominance of the Sapieha magnate family. Hoping to take advantage of the situation, August's first minister, Flemming, formulated a plan that ostensibly called for the king to play the role of arbiter in the conflict, all the while discreetly supporting the *szlachta*. This policy, it was argued, would administer a setback to the Sapiehas, the most dangerous of the king's potential opponents. Under the guise of restoring order Saxon troops would then move into Lithuania, suppress the *szlachta*, and impose military rule. In effect, the plan called for a coup d'état from above.

Initially, events favoured Flemming's design. In October 1700 the Lithuanian *szlachta* and allied magnates decisively defeated the army of the Sapiehas at Olkieniki. Soon afterwards the controversial Vilnius (Wilno) Declaration

of 22 November carried the surprising message that the Lithuanians un-
equivocally supported August II's claims to hereditary kingship and recognized
the need for absolutist reforms.[57] Recent research has shown that the declaration was most probably fabricated by August II's not overly numerous supporters in Lithuania and disseminated in the name of the entire Lithuanian
szlachta in hope of creating the impression that the king had widespread support in the grand duchy. His apparent position of strength seemed to be rein-
forced by the large number of Saxon troops that began to arrive in the land
under the pretext of maintaining order. For a while it appeared that the real
victor in the struggle between the Lithuanian *szlachta* and the magnates was
indeed August II.

Yet it was to be expected that when a king of Poland scored a major political
success, the oligarchy of the Commonwealth would become alarmed. As a
result of the developments in Lithuania the Polish magnates, in particular the
Lubomirski and Radziejowski families, launched a determined and successful
campaign to convince their *szlachta* clients that the new king was a man of unbridled ambition and that his actions represented a threat to the *szlachta*'s
precious "golden freedoms." Meanwhile, the presence of over eight thousand
Saxon troops in Lithuania itself soon gave cause for a crescendo of protests
about the damage and exactions that the Saxons imposed on the *szlachta*'s properties. In fact, some Lithuanians became so disillusioned with their king that
they turned to Peter I of Russia and signed a treaty with him that guaranteed
their rights. Confronted with a sudden deterioration of his position in
Lithuania, August II decided to abandon his plan to make the grand duchy
a base for his transformation of the Commonwealth.

There were, however, other options open to him. From the outset of his reign
August II had planned to concentrate his efforts on raising his prestige and
influence by means of external successes. In negotiating the *pacta conventa* with
the *szlachta*, he had promised to regain for the Commonwealth its lost sovereignty over Ukraine, Moldavia, Wallachia, and Livonia.[58] There were, in addition, other considerations that made him turn to foreign affairs. In general
the prerogatives of the kingship were much greater in foreign than in domestic
affairs. Because Saxony had a better-organized diplomatic service than did the
Commonwealth, the *szlachta*'s interference in the conduct of foreign affairs could
more readily be limited. Finally, the possibility of embarking on spectacular
foreign conquests was very much in keeping with the dreams that August II
had nurtured from his youth.

In view of these considerations it is understandable that, in 1698, August
would become an enthusiastic supporter of a proposed Christian coalition
which was to launch an offensive against the Ottomans in the Balkans.

However, just as he began to lay his plans to use the offensive to conquer Moldavia and Wallachia and attach them to the Commonwealth as his own hereditary lands, the Habsburgs began the negotiations which eventually led to the Peace of Carlowitz in 1699. Moreover, it was Habsburg diplomacy and not Saxon arms that regained for the Commonwealth the strategic fortress of Kamianets and part of Ukraine at Carlowitz. To make matters worse, as the price for regaining these lands August had to drop his plans for the conquest of Moldavia and Wallachia. Never one to brood over setbacks, he immediately looked elsewhere for new opportunities. For a brief period in 1699 it seemed that he might have a chance to launch a short, victorious campaign against his arch-enemy, the elector of Brandenburg, who had occupied the city of Elbag, which belonged to the Commonwealth. But the *szlachta* insisted on settling this conflict by means of negotiations.

In the midst of these frustrating events, an idea which would later play an important role in Saxon diplomacy began to take shape in August's plans. It is worth mentioning at this point as an example of the lengths to which August was willing to go in order to consolidate his power. Realizing that many of the major opponents of his absolutist designs in Poland received support from neighbouring absolutist powers such as Austria, Russia, and Prussia, who had no desire to see a strong ruler in the Commonwealth, August tried to win these powers over. He did so by offering to partition Poland-Lithuania among them on the condition that, in the portion which remained his, he would be able to rule in an absolutist fashion. Although this strategy became especially important in the period 1708 to 1713, there is evidence that as early as 1700 August II was willing to consider a partial partition of his new kingdom.[59]

Suddenly and unexpectedly, in January 1699 a project was brought to the king's attention that seemed to offer exactly what he wanted. A Livonian émigré, Johann Reinhold von Patkul, who will be discussed at length later, presented August II with a plan for what appeared to be quick, easy, and practically guaranteed means to conquer Swedish-held Livonia, one of the Commonwealth's lost provinces. With more than his usual enthusiasm the king committed himself to the project and, in so doing, set the stage for the Great Northern War, one of Europe's most decisive conflicts. During this war the long-brewing tensions between foreign absolutism and native nobilities in Eastern Europe would come to a head.

SAXONY: SELECTED STATISTICS[60]

Population and area circa 1700
Population: approximately 2 million: 65% rural (32,000 peasant households);

35% urban (98 cities)
Area: approximately 40,000 square kilometres

Army

Peacetime: 12,000; wartime: 24,000

In the confrontation between foreign sovereigns and East European nobles, the initiative clearly belonged to the former. By its nature absolutism was the more aggressive political system. Its dynamism was encouraged by competition, a factor with which the nobles did not have to live. The rivalry among the Habsburgs, Ottomans, Wettins, Vasas, and Romanovs was so fierce that each had to tighten its grip on its subjects or else face the possibility of losing them. Thus, dynastic rivalries engendered foreign absolutism in Eastern Europe in much the same way as they encouraged colonialism in the Americas.

War, the consequence of these rivalries, revealed the weakness of the native noble-dominated societies of Eastern Europe and forced them to accept the protection and sovereignty of foreign absolutist rulers. War also created the extraordinary circumstances which allowed these sovereigns to reorganize the government of their newly acquired lands. But conflict and competition were not the only catalysts of absolutist reforms. Absolutist rulers assiduously studied and imitated each other's administrative techniques. In the sixteenth century the Ottoman empire was considered a model of a well-run government, and European writers urged their rulers to copy the example. In the seventeenth century it was France which became the epitome of efficient and effective rule. Dynasties all over Europe hastened to apply Louis XIV's administrative innovations in their own lands. Soon they were busily learning from each other (Peter I's administrative reforms, for example, were copied almost in their entirety from the Swedes) how best, as it was often put, "to arrange things differently" in their lands.

To this end, the absolutist monarchs had to circumvent the restrictions which their initial compacts with the East European elites imposed upon them. For this purpose they had the option of using force. However, this was a costly alternative, and, as the numerous uprisings in Hungary, Ukraine, Poland, and Moldavia indicated, not always an effective one. Therefore, it was used only as the last resort. A preferable if slower method of wearing down the resistance of their subjects was to employ a variety of manipulative techniques – Cantemir, the *hospodar* of Moldavia, referred to them as "mechanica" – which were aimed at manoeuvring the nobilities into a position where they had no alternative but to acknowledge the unlimited authority of their sovereigns or at least to admit the futility of resisting them.

In order to implement some of these techniques the sovereigns advanced from secure positions – that is, they took advantage of prerogatives which were generally recognized as their own. Their goal was to obtain advantages which their compacts with the elites did not sanction. The most widespread use of this approach was associated with their manipulation of their duty to defend their subjects. As the Vasas established their garrisons in Livonia, as the Habsburgs continued their long struggle against the Ottomans in Hungary, and as the Romanovs became involved in yet another campaign against the Poles or Ottomans in Ukraine, they knew that the presence of their troops in the lands of their subjects, which would not normally have been tolerated, greatly increased their influence there. August II even plotted to involve the Commonwealth in a war so that, by bringing in his armies, he could strengthen his position with respect to the *szlachta* and the magnates. From the sovereigns' point of view the onerous duty of defending their subjects also provided them with the opportunity of intimidating them.

Although the nobles were often aware of the ulterior motives of their overlords, they found it difficult to protest against them. When they grumbled, as they often did, about the numbers and behaviour of their sovereigns' troops, the monarchs were quick to retort that they were merely fulfilling their obligation to defend them. This response was summarized succinctly in the phrase often used by the Habsburgs: "Nolentes volentes vis vos proteget sua majestas" (Whether you like it or not, His Majesty protects you). Moreover, the rulers could always threaten to withdraw their troops and leave the land open to invasion. Grudgingly, the nobles had to accept the lesser of the two evils and agree to the dangerous yet necessary presence of their overlords' armies in their midst for the duration of frequent and drawn-out wars.

An absolutist ruler could take advantage of offensive as well as defensive wars. For example, August II's plans to regain Livonia, Ukraine, and Moldavia "for the Commonwealth" rested on the assumption that if these lands were taken by conquest, the rule of the Saxon elector would become unlimited in them. A similar logic was apparent in the Habsburg refusal to return the recently retaken Hungarian lands to the *komitats* of the nobility; they had been conquered by Vienna, and Vienna considered that they should remain at its disposal.

Like wars, foreign affairs were generally considered to be primarily the domain of the sovereigns. None the less, East European nobles, citing the medieval principle of *quod nos tangit* ... (what concerns us cannot be resolved without us), often insisted on participating in negotiations when their own interests were at issue. As rulers tightened their hold on their subjects, the nobles' access to external contacts was one of the first privileges that the sovereigns tried to liquidate. Thus, in 1648 the Swedish chancellor, Axel Oxienstierna, adamantly refused to allow the estates of the realm to participate in the Westphalian peace talks; Tsar Aleksei Mikhailovich would not give in to the repeated requests of the Ukrainian *starshyna* to participate in the negotiations at Andrusovo in 1667; the Habsburgs excluded the Hungarian representatives from the talks at Carlowitz in 1699; and August II purposely used only his own Saxon diplomats when negotiating on behalf of the Commonwealth. The objectives of this policy of exclusion were to emphasize the point that the sovereign alone represented the interests of his subjects; to prevent the nobles from complicating the negotiations by pushing their own concerns to the forefront and possibly undermining the position of their overlord; and to isolate the nobles from foreign contacts and competing rulers. Ultimately, the isolation of the nobles from foreign contacts was meant to convince them that they could turn to no one but their own rulers with their grievances.

Another tactic used by the sovereigns was gradually to transform light, pro forma obligations of their subjects into more demanding burdens. A classic example of this political sleight of hand was the transformation by the Ottomans of Moldavia's initial "gift" of two thousand *galben* into an annual tribute of more than seventy times the original sum. When the Ukrainians accepted the tsar's sovereignty, they agreed to have only one Muscovite *voevoda* in Kiev. But after a little more than a decade Muscovite *voevoda*s and garrisons were established in all the major cities of the land. The Livonian *ritterschaft* was at first led to believe that the *Reduktion* would apply only to Swedish landowners. However, when the Livonians accepted the land reform in principle, they were surprised to learn that it would apply to their lands as well.

In certain cases overlords did not have to work around the restrictions imposed upon them by their compacts with the noble elites; for brief periods they could suspend these restrictions altogether. When nobles conspired or rebelled against their overlords, the *extraordinaria*, a pre-modern version of martial law, could be imposed. During the crisis which followed the death of Gustavus Adolphus, the *extraordinaria* were implemented in Sweden. The Habsburg pacification of Hungary and Croatia after the Wesselényi conspiracy was carried out with the aid of these measures. In 1713 August II purposely tried to provoke the *szlachta* into a revolt so that he could claim emergency powers. But the *extraordinaria* did have their limitations. They could only be used for a short time and in specific circumstances.

Of all the tactics available to the sovereigns, not one was used more frequently and more effectively than divide et impera. A technique as old as empires, it was used by East European rulers in several variations. Most often, sovereigns concentrated on exacerbating the socio-economic tensions which existed within the nobility or between it and other classes of society. The Vasas' support of the Livonian burghers in their conflict with the *ritterschaft* is one example of this approach. The tsars were especially adept at it, clandestinely supporting the Cossack rank and file against the *starshyna* and then turning the *starshyna* against the *hetmans*. August II, always eager to apply the proven techniques of his fellow monarchs, tried repeatedly to turn the *szlachta* against the magnates.

Another variant of the divide et impera technique was selective colonization and population transfers. Among its most avid practioners were the Habsburgs, who openly declared that the lands which had been retaken from the Ottomans would be turned over not to the Hungarians but to colonists from Swabia "so that the kingdom ... may become more tempered with Germans." Other sparsely populated areas of Hungary were made available to Serbs, Moldavians, Wallachians, and Slovaks. In Ukraine rumours were constantly flying about the tsars' intentions to transfer the Cossacks beyond the Volga and to give their lands to Russian settlers. Later in the eighteenth century, when southern Ukraine was opened to colonization, it was foreigners, mostly of Balkan origin, who were invited to settle it. While the transfer of population was a disquieting rumour in Ukraine, in Moldavia it became a fact. In the early sixteenth century the Ottomans expelled the inhabitants of southeastern Moldavia and brought in Nogai tribesmen to take their place. Every time the Moldavians rose against the Porte, the pillaging Nogai horde was loosed upon them. Thus, the already varied ethnic mosaic of Eastern Europe became even more complex as a result of absolutist policies.

Some sovereigns were forced to come to the rather unexpected realization that their newly acquired subjects were too numerous and their lands too large to be controlled effectively. In such cases rulers considered or actually implemented the partitioning of these lands. Most anxious to apply such an approach was August II, who soon realized that his Saxon base was insufficient to allow him to absorb the entire Commonwealth. He approached Russia and Brandenburg several times with offers to participate in the partitioning of Poland-Lithuania, on the condition that the choicest part would be reserved for him. At Andrusovo in 1667 Tsar Aleksei Mikhailovich, frustrated by the chaos and anarchy in Ukraine, agreed to the division of the land between Russia and Poland. The Habsburgs applied a variant of this technique when, after acquiring Transylvania, they refused to unite it with other Hungarian lands.

While systematically fragmenting their opponents, absolutist rulers repeatedly declared that their actions were guided by a concern for the "common good." It was perhaps this concept of common good that in the final analysis proved to be the most effective device in their struggle against the nobles. By identifying their centralizing policies with the general welfare they were able to equate the defence of local institutions with the nobles' concern for their own privileges. When and if this manoeuvre succeeded, the elite was deprived of a broad base of support. And this meant that the liquidation or emasculation of its institutions was only a matter of time. The coup de grâce to the nobility's hold on political power usually took the form of eliminating the nobles' right to elect their own principals, that is, officials such as the Hungarian palatine, the Ukrainian *hetman*, the Livonian *landmarschall*, or the Moldavian *hospodar*.

By applying the various tactics described above, absolutist rulers did not overwhelm the noble opposition as a matter of course. As the numerous Hungarian, Polish, Ukrainian, Livonian, and Moldavian revolts and conspiracies of the seventeenth century indicate, pressure exerted too recklessly by the sovereigns could lead to costly conflicts and frustrating setbacks. Yet, never losing sight of their well-defined goals, the rulers doggedly pushed on, increasingly tightening their grip on the lands of Eastern Europe.

IV

The General Crisis in Eastern Europe

In recent decades, historians of early modern Europe engaged in a major and protracted debate over the "general crisis" of the seventeenth century. In view of the unusually great number of revolts, rebellions, and revolutions that occurred in the course of the century, especially at its mid-point, such noted scholars as Eric Hobsbawn, H.R. Trevor-Roper, and Roland Mousnier argued that a general crisis did indeed take place. However, each of them had a different explanation for it. Hobsbawn saw it in Marxist, economic terms. He contended that the upheavals in England, France, Netherlands, Italy, Portugal, and Catalonia were brought on by the tension between the receding feudal and rising capitalist economic orders. Trevor-Roper argued that the crisis was essentially political and that it was brought on by the conflict between the luxurious, spendthrift "courts" and their parasitic bureaucracies on the one hand and the resentful, puritanical "country," which was excluded from courtly privileges, on the other. For his part, Mousnier saw the upheavals as encompassing all aspects of human life, while being reflected primarily in the confrontation between absolutist and republican ideologies.[1]

The provocative idea of a general crisis in Western Europe sparked a variety of responses. Some scholars rejected it completely. For example, the Dutch historian Ivo Schöffer questioned how one could speak of a general West European crisis at a time when Holland experienced its golden age.[2] Yet despite various exceptions and qualifications, many scholars did accept the notion that widespread upheaval was unusually prevalent in the seventeenth century. They continued to disagree, however, about its nature and causes.

Since historians frequently referred to the upheavals as revolutions, the focus of the debate turned next to the definition of revolution in the early modern period. It soon became evident that the term could not fruitfully serve as a catch-all for the wide variety of political, socio-economic, religious, ethnic, and regional conflicts that took place during the turbulent century. Moreover, as J.H. Elliot pointed out, it was dangerous to apply a twentieth-century conception of revolution to pre-modern situations.[3] Therefore, considerable effort has been expended in refining the definition of the term. Recently this task has been admirably carried out by Perez Zagorin.[4] In his survey and analysis of early modern revolutions, Zagorin establishes five distinct types:

1 Conspiracy and coup, limited largely to the action of noble and aristocratic elites;
2 Urban rebellion, either by plebeian and inferior groups against urban elites and governments or by urban communities against external royal and state authority;
3 Agrarian rebellion by peasants and others against landlord and/or state authority;
4 Provincial, regional, and separatist rebellion by provincial societies or dependent realms against their monarchical state center;
5 Kingdomwide civil war against monarchies based on noble and aristocratic leadership and involving the entire society.[5]

Up to 1660 these types of conflicts were a frequent occurrence in Western Europe. Thereafter, relative calm and stability reigned in the region. As will become evident below, for our purposes the first and fourth categories are of greatest interest. However, Zagorin was unable to deal with the conspiracies and coups at any length because, in the West European context on which he concentrated, they were not of great consequence. Yet in Eastern Europe the first category of revolt was exceedingly important. Fortunately, Zagorin's instructive discussion on provincial rebellions is germane to the conflicts which we will be examining.

Despite the progress in defining and categorizing early modern conflicts, historians have still to agree on the central question: what caused them? In their attempts to deal with this problem, they have generally been leery of monocausal explanations. But while stressing the variety of political, economic, and social conditions that brought on the differing types of conflicts, recent studies on revolution in early modern Western Europe have also noted that state building and, more specifically, societies' reactions to the process have been central, often predominant features of the upheavals. Zagorin, for example, states that "to speak of state building is to cite a fact that loomed large nearly everywhere upon the scene of revolutions in the sixteenth and seventeenth centuries ... Whether in its general operation or in its particular effects, no other single factor was of wider significance in contributing directly or indirectly to the preconditions from which the different revolutions of the time arose."[6] We would go further and argue that the prime cause of the general crisis in the early modern history of both Western and Eastern Europe was the transition from the noble-association form of government to that of the state-organization.

If state building was the single most important factor in creating the pre-conditions for revolution, what actually triggered the upheavals? Again, historians are loath to commit themselves to a single causal factor. But among those which they usually note, two are cited most frequently: one is the general economic decline which encompassed all of Europe after the boom years of the sixteenth century; the other, more immediate factor commonly cited is the unprecedented costs, especially the taxes, that accompanied the absolutist monarchs' frequent and demanding wars.

In the context of this study, the obvious question which arises is whether the concept of general crisis can be applied to the eastern as well as the western part of the continent. It is our contention that it can. Moreover, to an even greater extent than in the West, state building and societal reactions to it were the cause of widespread confrontation and conflict in the East. There were, of course, regional particularities which were associated with the East European conflicts. While the general crisis peaked in Western Europe in the 1660s, in the East the high point came about fifty years later, in the initial decades of the eighteenth century. This time-lag can be explained by the fact that the monarchies in the East embarked on absolutist state building (or, as in the case of the Ottoman empire under the Köprülü viziers, state renovation) about fifty years later than their Western counterparts. In addition, Eastern Europe has generally lagged behind developments in the West.

Another characteristic of the East European scene was its lesser diversity in the types of upheavals that occurred. Urban rebellions such as those in France in the 1620s and 1630s or in Naples in 1647 were almost totally lacking in the East, for the obvious reason that the towns there were too weak. In the West anti-royalist rebellions occurred both among native populations, whose rebellion was against autochthonous sovereigns, as in the English Revolution and the French Fronde of the mid-seventeenth century; and among dependent kingdoms, principalities, and provinces, which rebelled against foreign sovereigns, as in the case of the Catalan, Portuguese, Scotch, and Irish rebellions of the 1640s. In the East, however, by the early eighteenth century all the rebellions were only of the second variety. The comparatively less variegated manifestations of crisis in Eastern Europe were due to the region's less diversified and less complex social, economic, and political systems. Therefore, one can argue that, in general, broad historical patterns and trends stand out more clearly in the East.

In their discussion of the West European general crisis, historians have made effective use of an analytical device, developed by the French, which is often referred to as the structure-conjuncture relationship. This calls for defining the broad contradictions, disharmonies, and dysfunctions in society, that is, the structure of a conflict situation, and relating this to an immediate combination of events and circumstances, that is, the conjuncture that brings a conflict to a head. According to this relationship, the basic structure of the East European crisis may be characterized as essentially a conflict between two inherently contradictory political systems, those of the state-organizations and the noble-associations. At issue was which should possess ultimate, not merely formal, political authority in a given land. In the East this elemental confrontation was intensified by the fact that the aggressive, destabilizing force of the state systems was identified with foreigners. Such was the case with the Germans in Hungary and Poland, the Swedes in Livonia, the Russians in Ukraine, and the Ottomans in Moldavia. Thus, the usually strong negative reaction of the militantly conservative East European elites to any political innovations was intensified even more by their deeply rooted xenophobia (which many twentieth-century historians have interpreted as nationalism).

The conjunctional factors which triggered the confrontations and conflicts of the early eighteenth century in Eastern Europe were similar to those in the West. Economic decline, reflected in the sharp drop in exports to the West, was perhaps even more damaging to the East's agrarian, one-dimensional economy. Moreover, the general devastation brought on by protracted wars, famines, and epidemics – such as the Deluge in Poland, the Ruin in Ukraine, the Great Hunger in Livonia, or the catastrophic demographic and economic conditions which obtained in Hungary and Moldavia in the 1690s – was at least as disastrous as that suffered by the worst-hit parts of Western Europe after the Thirty Years' War. It was upon these decimated, exhausted populations of Eastern Europe that their foreign monarchs imposed, in the early eighteenth century, the crushing burden of the twenty-one-year-long Great Northern War, which, with its related conflicts, engulfed most of the region. While this conflict did not involve Hungary, that land was still staggering under the costs of the Ottoman wars. Thus, at a time when the resources of native noble-associations were stretched to their limits, the newly expansive absolutist state-organizations of their foreign overlords, egged on by their mutual great-power rivalries and ambitions, imposed unprecedented demands upon their East European subjects. As a result, in the early eighteenth century a general confrontation and crisis between the two political systems was unavoidable.

The general crisis in Eastern Europe was the culmination of a long series of seventeenth-century anti-sovereign uprisings: it included those of István Bocskai (1604), Ferenc Wesselényi and associates (1666), and Imre Thököly (1675 and 1697) in Hungary and *hetmans* Ivan Vyhovsky (1658), Iuras Khmelnytsky (1659), and Ivan Briukhovetsky (1666–8) in Left Bank Ukraine; it included the anti-Ottoman conspiracies in Moldavia of *hospodar*s Vasile Lupu (1645), Gheorghe Ştefan (1656), and Ştefan Petriceicu (1673); the Livonian anti-Polish uprisings (in 1601 and 1617); and the *rokosz* of Mikołaj Zebrzydowski (1606-9) and Jerzy Lubomirski (1665-6) in Poland. Although Bohemia does not fall within the purview of our survey, one might also add the Bohemian revolt of 1618. A sure sign of crisis is the relative calm that follows it. In Western Europe the widespread and frequent revolts, rebellions, and revolutions ceased after 1660. Similarly, in Eastern Europe the turbulence that characterized the region throughout the seventeenth and the climactic early eighteenth century died down dramatically after 1715.

CONFRONTATION IN LIVONIA

The wave of noble discontent that swept through Eastern Europe first welled up in Livonia. In the 1690s the Swedish *Reduktion* engendered between the *ritterschaft* and the crown a fierce debate which questioned some of the key assumptions on which their relationship was based and forced both sides to take up increasingly uncompromising positions. By 1688 almost five-sixths of all the estates in Livonia had reverted to the crown. Their former owners now had to lease them from the royal treasury. Not content with retrieving only the lands which the Swedish kings had distributed in Livonia, Swedish officials also raised claims to those lands which had been distributed by the Livonian Order, the original sovereign of the land. Incensed by what it viewed as arbitrariness, the Livonian nobility elected two delegates in February 1690 to plead its case before King Charles XI in Stockholm. One of these was the elderly and respected Baron Leonhard von Budberg; the other was Johann Reinhold von Patkul, a strong-willed, thirty-year old caption of the Riga garrison who was destined to become the embodiment of Livonian resistance to Swedish absolutism.[7]

After almost eight months of preparation, during which the Livonians searched in vain for the original of the *Privilegium Sigismundi Augusti*, the loss of which was a telling indication of how alien were bureaucratic procedures to these German noblemen, the two delegates set out for Stockholm in October 1690. Meanwhile, in that same year the Swedish government established a special commission to examine the validity of the rights and privileges of the German Baltic nobility. Thus, when the two sides confronted each other in Stockholm, each had carefully prepared its case. For almost a year Budberg and Patkul engaged the king's ministers in legalistic debates, submitted memoranda, buttonholed influential courtiers, and sought to gain the attention and sympathy of the king. Basically, their argument was that Livonia, by virtue of its special rights and privileges, which had been granted by Sigismund

Augustus in 1562 and confirmed by Charles XI in 1678, occupied a unique position in the Swedish empire. Its relationship, they argued, was not with Sweden and its parliament but only with the king. Therefore, measures and laws passed by the Swedish parliament, such as the *Reduktion*, ought not to apply to Livonia.

The king's officials, for their part, men like Chancellor Bengt Oxenstierna and especially Sweden's man in Livonia, Jakob Johann Hastfer, a Baltic German who served as governor-general of Livonia, struck back by questioning the authenticity of the *Privilegium Sigismundi Augusti* and by submitting the extant versions of the document to a special commission set up for this purpose. Because the commission was unable to resolve the issue, the matter went to the king himself. On 19 May 1691 Charles XI announced his decision. While accepting the authenticity of the *Privilegium*, the king reserved the right to confirm and accept only those rights and privileges which were compatible with the demands of the Swedish *reich*. One of the points that the king refused to confirm was the *ritterschaft*'s right to allodial holdings, on the grounds that it had not possessed this right originally, in the days of the Livonian Order. In other words, the *Reduktion* was to remain in force.

Although he was bitterly disappointed by this outcome, Patkul persisted. In a memorandum that clearly carried his mark he delicately hinted that, if the king was unwilling to respect Livonian rights, the *ritterschaft* might reconsider its ties with the Swedish crown. Even after Budberg had returned home, Patkul remained in Sweden, hoping to change the king's mind. Finally, in December 1691, after a few brief and what appeared to be encouraging encounters with Charles XI, he sailed for home. The period of legalistic sparring was over.

After the delegates' return, an assembly of the *ritterschaft*'s representatives met at Wenden on 11 March 1692 to hear their report. Patkul, who had by now emerged as the actual, if not formal leader of the *ritterschaft*, described his confrontations with the Swedish authorities and advised the assembly on further action. After some deliberation, and without requesting permission from the king or governor-general, the assembly decided to establish the new office of resident, to which four noblemen were to be elected to monitor attempts to infringe on the rights of the Livonian nobility. Even more bold was the memorandum which the assembly, apparently at the instigation of Patkul, dispatched to the king. Although it took the form of a letter of supplication, the Wenden memorandum was actually a bitter critique of Swedish rule in Livonia. It sharply attacked the *Reduktion*, the manner in which it was carried out, the favouritism shown by Swedish officials to other estates, and the anti-German and pro-Swedish policies of the government. ("If this goes on, in ten years there will not be a German left in the land ... since people of other nations and languages are appointed as pastors ... and to university positions.")[8] The memorandum concluded with a veiled threat that, if matters went any further, Livonia's personal union with the king would be placed in jeopardy.

The memorandum enraged Charles XI and Hastfer, the governor-general, even more, since it was the latter's implementation of Swedish policy that had been directly attacked. Returning from abroad, Hastfer was more determined than ever before to humble the *ritterschaft*, and Patkul in particular. In September 1692 he called a *landtag*, which he hoped would make a statement disassociating itself from the Wenden memorandum. But the Livonian nobles not only stood staunchly by their colleagues' statement; they flatly refused to surrender to the governor-general any document related to the matter. For Hastfer, the one positive outcome of the *landtag* was that, since a few Livonian noblemen, led by Ungarn-Sternberg, had voiced their reservations about the *ritterschaft*'s stand, he was able to report to the king that the Livonians were divided on the issue and that it was only a group of "malcontents" that was responsible for the "insulting" memorandum. The king then ordered the Livonian *landmarschall*, the *landrat*, and the residents to present themselves before a court of inquiry in Stockholm. Patkul, who had in the meantime fled to Kurland because of a conflict with a commanding officer, was granted a royal safe conduct so that he might be able to appear before the court.

By instituting these court proceedings, the Swedish government was not interested primarily in calling a few recalcitrant nobles to account. Its goal was much broader. It hoped to use the trial to discredit Livonian institutions and to pave the way for their eventual liquidation. Thus, the Livonians, who had hoped that their case would lead to an investigation of Hastfer's malpractice in their homeland, were surprised to learn that a commission of twelve of the highest government officials would try them on charges of *crimen laesae majestatis*, that is, of insulting the king's majesty. From the outset they were put on the defensive, and for four months they were forced into a position of defending not only themselves but their institutions as well. Patkul realized that, in spite of a brilliant defence, he would most probably receive the death penalty. Therefore, taking advantage of his safe conduct, he fled to Kurland. His fears had been justified. Soon after, the commission found him guilty of insulting the king and sentenced him to have his right hand cut off (for writing the insulting memorandum), as well as to die and to have his property confiscated and his writings publicly burned "so that it might be a threat and a warning to other disloyal and rebellious subjects."[9] Several of his colleagues also received the death penalty, but were later pardoned. In any case, the commission felt that it had unearthed a conspiracy against the king and that it could now take the necessary measures to prevent such a thing from recurring in the future.

Even before the trial was over in Stockholm, the Swedish government took steps to limit Livonian autonomy. Despite Hastfer's urging that the province be totally incorporated into the empire, the king decided on a more gradual approach. Instead of eliminating Livonian institutions outright, he planned to limit their authority and make them mere appendages of imperial rule. Thus, on 26 January 1695, within weeks of the trial, Hastfer announced the following measures in Riga: the office of *landrat* and resident were to be abolished; the *landmarschall* was to be replaced by a Swedish-appointed *hauptmann*; the *landtag* was to be deprived of most of its authority and given the function of a tax-receiving agency; a committee of twenty-one noblemen, picked by the governor-general, was to run the daily affairs of the *ritterschaft*; church affairs were to be taken over by the Swedish church; and preparations were under way to introduce the Swedish judicial system. It seemed that the bitter confrontation over the two paramount values of the *ritterschaft* – its land and its privileges – was over and that the Swedish crown had emerged the victor.

Were it not for one man, Swedish absolutism might perhaps have triumphed in Livonia without further impediment. The unusually stubborn, energetic, and talented Patkul refused to accept the fait accompli. Forced to flee abroad, he spent the next four years searching for ways to right the wrongs that the Livonian *ritterschaft* and he personally had suffered at the hands of the Swedes. Like all political émigrés he experienced the painful disorientation, sense of hopelessness, and frustration that came with exile. But unlike most émigrés, Patkul would get, or, more accurately, create for himself another chance to strike a blow for his cause.

In 1698, while staying at the home of Otto Arnold von Paykul, a Livonian expatriate and general in the Saxon army, Patkul experienced a stroke of good fortune. Completely by chance he met Jacob Heinrich von Flemming, August's first minister, who was recuperating at a neighbouring estate from his strenuous and successful efforts to win the Polish crown for his Wettin sovereign. Knowing of August's obsession with glory and conquest and of Flemming's desire to cater to his whims, Patkul approached the latter with a daring proposal. Would August be interested in the conquest of Livonia? Eloquently, he argued that a once-in-a-lifetime opportunity for an easy and yet important conquest lay at August's feet. Because of the death of Charles XI in 1697, Sweden's throne was now occupied by Charles XII, a sixteen-year-old boy, who, it seemed, was not of an age to provide the proper leadership. Moreover, the Livonians were unhappy with Swedish rule and would gladly support August. As for the Commonwealth, it would be grateful to its new king for regaining for it a long-lost province. In addition, August's image as a military leader would be immeasurably enhanced. Finally, Patkul added that king could establish his hereditary right in Poland and prepare for himself a most feasible way for introducing absolutism in the land.[10] Apparently, Patkul was not averse to helping rulers to introduce absolutism, so long as they did not try to do so in his own land. The proposal appealed to Flemming, and several months later he invited Patkul to meet the king.

On New Year's Day 1699 Patkul was presented to August in Grodno. After the usual formalities he handed the king an elaborate but, on the whole, realistic plan for the creation of a coalition of Saxony, Brandenburg, Poland-Lithuania, Denmark, and, with some reservations, Russia.[11] The general purpose of the alliance was to destroy once and for all the Swedish stranglehold on the Baltic. The immediate pretext for the proposed attack on Sweden was to be Poland-Lithuania's seemingly burning desire to regain Livonia. August was taken by the proposal; however, before committing himself, he wished to have more information about the views and desiderata of the Livonian *ritterschaft* in connection with this matter. For this purpose, Patkul and Flemming undertook a secret journey to Kurland. From there the Saxon minister travelled incognito to Riga to observe its defences, while Patkul apparently went to visit his supporters among the Livonian nobility. Despite the attention which Swedish, Baltic German, Estonian, and Latvian historians have lavished on the question of the identity and numbers of Patkul's co-conspirators during this period, little has been found in the way of concrete data. Most probably, not more than a handful of the members of the Livonian elite joined him or knew of his plans, but it seems that there were among them some of the most influential members of the *ritterschaft*. In any case, Patkul returned from his mission with several documents which August found very persuasive.[12]

One of these, dated 28 February 1699, was an unsigned declaration by "twelve Livonian patriots" who claimed that they spoke for the entire *ritterschaft* and who had empowered an unspecified person (Patkul) to negotiate with the Polish king on their behalf. Another document, signed by such notables as Gustav von Budberg, Otto von Vietinghoff, and Freidrick von Plater, thanked Flemming for his "work for our salvation," but the signers declined a meeting with the Saxon minister, considering it too dangerous. Most important was a third document, a set of instructions bearing the seal of the *ritterschaft* and authorizing the bearer (again, Patkul) to negotiate a series of articles with August, King of Poland.[13] Among the most noteworthy of these articles was the *ritterschaft*'s declaration that it was willing to acknowledge August and his dynasty as its overlords. A secret addendum to this clause stipulated that, if the Wettins lost the Polish crown, Livonia would remain under their and not the Commonwealth's overlordship. In its new position Livonia would be able to play the role of a bulwark against Sweden and, if need be, against Russia. Other articles stipulated that August guarantee Livonia's complete autonomy, freedom of worship, and the integrity of its laws. Moreover, the *ritterschaft* demanded the sole right to make military and civil appointments in the land. This was a direct blow against the proud, pro-Swedish burghers of Riga, with whom the Livonian nobility was often at odds. If August accepted these conditions, the *ritterschaft* would commit itself to raise and maintain a 6,500-man army and provide an unspecified amount of income for August's treasury.

Almost all the historians who have studied this document agree that it was most probably formulated by Patkul himself. None the less, it is generally acknowledged that the views reflected in the document were probably also representative of a large part of the Livonian nobility. In the opinion of the noted Baltic German historian Reinhard Wittram, had the treaty which Patkul signed with August on 24 August 1699 on the basis of these articles been put into effect, the Livonian *adelsrepublik* would have developed into "an absolutism of the *ritterschaft*."[14]

Once the pact between Patkul, the self-appointed representative of the Livonian *ritterschaft*, and August, in his role as king of Poland-Lithuania, was signed, a hurried, conspiratorial effort began to glue the rest of the coalition together. First August turned to the Commonwealth. It was, after all, in its name that the attack into Livonia was to be launched. Realizing that it would be pointless to try to convince the notoriously pacifist *sejm* to sanction an offensive war, the king secretly approached the primate of Poland, Michal Radziejowski, and, with the aid of a 100,000-*reichstaler* bribe, convinced him to help mobilize Polish public opinion for the war, or at least to stifle opposition to it. Meanwhile, in May Patkul was dispatched to Copenhagen to prepare the ground for an alliance of Denmark, Saxony, and Poland-Lithuania. After a brief and successful stay he returned to Warsaw and was immediately sent on to Moscow, together with the Saxon general Georg Carl von Carlowitz, to sound out the Russians. On 11 November 1699, in a secret meeting with Carlowitz and Patkul, who travelled incognito, the tsar enthusiastically agreed to join the attack on Sweden. Ironically, at that very same moment in another part of Moscow, a Swedish delegation was concluding the renewal of a Swedish-Russian peace treaty. Upon his return to Poland Patkul was officially appointed secret councillor of August 11. With this, he plunged whole-heartedly into the world of high politics, where for the next seven years he would cast a very long shadow.[15]

After the diplomatic groundwork had been laid, preparations began for the actual attack on Livonia. The primary target of the offensive was to be Riga, where Patkul claimed he had supporters who were ready to aid him. During late November and early December, under various pretexts and guises, about six to seven thousand Saxon troops moved unobtrusively to Kurland, close to the Livonian border. Overall command of the operation had been given to Flemming, while Patkul, having received a rank of colonel, led one wing of the Saxon army. In January 1700 several magnificent opportunities for capturing Riga by surprise presented themselves. These were lost because Flemming, who was enjoying himself in extended visits to nearby Polish magnates, had not been present to give the order to attack. Infuriated, "with tears almost running down his face," Patkul fired off several bitter, scolding letters to his commanding officer. Finally, on 9 February, Flemming arrived and the attack was launched. It failed miserably. The Swedish garrison, forewarned by several hours, had had time to prepare itself and thus deprived the Saxons of the advantage of surprise. Unable to take the city either by storm or by subterfuge, the Saxons had no choice but to settle in for a long siege. The Great Northern War had begun.

How did the Swedish authorities in Livonia view the situation, and what was the reaction of the *ritterschaft*, whom Patkul claimed to represent, to these events? Even before the outbreak of war, Erik von Dahlbergh, the new governor-general of Livonia, had been aware that the situation was dangerous. Dissatisfaction among the Livonian nobles had become rampant after the Swedish crown took away the greater part of their lands. Moreover, he was worried by the large number of restless, unemployed Livonian officers – fifteen lieutenant-colonels, ten majors, twenty-one *rittmeister*s, thirty captains, and sixty-nine lieutenants – in the land.[16] To make matters worse, in 1695 a terrible famine swept through the Baltic provinces, and its toll in Livonia was close to 25 per cent of the population. Despite the assertions of some Baltic German historians it has not been proven that the *Reduktion* was a contributing factor to the famine. None the less, the confusion engendered by it probably hindered the Livonians' ability to weather the calamity. Even the normally pro-Swedish burghers of Riga were dissatisfied with Swedish rule because of the exploitative grain prices set by Stockholm. Therefore, in 1698, as soon as Charles xii came to the throne, Dahlbergh requested that he grant the Livonians "special favour" by easing the burden of the *Reduktion* and reforming the chaotic Swedish-imposed judicial system. The governor-general also asked the young king to provide funds for improving the fortifications in Livonia and stationing another Swedish regiment there. Characteristically, Charles xii refused to make these concessions, but he did agree to the request for military reinforcements.

As for the *ritterschaft* itself, when Patkul and his Saxon supporters appeared in Livonia, its reaction was more of surprise and confusion than of elation. Although Dahlbergh complained of the nobles' listlessness in responding to his call to arms (only 315 noblemen came to the aid of Riga), few of them showed open enthusiasm for Patkul's endeavour, either. Evidently, Patkul's plan to bring Livonia into union with the Commonwealth did not sit well with the nobles. It soon became clear that, although they were disenchanted with Swedish rule, they liked that of the rabidly Catholic Poles even less, and under the circumstances Patkul's secret agreement with August could not be revealed. Furthermore, despite the unemployment of some Livonian officers, many others held positions in the Swedish army. In fact, one out of every three officers was a Baltic German, and about three-fifths of the Swedish troops were officered by Baltic Germans, of whom about one-quarter would die fighting for Charles XII.[17] Thus, it was little wonder that the Livonian *ritterschaft* was unsure of which way to turn. Its hesitation was evident at a conference called by Dahlbergh in June 1700 in Riga. The governor-general wanted the *ritterschaft* to issue a strong statement repudiating Patkul and his "treacherous enterprise." For weeks the nobles procrastinated, pleading that they did not have the "learned people" to formulate such a statement. Others left the city on the pretext of no longer being able to afford to stay there. Only with the greatest difficulty did Dahlberg finally extract the repudiation from them. And he had to formulate the statement himself. Thus, although they were only half-hearted in their support of the Swedes, the nobles were clearly unwilling to join Patkul. They preferred, in short, to sit back and await the outcome of the struggle. Their unwillingness to take a firm stand contributed in large part to the failure of the Livonian enterprise. None the less, Patkul, stubborn as ever, was determined to continue the struggle against Sweden on his own.

"GOLDEN FREEDOMS" VERSUS SAXON ABSOLUTISM IN POLAND-LITHUANIA

The conflict between August's absolutist tendencies and the Polish nobility's commitment to its "golden freedoms" became intense during the early eighteenth century. Yet, to a much greater extent than elsewhere in Eastern Europe, this confrontation was complicated by foreign occupations, rivalries between the pro-Swedish and pro-Russian parties, and intrigues by the powerful magnate "kinglets."[18] Thus, when the magnates and *szlachta* had to choose between the invading Swedes and their own dangerously ambitious king, the struggle between sovereign and elite became confused. Magnates who stood to gain high offices for supporting August did so despite their opposition in principle to everything that he stood for. Considerations such as these, plus the fact that August's absolutist plans were never really implemented, explain why the confrontation between royal absolutism and noble privilege, central as it was to the political developments of early eighteenth-century Eastern Europe, was less sharply delineated in the Commonwealth than in some other East European lands.

With the outbreak of the Great Northern War, the Polish dimension of this widespread struggle soon came to the fore. To the surprise and dismay of his Danish, Russian, and Saxon enemies, the eighteen-year-old king of Sweden's response to their surprise attacks was launched with lightning speed and devastating effectiveness. In the spring of 1700 Charles attacked the Danes on their home ground and quickly forced them to sign a humiliating peace treaty. Then he turned eastwards. In October a twelve-thousand-man Swedish army landed between the Saxons in Livonia and the Russians in Ingria. And on 20 November the young king scored a brilliant victory at Narva against a Russian army several times larger than his own. At this point Charles would gladly have pursued Peter I into the heart of Russia. But before he could do so, August II, against whom the Swedish king understandably bore a special grudge, would have to be dealt with. By July 1701 the Swedes had pushed the Saxons out of Livonia. As the elector-king retreated into Poland, Charles and his army paused in Kurland, where he and his staff contemplated how best to strike at August.

Charles XII came to the conclusion that, if he wished to neutralize the Poles or even gain their support, he would have to dethrone August and replace him with a more compatible monarch.[19] Because the Saxon elector-king had many powerful enemies in Poland-Lithuania, the plan seemed promising at the outset. The three Sobieski brothers, sons of the previous Polish king and contenders for the crown in 1699, contacted the Swedes in 1701 and offered their co-operation. The two Sapieha brothers, expelled from their Lithuanian holdings by August-supported magnates and *szlachta*, even signed a formal agreement with Swedes in 1701. In return for support in regaining their lands and offices, they promised to help the Swedes remove August from the throne. Also, the so-called patriots group, led by the two venerable politicians Stanisław Jablonowski and Rafal Leszczynski, preferred a Swedish presence to a Russian one in Poland. Finally, the large neutralist party among the *szlachta*, which wanted at all costs to avoid the devastation of war in its homeland, appeared willing to come to an understanding with Charles XII.

In view of these encouraging signs, instead of waiting for the Polish opposition to August to mobilize, Charles XII decided to force the issue himself. In January 1702 his troops entered Poland in pursuit of the Saxons, and on 9 July they defeated August's army at Kliszow. Yet neither this victory nor any other that followed was decisive enough to force August to his knees. Finally, Charles's patience wore out. At his behest an assembly of the *szlachta* was called in Warsaw on 16 February 1704, and duly voted to deprive August II of his royal crown.

The Saxon elector's countermove was quick and effective. On 28 February he kidnapped two of the Sobieski brothers in Silesia and threatened to kill them if the third brother accepted the crown, thus removing his greatest rivals. Moreover, August's supporters had begun to mobilize. In 1704 the previously formed Sandomir Confederation, which supported the duly elected king and his ally, Peter I of Russia, reorganized itself and stepped up its anti-Swedish activity. For Charles it became more difficult to find a new and malleable candidate for the throne. When the choice was finally made, it was a surprising one. Bypassing some of the more experienced and better-known magnates, the Swedish king selected the inexperienced, twenty-six-year-old Stanisław Leszczynski, *wojewoda* of Poznan, as his candidate. On 2 July 1704 at a rump electoral *sejm* – only eight hundred noblemen and four senators were present, as were, at a discreet distance, several regiments of Swedish infantry – Stanisław Leszczynski was elected king of Poland.[20] However, it was not until 1706, after Charles had invaded Saxony and forced August to abdicate formally as a result of the Treaty of Altranstadt, that Leszczynski gained a relatively secure hold on his throne. At long last it appeared that Charles XII had Poland under his control and could now turn against Russia.

At this juncture, one might well wonder how these conflicts between sovereigns were related to the conflict between sovereign and elite in Poland-Lithuania. The relationship was a direct one: August's real or alleged transgressions against the "golden freedoms" became his opponents' rallying cry and primary rationale for demanding his dethronement. For example, in turning to Charles for aid, the Sobieskis cited August's disrespect for Polish rights and liberties as the reason for their dissatisfaction with him. When they entered Poland, the Swedes distributed leaflets and manifestos which proclaimed their desire to defend Polish liberties against Saxon oppression. (Incidentally, Charles was in this case simply repaying August in kind, for when the latter invaded Livonia, he claimed that he was doing so to protect Livonian liberties from Swedish absolutism.)[21] The Swedish king stated that he would lend his support to his Polish allies "until their liberties are confirmed." And Swedish and pro-Leszczynski propagandists constantly sought to paint the Swedish king as the guarantor of Poland's freedoms. Even the highly influential primate of the Commonwealth, Cardinal Radziejowski, no friend of either Leszczynski's or Charles's, complained that, "from the beginning of his reign, His Majesty the King [August II] does nothing but break the laws and ravage the land by drawing his enemies from place to place while not providing for the land's defence, and all this leads to the destruction of our fatherland and of our freedoms."[22]

As might have been expected, when he was elected king, Leszczynski solemnly swore to struggle "for the salvation of liberty." Later, his propagandists constantly hammered away at August's levy of illegal taxes and requisitions, at his encouragement of German immigration to the Commonwealth, at the transfer of the royal crown and archives to Saxony.[23] There were even accusations that he had secretly abetted the huge Cossack uprising in Polish-held Right Bank Ukraine in order to undermine the nobility's position.[24] To be sure, these anti-absolutist pronouncements were to a great extent self-serving. They were a convenient way for Charles and Leszczynski to rouse the *szlachta* against August. None the less, their slogans struck a responsive chord among the nobility, for by 1705 Leszczynski's supporters numbered over fifteen thousand, and their numbers were growing.[25]

The widespread anti-absolutist sentiment, however, could not mask Leszczynski's basic weakness: the all-too-obvious fact that he was merely a puppet of the Swedes. His dependence on the Swedes was vividly reflected in the treaty which he concluded with Charles XII on 28 November 1705.[26] It stipulated that the Commonwealth and Sweden would provide each other with support in all future conflicts, that future kings of the Commonwealth would not sign any anti-Swedish alliances, that August's alliance with Russia would be repudiated because it was "dangerous to Polish freedoms," and that those supporters of August who left his camp would receive amnesty. Even more revealing of how subordinate the interests of the Commonwealth were to those of Sweden was the commercial part of the treaty. Sweden's mercantilist designs on the Commonwealth were clearly evident in the articles which stipulated that all of the Commonwealth's trade with the West would be re-routed through Riga and that Swedish merchants would be given privileged status in the Commonwealth. Thus, although the Swedes did not impose any territorial demands on the Commonwealth, as had been expected, few Poles were convinced that Charles XII was seriously concerned with the defence of Polish freedoms.

Another of Leszczynski's liabilities was that his efforts to recruit important supporters for his cause were severely hampered by Charles XII's notorious high-handedness. The young king made no secret of his dominance of Leszczynski and of the Poles in general. He stated openly, "Let them [the Poles] know that their friendship means little to the Swedes, and that the Swedes can do them more harm than anyone else."[27] A characteristic example of Charles's cavalier way of dealing with the pliant but persistent Leszczynski was the matter of the appointment of crown *hetman* (commander-in-chief). Leszczynski wanted this all-important post to go to Adam Sieniawski, *wojewoda* of Belz, who was reputed to be the richest and most influential magnate in the Commonwealth. But for reasons of his own Charles insisted that Leszczynski grant the office to Józef Potocki, *wojewoda* of Kiev. As a result, not only did Leszczynski lose the support of Sieniawski, but the latter became the leader of the pro-August forces. A similar problem arose in Lithuania. Leszczynski wanted the office of the Lithuanian *hetman* to go to a member of the Wisniowecki magnate family, which enjoyed great popularity among the *szlachta*. Charles, however, insisted that one of the hated Sapiehas have the office, a move which soon alienated many potential supporters in the grand duchy. In summary, Leszczynski's total dependence on Charles and the Swedish king's generally misguided interference in internal Polish politics explain to a large extent why Leszczynski, who was so successful in monopolizing anti-absolutist slogans and postures, was unable to attract the majority of the anti-absolutist magnates and *szlachta*.

While Leszczynski struggled with the burdens of Swedish patronage, August's supporters, organized in the Sandomir Confederation and led by Sieniawski, redoubled their efforts. Refusing to recognize the legality of Leszczynski's election, their pamphleteers responded to his claims that he stood for Polish rights by accusing him of making a mockery of free elections, of being a careerist, of encouraging the ruinous Swedish occupation, and of being anti-Catholic for siding with the Lutheran Swedes, who demanded freedom of worship for the Protestants of the Commonwealth. Even after Charles, in 1706, attained his major goals in Poland and forced August to abdicate, the Sandomir Confederation refused to accept Leszczynski as the king of Poland and looked for someone else to rival him. The man mentioned most often in this connection was Prince Ferenc II Rákóczi of Hungary.

After August's abdication there was an ominous development in the Commonwealth. Desperate for military assistance, the Sandomir Confederation became ever more dependent on Russian support. Peter I gladly gave it, and for the first time the Russians had the means of directly influencing the internal affairs of the Commonwealth. In the coming years, particularly after the Russian victory at Poltava in June 1709, this constantly expanding influence would make a sham of Polish sovereignty. In any case, it soon became clear that anti-Swedish sentiments were stronger in Poland-Lithuania than was the resentment against August's projected absolutist designs. As long as Charles XII maintained his military superiority, Leszczynski retained his uneasy throne. But almost immediately after the momentous Swedish defeat at Poltava, his fortunes plummeted and he was forced into political exile.

As Leszczynski retreated to join Charles XII in the Moldavian town of Bender, where the latter had sought refuge with the remnants of his army, August and his Saxon troops returned to Poland. With his second ascension to the throne the issue of August's absolutist tendencies, no longer sidelined by the Swedish invasion, again confronted the nobility. In fact, this time the confrontation would be more direct than it had been in the past. During the struggle between August and Leszczynski, which lasted from 1704 to 1709, the two rivals continually tried to outbid each other for the support of the most influential magnates. The awarding of prestigious offices was the common currency in this bidding. As a result, the influence of the magnates, already vast, became even greater during this period. This was especially evident in the case of those magnates who obtained the all-important offices of crown and field *hetman* in Poland and in Lithuania. Because of August's extended absence from Poland, for example, his crown *hetman*, Adam Sieniawski, not only led the loyalist troops of the Sandomir Confederation but for all practical purposes ruled the lands that were unoccupied by the Swedes. The same was true of Ludwik Pociej, August's crown *hetman* in Lithuania, whose power in the grand duchy was virtually unlimited. It was, therefore, almost inevitable that when August returned to Poland, there would be a clash between the *hetman*s and the king. When such a clash did occur in 1714, soon after Leszczynski's final efforts to recoup his losses, Sieniawski, Pociej, and other highly placed "royalists" suddenly became stubborn defenders of the status quo and dedicated tribunes of the *szlachta* and its "golden freedoms."

The issue that brought the conflict to a head was an old one, the quartering of Saxon troops in the Commonwealth.[28] As long as the remnants of Charles XII's and Leszczynski's troops were ensconced at Bender, from where they repeatedly threatened to invade Poland with the aid of the Ottomans and Tatars, the Saxon presence in Poland was grudgingly tolerated. The *szlachta* even agreed to pay the extraordinary taxes which August levied to support his troops. But when Charles finally left for Sweden in 1713 and Leszczynski sought refuge in Germany, and when the dangers of an Ottoman-Tatar invasion passed, the reason for keeping Saxon troops in the Commonwealth, at least from the *szlachta*'s point of view, also passed. Nevertheless, despite mounting complaints and unrest among the nobility, August stubbornly refused to remove his men from Poland. Again, as in 1700, rumours of a royalist coup d'etat began to circulate among the *szlachta* as its old suspicions of the king resurfaced.

Broadly speaking, there were two major sources of opposition to August's rule in post-1713 period. On the one hand there were the two *hetman*s, Sieniawski and Pociej, other major magnates, and their numerous clientele. Their policy was not so much to limit all the royal prerogatives, some of which, like patronage, were of great benefit to the magnates, but to play the king off against the *szlachta*. This allowed the *hetman*s and their fellow magnates to monopolize the crucial role of arbiters, which contributed so greatly to their influence. Thus, while Sieniawski, for example, sympathized with the growing anti-Saxon sentiment of the *szlachta* in so far as it complicated the king's position, he was unwilling to throw all his support to the nobility for fear that this might destroy the balance which worked so well to his advantage. Less finely tuned but more elemental was the opposition of the middle gentry. To this stratum of society, Saxon rule seemed a threat to its very survival. The long years of war and invasion which had been instigated by August, the famines and epidemics, brought widespread devastation to the Commonwealth. As always, it was the middle and marginal estate owners who, in relative terms, suffered the most. Moreover, the drastic drop in the price of grain on Western markets in the first decade of the eighteenth century brought the middle *szlachta* to the verge of economic ruin. At this critical juncture, August insisted on collecting heavy extraordinary taxes (*contributia*) for the support of his Saxon troops. For the hard-pressed middle *szlachta* this was the last straw. As for the lower *szlachta*, it was too poor to meet these demands, while the magnates were influential enough to avoid paying their share altogether. Focusing its inbred abhorrence of absolutism on the hated *contributia* and on the king who demanded them, the gentry proclaimed in the numerous pamphlets and resolutions of the *sejmiki* that it was ready to oppose these demands to the death.

By the fall of 1714 a *rokosz*, or general uprising, was definitely in the making. However, the closer the nobility came actually to rising against the king, the more hesitant was Sieniawski about lending it the support of the regular army. What caused him to hesitate was August's carrot-and-stick approach. On the one hand, the king was willing to leave the crown *hetman*'s powers intact; on the other, he made it clear that, should an uprising occur, it would readily be crushed by his well-trained German troops, thus providing him with the long-sought opportunity to impose military and then absolute rule on the Commonwealth. Impressed by the court's arguments, the cautious Sieniawski held back. Meanwhile, in one province after another in southeastern Poland the *szlachta* voted to declare a *rokosz* against the king. But because these local assemblies lacked leadership and the support of the regular army, they degenerated into a series of unco-ordinated local disturbances which were easily put down by Saxon troops.

Within a year, however, fighting flared up again, but this time on a much larger scale. On 10 September 1715 the nobility of Lithuania concluded an agreement with *hetman* Pociej in which the latter promised to use the regular Lithuanian army of eight thousand men to aid the *szlachta* if the Saxons tried to impose new exactions. It was agreed that if this aid proved insufficient, a general levee of the grand duchy would be raised to resist the Saxons. Overtures were also made to Peter I to secure his aid in case of an open conflict with the king. Faced with an exceedingly dangerous situation, August reacted as he had a year earlier. He engaged the Lithuanian *hetman* in negotiations, promised him major concessions, and succeeded in enticing him away from his alliance with the nobility. However, matters had already gone too far. The unrest, accompanied by skirmishes with Saxon troops, spread to Poland, where it took on even more serious proportions.

Unable to obtain the support of most of the magnates, the *szlachta* turned to the lower classes. Soon, large numbers of townsmen and wealthy peasants, who had also suffered from Saxon exactions, flocked to join the dissident nobility. The highlanders of the Tatra Mountains responded particularly strongly to the harassment by Saxon garrisons in their region. Even more importantly, despite Sieniawski's prohibition, the Polish crown army also joined the nobility. Encouraged by this broadly based support, the so-called Confederation of Tarnogrod was established on 25 November 1715. Its goals were, first and foremost, to defend the "golden freedoms," to demand that the king live up to the *pacta conventa*, and to "break out of Saxon tyranny."[29]

Among the most active leaders of the confederation were many of Leszczynski's old supporters, such as Wladisław Górzenski, Mikolaj Rosnowski, Jan Grudziński, and Michal Wiśniowiecki. Indeed, the main organizer of the movement, Stanisław Morsztyn, was a long-time supporter of the exiled pretender to the throne. From his refuge in Germany Leszczynski kept in close touch with events in Poland. There were indications that he was aware of plans to form the confederation weeks before it happened. His emissaries made repeated trips between Zweibrücken and Poland.[30] And he encouraged his former followers on against the Saxons and urged them not to forget him. In a letter to Górzenski he wrote, "Your Excellency should not doubt that God's grace will aid you against this tyrannical rule. And if you follow my advice, you will undoubtedly have success. Since you, my beloved brothers, are beginning to see how badly off you are under the German, I am encouraged to believe that you now want a Pole [as king] instead. And my main virtue is that I am a Pole."[31] Yet despite the importance of old-time Leszczynski followers in the confederation, there is little direct evidence to suggest that the movement was an attempted revival of his cause. As will be noted later, the confederation was too broadly based to be guided by the interests of one individual. In any case, by December 1715 several large-scale military clashes had occurred between the confederates and Saxon troops. Meanwhile, almost all of southeastern Poland and Right Bank Ukraine solidly backed the cause of the confederation. A bloody showdown between the forces of the king and the Tarnogrod Confederation appeared unavoidable.

At this juncture, first the *hetmans* and then the court and the confederates turned to Peter I for mediation. The tsar gladly agreed to provide his services. Initially, the negotiations proceeded slowly. But when the Russians entered Poland with eighteen thousand troops at the request of the *hetmans*, Georgii

Dolgorukii, the chief Russian negotiator, became master of the situation. It was chiefly because of his dictatorial handling of the matter that the Treaty of Warsaw was signed and confirmed at the so-called Dumb Sejm of 1 February 1717. As a result of the treaty August II was forced to withdraw almost all his troops from the Commonwealth. Henceforth he could keep only twelve hundred men of his personal Saxon guard and merely six officials of the Saxon chancery in the Commonwealth. This key stipulation deprived the Wettin dynasty of the means to impose *absolutum dominium* on the Commonwealth.

The complex and confused events of the second decade of the eighteenth century in Poland-Lithuania have attracted relatively little attention among Polish historians. According to Józef Gierowski, a leading specialist in the period, this is due to the unappealing decline that the Commonwealth experienced both internally and on the international level at this time.[32] Yet the decade was a watershed in the history both of the Commonwealth and of Eastern Europe as a whole. Briefly put, it was during this second decade that the Commonwealth, the largest noble-dominated society in the region, began clearly and irrevocably to lose control of its own affairs. Given the importance of this development, we might usefully recapitulate its main features here.

Prior to August II, Poland-Lithuania had had numerous foreign sovereigns such as, for example, Stefan Batory and the Vasas of Sweden. It had also had monarchs of both native and foreign origin who had attempted to impose absolutist reforms upon the land. But these sovereigns operated almost exclusively within the context of Polish society, which, as we have seen, provided little basis for the development of absolutism. The position of August II, however, was radically different. Even after his election in Poland he retained a power-base in absolutist Saxony, his hereditary domain. This gave him reason to believe that he could succeed where others had failed; that is, with Saxony acting as a staging area he could impose absolutism on the Commonwealth. In this manner he hoped to achieve great-power status equal to that of the other sovereigns in the region. To be sure, there was a problem of scale: tiny Saxony was expected to overcome the huge Commonwealth. But the Saxon ruler was convinced that with absolutism acting as a lever he could impose his will on Poland-Lithuania.

As might be expected, opposition to August's designs was quick to be mobilized both from beyond and from within Polish-Lithuanian society. Charles XII of Sweden resolved to crush the Saxon attempt to create a *gross-staat*. To aid in this task, the Swedish king pushed forward Stanisław Leszczynski as a rival and replacement to August II. Despite his royal title, Leszczynski was first and foremost a puppet of the Swedes and a leader of one of several magnate cliques in the Commonwealth. He was not – and this must be stressed emphatically to avoid misunderstanding – a leader of a nobiliary revolt against absolutism. However, in opposing August II Leszczynski and his followers ipso facto opposed Saxon absolutism. And although he was primarily interested in retaining his hold on the throne, Leszczynski, a scion of a staunchly republican, anti-royalist family, did make a point of emphasizing that he stood for the "golden freedoms" and against "German tyranny." Thus, in the paramount ideological confrontation of the time, in the struggle of absolutism and *szlachta* republicanism, Leszczynski sided with the latter.

A much more clear-cut and direct confrontation between these two principles occurred in 1715 with the formation of the Confederation of Tarnogrod. This was a classic case of the conflict between foreign absolutism and native nobility which characterized Eastern Europe at the time. In the words of Józef Gierowski, the confederation was "a movement aimed exclusively at the preservation, at all costs, of the untouchable privileges of the *szlachta* ... It should be viewed primarily as the movement of the middle *szlachta* against the Saxon regime."[33]

The confederates had widespread support, especially in the southern and eastern parts of the crown lands. Moreover – and this is a most unusual feature of the *rokosz* – the nobility turned to the townsmen and the peasants for support against the hated foreigners. Clearly, the confrontation had the makings of a long and bloody conflict. It is noteworthy that the followers of Leszczynski played an exceedingly important role among the Tarnogrod confederates. Their striking prominence in the movement has led some historians, most notably Józef Feldman, to argue that the confederation was a "machination" of Leszczynski and the Swedes.[34] However, recent work by Gierowski, while not denying the importance of Leszczynski's followers in the anti-absolutist uprising, stresses the broad, spontaneous, and middle-gentry nature of the movement.

Compared to other contemporary anti-absolutist clashes in Eastern Europe, that of the Tarnogrod confederates stands out, in that it was, in a limited sense, successful. After the Treaty of Warsaw of 1717, August II was in fact forced to abandon his absolutist policies. However, it was not the Tarnogrod Confederation, "the last spurt of *szlachta* democracy," but another absolutist power, Russia, that actually foiled the Saxon bid for great-power status. Henceforth, Russia would play the decisive role in the affairs of the Commonwealth. In the words of the authoritative *History of Poland*, "With the reign of Peter I the situation changed fundamentally ... with the result that the Poles could no longer control their own internal affairs."[35] In effect, the Poles had jumped from the frying pan of Saxon absolutist plans into the fire of Russian absolutist power.

MAZEPA'S UPRISING IN UKRAINE

As the demands of the Great Northern War increased and the threat of Charles XII's invasion of Peter I's realm became imminent, Mazepa, the leader of the Ukrainian elite, took the first steps towards preserving the interests of that elite. It was Stanisław Leszczynski who provided the Ukrainian *hetman* with the means of attaining his goal. Having inherited excellent contacts with Ukraine, the Ottoman empire, and the Crimean khanate from his father, Rafal, Leszczynski hoped to utilize these to raise his standing with the Swedes and to help to defeat their common enemy, Russia. It did not take him long to learn of Ukrainian disaffection from the tsar's rule, and he made it a point to entice Mazepa and the leading members of the *starshyna* over to his and Charles's side.[36]

In the fall of 1705, when the Ukrainian *hetman* was stationed with his troops in Polish territory near Zamostia, a Polish priest by the name of Franciszek Wolski was sent to him by Leszczynski with "secret and diversionary proposals." After questioning him in private, the *hetman* had him arrested and handed over to the Russian commander. As proof of his loyalty Mazepa sent these "diversionary proposals" to the tsar. He was not yet so desperate as to bite at the first bait. A year later Leszczynski tried again. This time Mazepa responded more positively. Apparently, the successful progress of the Swedish invasion of Russia forced the *hetman* to treat the possibility of a Swedish victory more seriously. As he later explained to a close associate, he took this initial step "so that it would show them [Charles XII and Leszczynski] my inclinations towards them and so that they would not treat us as the enemy and ravage poor Ukraine with fire and sword."[37] Still acting on his own and without revealing his plans to anyone, Mazepa cautiously sounded the *starshyna* on the possibility of an understanding with "the opposing side." Almost all of the major officers supported the idea. Encouraged but still keeping his contacts with Leszczynski secret, Mazepa began discussing with Leszczynski's Poles the terms on which he might consider joining them.

Because the negotiations were conducted in great secrecy and no documentary evidence of their progress has survived, historians have had to fit together bits and pieces of contemporary accounts in order to establish Mazepa's position in the bargaining. From the outset the question of Mazepa's goals was surrounded by controversy. Some contemporaries claimed that he wanted to establish a separate Ukrainian principality. Addressing his officers before the battle of Poltava, Peter I stated that Charles XII and Leszczynski wanted to "separate the Little Russian people from Russia and create a separate principality under Mazepa's rule."[38] One of the *hetman*'s own colonels, Hnat Galagan, who remained loyal to the tsar, noted in 1745 that the *hetman* went over to the enemy "in order to break us away from Russia and place us under his own rule, independent of all monarchs."[39]

A more common interpretation of Mazepa's goals is that he was to receive a princely title, while Ukraine would become the third and equal member of the Polish-Lithuanian Commonwealth. Several arguments make this interpretation the most convincing one: such an arrangement would have solved the Polish-Ukrainian relationship to the mutual benefit of both parties, and it would have preserved the socio-economic interests of the *starshyna*; moreover, it had a well-known precedent in the Hadiach Pact of 1658. Danylo Apostol, a leading colonel and central figure in the conspiracy, who later accepted the tsar's pardon, reported that Mazepa "presented us with a document from King Stanisław ... which contained guarantees for Ukraine of the same liberties that the Polish crown and the Lithuanian duchy enjoyed."[40]

Once this understanding with Leszczynski had been reached, closer contacts were established with Charles. These ties were instrumental in convincing the Swedish king to make his fateful decision to divert his attack from Moscow and move into Ukraine, where he expected to find support and respite. In the fall of 1708, as the Swedish and Russian armies converged on Ukraine, it became impossible for Mazepa to equivocate any longer. On 23 October the *hetman* gathered together all available troops and moved towards the Swedish lines. The die had been cast.

In his negotiations with the Swedes Mazepa had indicated that when he joined Charles, he would bring thirty thousand Cossacks with him. However, when the decisive moment arrived, the *hetman* had only seven thousand men at his disposal. The rest had, on the tsar's orders, been scattered on several fronts. Leaving three thousand men to defend his capital, Baturyn, Mazepa moved to the Swedish camp with only about four thousand men. Just before contact was made with the Swedes, the Cossacks were assembled and, for the first time, informed of the *hetman*'s intentions. In his speech Mazepa outlined the wrongs inflicted upon the Ukrainians by Moscow – the reduction of Cossack rights, the plans to alter the Cossack order, and the alleged plan to resettle the Ukrainians beyond the Volga – and he said:

The only solution for us is to rely on the compassion of the Swedish king. He has promised to respect our rights and liberties and to protect them from all those who would threaten them. Brothers, our time has come! Let us use this opportunity to avenge ourselves on the Muscovites for their longstanding oppression, for all the injustices and cruelties they have inflicted. Let us preserve for the future our liberty and our Cossack rights from their incursions.[41]

The Cossacks responded with silence; they were totally confused. To curse and grumble against the Muscovites was one thing, but to join foreigners, and heretics to boot, was an entirely different matter. It now became evident that the key to the conspiracy's success, its well-guarded secrecy, was also its drawback, for the Cossacks and, as it turned out later, the mass of Ukrainians were totally unprepared for this radical turn of events and so maintained a wait-and-see attitude.

It was with "great wonderment" that Peter I learned of "the deed of the new Judas, Mazepa, who, after twenty-one years of loyalty to me and with one foot already in the grave, has turned traitor and betrayer of his own people."[42] But the tsar and his associates quickly recovered from the shock. Prince Aleksander Menshikov attacked Baturyn and massacred all of its inhabitants, about six thousand men, women, and children. The news of Mazepa's defection, as it spread throughout Ukraine, was accompanied by the terrible tale of what had happened at Baturyn. At this point many would-be Mazepists must have reconsidered joining the *hetman*. In addition, ten dragoon regiments were dispatched to Ukraine, and within weeks of their arrival a reign of terror spread through the land. Confiscation of property, interrogations, executions, and exile became the fate not only of anyone just slightly associated with Mazepa's *izmena* (treason) but even of those merely suspected of uttering an uncomplimentary remark about the tsar.

Simultaneously with these intimidating measures, the tsar used a soft approach to the Ukrainian elite. In the first week of November 1708 Peter instructed his commanders "to summon courteously as many of the colonels and *starshyna* as possible ... for the completely free election of a new *hetman*, which will be conducted according to their ancient rights and privileges."[43] On November 11 the *starshyna* elected Ivan Skoropadsky as the anti-*hetman*. The tsar was not pleased with the choice because of the latter's formerly close ties with Mazepa, but, not wishing to irritate the loyal *starshyna*, he accepted the decision. Not long afterwards, however, Peter I dispatched V. Izmailov to act as permanent resident at the *hetman*'s court and in a set of secret instructions enjoined him "to observe most carefully that neither the *hetman* nor the *starshyna* nor the colonels evince any inclination to treason or agitation of the masses."[44]

The election of Skoropadsky set off a bitter propaganda war between Mazepa and the tsar. Peter I struck first, executing Mazepa in absentia in an elaborate ceremony prior to the election. During the election an even more elaborate ceremony, calculated to impress the deeply religious Ukrainian masses, was carried out, at which Mazepa's name was declared anathema. These events had a tremendous effect. Large segments of the Ukrainian population joined in the chorus of condemnation, and for centuries to come Ukrainian peasants would not mention the name of Mazepa without appending to it the epithet "accursed."

Before, during, and after the Skoropadsky election Peter I issued a series of manifestos denouncing Mazepa and his Swedish and Polish allies. Mazepa responded in kind. As military operations wound down for the winter, an intense war of manifestos took place in Ukraine. Even before Mazepa's defection several Swedish proclamations had penetrated into Ukraine and had caused the Russians some anxiety. When Mazepa joined the Swedes and provided them with numerous agents who, masquerading as merchants, musicians, or beggars, disseminated the Swedish propaganda, the problem became acute. The tsar sent orders to Ukraine urging the population "to stop its ears to these alluring letters." Anyone caught distributing the manifestos was immediately executed. Meanwhile, Menshikov urged the tsar to counteract the Swedish propaganda by issuing his own manifestos. "I advise you that, at this evil moment," he wrote the tsar, "it is necessary to keep the common people on our side by all kinds of promises and by the publication of proclamations which express all the *hetman*'s mischief against his people."[45] Soon afterwards the tsar instructed the printers of the Kiev Pechersk monastery to prepare large editions of his manifestos. These were read in all the towns and villages under Russian control. For months both sides bombarded the population with their arguments. Never before had such a fierce struggle been waged for the hearts and minds of the Ukrainian people.

While Mazepa repeatedly accused the tsar of trying to liquidate Cossack rights, of plotting to destroy the traditional order, and of planning to resettle the Ukrainians beyond the Volga, Peter I continued to proclaim that he had only the best interests of Ukraine at heart and went so far as to claim that "we can without shame assert that no people under the sun can boast of their liberty and privileges more than the Little Russian people under Our Imperial Highness."[46] In his own manifestos Skoropadsky stated that "Moscow, that is, the Great Russian people, is not inimical to our Little Russian interests" and added that "the Tsar promised with his own gracious lips and signed with his own hand the royal order that preserves our liberties and graciously guarantees our rights."[47]

The Swedes also entered the rhetorical fray. Bemoaning the "tearful state" of the Ukrainians under Russian rule, Charles promised "with God's help ... to protect and defend this oppressed nation until it can cast off the Muscovite yoke and return to its ancient liberties."[48] Both sides tried to emphasize that they had the interests of the Orthodox faith at heart, an argument which was easier for Peter than for the Lutheran Charles and his ally Mazepa to put forward. For months the salvos of rhetoric echoed through Ukraine as the manifesto war served to publicize the values that each side contended it stood for. However, factors more concrete than propaganda were to play the crucial role in convincing Ukrainians of whom to support.

Soon after Mazepa's defection it became evident that most Ukrainians were opting for the status quo, that is, loyalty to the tsar. An obvious reason for their choice was that most of Ukraine was occupied by Russian troops and orders had been issued by Menshikov to hand over anyone who had dealings with the enemy. The massacre at Baturyn also had a very intimidating effect. Alone, however, these preventive measures on the part of the tsar do not explain Mazepa's failure to mobilize popular support. Separate segments of the Ukrainian population also had their own particular reasons for remaining loyal to the tsar rather than siding with the *hetman*.

Mazepa had never been popular with the peasants and rank-and-file Cossacks. During his tenure of twenty-one years the process of subordinating the peasants and even the Cossacks to the socio-economic and political control of the *starshyna* had advanced markedly. As the leader of this elite and the wealthiest man in the land, Mazepa had been in the forefront of this development. Therefore, the tsar's manifestos describing the *hetman*'s treaty with Leszczynski as an attempt to "return Ukraine to Polish slavery" found ready acceptance among the masses. The reaction of the Ukrainian clergy was the same, despite the fact that Mazepa had long been a most generous patron of the church. After its subordination to Moscow in 1686, the Ukrainian church obediently followed orders from the north. This was reflected in the large number of Ukrainian prelates who participated in the ceremony of Mazepa's anathematization. Moreover, many churchmen were scandalized by Mazepa's co-operation with the heretic Lutherans and the hated Catholics. Nor could the *hetman* expect much support from the townspeople, who depended on the tsar to protect them from the economic and political encroachment of the *starshyna*. Thus, as had been the case so often in the past, the underlying social tensions in Ukrainian society worked to the tsar's advantage.

Both Peter I and Mazepa realized that the crucial social element in Ukraine was the approximately one thousand families who comprised the *starshyna*. It was on the support of the *starshyna* that Mazepa counted the most, since it had been the beneficiary of his generous distribution of common lands. Moreover, the *starshyna* was concerned with the tsar's infringement on Cossack rights and liberties, and the idea of joining the Polish-Lithuanian Commonwealth was attractive to it because it meant that it would obtain the same extensive privileges that the Polish *szlachta* enjoyed. It was not surprising, therefore, that almost all holders of high office in the *hetman*ate followed Mazepa into the Swedish camp. But the vast majority of the *starshyna*, surprised by the *hetman*'s move, hesitated.

Although he received reports that many members of the *starshyna* favoured the *hetman*, the tsar decided to win the Cossack elite over "with kindness." To those who remained loyal to him or at least did not follow Mazepa, Peter I gave generous allotments of confiscated lands and appointments to offices formerly held by Mazepists. Measures were also taken to entice those members back who had gone over to the Swedes. The tsar declared that all those who returned to his camp within a month of their defection would receive a full pardon and that their lands and offices would be returned to them. Seeing that matters were developing badly for the Swedes, a number of Mazepa's closest associates accepted the tsar's offer.

Not everything went as well for Peter I in Ukraine. In April 1709 Mazepa scored a major success which caused the Russians deep concern by winning the Zaporozhian Cossacks over to his and Charles XII's side. With the arrival of the Swedes in Ukraine the strategic importance of the Zaporozhians, a military fraternity of Cossacks based at the *sich*, a stronghold on an island in the Dnieper rapids (*za porohamy*, "beyond the rapids"), increased markedly. The *sich* controlled access to the Crimea and the Ottoman Empire (already there was talk that Charles XII was seeking an alliance with the latter) as well as to the Right Bank and the Don. The Zaporozhians were known as fierce fighters, and the approximately ten thousand men they could muster would be of considerable importance to whomever they chose to support. Under the influence of Kost Hordienko, their *koshovyi otaman*, or leader, a man who hated Moscow even more than he disliked the aristocratic Mazepa, they chose to join the Swedes.

The effects of the Zaporozhian decision were soon felt. Anti-Russian unrest flared up in the southern part of the *hetman*ate, especially in the Poltava regiment, which was closest to the *sich* and in which the Zaporozhian influence on the peasants was considerable. Bands of armed peasants and Cossacks, numbering close to fifteen thousand, caused serious disturbances in the area, and a number of towns in the region sided with the Zaporozhians. In several forts and towns Russian garrisons were massacred, and three Russian regiments were ambushed and smashed by the Zaporozhians. General Rönne, the Russian commander in the area, wrote to the tsar, "A great conflagration is developing here and it must be put out before it is too late."[49]

The tsar and his advisers agreed that since their attempts to win the

Zaporozhians over had failed, harsher measures would have to be taken to counteract the damage caused by their defection. On 12 April a Russian force of about twenty thousand, led by Brigadier Peter Iakovlev, was dispatched down the Dnieper to destroy the *sich*. After extended and costly efforts the *sich* was captured in mid-May, after most of the Zaporozhians had retreated under cover of night. Several hundred prisoners were executed. Some of them were nailed to planks and floated down the Dnieper as a warning to their colleagues. The tsar's vengefulness against the Zaporozhians was extreme. A standing order was issued to execute on the spot and in the most cruel manner any Zaporozhian caught anywhere. When informed of the fall of the *sich*, Peter I joyfully proclaimed, "Gone is the last nest of Mazepa's treachery."[50]

The destruction of the *sich* produced an effect similar to that of the destruction of Baturyn. Again the ability of the tsar to punish those who offended him had been demonstrated, as had been the inability of Charles XII to protect his supporters. And again those who considered joining the Swedes were discouraged. Khan Devlet Girei, while still professing willingness to fight the Russians, put off uniting his forces with those of Charles. Any hope of attracting the Don Cossacks had disappeared. The Ottoman Porte, promptly informed by the Russians of their victory, became more hesitant about aiding the Swedes.

In announcing the victory to the Ukrainian population, the tsar was careful not to gloat over his success. He realized that, for them, the *sich* had been a place of refuge from the overbearing demands of the *starshyna*. Therefore, on 26 May he issued a series of manifestos in which he carefully explained why the Zaporozhians had to be punished, concluding with the statement that "the Zaporozhians themselves are responsible for the disaster that befell them." For Mazepa and his followers the situation before Poltava looked very bleak indeed.

The battle of Poltava took place on 27 June 1709. The results of this battle, one of the most decisive in European history, are well known. Through his victory Peter I not only inflicted a crushing military defeat on Charles XII but also demolished the Swedish attempt to create an East European empire. Moreover, he liquidated the uprising of Mazepa and the leading members of the *starshyna*. One can imagine Mazepa's shock when it became clear that the battle had been lost: all his carefully wrought plans had been ruined, and his personal fate, if he were to be captured by the Russians, was too horrible to consider. Little wonder that when the Swedish king, unable to accept defeat, wished to return to the fray, it was the *hetman* who insisted that he flee. The retreat of the surviving Swedish forces and their Cossack allies to the Dnieper crossing at Perevolochna was relatively orderly. But at the crossing Menshikov's cavalry caught up with them. Several hours after Charles, Mazepa, and a select force of about one thousand Swedes and two thousand Cossacks had crossed the Dnieper and fled towards the safety of the Ottoman frontier, approximately thirteen thousand demoralized Swedes and close to three thousand Ukrainians surrendered to the Russians. Realizing the fate that awaited them (captured Zaporozhians were impaled on stakes), the remaining Zaporozhians fought to the death or hurled themselves into the Dnieper and drowned. By the end of the day, the Swedish army had ceased to exist.

Unaware of what had occurred at Perevolochna, Charles and his small force crossed into Ottoman territory near Ochakiv on 7 July, closely pursued by Russian cavalry. Had it not been for the aid of Mazepa and the Zaporozhians, the Swedish king would probably have been captured. After some hesitation the Ottoman authorities offered the refugees asylum and asked them to move closer to the Moldavian town of Bender, the seat of an Ottoman *serasker*. The Ukrainian phase of the Great Northern War was over. And immediately after this war came to an end in 1721, Russian rulers began the systematic liquidation of Ukrainian autonomy.

CANTEMIR'S REBELLION IN MOLDAVIA

With the flight of Charles and his surviving followers to Bender in Moldavia, the focus of the Russian-Swedish conflict shifted to the southeast. Recovering from the shock of the defeat at Poltava, the Swedish king launched an intensive diplomatic campaign to embroil the Porte in a conflict with Russia. On 19 November 1710 his efforts were crowned with success when the Ottomans, worried by the tsar's expansionism, declared war on Russia. Not wishing to be put on the defensive, Peter I hastily gathered an army of about thirty-five thousand and moved southwards to confront the Ottomans.

Despite its great distance from Russia, the Moldavian principality seemed to Peter I a promising place in which to engage the Ottomans. During the first decade of the eighteenth century dissatisfaction with Ottoman rule there reached a high point. Because of the losses in territory and revenue that it had suffered in Hungary and elsewhere, the Porte had an acute need to exploit its remaining vassal lands. Thus, the duties and tribute which the Moldavians paid to the Porte increased steeply during the final decades of the seventeenth and early eighteenth centuries.[51] Since these added burdens coincided with the sharp economic decline that characterized Eastern Europe as a whole during this period, the impact on the Moldavian population was double. Moreover, the long wars which the Holy League had conducted against the Porte during the final quarter of the seventeenth century led to tremendous devastation, famine, and outbreaks of pestilence in the principality. In writing about these difficult times, the boyar chronicler Miron Costin asked, "O Lord, who can express the suffering inflicted upon us by the heathens?" and hoped that "God will prepare for our land a different fate ... and give us, after this terrible period, a freer age."[52] Even the *hospodars* were hard pressed. They were replaced much more frequently than before, at times as often as once a year, in order to raise more money for the Porte. In this regard Moldavia was worse off than Wallachia, where the wily Constantin Brîncoveanu managed to maintain himself on the throne for over twenty-five years.

The Russians had good reason to feel that this resentment would work to their advantage. For decades Moldavian and Wallachian *hospodars* had approached them with requests for aid and appeals to accept them under their overlordship.[53] For example, in 1656, as a direct result of the Ukrainian-Russian union of 1654, an agreement was drawn up between Tsar Aleksei Mikhailovich and the Moldavian *hospodar*, Gheorghe Ştefan, in which, with Russian aid, Moldavia was to cast off Ottoman rule and come under the protection of the tsar. But Polish intervention, the loss of Right Bank Ukraine by the Ukrainians and Russians, and Moldavian dissension prevented the tsar from extending his sovereignty over the principality at that time. None the less, at least once a decade between 1670 and 1710 Moldavian *hospodars* turned to the tsar with complaints about Ottoman rule and requests for aid against "the heathen." As late as 1709, soon after the battle of Poltava, the *hospodar*, Mihail Racoviţă, contacted Peter in Kiev and offered to desert to the Russians and then return with a Russian army to liberate his land. Before this plan could be thoroughly discussed, however, Racoviţă was arrested by the Ottomans.

It was not only the Moldavians who turned to the tsar. Constantin Brîncoveanu, the long-time *hospodar* of Wallachia, also approached Peter I after Poltava and concluded with him a secret pact calling for Brîncoveanu to join the Russians if and when they appeared in the principalities.[54] Moreover, the Russians established close contacts with the Serbs and Montenegrins. And August II assured Peter that, in the event that the tsar launched a campaign against the Ottomans, he would send thirty thousand Polish and Saxon troops to his aid. In view of these promises of support there is little wonder that the tsar felt confident, even cocky, about war with the Porte. Indeed, he considered it an excellent opportunity to extend his sovereignty over all the Balkan Christians.[55]

A most encouraging development took place early in 1711, shortly before the tsar's army entered Moldavia. Dimitrie Cantemir, the recently appointed (on 23 November 1710) *hospodar* of Moldavia, secretly offered to join the tsar. When this move became known, just as in the case of Mazepa – the similarities in the behaviour of the *hospodar* and the *hetman* are striking – it caused the *hospodar's* subjects and Ottoman overlords considerable surprise. Because he had spent a large part of his life in Istanbul as a hostage during the reigns of his father and brother, the scholarly Cantemir had become so thoroughly assimilated into the Ottoman milieu that many at the Porte considered him one of their own. As a result, when the Ottomans learned of Brîncoveanu's dealings with the tsar, they had appointed Cantemir, at the insistence of Devlet Girei, the Crimean khan, to the Moldavian *hospodar*ship in order to serve as a check against the Wallachian. The fact that Brîncoveanu was known to be a bitter enemy of Cantemir's family had also worked in the latter's favour. Proof of how much the Porte wanted the supposedly reliable Cantemir to take over the Moldavian *hospodar*ship was its willingness to forgo the huge payments it usually demanded for the office. Had the Porte insisted on these, Cantemir would probably not have been able to raise the necessary funds anyway because his family was not as wealthy as the leading boyar families. At any rate, the Ottomans were soon to learn how badly they had miscalculated in appointing him *hospodar*.

Almost as soon as he arrived in Jassy, the capital of the principality, Cantemir took steps to establish contacts with the tsar.[56] He informed the Porte that he was doing so in order to obtain more information about the enemy. Apparently, the decision to join the Russians was not made on the spur of the moment. There are indications that while he was still in Istanbul, Cantemir had discreetly revealed his intentions to P.A. Tolstoi, the tsar's envoy. In any case, sometime in late February or early March of 1711 he dispatched a Captain Procopius and, somewhat later, an official named Ştefan Luca to meet the advancing Russians and negotiate a military and political alliance with the tsar. Peter I quickly agreed to the terms proposed by the *hospodar*, and on 13 April 1711, in Lutsk in Volhynia, the alliance was concluded, on the understanding that it would be made public only after the entry of the Russians into Moldavia.[57]

Both for its contemporaries and for later historians the treaty of alliance was a most revealing and controversial document, for it reflected not only the obvious tensions between the Porte and the Moldavians but also the conflicts of interest which existed within the Moldavian elite itself. Before elaborating on this point, however, let us briefly summarize the main points of the Lutsk treaty. For the tsar, the treaty provided for sovereignty ("protection") over Moldavia and military assistance from the *hospodar* for the duration of the upcoming campaign. Cantemir, for his part, requested and received the following terms: his family was to have hereditary claim to the *hospodar*'s title; "in accordance with old Moldavian custom" the *hospodar*s would exercise complete authority in the principality; and in case of Ottoman victory the tsar would provide the *hospodar* with appropriate compensation in Russia. As far as Cantemir and Peter were concerned, this version of the treaty would be the binding one.

There was, however, another version of the agreement, one which was recorded in his chronicle by Ion Neculce, a powerful boyar who served as Cantemir's *hetman* (commander-in-chief).[58] In this version the articles relating to the *hospodar*'s power were watered down, and two additional articles were inserted. One of these stipulated that the *hospodar* could not strip boyars of their position and noted that, "no matter what their transgressions," boyars could not be punished by the *hospodar* without the concurrence of the boyar assembly and the signature of the metropolitan. These two differing versions of the treaty and especially their contradictions about the *hospodar*'s prerogatives indicated that the Moldavian elite was not of one mind as it prepared to revolt against the Porte.

Just how pronounced the conflict was between Cantemir and the boyars is difficult to establish. Because of their relatively modest wealth the Cantemirs had never been fully accepted as members of the leading boyar circles. In fact, some contemporaries felt that Dimitrie's father, Constantin, had been elected *hospodar* because the wealthier magnates felt that they could control him more easily. Later, long after the uprising, when Dimitrie wrote his *Descrierii Moldovei* (History of Moldavia), he had little good to say about the Moldavian boyars, whom he called "birds of prey ... wild animals thirsty for the blood of the subjugated"[59] and whose greed, he argued, was responsible for the sad fate of Moldavia. However, at the outset of his brief eight-month reign Dimitrie Cantemir's relations with the boyars seemed to be good, even cordial. Neculce noted in his chronicle that after Cantemir's ascension to the throne "he appeared to be loving and kind to all and respected the boyars and did not anger the land with demands for money."[60]

If there was one feature of Cantemir's rule that did create tensions with the boyars, or at least confuse them, it was his insistence on keeping his ties with Peter I strictly secret. Until the decisive moment many boyars, taking account of his long stay at the Porte, considered him to be pro-Ottoman. Further, as the Russian army crossed the Moldavian border and, suffering from indecision, Cantemir kept putting off the announcement of his agreement with the tsar, suspicions arose among the boyars about where his sympathies really lay. Therefore, when he called an assembly and asked them what should be done when the Russians arrived, many of them advised him to adopt a wait-and-see attitude. Unsure of his intentions and lacking leadership, a large number of boyars scattered to the safety of their estates. As a result, Cantemir's procrastination cost him the support of a number of important members of the Moldavian elite.

At the beginning of June Cantemir abandoned Jassy and ensconced himself in a nearby castle. There he held one more council with the remaining boyars, among whom were such important figures as Ion Neculce, N. Costin, I. Sturdza, G. Rosetti, and I. Catardzi, and finally announced to them that he intended to join the Russians. According to Neculce, "The boyars were overjoyed and said to the *hospodar*, 'You have done well, Your Highness, for we feared that you might join the Turks, and we agreed among ourselves that, should you go over to the Turks, we would desert you and join the Muscovites.'"[61] It was also at this time that he discussed with the boyars the treaty with the tsar, going over it point by point. According to Costin, the discussion went as follows: "After the chancellor read an article, Dimitrie asked the boyars: 'Is this article good?' They said, 'Good.' But to each point that was not to the liking of the boyars, they responded that it was not good. And here they stayed and settled matters until they were better."[62] Apparently, the Moldavian elite was succesful in seeing that its interests were taken into account in the treaty. Indeed, they were so successful that a leading Romanian historian viewed this treaty as "the first codification of boyar privileges in Moldavia."[63]

After the *hospodar* and boyars had come to an understanding, Cantemir contacted the Russians, who had already crossed the Prut, and requested an escort of four thousand men to convey him and his followers to their camp. Here they were met with great pomp and circumstance by the Russian commander, B.P. Sheremetev, because Peter I had not yet joined his main army.

Just before he joined the Russians, on or about 4 June, Cantemir issued to the inhabitants of Moldavia a manifesto in which he explained the reasons for his decision to side with Peter I and called on them to rise up against the Ottomans. Because this document was probably the most comprehensive statement of the *hospodar*'s rationale for the uprising, it deserves closer examination. Cantemir urged the Moldavians to take up arms "not only for the salvation of the Christian peoples from the enslavement of the heathen, but also to avenge the entire past of oppression and humiliation, whose origin lay in the Turk's non-observance of the treaty concluded with Bogdan [Moldavia]."[64] We find here the same theme that was sounded in the other uprisings: an overlord accused of having broken an agreement made with his vassals sometime in the past. Cantemir implied that this breach of faith gave the Moldavians the right to revolt. This is a clear indication that even in Moldavia, which had to deal with an Oriental autocracy, such classic, albeit hazily enunciated feudal concepts as *ius resistendi* were meaningful arguments for revolt against the ruler. In fact, Cantemir regarded this argument as so useful that he fabricated certain aspects of Moldavian history in order to strengthen it. For example, in his proclamation he argued, quite inaccurately, that "Moldavia entered into relations with the Ottoman Empire because of goodwill and without the compulsion of anyone, and therefore it was the will of the Sultan that its churches, customs, and the law of the land were to remain as before."[65] Thus, the revolt was justified and necessary because the Ottomans had ignored these stipulations and had systematically exploited the Moldavians, diminishing their rights and piling tribute upon tribute. The proclamation ended with a threat to curse, expropriate, and execute all who did not join in the uprising.

At about the same time the Russians issued their own manifestos to the Moldavians. These were meant to convince the populace that no harm would come to its property and that the sole reason for Russian intervention in Moldavian affairs was "to deliver the Christian people from the heavy Turkish yoke."[66] Furthermore, the Russian manifestos echoed sentiments expressed in earlier proclamations to Moldavian as well as to other Balkan Christian peoples. They stated, in part: "We will not seek to benefit from these countries and peoples and we will not impose upon them any kind of autocratic rule. On the contrary, we will leave all these countries under their traditional orders and their previous leaders. And in cases where these peoples do not have leaders because of Turkish enslavement ... we will allow them, under our protection, to choose their own leaders from among themselves, and we will restore and preserve their old rights and privileges."[67] Thus, the Russians made it clear that they too stood for the preservation or restoration of the old order.

Soon afterwards, on 27 June, Cantemir, Metropolitan Gideon, and about fifteen leading boyars met to confirm the treaty of Lutsk with Peter I, who had just arrived to join his main force. From the start the *hospodar* made an excellent impression on the tsar, who considered him to be "very wise and well versed in counsel." In order to assist him in recruiting an army the Russians provided Cantemir with 230 bags of gold. The response from the Moldavians to his appeals for men was enthusiastic. Not only did most of the *mazyls* (gentry) who had military experience offer their services, but even townsmen and peasants literally begged to be accepted into the ranks of the anti-Ottoman forces. No doubt, the generous incentives offered by the *hospodar* – one hundred rubles for colonels, thirty for captains, ten for lieutenants, and five for rank and file – helped stir Moldavian military ardour. Within two weeks between six and seven thousand men had joined the *hospodar*. In addition, the Russian army had already raised four regiments, mostly of Moldavian refugees. In all of this anti-Ottoman activity, only a few of the leading boyar families held back and waited to see how matters would develop.

While Cantemir and most of the Moldavians rallied to the Russian side, the Ottomans, led by Mehmed Baltaci, moved into the principality with an unexpectedly large force. Estimates of its size varied, with Neculce citing a figure of 370,000 and the Russian commander, Sheremetev, providing a more conservative number of 140,000.[68] Despite the vast size of the Ottoman army Peter remained confident about his chances for success. He felt that he had another trump card to play. Constantin Brîncoveanu, the *hospodar* of Wallachia, had promised to join the Russians with thirty thousand men. In addition, twenty thousand Serbs were supposed to be on their way to the Russian camp. But at this crucial juncture, when he saw the size of the Ottoman army and learned of Mehmed Baltaci's determination to fight, Brîncoveanu reneged on his promise to the tsar.[69] Not only did he fail to come to Peter's aid, but the Serbs who were already on the march were prevented from crossing Wallachia and joining the Russians. Thus, by the end of June, instead of having close to one hundred thousand troops at his disposal, Peter had only about forty thousand, including the Moldavians, and he faced an enemy about four times more numerous.

During the first week of July the two armies manoeuvred into position, and on 9 July, as the Russians set up camp near the village of Stanileşti on the Prut River, the Ottomans surrounded them and launched a series of fierce attacks. Although the Russians managed to repel these onslaughts and to inflict large Ottoman losses, it soon became clear that their position was extremely precarious and that the tsar was in real danger of being captured. Although Cantemir and several of the tsar's German generals begged him to continue the battle, on the advice of Sheremetev Peter decided to initiate negotiations with Mehmed Baltaci. Troubled by a rebellion among the Janissaries, who were angry about the great losses they had incurred, the grand vizier was also in a negotiating mood. Therefore, on 11 July the grand vizier and the tsar came to an agreement that was to prove extremely costly to the latter. In return for being allowed to withdraw peacefully with his army, the tsar promised to give up all previous conquests he had made in the Black Sea area, including the Azov, Taganrog, and Dnieper fortresses. Moreover, he committed himself not to interfere in Ukrainian and Polish affairs, a promise he probably had no intention of keeping, and to evacuate Moldavia. There was, however, one point on which the tsar refused to budge. Mehmed Baltaci demanded several times that Cantemir be surrendered to the Porte. To this Peter replied that he would sooner lose all his lands up to Kursk than break his word to the *hospodar*.[70] On the tsar's orders Cantemir was then concealed in the baggage train of the Russian army and successfully extricated from the Ottoman encirclement as it withdrew. After a brief stay in Jassy to gather together his large family, Cantemir, accompanied by two dozen minor boyars and several thousand Moldavians, followed the tsar into the Russian empire, never to return to his native land.

As the Russians and Cantemir's followers retreated from the principality, the Ottomans began to take their revenge.[71] First of all, the Tatars were loosed on the land. In a matter of days lower Moldavia became the scene of the worst devastation within memory. In the meantime, Mehmed Baltaci waited in Stanileşti for the remaining boyars to pay him homage. For two weeks none of them dared to appear. When they finally did arrive, the grand vizier castigated them for the treasonous behaviour of the Moldavians and then appointed Lupu Costaki, a boyar, as *hospodar*. The latter begged to be spared the honour, but Mehmed Baltaci insisted, making him responsible for the good behaviour of his countrymen and for the collection of the huge sums needed to free the more than two thousand hostages that the Ottomans were holding. After the grand vizier departed, an Ottoman official arrived in Jassy to supervise the *hospodar* and the Moldavian elite. Rumours were rife that the principality would soon be turned into a regular Ottoman province. Although this did not occur, the Porte did take the opportunity to introduce basic changes in the way Moldavia was administered.

Only several months after his appointment Costaki was removed, and on 25 September 1711 Nicolae Mavrocordato was nominated *hospodar*. This appointment inaugurated the rule of the so-called Phanariots in Moldavia.[72] Henceforth, Moldavian and, from 1716, also Wallachian *hospodar*s were chosen exclusively from among the rich Greek families who lived in the Phanar district of Istanbul and who, primarily through their service as translators, had attained great influence at the Porte. Every three years or so one of these Greeks, usually from the Mavrocordato, Ghica, or Cantacuzene families, would be appointed to the office of *hospodar*, while members of their personal entourages would occupy the leading positions in the land. Together they proceeded to milk the country of as much wealth as possible, both for their own and for the Porte's benefit. Not only the general populace but also the boyars suffered under this new system, for they no longer had any say in the election of the *hospodar*, and since they could no longer influence him, they lost much of their power. Eventually, Greeks who settled in the principality replaced native Moldavians at the highest levels of the boyar class. The weakened Moldavian military forces were disbanded or assigned to guard the borders, while the Phanariots enlisted foreign mercenaries to form the core of their military units. The active foreign relations which the *hospodar*s had previously enjoyed now dwindled to an insignificant level, as the Phanariots saw no need for foreign involvement. In effect, the emasculation of the office of *hospodar* became complete, and as Moldavia was subjected to ever more strict control from the Porte, the Phanariot *hospodar*s became little more than Ottoman governors.

RÁKÓCZI'S REVOLT IN HUNGARY

Of all the East European conflicts in the early eighteenth century, the Hungarian revolt, or war of independence, as Hungarian scholars prefer to call it, was the largest, longest, and fiercest. Just a few facts underscore its magnitude: it lasted eight years, from 1703 to 1711; at its high point the Hungarians were able to put close to 80,000 to 100,000 troops into the field; after it was over, about 85,000 had died in battle and over 400,000 had perished as a result of famine and pestilence. The conflict also loomed large on the international level. Drawn into the vortex of diplomatic activity that surrounded it were French and Russian diplomats in particular, seconded by those of Saxony, England, Holland, Bavaria, Sweden, Prussia, the Crimean khanate, and the Ottoman Porte. But the Hungarian uprising also possessed so many of the typical features of the East European nobiliary revolts that it may well be considered the classic example of this type of conflict.

The conditions that sparked the Hungarian revolt were quite similar to those that initiated the other East European confrontations. Even more so than its neighbours, Hungary had been devastated by long years of warfare. Like other lands in the region, it was in the throes of economic regression. And during this difficult time the ever-increasing Habsburg demands for more taxes reached unprecedented levels. In view of a long tradition of rebelliousness it is not surprising that the Hungarians reacted violently to their plight. Thus, in 1697 a major peasant uprising took place in the Tokaj region, but it was quelled without much trouble. Three years later a magnate conspiracy aimed at recruiting French support for a general revolt against the Habsburgs was discovered and foiled. To the authorities in Vienna these incidents seemed to prove their increased ability to control their troublesome subjects. Little did they know that these events merely foreshadowed the most serious conflagration that the Habsburgs would ever have to face in Hungary.

Ferenc II Rákóczi, the leader of the Hungarian revolt, was both a likely and an unlikely candidate for his role.[73] The rich twenty-four-year-old prince of the Holy Roman Empire, who owned 20 estates, 38 castles, 681 villages, and over a million hectares of land, was the scion of one of Hungary's most illustrious families, noted especially for its anti-Habsburg tendencies.[74] Three of his forefathers had been princes of Translyvania during the early seventeenth century, when it was at the height of its power and posed a menace to Vienna. His father, Ferenc I, had been one of the leading members of the Wesselényi conspiracy, and after his death Rákóczi's mother, the famous Ilona Zrinyi, married Imre Thököly, the leader of an anti-Habsburg uprising in the late 1680s and early 1690s. For two years Ilona defended the fortress at Munkács against Habsburg troops; forced to surrender, she eventually joined her second husband in exile in the Ottoman Empire. Thus, Ferenc II Rákóczi was a natural leader for a new anti-Habsburg uprising.

It was precisely for this reason that the authorities in Vienna took him from his mother at the age of twelve and, under the watchful eye of Cardinal Kollinich, made every effort to alienate him from all things Hungarian. The young magnate was educated in a Jesuit college in Bohemia and later enrolled at the University of Prague. After a study tour of Italy he married a German princess, Charlotte Amalia von Hessen-Rheinfels. His knowledge of Hungarian was practically non-existent and, as his behaviour in 1697 illustrates, his ties with his fatherland were very weak. During the peasant revolt of that year, a number of Rákóczi's peasants begged him to lead him against their "German oppressors." The prince's reaction would have made his Jesuit educators proud: dressing himself in German clothes, he rushed post-haste to Vienna to proclaim his loyalty to the emperor. In order to avoid temptations and suspicion he asked that his Hungarian lands be exchanged for holdings in the Holy Roman Empire. Apparently convinced by this show of loyalty, the Viennese authorities decided that such an exchange would be unnecessary. For a while, at least, Habsburg officials were to regard the young magnate as one of their most trustworthy supporters in Hungary.

Yet soon afterwards Rákóczi's political loyalties underwent a complete transformation. In Hungarian historiography the man traditionally credited with this abrupt and radical change was Count Miklos Bercsényi, the vice-*iszpan* of Sáros. Intelligent, ambitious, and combative, this thirty-five-year-old (born 1665) magnate, who had attained his high rank and great wealth through his own efforts, not through inheritance, had an almost fanatical hatred of Habsburg absolutism and all things German.[75] At the turn of the century he undertook to organize a circle of like-minded magnates and made it a point to draw his neighbour Rákóczi into it. Apparently, under the continuous exposure to the older, more experienced Bercsényi, Rákóczi came to develop a burning resentment of Habsburg treatment of his countrymen and their rights.

From the outset the members of the plot, in which Rákóczi began to play an increasingly central role, assumed that the only way in which they could rid themselves of Habsburg domination was to gain the support of a powerful foreign ruler. Given Versailles' long tradition of sympathizing with and aiding Hungarian rebels because they weakened its arch-rival, the Habsburgs, and especially in view of the rising tensions between Vienna and Versailles over the issue of the Spanish succession, the obvious ruler to turn to was Louis XIV of France.[76] After contacts had been established with the French king and a favourable response had been received, the plot was discovered through the treachery of an intermediary. Bercsényi was able to flee to Poland, but Rákóczi was captured and jailed in Wiener-Neustadt, to await an almost certain death sentence. However, with the help of his wife and a Prussian officer he staged a dramatic escape and joined Bercsényi in Poland.

The two magnates decided to continue their efforts in the Commonwealth to attract foreign aid for their cause. They turned to the French envoy in Warsaw, Charles Du Héron, and found in him an enthusiastic supporter who quickly realized the value of a "Hungarian diversion" during the struggle which had just broken out for the Spanish succession. But France was far away, and aid, especially in the form of troops, would be hard to come by. Therefore, even before Rákóczi's escape, Bercsényi turned to August II for support. In a manifesto that might be called the credo of the Hungarian opposition, he outlined the grievances of his countrymen against the Habsburgs and the possibilities for August II of benefiting from the situation.

According to Bercsényi, what pained the Hungarians most was the loss in 1687 of the two "pearls" of their liberties: the right to elect their king and the abolition of the *ius resistendi*. Other complaints included the heavy tax burden; the extortions of the Habsburg soldiery; the spreading influence of the Jesuits and their anti-Protestant measures; the *Neoacquisitica commissio*; the exclusion of the Hungarian delegates from the Carlowitz negotiations, which led to the end of the Habsburg-Ottoman war; and the constant administrative innovations. The list of grievances concluded with the statement, "A nation such as the Hungarian, which does not fear to die for its liberty, cannot live in slavery. The magnates, gentry and the estates all hope to free themselves from the hated yoke. They are ready to risk all and wait only for the proper moment to act."[77] What did the Hungarians have to offer August II in exchange for his aid? Knowing of the king's boundless ambition, Bercsényi offered August the Crown of St Stephan, the chance to win easy victories in Hungary, and a possible personal union between Poland and Hungary. To obtain this, all August II had to do was to provide the Hungarians with military aid. But after the Livonian fiasco, the elector-king had become wary of proposals that promised easy gains. In fact, he did not even protest when Habsburg agents tried to abduct the two Hungarians.

Although their overtures had been rejected by the king, Bercsényi and Rákóczi found a much friendlier reception among a number of Polish magnates, especially those who had belonged to the pro-French party which had backed Conti for the Polish crown. These included Michał Radziejowski, the primate of Poland, Martin Kątski, the *wojewoda* of Cracow, Adam Sieniawski, the *wojewoda* of Belz, and especially his wife, Eliżbeta.[78] Partly to please their French allies and partly because of Eliżbeta's amorous interests in the young Rákóczi, for almost two years the Sieniawskis provided the refugees with much-needed protection at their castle in Berezhany in eastern Galicia, with political contacts, and with promises of men and money. Meanwhile, in Hungary, matters took an unexpected turn.

Because of the war with France the Habsburgs had begun to transfer their troops from Hungary to Italy and the Rhine. By the spring of 1703 there were only about five thousand Imperials left in the land. As a result, bands of rebellious peasants, dispossessed gentry, and even common bandits began to form and attack small Habsburg garrisons and, more often than not, the estates of unpopular noblemen. Following the example of Thököly's men, they called themselves *kuruc*. One of the largest of these bands, numbering over one thousand and operating in the northeast highlands, where Rákóczi had extensive land holdings, decided to approach the popular magnate, whose arrest and exile had made him a symbol of resistance to Habsburg oppression, to ask him to lead a general uprising. In March 1703 two *kuruc* leaders, Mihály Pap and György Bige, disguised as Ukrainian peasants, located Rákóczi in Berezhany and, buttressing their pleas with reports of Habsburg weakness, urged him to become their leader. Neither Rákóczi nor Bercsényi had any illusions about the quality of the men they were being asked to lead, but they did realize that to wait for foreign aid was futile, for none would be forthcoming unless they themselves initiated action. Therefore, Rákóczi accepted the *kuruc* offer and presented the two delegates with banners bearing his initials and the motto "Cum Deo pro Patria et Libertate." Meanwhile, Bercsényi composed a manifesto addressed to "all true Hungarians who love their native land and who wish for it to regain its ancient glory," and called on them to join the prince's standards.[80] Then, while Bercsényi visited several Polish magnates to organize men and money, Rákóczi made his way towards the Hungarian border and, on 16 June, re-entered his homeland.

His reception there was not inspiring. Waiting for him on the Hungarian side of the border were about five to six hundred bedraggled men belonging to Tamás Esze's band, the survivors of a bad mauling a week earlier at the hands of a noble levee led by Count Sándor Károlyi, the *iszpan* of Szatmár. As he surveyed his new army, the bemused Rákóczi noted, "Casting aside all thoughts of the dangers that surrounded me, I committed myself to this unshodden mass. An unequipped peasant army! Some had swords; others had scythes, and a few had firearms. But all lacked military experience and discipline."[81] But the appeal of Rákóczi's name soon began to have an effect, especially after Bercsényi appeared with fresh funds and about eight hundred Polish mercenaries, and even more so as rumours spread the news of the freedom Rákóczi promised to those peasants who joined him. Many of Rákóczi's early recruits were Ukrainian peasants from his holdings in the Carpathian highlands, men whose commitment to him became so strong and lasting that he referred to them as "fidelissima ac clementissima gens" (the most faithful and gentle of the people).

Emboldened by the growing numbers of followers, Rákóczi attempted to take the strong fortress of Munkács in late June 1703, but he failed in the attempt. Realizing that his peasant army, which now numbered close to six thousand, was incapable of taking such strong points as Munkács, Ungvar, or Košice, he simply bypassed them and pushed on to the Tisza River, crossing it on 15 July. Now wide, open plains stretched before him, and here the rebellion began to pick up momentum. By the end of July the *kuruc* took Debrecen, whose citizens not only failed to offer resistance but welcomed and aided the rebels. Meanwhile, another *kuruc* column, led by Bercsényi, took the important towns of Nagy Szombat and Pozsony. By the end of 1703 the *kuruc* army, numbering close to thirty thousand and scoring one victory after another against the heavily outnumbered Habsburg troops, held most of Hungary east of the Danube. Vienna, which at the outset of the revolt had considered it to be little more than a peasant disturbance, now panicked for fear that the Austrian provinces and even the capital itself might be overrun.

As the successes mounted, Rákóczi's rebellion underwent a transformation. At the outset the social basis of the uprising had been the peasantry, which was motivated largely by hopes of bettering its lot. But of crucial importance was the support of the nobility, the "political nation," without whose aid there could be no sustained resistance to the Habsburgs. Herein lay Rákóczi's dilemma: how to square the inherently antagonistic interests of the Hungarian nobles with those of the peasants and other dispossessed elements of society? As his proclamations in the early stages of the rebellion indicate, he was seriously interested in ameliorating the lot of the peasantry, although whether he was willing to go so far as to grant it complete freedom is debatable.[82] While his position on this matter, a remarkably enlightened one for the times, did not change in substance, the attention and emphasis he later gave it did, for in 1704–5, as he began to court the nobility more assiduously, he played down the socio-economic issue and urged his followers to desist from pillaging noblemen's estates and concentrate rather on fighting the foreign oppressors.

The uprising created a difficult situation for the nobility as well. As Rákóczi himself noted, "The nobility ... did not know which side to choose; it was equally afraid of the masses and of the Germans."[83] However, as the weakness of the

Habsburgs became more evident and the threat that the *kuruc* might pillage their estates more acute, the nobles came to a decision. During the fall of 1703 and throughout 1704 large numbers of the lower and middle nobility began to join Rákóczi. A great and welcome surprise came when Count Károlyi, an early antagonist of the rebels, came over to their side. Apparently, the Habsburg lack of recognition for his early victory over the *kuruc* and fear that his estates, most of which lay in Rákóczi-held territory, might be devastated led to this decision. Sándor Károlyi's example was followed by other members of the Hungarian aristocracy, and soon the leadership of the rebellion was almost completely in their hands. For example, whereas the early leaders of the *kuruc*, men like Tamás Esze, Albert Kiss, Mihály Pap, and János Bottyán, were peasants or impoverished nobles, by 1705 the *kuruc* army was led by twenty-six generals, eight of whom were counts, seven of whom were barons, and ten of whom belonged to the middle nobility. János Bottyán, a remarkably talented military leader, was the only representative of the lower classes in the military leadership. With this change in the composition of the *kuruc* and especially of its leadership, the rebellion lost its initial socio-economic, populist character and became primarily a political, anti-absolutist, noble-oriented movement.

That is not to say that the entire Hungarian elite sided with Rákóczi. A large number of magnates, particularly those with strong court connections, such as, for example, János Pálffy and Pál Eszterházy, together with their numerous clientele, remained loyal to the House of Habsburg. In popular parlance these loyalists were called *labanc*.[84] Meanwhile, in Transylvania, which the *kuruc* had invaded in 1703 and controlled for the most part of 1706, the Saxon townsmen and Romanian peasants also tended to side with the Habsburgs. Moreover, about eighty-five thousand Serbs, to whom the Habsburgs had granted refuge from Ottoman persecution in the Vojvodina, returned the favour by performing dedicated military service. Thus, by 1705, while the *kuruc* forces still retained the initiative although they usually lost pitched battles to the better-trained Habsburg troops, it was evident that neither side had the power to inflict a decisive defeat on the other. Therefore, in 1705–6 both sides took the opportunity to consolidate their positions, increase their diplomatic activity, and engage in negotiations.

During the lull in fighting the *kuruc* leaders intensified their propaganda directed at foreign rulers, whose sympathy and aid they hoped to elicit. As early as March 1704 they addressed a proclamation "to all Christian rulers and lands of the world"[85] to convince them, despite their inclination to be leery of rebellious subjects, that the Hungarian cause was a just one. The proclamation sounded what became the two main themes of *kuruc* progaganda: the inviolability of the contractual agreement between the ruler and his subjects and the right of subjects to resist their unjust rulers. In the twenty articles of the manifesto were listed the illegal acts committed by the Habsburgs in Hungary over the previous thirty years, that is, those actions which contradicted the terms under which they had obtained the Crown of St Stephan. In the conclusion of the document the Hungarians once more sought to justify their uprising by citing their ancient *ius resistendi*.

An even more striking example of the *kuruc* search for legitimacy was the assembly called by Rákóczi at Szécsény on 12 September 1705. The number of participants of rank was itself impressive: six bishops, thirty-six magnates, delegates of twenty-five *komitats*, and spokesmen from many towns. The peasants, however, were not represented. In its initial deliberations the assembly called for the re-establishment of Hungary's "lost liberties," a guarantee of which would be the recognition of Transylvania as a sovereign principality. Even though the assembly was not yet ready to vote for a complete break with the Habsburgs despite Rákóczi's insistence, it did refuse to recognize the new emperor, Joseph I, as king of Hungary, and it reserved for itself the right to carry out its own election. In a subsequent meeting it took steps to give the *kuruc* movement the semblance of legitimate government. Following the Polish example it formed the Confederation of Hungarian Estates for Liberty and chose Rákóczi as its "prince and leader." A council of twenty-five members, picked mostly from among the magnates and nobility, was also formed, to carry on negotiations with Vienna and to look after internal and external affairs. Finally, an "economic council" was established, to regulate the economic life of the land and to collect and redistribute its resources. One of the most important measures carried out by the council was the issue of a new, copper-based currency, which was to help finance the struggle against the Habsburgs.

The governmental structure which emerged as a result of the Szécsény assembly possessed considerable military power. At its high point in 1706 the *kuruc* army numbered about 100,000 and consisted of ninety-one infantry regiments, fifty-two cavalry regiments, and a number of artillery and auxiliary units. As it was still inferior to the Habsburg armies in terms of discipline, training, leadership, and provisioning but not in numbers or in spirit, Rákóczi took measures to narrow this gap. The *kuruc* were divided into regular, that is, regularly paid, and irregular forces; about ninety French officers, along with artillerists and engineers, were brought in to train the troops; the first Hungarian book of army regulations, based on a French model, was published; and factories were established for the production of arms and uniforms.[86] Rákóczi's desire to introduce modern organizational models was not confined to the military. Indeed, there are strong indications that he found certain absolutist principles and techniques attractive.[87] For example, he drafted far-reaching plans to regulate the economy, establish a postal system, and modernize education. Of even greater import were his attempts to exert tighter control over the broad autonomy which the *komitat* assemblies enjoyed, to abolish the electoral principle in the selection of the *komitats'* officials, and to introduce a general tax. But these centralizing, one may even say absolutist tendencies, which obviously contradicted the entire thrust of the uprising, could not be pursued openly, systematically, or successfully.

After its high point in 1706 the rebellion lost momentum. Broadly speaking, the causes for this were, to borrow a Marxist phrase, a "deepening of internal contradictions" among Rákóczi's followers, and unfavourable foreign developments. Moreover, Habsburg tactical superiority, both political and military, over the Hungarians had become increasingly evident and was reflected in the way that Vienna skilfully used the protracted and fruitless negotiations of 1705–6 to slow the tempo of the uprising and, rather than seek a modus vivendi, to reinforce its troops in Hungary and sow dissension among the Hungarian ranks.

Even without Habsburg instigation, there would have been enough reasons for the growing tensions that appeared in Rákóczi's camp. By now Rákóczi's orientation towards the nobility had become clear. With his muted acquiescence it had begun to reassert its control over the rebellious peasants, including those who had fought in the *kuruc* armies. This so cooled the ardour of the peasantry for the uprising that in 1707 Bercsényi openly acknowledged, "We have lost the love of the common people."[88] But Rákóczi soon discovered that it was much more complicated and frustrating to have to deal with his fellow nobles, who were quick to point out to their leaders that all nobles were equals, than to fight the enemy.

The problem of winning and maintaining a consensus among the Hungarian nobles directly confronted Rákóczi at the famous assembly of Onod. Convoked on 31 May 1707, its main goal was finally to make a clean break with the Habsburgs by formally declaring them deposed. One of the most important considerations that prompted the *kuruc* leadership to take this step was that as long as the Habsburgs remained the titular sovereigns of Hungary, foreign rulers considered the *kuruc* rebels, pure and simple, and thus inappropriate as negotiating partners. This had been the case when the Hungarians had turned to various foreign rulers for aid and to the French for a formal alliance. Therefore, both Rákóczi and Bercsényi vigorously argued for the dethronement of the Habsburgs and the invitation of a more suitable candidate – Maximillian-Emmanuel of Bavaria was mentioned most often – in their stead. For himself, Rákóczi sought the title of Sovereign Prince of Transylvania. However, the domestic implications of the proposed dethronement led to a furious and fractious debate among the Hungarians.[89]

In essence the issue was money. Upon hearing of the dethronement proposal, a vocal faction in the assembly, led by two delegates from the Turóc *komitat*, raised the following questions: If the Habsburgs were removed, who would assume the costs of the land's defence, which they had previously been responsible for? And who, for that matter, would pay for the continued costs of the struggle against Vienna? These questions hit upon a sore point with the nobility. Because the copper currency issued by the confederation several years earlier had lost its value as a result of oversupply, many noblemen and the confederation as a whole had suffered severe financial losses. Moreover, the French subsidies on which Rákóczi had always been dependent were clearly insufficient. With the confederation thus in dire financial straits Rákóczi proposed the imposition of a general tax for which peasants, townsmen, and nobles alike would be liable. In response to this proposal the Turóc delegates argued that heavy taxation was one of the main reasons why they had revolted against the Habsburgs in the first place and that a general tax would, in effect, contradict the aims of the uprising. In view of the seemingly endless costs of continuing the struggle, the Turóc delegates proposed that the idea of dethronement be dropped and that an accommodation with Vienna be sought instead. As the issue was debated, tempers flared, and in a moment of extreme agitation Bercsényi cut down one of the delegates with his sword. The next day the other *komitat* delegate was executed. After these traumatic events the assembly voted in favour of the general-tax proposal, and it was agreed that the lands of those nobles who did not pay the tax would be confiscated. The decision to dethrone the Habsburgs came soon afterwards, on 14 June 1707, and Rákóczi was formally recognized by the assembly as Prince of Transylvania (the estates of Transylvania had voted for the measure earlier). But the sharp differences of opinion over the issues raised at Onod, the brutal treatment of the dissident nobles, and the imposition of the general tax took their toll, contributing greatly to the growing alienation of many of Rákóczi's noble supporters.

As internal difficulties multiplied, Rákóczi intensified his efforts to obtain foreign support. French aid had played a crucial role from the very outset of the rebellion. It came in three forms: financial – from 15 November 1703 to 15 May 1705 Rákóczi received, more or less regularly, thirty thousand livres per month, and from May 1705 to 1708 fifty thousand livres per month – military – during the course of the uprising, about one thousand to fifteen hundred French soldiers and close to ninety French officers served in the *kuruc* armies; there were also plans for military co-operation on a much broader scale, calling for a link-up of Hungarian and French expeditionary forces on the Adriatic coast and a combined strike against Austria – and diplomatic – French diplomats, such as Charles Du Héron and Jean Louis Bonnac in Poland, Charles Ferriol at the Porte, and Pierre Des Alleurs in Hungary, worked energetically, if not always successfully, to gain foreign backing for the *kuruc* cause.[90] In this connection one of the most hotly disputed issues in the historiography of the Rákóczi rebellion has been the question of the extent to which the prince was dependent on and responsive to foreign interests. Many nineteenth-century historians, Austrians in particular, liked to argue that Rákóczi was little more than a puppet of the French in Eastern Europe and that the rebellion stayed alive only as long as it served the interests of the French. Not surprisingly, Hungarian works on the subject reject this view. The most recent Hungarian study of this question stresses that, in his dealings with foreign powers and with France in particular, Rákóczi's policy was based on Hungarian interests that were quite often antithetical to French interests.[91]

An example of this tendency was Rákóczi's ties with Peter I, which the French viewed with disfavour.[92] Initially, the tsar had vacillated between a pro-Hungarian and a pro-Habsburg policy. Shortly before the uprising, when Peter was still smarting from the Habsburg exclusion of Russia from the Treaty of Carlowitz, there were indications that he might support Rákóczi. However, in 1705 it appeared that Russia, eager for Vienna's support in the upcoming struggle with Sweden, might help the Habsburgs quell the rebellion. But finally, in 1707 the tsar settled on a more or less friendly policy towards Rákóczi. His reasons for this decision were somewhat complicated. Peter hoped that, with their close ties with the French, the Hungarians might be able to convince Versailles to act as mediator in the war between Sweden and Russia, a conflict which at that time was not going well for him. So desperate was he for Hungarian aid in obtaining French mediation that Peter made Rákóczi the most encouraging promises, offering him the Polish throne, which had been recently vacated by August II, support in the restoration of Hungarian rights and liberties, and even a formal alliance.[93] This was the only formal international agreement that Rákóczi was ever to conclude. However, after the battle of Poltava, when he no longer needed French mediation, Peter's interest in the Hungarians quickly faded.

What was more serious, French support for the rebellion also began to wane. In 1707 the war went from bad to worse for Louis XIV. By 1709 the French armies had suffered a series of defeats; part of France was occupied by the armies of Eugene of Savoy, and there was such a severe famine in the land that Louis XIV was obliged to sacrifice his gold table-settings for famine relief. Under these conditions continued financial aid to Hungarians was out of the question. Together with these diplomatic setbacks the Hungarians suffered military disasters. On 3 August 1708, near the town of Trencsén, they experienced the worst defeat of the war at the hands of the Habsburg forces under General Siegbert Heister. Meanwhile, as famine and disease spread through the land, desertions in the *kuruc* army became rampant, and it soon shrank to less than thirty thousand men. It was clear that the rebellion was in its final stages.

After the Hungarians lost another important, final battle at Romhányi on 22 January 1710, two opposing tendencies that had been gathering momentum came to the fore among the *kuruc* leadership. Rákóczi and Bercsényi, on the one side, placed all their hopes for the continuation of the uprising on their ability to gain foreign support. To replace the lost French aid they attempted to obtain Russian backing, and in early 1711 they left for Poland to plead their case before the tsar. The "peace party" in the *kuruc* camp, however, led by many prominent aristocrats, was convinced that the time had come for an accommodation with Vienna. Sándor Károlyi, one of the foremost members of this group, had been assigned by Rákóczi to command the *kuruc* army in his absence. Károlyi used this opportunity to establish secret contacts with János Pálffy, the Habsburg commander-in-chief. When the Habsburg negotiators offered the *kuruc* amnesty and the return of their property (Károlyi received additional inducements), Károlyi decided to accept the offer and to capitulate. Thus, on 1 May 1711, on a field near Szatmár the twelve-thousand-man *kuruc* army laid down its banners and dispersed. Meanwhile, in Poland Rákóczi and Bercsényi, to whom these terms also applied, rejected them and chose to continue the struggle against the Habsburgs from abroad.

Hungarian historians like to call the Treaty of Szatmár a compromise. The reason for this is most probably the lenient treatment accorded to the Hungarians by Vienna after the rebellion. Not only did former *kuruc* receive full amnesty and the restitution of their estates, but local administrations, that is, the *komitat*s, preserved their former prerogatives, although initially they were controlled by pro-Habsburg magnates. Even the general assemblies of the nobility again met regularly; but being controlled by pro-Habsburg magnates, they were much more responsive to Vienna's needs than to those of their homeland. In any case, on the surface at least it appeared that the status quo ante had been preserved in Hungary.

After 1711, however, far-reaching changes took place at the uppermost levels of government in Hungary. All of the highest administrative institutions were either moved to Vienna or placed under the direct control of Viennese authorities. The Hungarian chancellery, the main administrative body of the land, was now located in the Habsburg capital. Its chief executive and all of his associates were appointed by the emperor from among Hungarian magnates of proven loyalty. And although the Hungarian treasury remained in Hungary, at Pozsony, it operated more as a local agency of the Habsburg treasury. Vienna also retained control of the Hungarian army by stipulating that at least half of its men and officers had to be non-Hungarians. In addition, units of the imperial army were stationed in Hungary at the cost of the populace. In establishing the territorial organization of the lands of the Crown of St Stephan, the Habsburgs applied the principle of divide et impera. Transylvania was kept separate from Hungary and had its own administrative agencies in Vienna; the same was true of the Banat and the parts of Croatia and Slovenia that made up the "military border." In short, the most important vestiges of Hungary's former self-rule were eliminated, and it seemed that the land was about to suffer the fate of largely assimilated Bohemia.

Although East European historians have long been preoccupied with the resistance of their respective countries to foreign absolutism, and especially with the "liberation struggles" discussed above, they have never grouped, let alone examined them as a whole. Why this unwillingness or inability to establish similarities among these five contemporaneous anti-absolutist clashes? The most likely explanation is that East European historiography, formed during the age of nationalism, focused primarily on national rather than regional developments. Although the imposition of Marxist perspectives after the Second World War corrected these myopic tendencies to a certain extent, it did so only in the field of socio-economic history. Marxist historians did not and could not work on broad comparative studies of political structures that did not fit into the Marxist scheme. Thus, because national historiographies in Eastern Europe were too narrow in their perspectives and Marxist historiography too one-dimensional, the close relationships among the early eighteenth-century conflicts in the region have been ignored.

There could, of course, be another reason why these conflicts have not been treated together – namely, that they were unrelated. But once we consider the evidence presented above, this position is no longer tenable. These five confrontations in Eastern Europe were all primarily reactions of the native nobilities against foreign absolutism, state-building, and oppression. This alone puts them into a separate category, especially since each case represents the final attempt of that elite to forestall the spread of absolutism. In short, what the decade of the 1640s was to Western Europe, that of the 1710s was to the East.

The relationships among the five contemporaneous East European clashes of sovereign versus nobility were more tightly interwoven than those among the analogous rebellions commonly associated with the "general crisis" in the West. Like the rebellions in France, Catalonia, Scotland, and Ireland, the conflicts in Livonia, Moldavia, Ukraine, Poland, and Hungary occurred mostly within the same decade. However, unlike their Western counterparts, they also took place within the same historical context, that of the Great Northern War. This fact necessitates a re-evaluation of the vast, crucial, twenty-one-year-long struggle for control of much of Eastern Europe. Usually it is viewed simply as a great-power confrontation between Sweden and Russia and their allies. While this is correct as far as it goes, the war, as we have seen, had another dimension to it: not only was it a conflict of one absolutist, empire-building sovereign against another, but at its most decisive junctures it also involved the struggles of native elites against foreign monarchs. Thus, Livonian unrest and Patkul's machinations ignited the war; Polish resentment against August II's absolutist schemes helped to mobilize support for Leszczynski and his Swedish patrons; the contingencies of the war also allowed August to bring his Saxon troops into Poland, which led to the formation of the Tarnogrod Confederation; Leszczynski's contacts with Mazepa led the Ukrainian *hetman* to rise against Peter I and brought about the fateful battle of Poltava; the flight of Mazepa and Charles XII to the Ottoman empire brought on the Ottoman-Russian conflict and Cantemir's anti-Ottoman moves; even Rákóczi, whose revolt was not a part of the Great Northern War, had extremely important and close contacts with major parties involved in the conflict.

The opposition of the leaders of the East European nobilities to their sovereigns primarily represents a rejection of absolutism, but in all cases their motives were necessarily complex, often running the whole gamut from altruism to calculated self-interest, as indeed did those of their noble peers and associates. In the voluminous literature dealing with these confrontations, however, the leaders' motives for their anti-absolutist positions are usually interpreted in terms of mutually exclusive extremes: either as patriotism, by historians who are nationalistically inclined, or as self-interest, by scholars whose sympathies lie with the absolutist sovereigns or who are of a more sceptical bent. Thus, while the former stress the leaders' frequent protestations that they acted "for the good of all," the latter point out that it was Mazepa's hope to obtain a principality for himself in the Commonwealth, that Rákóczi yearned for sovereignty over Transylvania, that Cantemir wanted to lay hereditary claim to the Moldavian *hospodar*ship, and that Patkul aspired to high office. Because this issue of patriotic motivation versus personal interest has been the subject of much debate, it should be noted that in early eighteenth-century Eastern Europe the distinction between public and private interests was not as clearly drawn as it is in modern times. This can be understood in light of the underdevelopment of public (or state) institutions in the region and the concomitant lack of a well-defined concept of common good. It is not surprising, therefore, that the leaders of the nobility, as is especially evident in the treaties which they signed with allied monarchs, often treated their personal interests in the same breath as the interests of their lands.

But the nobles themselves were often more zealous than their leaders in their support of the impulse to revolt. Such was certainly the case with the Ukrainian *starshyna*, the Moldavia boyars, and Bercsényi's circle of Hungarian magnates. As a rule their grievances were more typical of their societies as wholes, or of their elites, at any rate, than were those of the leaders. The sight of their homelands being despoiled by foreigners must certainly have evoked in them patriotic concern. Simple but virulent xenophobia (often confused with nationalism by later historians) also fuelled anti-absolutist sentiments not only among the nobility but at all levels of East European society. On a more concrete level, the unprecedented economic obligations imposed by distant monarchs enraged noblemen, townsmen, and peasants alike. But the immediate and universal complaint stemmed from the burdens of supporting the sovereigns' wars – more specifically, of quartering and provisioning their troops. That this difficult task fell to the nobles at a time when their real incomes had begun to drop as a result of depressed food prices in the West only compounded their resentment, which soon changed to animosity. And for this animosity to turn into open revolt, all that was needed were opportunities that promised fair chances of success. The wars that engulfed Eastern Europe in the early eighteenth century provided just such opportunities.

If the nobles' immediate motives for rising against their sovereigns varied, the rationales they themselves proffered for doing so did not. In all cases these were based on the strong legalistic sense that most noblemen in Europe possessed: the conviction that they were being wronged before their own laws and customs, that their compacts with their sovereigns were being broken or ignored, and that their monarchs were resorting to the principle of might over right. It followed, in the logic of noble values, that if a ruler behaved unjustly, that is, contrary to the laws of the land, nobles had not only the right but the duty to rise against him. Thus, the one basic principle at the heart of the nobiliary revolts was the medieval *ius resistendi*, adherence to which, in varying degrees of articulation, was common to the noble elites of both the East and the West. Indeed, the actions of Rákóczi, Patkul, Mazepa, and Cantemir were the last gasp of the *ius resistendi* in Eastern Europe.

To establish the goals of the anti-absolutist movements, we need only glance at the treaties which the noble leaders concluded with their foreign allies. These include Patkul's compact with August II (24 August 1699), Leszczynski's with Charles XII (28 November 1705), Mazepa's with Charles XII (24 April 1708), Rákóczi's projected treaty with Louis XIV (18 July 1708), and Cantemir's with Peter I (13 April 1711). Without exception, each of these documents stresses that the goal of the particular alliance and, by implication, of the movement as well is to rid the land of "current tyranny," restore its liberty, and guarantee its traditional rights and privileges. In every one of these treaties liberty is identified with the restoration of the old order. We may say, therefore, that the "wars of liberation," as some historians like to call them, were actually wars of *conservation*. Ironically, the foreign monarchs to whom the anti-absolutist leaders turned in their search for allies were among the most absolutist in all of Europe.

The East European conflicts can all be subsumed under one category, that which in Zagorin's typology of early modern revolutions is called the provincial rebellion. According to him, provincial rebellions, despite their many differences, "all shared the fundamental common property of originating in the grievances of subordinate or provincial kingdoms within dynastic unions. Either the absentee ruler and paramount state were guilty of unaccustomed demands and innovations that violated the autonomous liberties of the provincial kingdom, or they inflicted upon it an increasingly repressive government that finally became intolerable."[96] A key factor in the provincial rebellions was that they were aimed at forces which were external to the given society. While all the East European conflicts fit this category, perhaps the best example of it, because of the role played by a dynastic union of two theoretically independent political entities, is the conflict between Poland-Lithuania and August of Saxony.

The Hungarian uprising combined the features of a provincial rebellion with those of what Zagorin calls a "revolutionary civil war." It qualifies as the latter because it involved broad social participation and covered large geographical areas, because the rebels exhibited a high degree of organization and expounded a fully developed ideology, and because it constituted a "massive societal reaction to the forward march of monarchical state-building."[95] Moreover, revolutionary civil wars in early modern Europe generally lasted more than five years, involved plebian radicalism, great-power participation, and the erection of rival and alternative governments to those of the incumbent regimes. Examples of such conflicts are the Netherlands rebellion of 1566–1609, the English revolution of 1640–60, and the French Fronde of 1648–53. Among these relatively few revolutionary civil wars we can also include the Hungarian revolt of 1703–11.

Another form of resistance to absolutism is the anti-sovereign conspiracies of aristocrats and nobles. In terms of our subject this is an exceedingly important type of revolt, since the events in Livonia and especially in Ukraine and Moldavia were a combination of provincial rebellion and conspiracy. As representatives of politically and militarily hopelessly weaker entities, Mazepa, Cantemir, and Patkul could not dare, as could the Hungarians and Poles, to confront their sovereigns openly and directly. In this regard it is interesting to note a glaring example of inconsistency in the historiographical evaluation of anti-absolutist conspiracies. Of all the East European uprisings those of Mazepa and Cantemir are the most strikingly similar. Both leaders resolved to rid themselves and their lands of oppression by concluding secret alliances with their sovereigns' worst enemies. Both attracted their foreign allies to their land and to fateful confrontations with unfulfilled promises of widespread support. And both joined them in hasty flight after witnessing the catastrophic defeats of their allies. Yet despite these similarities, traditional Russian and modern Soviet historiography virulently condemn Mazepa, painting him as the epitome of treachery and treason. Meanwhile, Cantemir is idolized in Soviet historical writing. The reasons for these very different interpretations are not difficult to find. Because Mazepa attempted to break Ukraine away from Moscow, while Cantemir sought to place Moldavia under Russian overlordship, the former is pilloried while the latter is praised. Clearly, such an obvious intrusion of modern politics into historiography does little to help Soviet scholars to understand the key political issues of the early eighteenth century.

The use of conspiracy to initiate noble uprisings was not, as the Soviets argue in the case of Mazepa, an ipso facto indicator of evil or reactionary intentions. It was rather, a reflection of basic changes in the political environment of Eastern Europe. Prior to the eighteenth century, when foreign control of East European lands was limited, opposition to sovereigns could be mounted more or less openly. But by the early eighteenth century the absolutist presence in the region had become so widespread that those who wished to oppose their rulers had to lay their plans in the utmost secrecy. Another reason for caution was that, since they had immeasurably more to lose than the peasants who engaged in spontaneous outbursts, the leaders of the nobiliary revolts usually reached their decisions to rise against their overlords only after much deliberation and even more hesitation. In addition to offering the obvious advantage of preventing detection, secrecy provided the participants with the option of altering, postponing, and even abandoning their designs as they saw fit. Little wonder that throughout Europe noble opposition frequently began in small, tightly knit conspiratorial groups. But conspiracy had its drawbacks, too. It did not allow its participants to prepare the majority of their fellow noblemen suitably for the impending uprisings. As a result, when the revolts broke out, many nobles were confused as to their aims and hesitated to commit themselves.

While the extent, format, and modus operandi of the East European rebellions differed, their timing did not. Without exception they occurred when the rebels' sovereigns were involved in war or when the rebels' foreign allies were nearby. By waiting for such circumstances to develop, the leaders of the uprisings acknowledged their inability to mount serious opposition of their own. It will be recalled that Mazepa made his move only after Charles XII had entered Ukraine; Cantemir waited until Peter I had crossed the Dniester into Moldavia; and Rákóczi's uprising erupted after the Habsburgs had become involved in a war with the French. Patkul went a step further by helping to start the Great Northern War himself. Thus, war was the midwife of the East European nobiliary revolts.

It was their narrow domestic base of support that necessitated the dependence of the nobiliary uprisings on outside aid. Except for the numerous *szlachta* of Poland-Lithuania, the East European nobilities constituted less than 4 per cent of their respective societies. Since they had already alienated the townsmen and antagonized the peasants even more, they could expect little in the way of support from within their own societies. As absolutist monarchs began to identify with the interests of society as a whole (Moldavia was an exception), the nobility felt its political isolation sharply. Furthermore, during the insurrections, although sympathizing with the anti-absolutist cause, many noblemen failed to commit themselves, opportunistically playing a game of wait-and-see instead. Consequently, the rebel leaders had no recourse but to seek aid abroad.

By lending their support to the nobles in revolt, foreign monarchs hoped to benefit in several ways. The short-run advantages they counted on were primarily of a tactical nature: if encouraged, the insurrections behind their enemies' lines would sow confusion among those enemies and force them to divert some of their forces. In the long run, aid to the rebellious lands could be converted into influence and possible expansion into these lands. However, co-operation between the leaders of the uprisings and foreign monarchs could create problems for both parties. Neither the rebels nor their foreign allies could be sure, once they had committed themselves, that aid which had been promised would be forthcoming or sustained. When France, for example, ran into difficulties during its war with the Habsburgs, it promptly cut off aid to the Hungarians and left them in a hopeless situation. Foreign sovereigns who meddled in their foes' internal problems were also subject to disillusionment and loss. Convinced by Patkul's assurances that the Livonians were ready to reject Swedish rule, August II launched an invasion of Livonia only to find, to his dismay, that the Livonians preferred the Swedes to the Saxons. Charles XII drastically altered his plans for the invasion of Russia and moved into Ukraine on the assumption that Mazepa would join him with thirty thousand Cossacks and plentiful provisions. As it happened, all the *hetman* could muster was three to four thousand unenthusiastic followers.

Another matter of concern to some of the intervention-minded monarchs was the loss of face they might suffer within the feuding fraternity of the crowned heads of Europe on account of their ties with the rebels. With the memory of the Fronde still fresh in his mind, Louis XIV was clearly uneasy about his ties with the Hungarian rebels, despite his personal admiration for Rákóczi. Most sensitive on this score was Charles XII. His initial reaction to the proposal to establish contacts with Mazepa was to reject it outright on the grounds that the *hetman* had risen against his rightful lord. He voiced similar misgivings about proposed dealings with Rákóczi. Peter I seems to have been least concerned about these breaches of monarchical propriety. Not only did he unhesitatingly extend support to Cantemir, but he was also quick to offer his hospitality to Patkul and Rákóczi. The more common reluctance of other monarchs was, however, well grounded, for the decision of rulers to aid rebels against their royal brothers had far-reaching implications. For one monarch to abet a rebellion against another was tantamount not only to lending it legitimacy but also to acknowledging the right of subjects to resist their overlords, to invoke, formally or in practice, the *ius resistendi*. By opting for the immediate benefits which accrued to them from supporting the noble uprisings, interventionist monarchs were setting a dangerous precedent, for, like a double-edged sword, this encouragement of insurrection could also be used against them.

At the same time that they guaranteed the rights of their enemies' subjects when it suited their interests, interventionist monarchs repressed those of their own elites. Peter I, for example, promised to preserve the privileges of the Moldavian boyars while systematically liquidating those of the Ukrainian *starshyna*. Similar contradictions existed in the policies of other interventionist monarchs. Certain acts of intervention, however, seem in the general opinion of the times to have been more justifiable than others. This was especially true in so far as religion was concerned. Thus, when Peter I invaded Moldavia, his argument that this had been done for the sake of the oppressed Orthodox Christians of the land was well received by the local populace. By contrast, when August II, the newly converted Catholic king of Poland, tried to take advantage of the tensions between the Lutheran king of Sweden and his Lutheran Livonian subjects, he was regarded as an interloper. The reaction was the same when the Lutheran Swedes became embroiled in the conflict between the Orthodox Ukrainians and their Orthodox tsar. It is clear that long after the religious wars in the West were over, religion and politics continued to be closely intertwined in the East.

In rising against their sovereigns, what domestic support could the East European rebels count on? As we noted earlier, townsmen, who were so prominent in anti-absolutist revolts in Western Europe, were a negligible factor in the East. There the impoverished towns had become so alienated by the nobility that despite royal exactions they generally preferred to side with their sovereigns. Perhaps the most striking example of this tendency is the burghers of Riga, who staunchly defended their city against Patkul and his Saxon allies, thereby foiling his plans and demonstrating their loyalty to their Swedish sovereign. In Ukraine the townsmen of Kiev, Poltava (where the burghers fought particularly bravely against the Swedes), and other towns sided with the tsar. The situation was somewhat less clear in Moldavia, Poland, and Hungary. In general, certain towns in these lands provided assistance to the anti-absolutist forces. But in every case this aid was limited to the early stages of the revolt. In Hungary, for example, as time went on and the old animosities between the two estates resurfaced, the towns usually adopted a neutralist or even antagonistic stance to the nobles' revolts.

As was the case with the burghers, the attitudes of the East European peasantry towards the nobiliary revolts varied considerably at the outset but, with time, generally became either ambivalent or antagonistic. In Livonia the Latvian and Estonian peasants openly and vigorously opposed the aspirations of the German *ritterschaft*. This was not suprising, for the exploitation of the peasantry by the nobility there was among the most severe in Europe, while the policy of the Swedish sovereigns towards peasants was among the most enlightened. In Ukraine the peasants had no special reason to be grateful to the tsar; however, they did have good grounds for detesting the *starshyna*, and Mazepa in particular. Until Mazepa's *hetman*cy the Ukrainian peasantry had been among the freest in the region and thus was particularly sensitive to and resentful of Mazepa's and the *starshyna's* unbridled attempts to whittle away at their freedoms. In Hungary, by contrast, it was the peasants and other dispossessed elements of society that provided the impetus for Rákóczi's uprising. It was also the peasantry that launched a number of attacks on Saxon troops in Poland in 1714, thereby indirectly aiding the cause of the rebellious *szlachta*. Yet these instances in which the socio-economic interests of the peasantry and the political grievances of the nobility coincided were short-lived. Worried by the sight of armed peasants, Hungarian and Polish nobles moved quickly to gain control of the uprisings, and, despite the enlightened efforts of men like Rákóczi, they soon alienated the peasantry. Thus, compared to their Western colleagues, the East European nobles, particularly those who revolted against their monarchs, were politically and socially more isolated. This proved to be one of the major weaknesses of their uprisings.

In Eastern Europe ethnic hatreds played a much greater role in the anti-absolutist conflicts than they did in the West. All of the East European sovereigns and most of their bureaucrats were foreigners, and the insurrections in the East thus had a strong xenophobic impulse. It remains puzzling, however, given the many common features of the East European conflicts with foreign absolutism, that there was so little mutual aid and co-operation among the rebels. On the one hand,'this can be explained by the extreme provincialism of the thinking of the noble elites in particular and of East Europeans in general. It was simply beyond their comprehension that absolutism, as a whole new system of government, could be encroaching upon their region as a whole. On the other hand, the concrete political situations in which rebel leaders found themselves usually precluded co-operation. Often they worked at cross purposes, the absolutist enemy of one nobility being the major ally of another elite. Thus, August II posed a threat to Polish rights and liberties at the same time that he promised to restore Livonian privileges, and Peter I systematically liquidated Ukrainian autonomy while committing himself to the liberation of Moldavia from Ottoman oppression. The Ottomans, meanwhile, became the traditional supporters of Hungarian liberties against Habsburg absolutism. None the less, the rebels may have influenced, if not aided each other indirectly. Their uprisings, so close in time and space to each other, created a climate of unrest and provided stirring examples of resistance to oppressive sovereigns. This may well have encouraged the spread of revolt in the region.

The most salient characteristic shared by the East European nobilities' attempts to halt absolutism was that they failed. Earlier, we noted the decisive advantages which the foreign state-organizations of the Habsburgs, Ottomans, Romanovs, Vasas, and Wettins enjoyed over the Hungarian, Moldavian, Ukrainian, Livonian, and Polish noble-associations in marshalling military and financial resources. In the context of the failure of the uprisings this point bears repeating because apologists for the rebels tend to overlook it, arguing instead that the rebels were simply overwhelmed by the more numerous forces of the vast empires to which they belonged. Arguments such as this ignore a crucial consideration – namely, that along with the revolts the imperial rulers had to deal with a wide array of other, equally pressing problems. Their ability to cope more or less successfully with all of these difficulties simultaneously is a striking demonstration of how much more effectively organized than their noble opponents they were. That their advantages were not only of a quantitative but also of a qualitative nature is the basic reason for their success and for the defeat of the noble elites of Eastern Europe.

The anti-absolutist conflicts precipitated an important change in the relationship between the imperial state-organizations and the noble-associations in the region. Previously, each of the noble-associations had participated in the government of its land on the highest levels, making decisions on foreign policy, maintaining and controlling its military forces. The Poles elected their own sovereigns; the Hungarians had the right to confirm theirs. Throughout the seventeenth century the government of the East European lands represented a condominium of the state-organizations and the noble-associations. And it would certainly not be accurate to say that after the unsuccessful revolts the noble-associations were removed from this partnership in government. Indeed, after the clashes of the early eighteenth century the empires and native elites of the region reached a remarkably workable accommodation. But the ground rules of this new condominium of government were changed decisively. The imperial state-organizations now monopolized all of the highest decision-making functions, that is, those pertaining to the choice of monarchs, to foreign and military affairs, and to financial policy, while the influence and prerogatives of the noble-associations became limited to local government. In effect, the nobles of Eastern Europe were demoted from full to junior partnership in the government of their lands. This was the major result of their failure to halt the spread of absolutism in the region.

There are, of course, many qualifications that can be added to this general pattern. In the case of Poland-Lithuania, Saxon absolutism did not triumph. This was, however, primarily due not so much to Polish as to Russian opposition. August II's failure did not mean that the Commonwealth escaped the onslaught of absolutism, however. Russian "protection" and interference in the internal affairs of the land led to what became, in effect, the loss of sovereignty. Thus, long before the Partitions, the Commonwealth had become a plaything in the hands of its absolutist neighbours.

The fate of the Livonian *ritterschaft* constitutes another notable divergence from the general East European trend. After the failure of Patkul's venture it seemed that the days of Livonian autonomy were numbered. Between 1700 and 1710 most Livonian institutions either were dismantled or became inoperative. But when he conquered the land in 1710, Peter I restored almost all of the traditional institutions and the prerogatives of the *ritterschaft*, to the great surprise of the Livonians (even Patkul had feared Russian rule more than Swedish overlordship). The tsar did so in order to pacify the Livonians as quickly as possible and to gain the co-operation of their Westernized elite. However, even this atypical resurgence of noble influence was strictly limited to local affairs. As far as the new Russian sovereigns were concerned, the so-called Capitulations of 1710 were not an inalienable right of the *ritterschaft* but a retractable gift from the tsar.

The significance of the failure of the East European anti-absolutist movements was epochal. The will of the region's elites to resist foreign absolutism suffered a crushing blow. Whereas before the early eighteenth century nobiliary revolts had been a frequent occurrence, they now ceased completely. The defeat of the noble elites marked a watershed in the history of Eastern Europe; it underscored the inability of the East Europeans to create power centres of their own and marked the lands of the region as ripe for assimilation by the empires that surrounded them.

V

The Émigré Epilogue

There was yet another trait shared by the East European nobles in their resistance to foreign absolutism: all of their leaders became political émigrés. Rákóczi, Leszczynski, Mazepa, Cantemir, and Patkul were all eventually forced into exile. Viewed broadly, their fate was not unusual for a region which has traditionally been one of the world's richest spawning grounds for émigrés.[1] As we have argued earlier in this study, the explanation for this peculiarly East European phenomenon lies in the chronic inability of its inhabitants to establish lasting power-centres in their region. As a consequence, they were doomed to be victimized for centuries by stronger neighbours. Herein lies a key distinction between Western and Russian émigrés as opposed to those from Eastern Europe: the former were forced into exile primarily as a result of internal conflicts in their homelands, the latter usually as a result of resistance to foreign domination.

Among the successive waves of East European émigrés, those of the early eighteenth century have a special significance. In several respects they were prototypes. Their emigration was the first generalized one in the region, and it prefigured the widespread emigrations of the mid-nineteenth and mid-twentieth centuries. Their methods of operation, their dilemmas, even their lifestyles served as a prelude to those of the later emigrations. Indeed, it can be said that Rákóczi, Leszczynski, Patkul, Cantemir, Mazepa, and his successor, Pylyp Orlyk, introduced a new archetype into East European history, that of the political émigré and, more specifically, the political émigré struggling abroad to liberate his homeland from foreign domination. The careers abroad of the exiled leaders can be divided into several more or less distinct phases. The goal of the following section will be to characterize these phases as well as to establish the circumstances in which the émigrés operated abroad, the goals they hoped to achieve, and the actual results they attained.

Johann Reinhold von Patkul 1660–1707

Ivan Mazepa 1639-1709

Stanisław Leszczynski 1677–1766

Dimitrie Cantemir 1673–1723

Ferenc Rákóczi ii 1676–1735

PHASE ONE: IN SEARCH OF A SECOND CHANCE

The initial stage of the East European émigrés' exile was characterized by the hope that all was not lost, that with the aid of foreign supporters they could recoup their losses. And as long as the widespread European conflicts of the early eighteenth century continued, these hopes were well founded. Intent on using them as a diversion, the foreign allies of the émigrés supplied them with financial, military, and political support. Meanwhile, in some cases the émigrés' enemies had to acknowledge the possibility of renewed negotiations with their exiled subjects. In short, war or the possibility of war preserved the political relevance of the émigrés and their causes. However, when peace ensued as a result of the treaties of Passarowitz in 1718 and Nystad in 1721, this relevance quickly faded, and the first, hopeful phase of their exile came to an end.

Patkul

In the Livonian case, Patkul himself constituted the entire emigration. None the less, so manifold and far reaching were the activities of this headstrong and talented man in exile that one could easily gain the impression that it was a sizeable group of Livonians that was agitating and plotting against Sweden throughout Europe.[2] The very circumstances in which this scion of an old but impoverished Livonian family came into the world presaged an unusual career: Johann Reinhold von Patkul was born in 1660 in a Swedish prison in Stockholm. His father, the *landrat*, Wilhelm Friedrich von Patkul, had been incarcerated on charges of treason, and Wilhelm's wife, Gertrude, was allowed to join him while the case was under investigation. Shortly after the birth of his son the elder Patkul received a pardon and returned to Livonia with his family. The young Patkul already showed a growing and marked contentiousness; it seems that he simply could not walk away from a fight. After his father's death he engaged in a bitter legal battle with his elder brother over the family estate; when he joined the Swedish regiment in Riga, he soon became involved in an altercation with his commanding officer; and when the conflict between the Livonian *ritterschaft* and the Swedish crown broke out, Patkul was quick to jump into the fray. He was thus acting completely in character when he decided to struggle on against Sweden after his escape, even if he had to do so alone.

After he slipped out of Stockholm on 15 November 1693 and crossed over to Kurland, where he found shelter on the estate of a distant relative, Patkul had to reassess his position. To return to Livonia was out of the question. The Swedish government had issued the strictest orders forbidding anyone, under penalty of death, to provide aid to the fugitive. Correspondence with him and even any public mention of his activities were forbidden. Stockholm was clearly determined to isolate him from the rest of the Livonians and thereby to encourage them to forget the entire Patkul affair as quickly as possible. Although several sympathetic letters did reach him from Livonia, it soon became evident to Patkul that the vast majority of his countrymen, believing the contest with the Swedish crown to be lost, had decided to avoid any contact with him. It was, for a man who had sacrificed so much for his homeland, a bitter pill to swallow.

But what could a single individual do against the forces of the Swedish crown? Patkul concluded that the most effective way for him to strike at the Swedes was to tarnish their reputation in European public opinion. He planned to publicize the arbitrary and unlawful manner in which the Swedish crown had handled the matter of Livonian rights in general and his own case in particular. For this purpose, in the summer of 1694 he travelled to the universities of Halle and Leipzig to present the documents of his trial to famous legal experts for their evaluation. Their opinions favoured his case. But although the decision was personally satisfying, Patkul soon discovered that without money he would be unable to gain access to the European press.[3] Never one to waste time, Patkul, while awaiting the jurists' verdicts, attended lectures at Halle in law and in theology, the latter a favourite subject from his student days in Kiel in 1667–70.

It is unclear how long Patkul stayed in Halle. Apparently, money problems forced him to seek employment, and he joined the regiment of the count of Hessen-Kassel. After fighting in several campaigns against the French, during which he specialized in the construction of fortifications, he left military service as soon as the war ended in 1697. Charles XI died in that same year, and Patkul, exhausted by war and by his wanderings, attempted to obtain amnesty. His efforts were rejected, however. But by a stroke of good fortune he managed to win the favour of the all-powerful Prussian minister Eberhard von Danckelmann, who awarded him a modest subsidy and invited him to spend some time at his estate near Lausanne in Switzerland. It was here, living under the false name of Fischering in order to avoid Swedish agents, who were constantly searching for him, that Patkul spent some of the most pleasant days of his life. In the mornings he translated the works of Samuel von Pufendorf into French and discussed them in a circle of sophisticated friends. One of these was Heinrich Huyssen, a tutor in Danckelmann's household and later one of Peter I's publicists. Afternoons were spent in the charming company of the ladies of Lausanne. But this idyllic existence came to an end in the final months of 1697, when von Danckelmann lost his post. Once again Patkul was forced to seek the help of well-placed friends, and again he was lucky. Through a chance meeting with another Livonian, Otto Arnold von Paykul, a general in the Saxon army, Patkul became acquainted with Jakob Heinrich von Flemming, August II's chief minister.[4] This meeting quickly propelled him into the world of high politics.

Mazepa and Orlyk

After their defeat at Poltava, Mazepa and Charles XII, accompanied by about eight thousand bedraggled followers, were granted asylum by the Ottomans in the Moldavian town of Bender. Most numerous of the refugees were the Ukrainians. They consisted of several distinct groups. Fewest in number were about forty-five members of the *starshyna*. Another category of exiles was the roughly five hundred rank-and-file Cossacks from the *hetman*ate, members of Mazepa's mercenary regiments, and chancellery officials. By far the largest group was the Zaporozhians. After the destruction by the Russians of their stronghold on the Dnieper, about four thousand Zaporozhians had followed Mazepa to Bender.[5]

Foreseeing the worst, Mazepa brought along a vast fortune in gold and jewels.[6] But it was a small comfort to him. Already ill upon his arrival at Bender, the aged *hetman* was well aware that his days were numbered. His political career, now drawing to a close, had been one of the most colourful in Ukrainian history.[7] It began when Mazepa, born in 1639 into an old Ruthenian-Ukrainian noble family, entered the service of the Polish king, Jan Casimir, as a page. This service allowed him to spend several years of study in Western Europe and to gain valuable experience as a diplomat. Upon his return to Ukraine in 1668 and his subsequent capture by pro-Russian Cossacks, Mazepa used his Western polish and diplomatic skills to great advantage. Not only did he gain the favour of Ivan Samoilovych, the *hetman* of Left Bank Ukraine, but he also charmed the Muscovite officials who interrogated him in Moscow. Soon after his return to the Left Bank, Mazepa became Samoilovych's chancellor, and in 1687 he replaced him as *hetman*.

When Peter I came to power in 1689, Mazepa developed a close personal relationship with the young tsar. But although Peter showered him with gifts, titles, and lands, making him the richest man in Ukraine in the process, Mazepa never felt secure under autocratic Russian rule. It was this sense of insecurity that influenced his decision to revolt against his sovereign.

On 22 September 1709 Mazepa died near Bender. His successor-in-exile was Pylyp Orlyk, the former *hetman*'s chancellor. Orlyk was not, to use a favourite phrase of the times, a "true son of the fatherland" – that is, he had not been born in Ukraine. Born in 1672 into a respected but impecunious noble family in Lithuania, he came to Kiev as a youth to continue his education at the famous

Kiev Academy. Ambitious and gifted, he married into the Cossack elite and in 1706, with Mazepa's backing, was chosen chancellor. By virtue of his office Orlyk became Mazepa's right-hand man and played an important role in the preparation of the latter's uprising. It was natural, therefore, that upon the old *hetman*'s death he should be chosen to lead the exiled Ukrainians.

One of Orlyk's first political actions was to obtain, on 10 May 1710, Charles XII's assurance that he would not make peace with the Russians until "the Muscovite yoke was removed from Ukraine and the land's ancient liberties were returned."[8] Prior to his election Orlyk also concluded, on 5 April 1710, a formal agreement with his electors in which the conditions under which he assumed authority were clearly stated.[9] Modelled on the Polish *pacta conventa*, the so-called Bender Constitution was designed to prevent the accumulation of power in the hands of the *hetman*. As such it was a good indication of the political changes that the Ukrainian émigrés hoped to effect if and when they returned to their homeland.[10]

In 1711 the Bender refugees mounted a second effort against the Russians. This unexpected development was to a great extent the work of Charles XII. It was he who persuaded the Ottomans to declare war against the Russians on 19 November 1710. Also as a result of the Swedish king's prodding, Orlyk's Cossacks concluded a treaty of alliance with the Crimean Tatars on 23 January 1711 and prepared, together with Potocki's Poles, to invade Ukraine. The campaign was to serve as a prelude to the great offensive which the Ottomans planned to launch later in the year.

On 31 January a force of four thousand Zaporozhians led by Orlyk, two to three thousand Poles commanded by Józef Potocki, and twenty to thirty thousand Tatars set out from Bender. Initially, Orlyk and his allies made excellent progress in Right Bank Ukraine, where without much difficulty they overwhelmed several Russian garrisons. Even more heartening was the widespread support Orlyk received from the Ukrainian populace. Thousands of Right Bank Cossacks, unhappy with the Russians, joined him, and soon Orlyk's forces increased more than fivefold. It seemed likely that even Kiev might fall to the invaders. However, just as Orlyk's fortunes looked brightest, internal problems among the allies loomed up. As Russian resistance stiffened, the Tatars, unable to acquire easy booty, began to pillage the Ukrainian populace that had welcomed Orlyk. As a result, the Cossacks who had joined Orlyk now abandoned him in order to protect their families from the Tatar depredations. As the *hetman*'s forces shrank, the Tatars decided to break off the campaign and return to their homes. Unable to press forward on his own, Orlyk had no choice but to return to Bender.[11]

Although he was unable to re-establish himself in Ukraine by means of force, it appeared in 1712 that Orlyk might attain his goals by means of diplomacy. The Ottoman offensive had led to the Russian defeat at the Prut. As a result of this setback, one of the concessions that Peter I made to the Ottomans was to renounce all claims to Right Bank Ukraine. One of the most important goals of the Porte now was to establish a Cossack buffer principality in the area under the rule of Orlyk. However, August II and the Poles, who also claimed the area, refused to acquiesce to the Ottoman plan. After more than a year of stubborn negotiations with the Poles, the Porte was forced to abandon its Ukrainian project and to conclude a general peace. At this point there was no reason left for either Charles XII or Orlyk to remain in the Ottoman empire. Therefore, on 25 October 1714 Charles returned to Sweden, and after arranging to leave the Zaporozhians under Crimean overlordship, the *hetman*-in-exile followed in his patron's footsteps.

Orlyk, his numerous family, and about a dozen close associates remained in Sweden from 1714 and 1719. As long as Charles was alive, they received modest but regular subsidies. However, when the king was killed in 1718, support for the Ukrainians was drastically reduced, and they were even encouraged to leave. Therefore, when Hanover, Austria, and Saxony formed an anti-Russian alliance in 1719, Orlyk and his band of compatriots moved to the continent to offer their services to the allies. But the alliance soon crumbled, and when Orlyk met with the representatives of George I in Hanover, he received assurances of goodwill but little else. His stay in the Habsburg empire was even more disheartening. As soon as Orlyk crossed the Bohemian border, the Russian ambassador in Vienna protested against his presence in the empire. Meanwhile, Russian agents, who had been following Orlyk for some time, prepared to abduct him, just as they had kidnapped Andrii Voinarovsky, Mazepa's nephew, in Hamburg in 1716. Only a last-minute warning allowed Orlyk to escape his would-be kidnappers. Embarrassed by the incident, Habsburg officials insisted that Orlyk leave the empire. In his diary the harried émigré sadly noted that, "without a place to rest my head safely, I have become an object of contempt for the world and its people. For the sake of security I must move from place to place, using a false name and playing the role of a foreigner."[12]

Leaving his family behind in the safety of a Bohemian monastery, Orlyk moved on to Poland. Although he was warmly received by the Poles, they made it clear to him that they could not guarantee his safety. For emphasis they pointed out that a year earlier, in 1720, the Russians had kidnapped Hryhor Hertsyk, one of the *hetman*'s closest associates, in Warsaw in broad daylight. At this point Orlyk was so demoralized that he attempted to obtain an amnesty from the tsar. But Peter dashed his hopes. There was now only one option left.

On 22 March 1722 Orlyk entered the Ottoman empire. Surprised by its unexpected guest, the Porte decided to detain him "temporarily" in Salonika until it could use his services. It would be twelve years before Orlyk would be able to extricate himself from Ottoman hospitality.

Leszczynski

The career of Stanisław Leszczynski as an émigré began in the fall of 1709.[13] After the battle of Poltava he took refuge in the Swedish-held town of Szczecin (Stettin) on the Baltic coast. His entourage consisted of his family and about three hundred officials, soldiers, and retainers. While Charles XII launched energetic efforts from Bender to involve the Ottoman Porte in a war with the tsar, Leszczynski idled away his time in his Baltic refuge, now and then dropping vague hints to August II about his desire to negotiate a settlement. Charming and easygoing, Leszczynski was neither assertive nor overly ambitious. It was probably these traits that had led Charles to choose him for the kingship. Certainly, compromises and negotiations were much more to Leszczynski's liking than was warfare. Therefore, at the outset of exile his reaction was to wait and see how matters developed rather than to continue the fight.

Meanwhile, the Polish contingent in Bender increased markedly when in November 1710 Józef Potocki, the *wojewoda* of Kiev and one of Stanisław's most energetic supporters, arrived with about two thousand bedraggled followers. Theirs had been a difficult journey. In the fall of 1709 Potocki and his men had parted with Stanisław and fought their way through Poland, crossing the Carpathians into Hungary. There they received aid from Rákóczi, but only on the condition that the Poles join the *kuruc* forces. Finally, after almost a year of difficult service in Hungary, Potocki and his men managed to take leave of Rákóczi and join Charles in Bender. In early January of 1711 they joined the combined Tatar-Ukrainian force that was sent back into Ukraine to prepare the ground for the Ottoman offensive that was to follow.[14]

Simultaneously with this thrust from the south, Adam Smigielski, another of Leszczynski's military commanders, launched a raid into Poland from the north. Although he penetrated deep into enemy territory with several thousand men, Smigielski was unable to win any decisive victories. More importantly, he was unable to rouse much enthusiasm for Stanisław's cause among the war-weary Polish nobility. Indeed, the major outcome of this raid was the marshalling of Saxon and Russian forces for a possible retaliatory attack against Szczecin. Worried by this prospect, Leszczynski gathered together his family and his rapidly shrinking entourage and moved to Straslund, after which he set sail for Sweden, arriving in Stockholm in October of 1711.

The stay in Sweden was not a pleasant one for Leszczynski. Many of Sweden's leading statesmen had always regarded their king's obsession with Polish affairs and especially his commitment to Leszczynski as a major source of their troubles.[15] In monetary terms alone the cost of supporting the Polish king was extremely high for the depleted Swedish treasury: by 1709 it had cost the Swedes close to 700,000 *talers*. Still, upon his protégé's arrival in Sweden Charles sent word to Stockholm that Leszczynski was to participate in the council of state as his personal representative and to receive 104,000 *talers* annually plus provisions. The hard-pressed members of the regency council grumbled that they could hardly support their own king, let alone a foreign one.

On the instructions of Charles, Leszczynski spent much of his time urging the reluctant council to mount one more offensive against the enemy. In September 1712, mobilizing their last resources, the Swedes sent off a sixteen-thousand-man expeditionary corps across the Baltic under General Magnus Stenbok. Bidding farewell to his family, Leszczynski accompanied the force. After achieving a resounding victory over the Danes at Gadebusch in Mecklenburg, the Swedes became bogged down in the cleverly baited negotiations initiated by August ii. The elector-king proposed, quite insincerely, an anti-Russian alliance. This led to a loss of momentum for the Swedes and eventually, in May 1713, to Stenbok's capitulation to the Danes.

As matters went from bad to worse Leszczynski engaged August ii in negotiations of his own. At issue was the settlement Leszczynski wanted to obtain for giving up his claims to the Polish crown. After protracted haggling with Flemming an arrangement was agreed upon: in return for recognizing August ii's sole claim to the Polish crown, Leszczynski was to get back all his lands and former offices in Poland, as well as 100,000 ducats to cover damages to his lands and an annual pension of 150,000 *talers*. The agreement, which was signed on 5 December 1712, carried only one condition: that Charles approve it. To obtain this approval, Leszczynski made his way to Bender. There he learned that Charles was unwilling to condone his agreement with August ii. Unwilling to defy his protector, Leszczynski completely reversed his policy and again adopted a militantly anti-August position. An Ottoman offer of military support against his Saxon rival also helps to explain this sudden reversal of policy. But in return for their aid the Ottomans demanded that Leszczynski agree to cede Right Bank Ukraine to Orlyk and his followers, who would then turn the land into an Ottoman-dominated principality and a bulwark against Russian expansionism. Leszczynski agreed, and in the spring of 1713 he was ready to march into Poland at the head of a horde of Crimean Tatars and Ottoman Janissaries to fight for his crown. Meanwhile, in Poland his old supporters, led by his uncle, Jan Jabłonowski, began to organize a fifth column. However, as

Leszczynski and his Muslim allies approached the Polish border in July 1713, the news came that Stenbok had surrendered. Moreover, English and Dutch diplomats at the Porte pressed for peace, while the Saxon and pro-August troops in Poland appeared to be well prepared for the attack. Suddenly, the Porte and the Crimean khan lost their ardour for the whole undertaking and ordered a retreat. As interest in Leszczynski and the invasion evaporated, the king-in-exile was left empty handed, having lost his chances both to negotiate with August and to fight on against him.

Disgusted with the behaviour of his erstwhile Muslim allies, Leszczynski made plans to leave "their accursed pagan land" as soon as possible. But where could he go? A way out of his dilemma was provided by Charles XII. Charles offered the Polish émigré the hospitality of Zweibrücken, a tiny Swedish holding on the Rhine. Leszczynski and his small entourage accepted the offer and left for Germany in January 1714. At Zweibrücken Leszczynski gathered around him a minuscule court of several dozen people. The Duchy of Zweibrücken provided a modest but steady income of about twenty thousand *talers* annually. However, it was not long before the chronic problems of the émigré condition set in. Leszczynski's wife suffered from homesickness; in June 1717 his gifted elder daughter, Anna, died suddenly; and in August of the same year, as he was about to visit her fresh grave, a group of French adventurers who had been hired by Flemming tried to kidnap him. Their orders, in the event that this failed, were to assassinate him. Luckily, Leszczynski had been forewarned, and the attempt miscarried. After this traumatic incident the Polish émigrés moved to a nearby castle at Bergzabern, and soon afterwards Leszczynski learned that his friend and protector, Charles XII, had been killed in Norway by a stray bullet. With his patron gone, he now faced the distinct possibility that support for him, be it diplomatic, financial, or military, would no longer be forthcoming and that he would have to face the future as a penniless and homeless émigré.

"Desperate as a fish out of water," as his biographer, Jósef Feldman, put it, Leszczynski cast about for support. He bombarded the new regent of Sweden, Charles's sister, Ulrike Eleonora, with the most imploring letters, pleading that "if Sweden no longer deems me worthy of its aid, it should take pity on my misery, for I no longer have the means to survive and I am constantly persecuted by my enemies."[16] Ulrike Eleonora made a sincere attempt to help him. About fifty thousand livres from the French subsidy to Sweden was secretly diverted to him. Swedish diplomats in Paris tried to find him a new refuge because Zweibrücken had passed into the possession of one of Charles XII's nephews. As a favour to its Swedish allies Versailles granted him asylum in France and allowed him to settle in the town of Wissemburg in Alsace. In response to vigorous Saxon protests the French court declared that "France

has always been a shelter for unfortunate princes." However, apart from granting him refuge, the French totally ignored their new guest.

With the signing of the Treaty of Nystad between Russia and Sweden in 1721,
Leszczynski suffered another setback. Despite Swedish efforts, his interests
were not discussed during the negotiations or included in the treaty. Oblivion
and penury now stared him in the face. Swedish financial assistance had come
to an end with the conclusion of the war; his lands in Poland had been
devastated and produced only half of their previous income, while carrying
a debt of 300,000 *talers*; his debts in Wissemburg also mounted. Leszczynski's
future had never looked more grim.

Cantemir

Long years of separation from his homeland were not a new experience for
Dimitrie Cantemir. When he left Moldavia in July 1711 at the age of thirty-seven,
he had already lived twenty years abroad, most of them spent in Istanbul as
a hostage during his father's elder brother's *hospodar*ships. Nevertheless, the
impact of witnessing his plans crumble as a result of the Russian defeat at the
Prut must have been traumatic. As the Russian army retreated from Moldavia,
Cantemir dashed to Jassy with a small detachment of men, collected his family
and whatever valuables and money he could, and two days later joined Peter
I's retreat, leaving his homeland forever.[17]

Estimates of the number of his countrymen who followed him vary greatly.
Some sources place the figure as low as twenty-four, while others cite an unlikely
figure of eleven thousand.[18] According to the Russians, Cantemir arrived in
their land with an entourage of 448 boyars, officials, and military officers.
Included in this number were about 20 to 30 boyars, mostly of junior rank.
Hetman Ion Neculce was the only senior boyar. However, the figure of 448 does
not include the rank and file or the women and children who joined in the
exodus. Thus, the total number of Moldavians who followed in Peter's wake
was, according to Russian sources, about two thousand.[19]

The flight from Moldavia was not without its anxious moments. As the
refugees travelled through Right Bank Ukraine, a large band of Orlyk's
Zaporozhians, hoping to earn a rich reward from the Ottomans for capturing
the *hospodar*, gave chase to Cantemir's party. In July 1711, after brief stays in
several Ukrainian towns, the Moldavians reached Kharkiv in eastern Ukraine.
At this point the exhausted Cantemir addressed a letter to the tsar in which
he asked him, "What am I to expect from this constant wandering?"[20] In his
response Peter made it clear that he intended to recompense the Moldavians
for their losses. Cantemir was assigned an impressive house and several

hundred villages near Kharkiv. Ironically, much of the land the Moldavian refugees received had once belonged to the Mazepist émigrés.[21] The tsar also presented Cantemir with a house in Moscow, an annual pension of six thousand rubles, the exalted title of prince, and a jewel-encrusted portrait of himself. But perhaps Peter's most impressive gift to the *hospodar* was the exclusive right to govern and judge the Moldavians who arrived with him. Rarely if ever had anyone received such extraterritorial rights in Russia. Other Moldavian émigrés also received appropriate grants of land in Ukraine.

In 1712 Cantemir received further evidence of the tsar's goodwill. During a trip to Moscow he was given over two thousand peasant households in the vicinity of the capital. Wishing to be closer to the centre of political power, he moved to Moscow in the spring of the same year, while the rest of the Moldavians remained in Ukraine. As might be expected, the tsar's generosity irked some of the leading members of the Russian elite. According to Neculce, who had become increasingly estranged from Cantemir, "The other important Muscovites hate him [Cantemir] because the tsar loves him and has given him a higher title than they have."[22] But despite the negative attitude of some of the Russian boyars, the tsar persisted in favouring the Moldavian leader.

During the early stage of his exile, if there was one favour that Cantemir desired from Peter, it was his support in reinstating him as *hospodar* of Moldavia. In 1712 it appeared that he might even achieve this goal. In April of that year Cantemir visited the tsar in his new capital on the Neva. During this visit he had a secret conference with Peter and some of his closest advisers about the possibility of launching another thrust against the Ottomans and the Crimeans. But the opposition of Field Marshal Boris Sheremetev and Admiral Feodor Apraksin, who forcefully argued that it would be foolhardy to antagonize the Porte while the conflict in the north was far from settled, convinced Peter to abandon his plans.

His hopes dashed, Cantemir returned to his Ukrainian estates. Here he immersed himself in his studies, completing some of his most famous works during this relatively calm period of his life. But he did not desist from dreaming about a return to Moldavia. Therefore, when war broke out between the Porte and the Habsburgs in 1716, Cantemir again urged Peter to intervene. In a letter to the tsar dated 6 October 1716 he argued that the Tatar raids into Ukraine that were taking place at this time provided Russia with an excellent excuse for attacking the Muslims.[23] Again, Peter's response was encouraging. Apparently on the latter's instructions, Cantemir moved closer to the Moldavian border sometime in the fall of 1716, and news of his proximity quickly spread through the principality.[24] There are also indications that he participated in a raid into the Crimea at this time. Meanwhile, contacts with important Moldavians within the principality were established. Thus, when Peter returned from abroad in January 1718, Cantemir informed him that he had received emissaries from the Moldavian metropolitan and from some leading boyars. They had pleaded with him to intercede with the tsar to extend Russian protection over Moldavia. In reporting on his talks with his countrymen, Cantemir also added that they still considered the terms of the treaty of 1711 to be in effect.[25]

The *hospodar* also played on the emerging Russian-Habsburg rivalry in the Balkans, pointing out to Peter that it would be in Russia's interests and in the interests of Orthodoxy to move into Moldavia before the Catholic Habsburgs did. The tsar seemed convinced. From his position in Right Bank Ukraine near the Moldavian border Cantemir was instructed to inform the Moldavian boyars that in 1719 a Russian army would enter Moldavia.[26] But just as this joyful news reached the *hospodar*, a report arrived from Passarowitz informing him that the Habsburgs had signed a peace treaty with the Porte. Again his hopes for a war against the Ottomans and a chance to return to Moldavia were shattered. In the midst of these bitter disillusionments Cantemir concluded that it was pointless for him to base all his hopes on the slim chance that Russia might some day install him again in Moldavia. He decided, therefore, to become involved in Russian politics and to pursue his studies.

Rákóczi

When he left Hungary in February 1711 in search of support for the faltering Hungarian cause, Rákóczi fully intended to return to his homeland. However, Károlyi's unauthorized conclusion of the Szatmár Treaty with the Habsburgs in May completely upset the prince's plans. Suddenly, he was confronted with a difficult decision: either to accept the amnesty which the Habsburgs were offering him on the condition that he give up his claims to Transylvania and return to his estates, or to continue the struggle from abroad. Thus, unlike the other leaders of nobiliary revolts, Rákóczi had the tempting possibility of quietly laying down his arms and returning to the status quo ante. However, his idealistic nature and aristocratic pride would not allow him to take the easy way out. Instead, he chose to fight on. It was a decision that consigned him to twenty-four years of bitter, frustrating exile and a lonely death far from his native land.

Rákóczi and his entourage of about one hundred courtiers, officials, and noble guardsmen were not the only Hungarians to arrive in Poland in 1711.[27] After Szatmár about three thousand *kuruc* officers, senators, and soldiers also crossed the borders into the Commonwealth. They established themselves in Iaroslav in eastern Galicia, in an area where Rákóczi accompanied the tsar in his travels through Poland. Realizing that the Hungarian cause was lost, Peter carefully refrained from making any commitments to the prince. He did, however, offer him asylum and, as in the case of Cantemir, large grants of land in Ukraine. Rákóczi politely declined the offer, parted with the tsar, and in December, travelling under the name of Count Saros, made his way to Gdansk.

Although the stay in Gdansk, where Rákóczi was feted by the local Polish aristocrats, was largely pleasant, it also had its darker moments.[28] From Iaroslav Berczényi wrote to warn Rákóczi that "one must be very careful of the imperial officers who are in Gdansk. Your Excellency should always be on guard, especially at night, lest an unfortunate accident occur."[29] At the outset of his exile Rákóczi scoffed at such warnings, replying to Bercsényi that he looked forward to meeting "these gentlemen" in person. However, he later learned to take the warnings more seriously. Even more worrisome for the prince was his own financial plight and that of his followers. French subsidies were few and far between. In May 1712 the financial situation became so critical that Rákóczi had to disband part of his entourage and send sixty of his noble guards back to Hungary. Describing their mournful parting with their beloved prince, Adam Vay, Rákóczi's chamberlain, wrote, "Even at the most sorrowful funerals I have not seen such tears and laments as on this occasion."[30]

In 1712 negotiations began in Utrecht to conclude the War of the Spanish Succession. Convinced that the issue of Hungary would surface at these talks, Rákóczi resolved to get closer to the negotiations. Therefore, in late 1712 he left Gdansk for France, and on 13 January 1713 he debarked with his entourage at Dieppe. Exactly one month later he was in Versailles, where he was received by Louis XIV with all the honours due to a prince. Among the first issues he discussed with the king was the matter of finances. Louis agreed to provide him with a subsidy of seventy-two thousand écus annually.[31] Although the grant was a generous one, its significance was diminished by the fact that Rákóczi had to use a substantial part of it to support his entourage and some of his more important followers who had stayed behind in Poland. It was, however, diplomacy rather than finances that interested Rákóczi most.[32] After France concluded the Peace of Utrecht with Holland and England, it had only Austria left to deal with. The question was, would Versailles continue the war now that it was one-on-one with the Habsburgs, or would it decide to make peace with its arch-enemy? Rákóczi argued for war. He repeatedly tried to convince Louis XIV and Jean Baptiste Torcy, the king's foreign minister, that if the French provided a renewed Hungarian uprising with sufficient aid, victory over the Habsburgs would practically be assured.[33] But both the French and the Austrians were too exhausted to fight on. In early 1714 they commenced peace negotiations at Rastadt.

Rákóczi quickly adapted to the new situation. His goal was now to convince the French to raise during the talks the issues of Habsburg rule in Hungary and of his claim to Transylvania. Louis XIV did, in fact, instruct his envoys to discuss Hungarian rights, but he felt that it was pointless to talk about Rákóczi's claims to Transylvania. In any case, the Habsburg diplomats were prepared for such an eventuality. As soon as the French envoys mentioned Habsburg oppression in Hungary, the Austrians brought up the matter of the French occupation of Catalonia. Unwilling to broach the Catalonian issue, the French agreed to drop the matter of Hungary. Thus, in the Peace of Rastadt (March 1714) and the Peace of Baden (September 1714) that confirmed it, Rákóczi's interests were ignored. It was clear that in political and diplomatic terms he had been abandoned by his French protectors.

The disappointing outcome of the peace talks severely depressed the Hungarian leader. Within a year matters took another turn for the worse. In September 1715 Louis XIV, who had personally been quite fond of the prince, died. It seemed pointless for Rákóczi to continue to stay at Versailles. Indeed, at this low point Rákóczi began to wonder about the deeper meaning of his life. Disillusioned with politics and in need of spiritual regeneration, he decided to enter a Camadulian monastery in Grosbois, near Paris. From April 1716 to August 1717 "Count Saros" immersed himself in deep and sincere spiritual contemplation. It was evident to all that the incredible exertions of recent years had strained him to the limit.

But Rákóczi's will to fight was far from broken. In the summer of 1716 war broke out between Vienna and the Porte. Soon both Rákóczi in France and Bercsényi in Poland began to receive letters from the Porte urging them to prepare their countrymen for an Ottoman-backed uprising against the Habsburgs. The prince quickly adjusted from a contemplative to a combative frame of mind. He sent instructions to Poland for his old comrades Miklos Bercsényi, Mihaly Csaky, Antal Eszterhazy, Simon Forgach, and others to organize their men and move to Khotyn on the Polish-Ottoman border. Rákóczi's old Ottoman specialist, János Papai, was again sent to the Porte. Within weeks of emerging from the monastery the prince, escorted by an Ottoman *aga*, was on his way to Adrianople to meet with the sultan.

Unfortunately for Rákóczi and his colleagues, their efforts were in vain. Before they could formulate their plans the Ottomans had signed with Austria the Peace of Passarowitz (1718). This same peace that had buried Cantemir's hopes of returning to Moldavia now crushed the dreams of the Hungarian exiles. The Ottomans were now confronted with the problem of what to do with the émigrés, who, because of their proximity to the borders of their homeland, posed a threat to international stability, yet whose services might in the future be of use to them. They applied the same solution that was later used in Orlyk's case. Rákóczi and his companions were "invited" to take up residence in isolated Rodosto on the Black Sea. Thus, the Hungarian leader began his long and frustrating sojourn in the "land of the accursed infidel."

In summary, the initial phase of the émigrés' activity abroad witnessed their transformation from rebellious leaders of native elites to helpless pawns of foreign powers. This metamorphosis was most evident in the cases of Rákóczi, Orlyk, and especially Leszczynski (whose credentials as an anti-absolutist leader were the weakest and whose experience as a foreign pawn the longest), the three men whose attempts to recoup their losses would be the longest and most persistent. For these three the foreign power which seemed to be a most promising source of military and political support was the Ottoman Porte. Confronted in the north by the Habsburgs and the even more threatening Russians, the Ottomans were quick to see the potential usefulness of the Hungarian, Polish, and Ukrainian "malcontents." Diplomatic support for and encouragement of co-operation between the émigrés and the Ottomans usually came from France, the traditional ally of the Porte against Habsburg and Russian expansionism. In the cases of Patkul and Cantemir, Russia was the key supporter. Because the main areas of Peter's expansionist plans were the Baltic and the Black Sea areas, Patkul in the north and later Cantemir in the south presented the tsar with potentially useful options.

The obvious feature common to each instance of foreign support of émigré activity was that such support was geared to the interests of the great powers rather than to those of the East European émigrés. Thus, from the outset of exile it was evident that the cause of East European rights and liberties and the struggle against absolutism could only be raised again if and when other foreign absolutist powers allowed it.

PHASE TWO: THE STRUGGLE TO SURVIVE

During this period the émigrés' hopes of attaining their maximal goal of returning to political power in their homelands faded. At home their former supporters had reached a modus vivendi with their absolutist sovereigns, while in the international arena their former patrons had opted for peace. These developments threatened the émigrés not only with prolonged exile but also with extinction as politically significant entities. Therefore, during this second phase their minimal goal – to look after their personal interests – became their primary focus of concern.

Patkul

The Livonian leader was an exception to this general trend. For him the second phase of exile brought numerous opportunities to pursue his cause, mainly because Patkul's exile preceded the Great Northern War and he therefore had before him options that were not available to the other émigrés, whose exiles commenced only in the concluding phases of the war.

Disappointed by the slipshod manner in which the Saxons had conducted the invasion of Livonia, Patkul entered Russian service in the summer of 1701[34]. Soon afterwards Peter I dispatched him on the first important mission to recruit high-ranking European officers for the Russian army. Before setting out, he savoured a moment of personal satisfaction when, on 27 April 1702 in Moscow, a group of Swedish prisoners of war were forced to witness the public denunciation and burning of the Swedish polemics against him.[35] On his journey west Patkul stopped in Baturyn, Mazepa's residence, where he spent ten days in talks with the *hetman*. In Vienna, on his own initiative Patkul set in motion talks that were aimed at bringing the Habsburgs into the Northern War on the side of the Russians and the Saxons. Pleased with the Livonian's initiative, Peter recalled him to Russia, promoted him to the rank of permanent privy councillor and major-general, and in August 1703 dispatched him again to the West, this time with full plenipotentiary powers, to look after the tsar's diplomatic interests in Europe.

During this second tour Patkul succeeded in convincing the Poles to declare war on Sweden. (Originally August II entered the conflict in his capacity as elector of Saxony, not as king of Poland). However, an attempt to gain Prussian support against the Swedes failed. Patkul blamed this failure on the disorganization and ineptness of the Russian diplomats and, with the tsar's blessings, set about to organize a network of Russian diplomatic residents all over the continent. In the summer of 1704 the energetic and talented Livonian switched from diplomacy to warfare. On the tsar's orders he took over command of the Saxon artillery and helped his former patron, August II, to recapture Warsaw from the Swedes in September of 1704. Several weeks later he became the commander of a Russian expeditionary force of twelve thousand operating in Poland. This set the stage for a conflict, fuelled by old resentments, which burst out between Patkul and his Saxon allies. Unable to obtain support and provisions from August II for his literally starving troops, the Livonian retreated to Habsburg territory. The move infuriated the Saxons, who considered it an unauthorized wilful attempt by Patkul to withdraw from the front. Therefore, on 8 December 1705, on the orders of the Saxon generals and without the knowledge of August II, Patkul was arrested by Saxon soldiers and incarcerated in Sonnenstein Castle in Saxony.

This unprecedented arrest of a minister of the tsar quickly became a cause célèbre in Europe. Protests poured in from the Habsburg and Russian courts, and European newspapers discussed the event in great detail. August, however, stood behind his ministers and generals. Patkul, for his part, prepared to spend what he thought would be a brief time in prison until the episode could be cleared up. But in the late summer of 1706 his predicament took a sudden turn for the worse. Charles launched a surprise offensive into Saxony, and Patkul faced the very real possibility of capture by the Swedes.

With his hereditary lands at the mercy of the Swedes, August II was forced to negotiate. As expected, Charles was harsh and unyielding. He demanded that August renounce his claim to the Polish throne, break his alliance with Russia, and provide the Swedes with provisions and quarters in Saxony. Finally, Charles insisted that "the Swedish subject ... General J.R. von Patkul" be surrendered to the Swedes. After some hesitation August acquiesced. Once again Peter I sent off a series of irate letters to the Habsburg, English, and Danish courts, complaining about the "unheard-of treatment" of his "innocent minister," and requested that they intercede with Charles on Patkul's behalf.

But Patkul's fate was sealed. Shortly before, his old comrade and fellow Livonian refugee, Otto Arnold von Paykul, had been captured and executed by the Swedes. There was every reason to believe that a similar fate awaited Patkul, who had caused the Swedes immeasurably more harm. Charles XII proved to be even more vengeful than expected. Not only did he confirm the death sentence imposed on Patkul back in 1694, but he also ordered that before his execution the Livonian was to be broken on the wheel. The night before his death Patkul had a long, soul-searching conversation with the Swedish chaplain. During the conversation he stated, "It is the *Reduktion*, which has impoverished so many, that is responsible for the crimes which are now laid at my feet."[36] Repeatedly, he swore that he had fought for the rights of his fatherland and his brother noblemen. With tears in his eyes he asked, "What else could I have done?" The next day, on 10 October 1707, after a horribly inept and excruciatingly prolonged torture, Patkul died.

Cantemir

Although Cantemir disliked living in Russia, he concentrated with great single-mindedness after 1718 on making his way to the top of his host country's social and political ladder.[37] In 1719 Cantemir moved to St Petersburg, where he met Anastasia, the beautiful, vivacious eighteen-year-old daughter of Prince Ivan

Trubetskoi, field marshal of the Russian army. Within days of meeting her the forty-six-year-old widower (his first wife, Cassandra Cantacuzene, had died in 1713) proposed to Anastasia, and on 14 January 1720, with Tsar Peter and his wife serving as sponsors, the couple was married. To please Peter and perhaps to symbolize the beginning of a new phase in his life, Cantemir shaved off his beard, cast off his Moldavian robes, and henceforth dressed in the European fashion.

During the next few years the former *hospodar* became deeply involved in Russian affairs. In 1720 he polemicized at length with Feofan Prokopovich about the best means of bringing up Russia's youth. It was at Cantemir's urging that Peter I assumed the title of emperor in 1721.[38] And Cantemir's activism bore fruit. On 21 February 1721 Peter appointed him privy councillor and member of the senate. This appointment made the Moldavian émigré a member of a select group of men, such as A.D. Menshikov, G.I. Golovkin, P.P. Shafirov, and P.A. Tolstoi, who together with the tsar governed Russia.[39]

As a member of the senate Cantemir participated in a series of important reforms. His signature appeared on decrees that regulated the status of church serfs, established the College of Commerce, and abrogated the autonomy of the Don Cossacks. Perhaps the most important decision in which he took part dealt with the question of imperial succession. Apparently, he was one of the senators who supported the change in the system of succession that would allow the tsar to appoint his successor during his lifetime. The politically agile Moldavian had more than a passing interest in this decision. Through a court intrigue initiated by Peter Tolstoi and designed to remove his rival, Aleksander Menshikov, and the latter's patroness, Empress Catherine, from the tsar's favour, Cantemir's eldest daughter, Maria, was brought to Peter's attention. Maria was no beauty; however, she had what Catherine woefully lacked – intelligence and education. This, it seems, was what Peter needed at this point in his life, for he quickly fell in love with her. Because Catherine was childless, Peter even offered to marry Maria if she were to bear him a son. Thus, in 1722 it appeared that Cantemir had every chance of becoming the father-in-law of the Russian emperor.

Rákóczi and Orlyk

The immediate goal of both Rákóczi and Orlyk after they were interned in the Ottoman empire was to extricate themselves from the "godless Babylon." Up to the Ottoman-Habsburg peace treaty of 1718 Rákóczi still had hopes of concluding a formal treaty with the Porte and, with its support, of regaining Transylvania. The treaty, however, dashed these hopes. Even before it had been signed, the Ottomans openly scoffed at Rákóczi's ambitious plans to raise a new *kuruc* army when he could hardly maintain his entourage of eighty men.[40] None the less, the Ottomans treated Rákóczi well in Rodosto. They provided him with a generous subsidy, set aside an entire street in the town for his followers, assigned a detachment of Janissaries to guard against assasination attempts, referred to him as "King of Transylvania," and allowed visitors from abroad to come and go freely.[41] Yet Rákóczi himself was not allowed to leave Rodosto. In 1722 his options became even more limited when the French, who had recently concluded a peace with Austria, coldly refused to invite him back to France.[42]

The longer Rákóczi stayed in Rodosto, the more unrealistic became his plans. He attempted to mediate between Russia and the Ottoman Empire and then to convince both of them to strike against Austria.[43] When no one, including his closest associates, treated these proposals seriously, Rákóczi tried to have the Porte appoint him prince of Moldavia and Wallachia, hoping that he could use this position as a stepping stone to the princedom of Transylvania.[44] Finally, in 1728 he became so discouraged that he was willing to give up his political ambitions altogether if he were allowed to return to "Christendom" and live as befitted his station in life. To achieve this goal, he planned to marry Constantina Jabłonowska, one of the wealthiest women in Poland and a distant relative of Stanisław Leszczynski. It was clear to all but Rákóczi that such a marriage would complicate August II's relations with Vienna and that the latter would therefore never allow it. Moreover, Rákóczi never received any confirmation that Jabłonowska was willing to accept his proposal of marriage in the first place.[45]

The prince did experience a few happy moments in Rodosto, however. In 1727 his son, György, escaped from Vienna and joined him there. But even this event had its dark side. The youth's restless nature soon brought his father more problems than satisfaction. Moreover, the tutor whom Rákóczi hired for the youth, a Dane named Wilhelm Bohn, turned out to be a Habsburg agent.[46] With the help of Bohn's reports the Habsburgs were well informed about the Hungarian leader's slow slide into political obscurity.

Orlyk's predicament was, in certain ways, similar to Rákóczi's. He too whiled away long, frustrating years in Salonika, his place of internment. However, because he never attained the prestige and renown of Rákóczi, the conditions of his confinement were correspondingly less comfortable. Orlyk's subsidy was a fraction of that which Rákóczi received; his entourage consisted of only two to three personal servants (his family and remaining associates were scattered throughout Europe); and a modest inn constituted his quarters. But then, unlike Rákóczi, the Ukrainian leader had never claimed to be a sovereign ruler.[47]

The two exiles quickly established contact. Immediately after Orlyk's arrival in Salonika in 1722, Rákóczi sent him a gracious letter of greeting. Orlyk replied in kind, and for several years the two continued to exchange pleasantries. But since Orlyk wanted to maintain good contacts with the Habsburg court at this point, while Rákóczi hoped to win Russian support, any serious co-operation between them was out of the question.[48]

Dispirited by his confinement, Orlyk concluded that his only hope was to seek Russian amnesty. After Peter's death in 1725 his chances of reaching this objective suddenly soared. There were even rumours that he might return to Ukraine as *hetman*, since the office was unoccupied. All of these hopes rested on the support that Charles Fredrick, duke of Holstein and a favourite of Empress Catherine I of Russia, seemed willing to provide the Ukrainian émigré, whom he had known personally from the days of the Great Northern War. Moreover, General Sztenflicht, Holstein's envoy to St Petersburg, was at the time courting Orlyk's daughter, whom he eventually married.[49] But court intrigues in St Petersburg led to the duke's fall from favour. This in turn ruined Orlyk's chances for an amnesty. By 1727 he was mired in a state of hopelessness and depression.

Leszczynski

After his patron, Charles XII, was killed in 1718 and especially after the negotiators of the Nystad Treaty with Russia (1721) totally ignored his interests, Stanisław Leszczynski's plight became as unenviable as those of Rákóczi and Orlyk. A biographer of the Polish king-in-exile describes thus his situation in the early 1720's: "Amid illusions which contrasted ever more glaringly with reality, one year passed after another. One could conclude that Stanisław's active [political] life had come to an end. The nominal sovereign of the Commonwealth ... was slipping into obscurity. Actually, Stanisław Leszczynski – one called him 'King' only out of politeness – had become a private individual dependent on charity, an exile without any prospect of returning home."[50] Perhaps the extremely religious Leszczynski gained some solace from the fact that, unlike Rákóczi and Orlyk, he was not confined to the "barbarous Babylon" of the Ottoman Empire but lived instead in the town of Wessenburg in French Alsace. However, his material situation was most desperate. Only with great difficulty was he able to feed his family and small entourage of about fifteen threadbare attendants and companions.[51] In fact, during the years at Wissemburg Leszczynski's concerns about how to keep his creditors at bay often overshadowed political issues.

Then, on 23 March 1725, the unbelievable happened. A courier arrived from Versailles with an astounding request: would Leszczynski agree to have his only daughter, Maria, marry Louis xv? Dumbfounded, Leszczynski fainted when he first heard the proposal. For years he had been trying to arrange a suitable marriage for Maria, who, incidentally, was neither beautiful nor talented, but he had never expected anything like this. When his daughter arrived and saw her father effusively giving thanks to God, she asked whether news had arrived summoning him back to the Polish throne. "No, my daughter," he replied, "heaven has been even more generous to us. You are the Queen of France!"[52]

In an effort to offer an explanation for this incredible turn of events, many historians have argued that court intrigue at Versailles had a decisive impact on the decision.[53] The regent, the duke of Bourbon, and especially his clever mistress, Madame de Prie, wanted the sixteen-year-old Louis xv to have a wife who would be malleable, lacking in powerful backers and eternally grateful to Bourbon for arranging the marriage. To the regent and his mistress the rather mediocre, impoverished daughter of the Polish king-in-exile fitted these specifications perfectly. Dynastic interests also played an important role in the decision. The sickly Louis xv had previously been engaged to the eight-year-old infanta of Spain, and it was feared that he might die before his bride-to-be was capable of providing France with a successor. Therefore, a wife of child-bearing age had to be found quickly. Finally, the possibility that France would at long last have the opportunity of placing its own candidate – although not necessarily Leszczynski – on the Polish throne intrigued some French statesmen.[54] In any case, on 4 September 1725 Leszczynski became the father-in-law of the mightiest ruler in Europe. This was an event of great portent for Eastern Europe, since, in view of August II's failing health, the question of the Polish succession loomed large on the political horizon.

PHASE THREE: THE LAST HURRAH

In the final phase of their activity abroad, the East European émigrés experienced a revival of their political activity and significance. However, their brief return to political prominence produced only minimal results. Indeed, it served as little more than their swan-song on the East European political scene.

Cantemir

By 1722 the Moldavian *hospodar* had reached the pinnacle of his influence in Russia. That his daughter Maria, who was the tsar's mistress, had become pregnant was a great asset to Cantemir. Jacques de Campredon, the French ambassador to Russia, informed Louis xv that "Empress Catherine ... fears the tsar's inclination for the prince of Moldavia's daughter. Her father is clever.

If she [Cantemir's daughter] should bear a son, the tsar, at the insistence of the prince of Moldavia, could repudiate his wife in order to marry this favourite mistress, who could give him a male heir to the throne. This fear is not without basis ... I myself have had occasion to observe the influence that the prince of Moldavia enjoys with the tsar."[55]

In the summer of 1722 Peter I launched another of his numerous campaigns. In the early eighteenth century, Safavid Iran had slipped into anarchy. Hoping to profit from the turmoil, both Russia and the Ottomans moved in to occupy Safavid lands and to check each other's influence in the area. Peter, accompanied by Cantemir, proceeded down the Volga with an army of twenty-three thousand men. The ensuing campaign provided Cantemir with one last opportunity to strike against his old Ottoman enemies.

As the Russians entered Safavid territory, Cantemir's role in the campaign took on great importance. Because of his intimate knowledge of Oriental affairs he was constantly at Peter's side as his adviser and as a member of the war council. Moreover, the tsar appointed him chief of the field chancellery, with special responsibility for preparing manifestos in Turkish and Iranian.[56] Over one thousand copies of these pamphlets were distributed to the Muslim population. In addition to propaganda, Cantemir was also charged with carrying out military intelligence.

In the midst of the campaign disturbing news arrived from Astrakhan, where the tsar's entourage had been left. Maria Cantemir had given birth to a stillborn child. Peter was deeply disappointed, and the entire Cantemir family fell into disgrace.[57] To make matters worse, Dimitrie Cantemir was struck by a sudden illness. Under the circumstances, he decided to leave the army to recuperate on his estate in Ukraine. He died there on 21 August 1723.

The Cantemir story had a sequel. In 1739 another Russian-Ottoman war broke out. Shortly before the conflict two nephews of Dimitrie Cantemir, Constantin and Dimitrie, the sons of his brother Antioh, escaped from the Ottoman empire and offered their services to Field Marshal Wilhelm von Münnich, the commander of the Russian army. Constantin, the elder of the two, played a prominent role in the conflict. He helped to organize a regiment of Moldavian émigrés living in Ukraine and secretly dispatched a number of them to Moldavia to recruit new adherents and to spread anti-Russian propaganda.

In August 1739 Constantin accomplished something that his uncle had only dreamed of doing in 1717. With a unit of one thousand men he moved ahead of the advancing Russian army of fifty-six thousand and, in a surprise move, captured the Moldavian capital of Jassy. While the current *hospodar*, Gheorge Ghica, and most of the senior boyars fled to the side of the Ottomans, many of the junior boyars and most of the clergy welcomed Constantin, whose name assured him immediate popularity, and the advancing Russians. On 5 September 1739 it seemed that Dimitrie Cantemir's old plans would finally come to fruition. Twenty-two representatives of the Moldavian elite concluded a projected treaty with Münnich whereby Moldavia recognized Russian sovereignty and the boyars were assured of their traditional privileges. But because of a sudden deterioration of Russia's diplomatic position, the treaty was never ratified. Münnich's army was forced to withdraw, and Moldavia returned to Ottoman control. After these events the fate of the two Cantemirs was unremarkable. Constantin died in 1776 after retiring from the Russian army with the rank of general. His brother Dimitrie attained the rank of major and died in 1758.[58]

It is noteworthy that it was Dimitrie Cantemir's nephews and not his famous and talented son Antioh, who continued to fight for his cause. In part, this was because Antioh was serving as Russia's ambassador in London and Paris during the war. Certainly, there can be no doubt that he cherished and respected what his father had stood for. In England he saw to the publication of his history of the Ottoman empire, and in France he polemicized with Voltaire about the latter's misrepresentation of his father's actions. In a letter to Antioh, his sister Maria even raised the possibility of a return to Moldavia: "Perhaps some day we will see each other in our old homeland and we will live there in peace. But it seems to me that he who would become prince of the country must, above all, take on the task of ruling. Thus, if your destiny is to be prince of our homeland, it will be necessary to bid farewell to the comfortable pleasures of a philosopher's life."[59] In time, Antioh made his choice. He became one of the leading writers of eighteenth-century Russian literature. And after 1739 his father's cause was left without a standard-bearer.

Leszczynski, Orlyk, and Rákóczi

In the late 1720s and early 1730s the Polish, Ukrainian, and Hungarian émigrés had occasion to recognize their common interests and to co-operate. The circumstances which encouraged this unusual demonstration of East European solidarity were associated with Leszczynski's attempts to regain the Polish crown. In 1727 August II became seriously ill, and the question of his succession surfaced as a major issue in European politics. Convinced that his chances of returning to Poland were good, Leszczynski began to lobby for support. He pointed out to the French that the long-cherished goal of France's Eastern policy – the creation of an anti-Russian and anti-Habsburg barrier consisting of Sweden, Poland-Lithuania, and the Ottoman empire – could easily be achieved if he were king of Poland. Moreover, Louis xv's prestige would be enhanced if his father-in-law were to become king. Although Cardinal Fleury, France's first minister, was not convinced by these arguments, pressure from Versailles forced him to provide Leszczynski with cautious French support.[60]

It was much more difficult for Leszczynski to convince Austria and particularly Russia to agree to his return to the Polish throne. To this end, he employed an interesting argument. In his communications with the Russian and Austrian courts he stressed that August II would undoubtedly attempt to ensure his son's succession to the Polish throne. Leszczynski argued that if this occurred, it would lead to the establishment of hereditary rule and, along with it, the imposition of absolutism in the Commonwealth. In fact, in the final years of his reign August II actually did make preparations for an absolutist coup in Poland. Leszczynski warned that if a land as large and as populous as the Commonwealth became an absolutist state, it would upset the balance of power in Europe, not to mention the difficulties this would create for Russia and Austria. But if he were elected, the Commonwealth's traditional rights and privileges would be assured and the international status quo preserved.[61] Despite Leszczynski's arguments, the Russian and Austrian courts made it clear that they would not accept a "creature" of Charles XII on the Polish throne. It was at this point that Orlyk and Rákóczi entered into Leszczynski's plans.

On 1 June 1726 Orlyk noted the following in his diary: "After Mass, a Frenchman who works for various French merchants here in Salonika came running to my lodgings and informed me that some officer had arrived from France ... with a letter for me. I guessed that if it was from France, it could be from none other than King Stanisław, and indeed it was."[62] In his letter Leszczynski proposed to Orlyk that he should again concentrate on raising "a revolution in Ukraine." By this Leszczynski meant that in case of open conflict with Russia, Orlyk, supported by the Tatars and Ottomans, was to organize a diversionary movement among the Ukrainian Cossacks to prevent the Russians from concentrating their full strength in Poland and thus preventing Leszczynski's return. If Orlyk agreed, Leszczynski would spread the idea of a potential revolution in Ukraine among the courts of Europe as proof that Russia would find it difficult to oppose his return. Thus, Orlyk's cause would benefit from Leszczynski's success. Orlyk was not enthusiastic about the letter from France. He had already spent many fruitless years trying to propagate the idea of a Ukrainian uprising against the Russians. Furthermore, he had never had great confidence in Leszczynski or in his chances for success. In his diary Orlyk noted that Leszczynski's suggestion was "a political trick by means of which they [Leszczynski and his French supporters] want to draw me to their side against Moscow and, taking advantage of me, use me for their own ends."[64] Finally,

Leszczynski was urging Orlyk to remain in the Ottoman empire, while Orlyk himself wanted nothing more than to leave it.

But Leszczynski persisted. In March 1727 he assured Orlyk that France and its allies would be willing to provide him with financial and diplomatic aid, also noting that "Your Excellency should not delay in demonstrating by means of memorials to the French, English, and Dutch envoys your readiness, for the sake of public welfare, to create a diversion against Moscow by means of a great Ukrainian revolution."[65] As his hopes for amnesty dimmed, Orlyk decided to give Leszczynski a more encouraging reply. The result was a remarkable document which provides both a vivid and generally accurate expression of Ukrainian discontent with Russian overlordship and an insight into Orlyk's manipulation of the idea of a revolution in Ukraine for his own immediate purposes.

Orlyk's letter begins with a profuse expression of gratitude not only for Leszczynski's concern for his personal fate but also for his wish to help the "Cossack nation" to regain its ancient liberties. The letter then launches into Orlyk's main theme: "There can be no doubt of a revolution in Ukraine; its sparks are already smoldering and need only to be fanned."[66] After this comes a detailed account of how Moscow had turned Ukraine into a "place of carnage" and how it had done away with Ukrainian rights and privileges and undermined the Ukrainian elite, assigning Muscovites to rule the land in its stead. As a result, great numbers of Cossacks had fled to the Zaporozhian *sich*, which was now filled to overflowing. Orlyk estimated, or rather exaggerated, that there were over sixty thousand well-armed and experienced soldiers there, "for in Ukraine every peasant is a soldier." Finally, he made what his Polish colleagues may have considered to be an unfortunate analogy: Ukraine, Orlyk declared, now awaited him as it had once awaited Khmelnytsky. Armed with this and similar letters, Leszczynski convinced the French that the possibility of a Ukrainian revolution was very real and encouraged them to back him and Orlyk more resolutely.

Although Leszczynski was more concerned about the possibility of Russian than of Habsburg intervention in Poland, he also worked to obtain the support of Rákóczi.[67] Apparently, the latter did not need much persuading. In 1729 Rákóczi began to shower the Porte with letters urging it to support Leszczynski's claim to the Polish throne. The reasons for his support of the ex-king were not difficult to fathom. If the Ottomans helped Leszczynski, this would lead to a clash between them and the Habsburgs, and in this event the services of the Hungarian émigrés would again be in demand at the Porte and in France as well.

Even before the Porte made any commitments to Leszczynski, Rákóczi began to fantasize about leading an Ottoman army of forty thousand into

Hungary, whose populace, he was convinced, yearned for his return. Should the Ottomans be unable to provide him with such a force, he planned to solicit French support. Specifically, he hoped to convince the French to land a force of fifty thousand on the Dalmatian coast, where Rákóczi's Croatian supporters would join it in an attack against the soft underbelly of the Habsburg defence in Hungary.[68] In a vein similar to Orlyk's he wrote to France: "There is no doubt that the feelings of the [Hungarian] nation are the same today as they were before. Its grievances were mitigated somewhat at first [after Szatmár], but since the Treaty of Passarowitz matters have reverted to their previous state. I am no less enthusiastic about my fatherland, and I am still bound by my pledge to uphold the liberty and rights of my principality."[69] Although neither the French nor the Ottomans gave any indication that they treated Rákóczi's proposals seriously, the Habsburgs, who had planted a spy in the prince's household, were clearly disturbed by his plans.[70] Thus, in the late 1720s the three East European émigrés co-operated, with a certain degree of success, in summoning up the spectre of both a Ukrainian and a Hungarian rebellion, thereby aiding Leszczynski in his efforts in Poland.

In 1730 Leszczynski recruited Orlyk's son, Hryhor, an officer in the Polish army, for his cause.[71] After a series of briefings in France Hryhor was dispatched to Istanbul to urge the Porte to release his father so that he might join the Zaporozhians on the Lower Dnieper and, with the Tatars, prepare for a thrust against the Russians. This was the first of many important missions Hryhor would perform for the French, Leszczynski, and his father. But apart from providing Hryhor with an opportunity to discuss matters with his father in Salonika, the mission did not produce any concrete results. The Ottomans were not prepared to irritate the Russians by releasing the elder Orlyk. Upon his return to France in December 1730 Hryhor was debriefed by Leszczynski, by the French foreign minister, Germain-Louis Chauvelin, and by the ever-sceptical Fleury. He also had the honour of being received at Versailles by Louis XV and Queen Maria. Within weeks of his return Hryhor was again sent to the East. This time his destination was the Crimea, and his mission was to convince the khan to arrange for his father's release. During his three-month-long stay in the khanate Hryhor did manage to obtain the khan's promise to help Orlyk and Leszczynski in every way he could. Armed with this encouraging news, he returned to France.

Finally, on 1 February 1733 August II died. The following summer Leszczynski, disguised as a merchant, dashed across Europe in order to arrive in Warsaw before the electoral *sejm*. The indefatigable Hryhor was one of his companions on this hazardous trip. Leszczynski's appearance in Warsaw in August 1733 caused a sensation. In contrast to the situation in 1705, this time he was the popular choice of the *szlachta*, which had had its fill of foreign rulers and wanted only a "Piast" – that is, a native Pole – to occupy the throne of the Commonwealth. On II September, before a vast throng of noblemen, Leszczynski was for the second time proclaimed king of Poland and grand duke of Lithuania. This was the moment he had longed for. But jubilation soon gave way to grief. Shortly after his election Russian troops crossed the border and moved on Warsaw. Leszczynski was now forced to flee to Gdansk.

For the second time Leszczynski learned that it was much easier to win the crown of Poland-Lithuania than to retain it. Instead of providing him with a strong supporting army, France sent a nominal force of two thousand to Gdansk, which was soon surrounded by Russians. Meanwhile, in the south the much-awaited diversion failed to materialize. Although the Ottomans finally allowed Orlyk to leave Salonika in March 1734 to join his "army," the move came too late. Just as Orlyk was to arrive at the *sich*, the Zaporozhians succumbed to Russian offers of complete amnesty. In May 1734 they swore allegiance to Empress Anna Ivanovna and returned to Ukraine.[72] Rákóczi, too, failed to mobilize any forces.[73] These disheartening developments were for him the final disillusionment in a tragic career, and on 8 April 1735 Ferenc II Rákóczi, prince of Transylvania, passed away in Rodosto.

The co-operation of the East European émigrés did not end at this point. In November 1734, when Leszczynski's supporters formed the Confederation of Dzikow to fight for their duly elected king against Russian intervention, it was Hryhor Orlyk who acted as their main liaison with their king. It is noteworthy that the Dzikow confederates appealed for aid against the Russians not only to France, Sweden, and the Ottomans but also to the "oppressed estates" of Hungary, Bohemia, Livonia, and Ukraine. As Józef Feldman has sardonically remarked, it was as if the confederates were preparing the ground for the slogan which later generations of East European "freedom fighters" were to address so often to their equally oppressed neighbours: "We are fighting for our freedom – and for yours."[74] However, the *szlachta* levies of the Dzików Confederation were no match for the regular Russian regiments. After installing Friedrich August of Saxony on the Polish throne, the Russians forced Leszczynski and his French backers to the negotiating table. As a result of the talks of 1735, Leszczynski was forced to give up his claim to the throne. In return he was allowed to keep the empty title of king of Poland and received the duchy of Lorraine, where he retired to immerse himself until his death in 1766 in scholarly pursuits and political theorizing.

Ensconced in his comfortable "capital" of Luneville, Leszczynski could afford to cease his political adventurism. But the other émigrés could not. The two

Orlyks and Ferenc Rákóczi's two sons, József and György, continued their struggle against the Russians and Austrians respectively. Their efforts now took place in a new context, that of the Russo-Ottoman War of 1735–39 and the Ottoman-Habsburg War of 1737–9. Hostilities were initiated by the Tatar khan, Kaplan Girei, who launched a series of raids into Ukraine while the Russians were engaged in Poland. The Russians retaliated and the Porte came to the defence of its Crimean vassal. After some hesitation Russia's ally, Austria, declared war on the Ottomans, and the whole of southeastern Europe became embroiled in the conflict.

Confronted by a war on two fronts, the Ottomans eagerly sought to utilize the services of Pylyp Orlyk and Rákóczi's eldest son, József. Since Orlyk had no military force at his disposal, his services consisted mainly of advising the Ottomans on the fighting on the Ukrainian border and of producing anti-Russian propaganda, in which role he was apparently quite effective. Even before the outbreak of war between Russia and the Porte, Empress Anna Ivanovna complained that "Orlyk ... not only secretly continues to spread his intrigues and malicious suggestions against our empire, but this year [1734] he was sent to the Crimean khan and there, in proximity to our borders, he creates among our Little Russian subjects unrest and incitement to hostile acts against us, especially encouraging conflict and disagreement between us and the Porte."[76] In 1738, during a lull in the fighting, the Ottomans decided to use Orlyk elsewhere. In February the grand vizier ordered Orlyk to move to Vidin to join József Rákóczi, whom the Ottomans were preparing to send into Transylvania, as his adviser.[76] Orlyk, for his part, was irritated by the assignment. In a letter to the grand vizier, he enumerated the reasons why he thought the appointment inappropriate: "I am more than slightly distressed by my appointment as adviser to Prince Rákóczi. This assignment is neither valid nor compatible with my rank. I have always been considered a leader of a nation by the Porte and, as such, have rightful claims against Russia. It is not in my interests, which are at one with those of the Porte, to be kept away from Ukraine, where my presence is necessary under the present circumstances."[77]

The matter was resolved unexpectedly when on 10 November 1738 József Rákóczi contracted the plague and died.[78] But this did not signal the end of the ties between the Ukrainian and Hungarian émigrés. In January 1739 Habsburg border officials in Bohemia, Moravia, and Silesia received an interesting circular that stated that Rákóczi's youngest son, György, had left France after his brother's death and was on his way to join the Ottomans "to become their unworthy and un-Christian tool, as had been his deceased brother."[79] Moreover, Hryhor Orlyk, "a famous Cossack who was often used by France in Polish affairs," was probably accompanying Rákóczi as his mentor. Unfortunately, no further information is available about the mission which the young Hungarian and Ukrainian émigrés had undertaken.

After 1739 the Orlyks alone continued to be politically active. The sixty-seven-year-old Pylyp Orlyk continued to offer his services to any power that had a quarrel with Russia. In 1740 a new opportunity appeared – or rather, an old one reappeared. Sweden, the original patron of the Mazepists, declared war on Russia. However, before Pylyp and Hryhor Orlyk could establish a working relationship with the Swedes, the conflict was over. With it disappeared Pylyp Orlyk's last chance to play a meaningful political role. On 7 June 1742, basing his report on information he had received from Jassy in Moldavia, the French ambassador to the Porte informed his government that "M. Orlick est mort."[80] After his father's death Hryhor and several aged Ukrainian émigrés continued to work against Russian interests and to remind European statesmen of Ukraine's "lost rights and liberties." In 1758, after the death of his last two comrades, Hryhor sadly noted in his journal that "of the entire phalanx of those who wished to liberate our land, only I remain."[81] Soon he too was gone. On 14 November 1759 Hryhor Orlyk, awarded the title of count and rank of general for his services to France, died as a result of wounds received while fighting for the French in the Seven Years' War. Thus did the final chapter in the history of the first generation of East European émigrés come to an end.

THE ÉMIGRÉS' LITERARY LEGACY

During their long years abroad the émigrés acted as advisers and "area specialists" for their foreign patrons and hosts. They gathered intelligence about their enemies and, in some cases, participated in covert activities against them. They also undertook another characteristic émigré activity – writing. Whether preparing propaganda for their own and their patrons' causes or producing serious scholarly, political, and literary works, all of the émigrés engaged in literary activity during their exile. Several of them even became highly successful in their endeavours.

Cantemir

Cantemir was the most productive of the group.[82] He was well suited for the scholar's calling that he embraced during his exile. Educated in Istanbul by leading Greek and Ottoman scholars, he was intimately acquainted with the classical Greek, Latin, and Islamic cultural traditions. Few of his contemporaries could match his linguistic skills. Apart from his native Romanian, he knew Greek, Latin, French, Italian, Russian, Turkish, Persian, and Arabic.

In addition, he was an industrious and self-disciplined individual who had first-hand experience in the areas about which he wrote. His works marked not only a high point in Romanian cultural history but were also major events in European scholarship.

Prior to his exile Cantemir had already completed several essays which dealt primarily with philosophical themes. One of these, the *Istoria ieroglifica*, a satirical allegory (perhaps it was from his father that his son Antioh later inherited the gift for satire), also touched on such matters as the greed and pettiness of the boyar oligarchy and of the rival Brîncoveanu clan in particular. But it was only after his arrival in Russia that Cantemir completed his most famous works. These dealt for the most part with three main topics: Moldavian history and society; Ottoman and Islamic history and culture; and the nature of monarchical government. No longer did these works abound in the metaphysical speculation that had characterized his earlier essays. In Russia Cantemir wrote not just for his own intellectual satisfaction but with an eye for current issues that he might use to serve his and the tsar's political interests.

In 1714 Cantemir completed his *Monarchiarum physica examinatio* (An Examination of the Nature of Monarchy), which, like most of his studies, was written in Latin. Ostensibly a survey of the world's great empires and an analysis of monarchical rule, it was actually a panegyric to Peter I and Russia. In it Cantemir argued for the necessity of attacking the Ottomans because they blocked Russia's path to greatness. Ironically, this fierce opponent of Ottoman despotism also claimed that absolutism was the most effective form of government. Upon closer examination, this is not a surprising position for the defender of Moldavian rights and privileges to have taken. Even before 1711 Cantemir had implied that Moldavia would be able to expel the Ottomans only if the *hospodar* could discipline the fractious boyars. Moreover, it was no secret that he had hoped to establish himself and his line as strong hereditary rulers of Moldavia. In his treaty of alliance with Peter I, Cantemir had gone so far as to include a clause with this stipulation, and it was only the vehement protests of the boyars that had forced him to retract it.

Cantemir's anti-boyar sentiments were most evident in his *Descriptio Moldaviae* (1716), a history of Moldavia commissioned by the Berlin Academy of Sciences, to which Cantemir was elected with the help of Gottfried Leibnitz and Heinrich von Huyssen. In this work, considered a milestone of Romanian historiography, the *hospodar* stated that boyar anarchy and greed were just as responsible for Moldavia's woes as was Ottoman rule. Cantemir also intertwined scholarship and politics in his most famous work, *The History of the Growth and Decay of the Othoman Empire*, written in Latin in 1716 and published in English in 1734. Until the appearance of Josef Hammer-Purgstall's monumental study about a century later, Cantemir's work was regarded as the most authoritative account of the Ottoman empire. Its central thesis was that from 1672, primarily because of the greed and self-interest of their ministers, the Ottomans were in a state of irreversible decline. A remarkably prescient observation for the time, it was also meant to encourage Peter I to launch another war against the Porte, thereby giving Cantemir a chance to return to his homeland. Another historical work, *Hronicul Romano-Moldo-Vlahilor* (Chronicle of the Romanians, Moldavians, and Vlachs), was begun in 1717. Cantemir's last major work, the *Kniga sistima ili sostoianie muhammedanskoi religii* (Concerning the System of the Mohammedan Religion, St Petersburg 1722), was also not without its utilitarian aspects. Completed on the eve of Peter I's Persian campaign, it was meant to instruct readers about Muslim beliefs and values. During the campaign Cantemir assiduously studied ancient Islamic archaeological inscriptions. This data he collected in his *Collectanea Orientalia*, a compendium which marked the beginning of Oriental studies in Russia. But regardless of whether Cantemir wrote his works for scholarly or for political motives, their value in terms of providing precious data and rare insights was indisputable, and the prominent place which he occupied in European scholarship was well deserved.

Leszczynski

Settled in the small but highly developed duchy of Bar and Lorraine, supported by France with an annual subsidy of two million livres, Leszczynski too developed a taste for political theory and treated his tiny "kingdom" as a laboratory for experiments in good government.[83] He provided his subjects with free schools, a network of hospitals, and a financial institution for merchants in distress. All this was accomplished without going into debt or raising taxes. Little wonder that his subjects remembered him as "le bon roi, Stanislas." He was, however, more interested in impressing his Polish countrymen than his French subjects, by demonstrating to the Poles what a good ruler they had lost twice already in the past but might still regain in the future.

An excellent education, a reflective nature, and association with such men as Montesquieu, Voltaire, and Hénault, drew Leszczynski to intellectual endeavours. In 1748 his most important work, the *Głos wolny wolność ubezpieczający* (The Free Voice Guaranteeing Liberty), appeared in Nancy; its purpose was "to set forth the best possible means for eliminating the abuses of the government of Poland."[85] For a man who still hoped to become king of Poland, this was an extremely sensitive undertaking. The fact was that in exile Leszczynski had reached a conclusion that contradicted views he had earlier held and that was anathema to the *szlachta* – namely, that the only antidote to the disorder that prevailed in the Commonwealth was a strong king. Apparently, the opportunity he had had to observe absolutist governments led him to acknowledge their superior effectiveness. But how was he to impress this upon his fanatically anti-absolutist countrymen? Tactfully and artfully, he began the *Głos wolny* with a flowery tribute to traditional Polish liberties, followed by stirring references to the Commonwealth's glorious past. Only after having won over his *szlachta* readers with praise of the old ways did he broach his main topic: Poland had been so great in the past because of the harmonious balance that had existed between king and nobles; it was because this balance had been upset that it was now beset with difficulties and disorder.

Under the guise of tackling the problem of the balance of power Leszczynski went on to propose a far-reaching program of reforms for the Commonwealth. He recommended the establishment of a balanced budget, an income tax of 10 per cent, a standing army of ninety thousand, the abolition of private magnate armies, and the transfer of the church's wealth to the national treasury. On the issue of royal prerogatives he was purposely ambiguous. On the one hand he favoured elected kings, with the stipulation that the candidates be Poles, and advocated a complicated system of checks and balances. On the other he argued that the king should have complete control of foreign affairs and military appointments. Thus Leszczynski created the impression that he favoured an even distribution of power, while the net effect of his proposals was actually to provide the king with more prerogatives than he currently enjoyed. Although the *Głos wolny* did not have an immediate impact on the Poles, many historians consider it to be the forerunner of the sweeping reforms introduced later in the Commonwealth. It is noteworthy that Stanisław Konarski, the moving spirit of the reform movement, was a long-time supporter of Leszczynski and his frequent guest at Luneville.

When writing in French Leszczynski was more open in his praise of absolutist government. However, he was also aware of its drawbacks. In his *Memorial de l'affermissement de la paix générale* (1748), an interesting if fanciful project for universal peace,[86] he acknowledged that absolute monarchies were much more likely to start wars than were republics. The sharp distinction that he drew between the two systems is noteworthy, and gave him the opportunity to stress the aggressiveness of the monarchies. In his view, general peace could be established only when the two leading monarchies in Europe, the Habsburg and the Bourbon, recognized each other as equals and concluded an eternal alliance.

Most of the other, almost forty works that Leszczynski completed also dealt with politics and, to a lesser extent, with philosophical topics. Many of them were exercises in dilettantism. Even the most sympathetic of his biographers would not describe him as a first-rate thinker. Yet most scholars agree that he was a noteworthy representative of the political thinking of the Enlightenment. It is to his credit that he was successful in making the transition from an extremely tradition-bound view of politics to one that reflected the most advanced European ideas on the topic.

Rákóczi

One of Rákóczi's biographers noted that his works were "an attempt to settle accounts with himself and with events."[87] He was well prepared for such a task. The schooling that the Jesuits and professors at Prague had provided him with was excellent; his command of Latin, French, German, Italian, and several Slavic languages was impressive; and the insights he garnered from his leadership of the revolt were unique. Yet it is the highly personal and spiritual nature of some of his writings that gives them a dimension that is lacking in the works of both Cantemir and Leszczynski and that makes them an especially moving reflection of the torments of an exile.

The efforts to settle accounts with himself was most evident in his *Confessio peccatoris* (Confessions of a Sinner). Begun in France at the outset of his exile and completed in Turkey after the disappointments of 1718, the work bemoaned the trials and tribulations of the émigré existence. A belletristic account of one disappointment after another, it is frequently interspersed with passages of deep religiosity and mysticism of the Jansenist variety. Its conclusion consists of a series of Latin and French prayers composed by the author during this difficult period in his life. Rákóczi's memoirs, by contrast, are, unlike the *Confessio peccatoris*, not a reflection of personal crisis and religious experience but rather an effort to counter Habsburg distortions and to delineate his personal role in the revolt.[88]

This typical émigré desire to set the record straight was very pronounced in Rákóczi. During the revolt he had founded the *Mercurius*, Hungary's first periodical, to serve as a forum for the Hungarian view of the conflict. He also had the *Recrudescunt*, a list of the "crimes against the Hungarian crown" which were formally attributed to the Habsburgs at Onod, translated into several European languages and distributed throughout Europe. When, under Habsburg influence, the French *Gazette* referred to the Hungarians as "malcontents," Rákóczi appealed to Versailles to force the paper to refer to his men as "confederates" instead. The major attempt by the exiled Hungarian leader to establish what he felt was an accurate account of the revolt was his *Histoire des revolutions de Hongrie*, published posthumously in 1739. With a chronology of the major events in Hungarian history as a framework, Rákóczi strove to prove the legitimacy of his uprising and of wars of liberation in general. To buttress his arguments, he provided the texts of the major documents relating to the revolt as an addendum to his work.

Less imposing than its title would suggest was his *Testament politique*. Written in Rodosto and addressed to his sons, who were still in Vienna, it was a treatise on court etiquette. But like Cantemir and Leszczynski, Rákóczi could not avoid making a statement about the nature of political power. Formulated in his *Politique tirée de L'Ecriture Sainte*, it was very similar to those of the other two émigrés. He too agreed that a ruler should have absolute power. But in order to explain why he had risen against the Habsburgs, Rákóczi added that this power should be challenged when the ruler acted against the interests of the people. This argument allowed him to justify his own absolutist tendencies during the revolt, while condemning those of the Habsburgs. In conclusion he reiterated what seems to have been the motto of all the émigré leaders, that he had fought not for his own power or rule but for liberty and country.[89]

Patkul

Unfortunately for Patkul, his life ended too soon for him to develop to the full his undisputed talents as a writer and pamphleteer. He certainly had the ability and the inclination to write.[90] Upon his arrival in Halle he inundated legal scholars at the university with briefs based on international law, charging Swedish mistreatment of himself and of Livonia. His arguments were presented so persuasively that he convinced the experts. During his stay in Geneva he immersed himself in the translation of Samuel von Pufendorf's treatise on politics. Although the project was probably never completed, it is characteristic that yet another émigré leader should be drawn into a discussion of the nature of politics.[91]

Orlyk

Both by inclination and by training Pylyp Orlyk was a man of the pen.[92] In his youth his performance at the Kievan Academy was so outstanding that it earned him the attention and later the friendship of the renowned Stefan Iavorsky, one of the most learned and cultivated men in the empire. Beginning as a secretary in the chancellery of the metropolitan of Kiev, Orlyk assured his meteoric rise to the chancellorship of the *hetman*ate by writing elegant panegyrics dedicated to Mazepa and other important individuals. In the first years of exile in Bender it was he who formulated the so-called Bender Constitution of 1710, which was to regulate political relationships in Ukraine in the event of the émigrés' return to power. Although it was never implemented, it has generally been considered one of the most complete statements of Ukrainian Cossack political values ever written. With the memory of Mazepa's imperious rule still fresh in their minds and with the fanatically anti-authoritarian Zaporozhians close at hand, Orlyk and his associates agreed in the constitution to a diminution of the *hetman*'s powers. Later, however, when he had had a chance to observe the governments of Europe and was no longer intimidated by the Zaporozhians, Orlyk too implied in his numerous manifestos that for the sake of better government in Ukraine the *hetman*'s powers should in fact be expanded.

In 1721, at a time when he was trying to obtain amnesty from the tsar, Orlyk produced a detailed account of Mazepa's preparations for his uprising. His chronicle took the form of a lengthy epistle to Stefan Iavorsky, who was at the time the head of the Russian church. Thoroughly tendentious, it was meant to maximize Mazepa's role in fomenting the uprising and to minimize Orlyk's. None the less, it contains a wealth of detailed, revealing, and generally convincing information about Mazepa's views and objectives. Despite Orlyk's ulterior motives for writing it, the letter to Iavorsky remains the single most important source for the history of the uprising. Significant as well is Orlyk's voluminous diary, over two thousand pages in length, which encompasses his twelve-year stay in Salonika.[93] In it he pedantically recorded his daily activities, thoughts, observations, rare moments of joy, and the much more frequent periods of depression that he experienced in Salonika. He also copied into the diary all of his incoming and outgoing correspondence. As a result, it constitutes a kind of private archive containing the numerous briefs which he dispatched to leading European statesmen. Many of these briefs represent mini-histories of Ukraine and its struggle against Russian absolutism; they reveal as well Orlyk's views on the current political situation in the Ottoman empire, Russia, and Poland.

Orlyk contemplated writing a history of the Orthodox church. A voracious reader, he went through all the libraries he could find. In order to keep up with the European press he learned French and Italian in addition to the Polish, Russian, Ukrainian, Latin, and Greek he already knew. Reading in the diary about the pleasure that he derived from books and intellectual discussion, one cannot avoid the impression that Orlyk would have been much happier as a scholar than as a political leader. It might also be noted that Orlyk's son, Hryhor, had the writer's urge as well. Despite his itinerant style of life, he planned to write a history of the Ukrainian Cossacks and even began gathering materials for it. Nothing came of the project, however, and the closest he came to historical writing was to act as Voltaire's informant about Eastern Europe.[94]

The impressive literary legacy of the East European political émigrés raises questions about their motivation for writing. Certainly, their excellent educations, high intelligence, and reflective natures predisposed them to this activity. Yet perhaps more of an explanation lies in G.B. Shaw's aphorism, "Those who can, act; those who cannot, write."[95] Or, in the words of a seventeenth-century Englishman, "The business of banished men is books." For many an émigré writing has been a surrogate for the ability to act. It has allowed exiles to continue the struggle against the enemy in the realm of ideas if not of politics, to combat his propaganda if not his armies, and to claim that right if not might was on their side. In terms of psychology, writing about their country was a way for homesick émigrés to revisit their homelands at least in their thoughts and dreams if not in reality.

Another approach to understanding the marked propensity of the émigrés for writing is through the concept of the "marginal man," which social psychologists developed early in this century. According to this concept, "The marginal man is a personality type that arises at a time and a place where, out of the conflict of races and cultures, new societies, new people and cultures are coming into existence. Fate condemns him to live, at the same time, in two worlds ... Inevitably he becomes, in his cultural milieu, the individual with the wider horizon, the keener intelligence, the more detached and rational viewpoint."[96] The applicability of this concept to the group of men we have been studying is striking. Even before they were forced into exile, they straddled two cultures. Cantemir was as much at home in Ottoman Istanbul as he was in Moldavia; Rákóczi grew up in the German court society of Vienna and returned to Hungary only as a young adult; before becoming *hetman*, Mazepa spent years at the Polish court and in travels throughout Europe; Orlyk was the scion of a Polonized Czech family that eventually settled in Lithuania, where he studied in a Jesuit college before coming to Orthodox Kiev and acclimatizing to Ukrainian Cossack society; Patkul was born in Sweden and studied in Germany; and Leszczynski travelled extensively in Europe before commencing his political career and becoming culturally as much a Frenchman as he was a Pole. It is likely that these cross-cultural experiences broadened the horizons of these men and propelled them into the leadership positions that they came to occupy. Of the function that such figures may perform one of the formulators of the concept of "marginal man" writes: "Because of his in-between situation, the marginal man may become an acute and able critic of the dominant group and its culture. This is because he combines the knowledge and insight of the insider with the critical attitude of the outsider. His analysis is not necessarily objective – there is too much emotional tension underneath to make such an attitude easy of achievement. But he is skillful in noting the contradiction and the 'hypocrisies' in the dominant culture."[97] The inner turmoil and crisis that all of the nobiliary leaders experienced as a result of their political failure and exile sharpened their perceptions all the more. But their crises also forced them into the disengagement and temporary withdrawal that often follow periods of extreme stress. A strong and talented individual can often "return" to the cause of his crisis and not only adjust to it but also attempt to provide a creative solution to it.

In a sense the writings of the East European émigrés represented an attempt to find just such a solution. This is most evident in their discussions of absolutism. Since all of them found refuge in lands under absolutist rule, they had ample opportunity to observe it at first hand. Although they had initially rebelled against it, they eventually acknowledged that strong monarchical rule was a more effective form of government than the associative systems which they had sought to defend. In their writings they tried to pass this realization on to their countrymen. Their espousal of absolutism did have some qualifications, however. Such rule had to be native-based and not imposed by foreigners. It had to be implemented with the consent of the people and for their good. All of the émigré leaders implied, of course, that they themselves were best suited to introduce this more effective form of government to their people. Their proposals came too late to regenerate the political systems prevalent in their homelands. But that they came at all was a tribute to the intelligence, dynamism, and commitment of the men who formulated them.

Chronology

Livonia

1237	German knightly orders established in Livonia.
1419	System of local diets instituted.
1472	Right of resistance confirmed.
1435–1500	Major concessions to the nobility.
1652	The *Privilegium Sigismundi Augusti*.

Moldavia

1359	Establishment of the principality of Moldavia.
1432–57	Period of strong boyar influence and growth.
1646	Codification of boyar rights.

Ukraine

1648	Establishment of the Cossack *hetman*ate.
1670–90	Beginnings of a hereditary *starshyna*.
1700s (early decades)	Formation of hereditary hierarchy of Notable Military Fellows.

ABSOLUTISM IN EASTERN EUROPE

Ottomans in Moldavia

1456	Moldavians pay first tribute to Ottomans.
1476	Renewal of Moldavian tribute payments.
1484	Ottomans occupy forts of Kilia and Bilhorod.
1538	Ottomans establish their own districts in Moldavia, strengthen control over *hospodars*.
1656–1703	The Köprülü revival; Ottoman rule intensified.

Habsburgs in Hungary

1526	Habsburgs gain sovereignty over western Hungary.
1556	War council in Vienna organizes defence of Hungary.
1671–2	Habsburg military occupation of Hungarian lands; fiscal reforms.
1687	Diet of Poszony: Hungarian nobles recognize Habsburg hereditary rights to Hungarian throne, renounce right of resistance. Transylvania under Habsburg control.
1688	The *Neoaquisitica commissio*: Habsburgs redistribute newly acquired Hungarian lands.
1689	Habsburg administrative reorganization in Hungary; German settlers brought in.

1696   Taxes imposed on lower nobility.

Vasas in Livonia

1621   Sweden conquers Livonia.
1680   The *Reduktion* implemented in Livonia.
1690   Swedenization of Livonian cultural and religious institutions
            begins.
1694   Livonian representative institutions dismantled.

Romanovs in Ukraine

1654   Ukraine accepts Romanov sovereignty.
1663   The *malorossiiskii prikaz* established.
1686   The autonomy of Ukrainian Orthodox church eliminated.
1687   Russians expand influence over election of *hetmans*.
1700–8   Plans to reorganize Ukrainian Cossack army and adminstration.
1708   Tightened Russian control over *hetman*.

Wettins in Poland-Lithuania

1697   August II elected king of Poland-Lithuania.
1698   Saxon troops brought into Lithuania.
1700   Vilnius [Wilno] Declaration alleges Lithuanian support for hereditary
            monarchy and absolutist reforms.
1700   Invasion of Livonia; plans to strengthen royal power.
1706   August II forced to abdicate.
1709–10   August II returns to throne; plans to partition Commonwealth.
1713   Renewed efforts to introduce absolutist reforms.

THE GENERAL CRISIS IN EASTERN EUROPE

Livonia

1690   Livonian delegates defend *ritterschaft* rights in Stockholm.
1692   Wenden *landtag* supports Patkul's call for resistance.
1694   Trial of Patkul and his flight from Stockholm.
1699   Patkul establishes contact with August II.
1700   January: Patkul joins Saxon invasion of Livonia; Great Northern War
            begins.
            Livonian *ritterschaft* forced to disassociate itself from Patkul.
            September: Saxons retreat from Livonia.

Poland-Lithuania

1702	Swedes invade Poland.
1704	Swedes enforce election of Leszczynski as king.
1704-10	Poland-Lithuania split into rival political camps; spread of anarchy.
1706	Treaty of Altranstadt: August II forced to resign.
1715	Confederation of Tarnogrod: *szlachta* rises against Saxon absolutism.

Ukraine

1706	Mazepa establishes secret contacts with Leszczynski and Swedes.
1708	October: Mazepa defects to Swedes.
1709	April: Zaporozhians join Mazepa.
	June: Battle of Poltava.

Moldavia

1710	November: Cantemir appointed *hospodar*.
1711	April: Cantemir's secret treaty with Peter I.
	June: Russians arrive in Jassy.
	July: Battle near Prut; Russians and Cantemir defeated.

Hungary

1703	Rákóczi begins revolt.
1704	Rákóczi elected prince of Transylvania.
1706	Rákóczi forces conquer Transylvania.
1707	Diet of Ónod declares dethronement of Habsburgs.
1708	Rákóczi loses Battle of Trencsén.
1711	Peace of Szatmár.

THE TRIUMPH OF FOREIGN ABSOLUTISM IN EASTERN EUROPE

Livonia

1694-1710	Sweden practically eliminates Livonian autonomy.
1710	New Russian overlordship rejuvenates Livonian autonomy, later liquidated by Catherine II.

Ukraine

1708	Russian military occupation of Ukraine.

1722   After end of Great Northern War, liquidation of Ukrainian autonomy begins.

Moldavia

1711   Sharp decline in Moldavian autonomy; Phanariot regime begins.

Hungary

1711   Sharp decline in Hungarian autonomy; Habsburg centralization begins.

Poland-Lithuania

1713–17   Saxon absolutist designs thwarted, but Russian influence in Commonwealth grows; sharp decline in sovereignty of Poland-Lithuania begins.

THE ÉMIGRÉ GENERATION

Johann Reinhold von Patkul (b. 1660)

1702   Joins Russian service.
1703–5   In diplomatic and military service of Peter I in Western Europe and Poland.
1705   December: arrested by Saxons.
1706   September: handed over to Swedes.
1707   October: executed by Swedes in Poland.

Dimitrie Cantemir (b. 1673)

1711   Granted lands in Ukraine.
1712   Moves to Moscow.
1716–17   On alert for possible Russian invasion of Moldavia.
1718   Treaty of Passarowitz; Cantemir concentrates on career in Russia.
1719   Moves to St Petersburg.
1720   Marries Princess Anastasia Trubetskoi.
1721   Daughter Maria becomes mistress of Peter I.
1722   Accompanies tsar on Persian campaign.
1723   Dies in Ukraine.
1739   Nephew Constantin stages brief return to Moldavia.

Ferenc Rákóczi II (b. 1676)

1711	Begins exile in Poland.
1713	Arrives in France.
1714	Treaties of Rastadt and Baden ignore his interests.
1716–17	Retreat in monastery near Paris.
1717	Prospects of Ottoman-Habsburg war; arrives in Constantinople.
1718	Treaty of Passarowitz defuses war threat.
1720	Interned in Rodosto.
1728	Contacts with Leszczynski.
1735	Dies in Rodosto.
1738	Son József participates in Ottoman offensive against Habsburgs.

Ivan Mazepa (b. 1639) and Pylyp Orlyk (b. 1672)

1709	September: Mazepa dies.
1710	Orlyk elected to lead Ukrainian émigrés.
1711	Campaign into Right Bank Ukraine.
1712–13	Ottoman diplomatic attempts to establish Orlyk on Right Bank.
1714–19	Stay in Sweden.
1720–1	Search for support in Europe.
1722	Interned by Ottomans in Salonika.
1726	Contact with Leszczynski.
1734	Released by Ottomans, moves to join Zaporozhians; Zaporozhians return to Russian overlordship.
1739	Aids Ottoman in war against Russians.
1742	Dies in Jassy.
1744–56	Son Hryhor active in anti-Russian affairs.

Stanisław Leszczynski (b. 1677)

1710	Begins exile in Szczecin.
1711	In Sweden.
1712	With Stenbok's expeditionary force on Baltic coast.
1713	In Bender; prepares to lead Polish-Tatar force into Poland.
1714	In Zweibrücken.
1718	Death of Charles XII; Leszczynski moves to Weissenburg in Alsace.
1725	Daughter Marie marries Louis XV of France.
1726	Begins preparation for contest for Polish crown.
1733–5	Struggle against August III and Russians for crown.
1736	Abdicates claims to Polish crown.
1737	King of Lorraine.
1748	Publishes *Głos wolny*.
1766	Dies in Lorraine.

Glossary

aga	an Ottoman official.
bene possessienti	Hungarian nobles with considerable landholdings
devşirme	the recruitment of Balkan Christian boys for training as Ottoman slave-soldiers (Janissaries) and slave-administrators
divan	the Ottoman imperial council
dvoriane	Russian gentry or lower nobility
erbländer	the hereditary lands of a dynasty
familiares	servitors of Hungarian magnates
folwark	demesne or landed estate organized primarily for the production of cash crops
grundherrschaft	demesne or landed estate, a large part of which was usually rented out to peasants.
gutsherrschaft	same as *folwark*
*hayduk*s	an intermediate class between free peasants and nobles who performed military service in Hungary but did not have noble privileges
heneralna starshyna	the Ukrainian Cossack general staff; it functioned as a *hetman*'s cabinet of ministers
hetman	the highest administrative, military, and judicial office in Cossack Ukraine; in Poland-Lithuania and Moldavia, the commander-in-chief of the army
hospodar	the highest office in Moldavia
iç oğlans	trainees for the highest levels of service in the Ottoman court and bureaucracy
iszpan	the highest office in a Hungarian country (*komitat*)
ius militare	laws that applied to medieval military servitors
ius resistendi	the legal right to resist a sovereign if he did not adhere to the conditions of his rule

karalashi	servitors of the Moldavian *hospodar*s
kholop	Russian term for slave; commonly used in reference to the tsar's subjects
knez	hereditary leaders of clans in medieval Moldavia
komitat	Hungarian county that was the focal point of noble activity
koshovy otaman	the elected leader of the Zaporozhian Cossacks
kul	Ottoman slave
kurtiany	servitors of Moldavian *hospodar*s
kuruc	Hungarian insurgents in the sixteenth to eighteenth centuries; probably derived from *crusader*
labanc	pro-Habsburg Hungarians
lan	twenty-six hectares or sixty-five acres of land
landmarschall	the elected principal representative of the Livonian nobility
landtag	the general assembly of the Livonian nobles
landrat	an elected representative of the Livonian nobility
landesstaat	a land possessing a well-developed autonomous government
liberum veto	the right of any deputy to the Polish-Lithuanian parliament to break off its proceedings and annul its decisions by expressing his dissent
manntagen	medieval local assemblies of German Baltic vassals
mazyls	impoverished Moldavian boyars and middle-range landowers
miles	military servitor in medieval Hungary and Moldavia
militärgrenze	Habsburg frontier lands under military administration
monarchia mixta	a mixed form of monarchical and oligarchic rule
nemesh	middle-range landowners in Moldavia
obywatel	Polish term for citizen
pacta conventa	terms and conditions that constituted in the Polish-Lithuanian Commonwealth a contract between the king-elect and the parliament
polkovnyk	a colonel in the Ukrainian Cossack army; also a high administrative and judicial official
rada	general assembly of the Ukrainian Cossacks
ritterschaft	an association of knights; a term for the German Baltic nobility
rokosz	a league of nobles in Poland-Lithuania called together to resist the encroachments of a king or magnates
rycerz	a Polish term for knight or military man
rzeczpospolita	commonwealth; Poland-Lithuania
sachsenspiegel	Saxon code of medieval laws widely used in Eastern Europe
serasker	high Ottoman administrative and military official
şeriat	Islamic code of law
sejm	the parliament or legislative assembly of the Polish-Lithuanian Commonwealth

sejmik	the local dietine or assembly in the provinces of Poland-Lithuania
servientes regis	royal military servitors in medieval Hungary
sich	the stronghold of the Zaporozhian Cossacks on the lower Dnieper
sipahi	Ottoman landowner who rendered military service as cavalryman
*sloboda*s	free, uncolonized lands in Cossack Ukraine
sotnyk	a Ukraine Cossack captain and chief administrative and judicial official in the home territory of the company
starshyna	the officer elite in Cossack Ukraine
szlachcic	the singular of *szlachta*
szlachta	the nobility of Poland-Lithuania
tainyi prikaz	the secret chancellery; an important unit of the Muscovite administrative system
*timar*s	allotments of land given to Ottoman feudal warrior-administrators.
universitas vassalorum	an association of vassals in medieval Livonia constituted to protect their common interests
viritim	the free election of Polish kings by the direct vote of the nobility
voevoda	a high Muscovite administrative official; a governor of a province
wojewoda	a high administrative and military official in Poland-Lithuania; a governor of a province
yasak	Turco-Mongol customary law
zemianin	Polish term for landowner
zemskii sobor	the general assembly of the land in Muscovy
znatne viiskove tovarystvo	a pool of Ukrainian Cossack elite members from which office-holders were chosen

Notes

Diariusz	Diariusz podróżny ... Mémoires et documents, Pologne, vols. 7–12. Archives du Ministère des affaires étrangères, Paris
"Istochniki"	B.D. Bantysh-Kamenskii. "Istochniki malorossiiskoi istorii, 1691–1722," *Chteniia v imperatorskom obshchestve istorii i drevnostei rossiiskikh* (1859)
Neues Archiv	*Neues Archiv für Sächsische Geschichte und Altertumskunde*
Ossolineum	Zaklad Narodowy imienia Ossolinskich
PWN	Panstwowe Wydawnictwo Naukowe
PIW	Panstwowy Instytut Wydawniczy
"Perepiska"	A.O. Bodianskii. "Perepiska i drugiia bumagi shvedskogo korolia Karla XII," *Chteniia v imperatorskom obshchestve istorii i drevnostei rossiiskikh* (1847)
Pisma i bumagi	*Pisma i bumagi imperatora Petra velikogo*
SRIO	*Sbornik Russkogo istoricheskogo obshchestva*
Studii	*Studii şi materiale de istorie medie*
Studia Historica	*Studia Historica Academiae Scientiarum Hungaricae*
ZNTSh	*Zapysky Naukovoho Tovarystva imeni Shevchenka*

CHAPTER ONE: THE SOCIO-ECONOMIC BACKGROUND

1 For a discussion of the concept of Eastern Europe see Josef Macůrek, *Dějepisectví evropského východu* (Prague: Naklad Historickeho Klubu 1946), pp. 15ff.; Oscar Halecki, "Der Begriff der osteuropäischen Geschichte," *Zeitschrift für osteuropäische Geschichte*, n.s., 5 (1934): 1–21; Jaroslav Bidlo, "Was ist die osteuropäische Geschichte?" *Slavische Rundschau* 5 (1933): 361–70; Otto Hoetzsch, "Begriffsbestimmung und Periodisierung der osteuropäischen Geschichte," *Zeitschrift für osteuropäische Geschichte* 8 (1934): 88–102; József Perényi, "L'est européen dans une

synthèse d'histoire universelle," *Nouvelles études historiques* 2 (Budapest 1965): 379–405.

2 See Gordon East, "The Concept and Political Status of the Shatter-Zone," in *Geographical Essays on Eastern Europe*, ed. Norman Pounds (Bloomington: Indiana University Publications 1961), pp. 1–23; and Hugh Seton-Watson, *The "Sick-Heart" of Modern Europe* (Seattle and London: University of Washington Press 1975).

3 The best treatment of this issue is Marian Małowist, *Wschód a Zachód Europy w XII-XVI wieku: Konfrontacja struktur spóleczno-gospodarczych* (Wrocław: Ossolineum 1973), espec. pp. 20, 253; see also Henryk Samsonowicz, "Europa Jagiellonska – Czy jednóscia gospodarcza?" *Kwartalnik Historyczny* 84 (1977): 94–100.

4 See Samsonowicz, "Europa Jagiellonska," p. 96, and especially Małowist, *Wschód a Zachód*, p. 253. Also consult Henryk Samsonowicz, "Das polnische Bürgertum in der Renaissancezeit," in *La renaissance et la réformation en Pologne et en Hongrie* (Budapest: Akadémiai Kiadó 1963), pp. 91–6. See in the same publication Jenö Szücs, "Das Städtewesen in Ungarn im 15-17 Jahrhundert," pp. 97–164; an older but still useful treatment of the question is Stanisław Herbst, "Miasta i mieszczanstwo renesansu Polskiego," in *Odrodzenie w Polsce*, ed. Stanisław Arnold (Warsaw 1955), vol. 1, pp. 336–61.

5 See Malowist, *Wschód a Zachód*, pp. 25ff., and Samsonowicz, "Europa Jagiellonska," passim.

6 See B.H. Slicher van Bath, *The Agrarian History of Western Europe, A.D. 500-1850* (New York: St Martin's 1963), p. 198.

7 Ibid., p. 197.

8 The literature on the effects of the Price Revolution on Eastern Europe is vast. Małowist's work on this topic has been ground breaking. A restatement and elaboration of Małowist's findings is available in Immanuel Wallerstein, *The Modern World System*, 2 vols. (London and New York: Academic Press 1976–80), pp. 99–110. Other important studies on this subject are Wilhelm Abel, *Agrarkrisen und Agrarkonjunktur* (Hamburg and Berlin: Verlag P. Parey 1966); Stanisław Hoszowski, "Rewolucja cen w Polsce w XVI-XVII wieku," in *VIII Powszechny zjazd historykow polskich* (Warsaw 1960), pp. 105–40, and his "L'Europe centrale devant la révolution des prix (XVIᵉ-XVII wieku," in *VIII Powszechny zjazd historykow polskich* (Warsaw 1960), pp. 105–40, and his "L'Europe centrale devant la révolution des prix (XVIᵉ-XVIIᵉ siècles)," *Annales* 16 (1961): 441–67; V.V. Doroshenko, "Deistvie 'revoliutsii tsen' v vostochnoi Pribaltike v XVI v.," *Ezhegodnik po agrarnoi istorii vostochnoi evropy* 1 (1961): 114–24. A Czech view on this question is Josef Petran, "K problemum tzv. 'cenove revoluce' ve stredni Evrope," *Numismaticky sbornik* 8 (1964): 47–54.

9 Wallerstein, *Modern World System*, p. 99.

10 A collection of important studies dealing with the trade between Eastern and Western Europe is Ingomar Bog, *Der Aussenhandel Ostmitteleuropas, 1450-1650* (Cologne and Vienna: Bohlau Verlag 1971). Other studies dealing with this topic are Zsigmond Pach, "The Role of East-Central Europe in International

Trade in the 16th and 17th Centuries," *Nouvelles études historiques* 70 (Budapest 1970): 217-63; Miroslav Hroch, "Obchod mezi Vychodni a Zapadni Evropou v obdobi počatku Kapitalismu,"*Československy Časopis Historicky*11 (1963): 480-511; Arthur Attman, *The Russian and Polish Markets in International Trade, 1500-1650* (Göteborg: Institute of Economic History 1973); Władislaw Rusinski, "The Role of Polish Territories in the European Trade in the 17th and 18th centuries," *Studia Historiae Oeconomicae* 3 (Poznan 1969): 115-26; Stanisław Hoszowski, "Handel Gdansku w okresie xv-xviii," *Zeszyty Naukowe w Krakowie* 11 (1960): 3-67.

11 See Hoszowski, "Handel Gdansku," and Marian Małowist, "The Economic and Social Development of the Baltic Countries from the 15th to the 17th Centuries," *Economic History Review* 12 (1959): 177-89. Also see Antoni Mączak, "Der polnische Getreide Export und das Problem der Handelsbilanz (1557-1647)," in Bog, *Der Aussenhandel Ostmitteleuropas*, pp. 28-46; also consult Andrzej Wyczanski, *Polska-Rzecza Pospolita Szlachecka 1454-1764* (Warsaw: pwn 1965), p. 28.

12 For the role of the Dutch in the Baltic trade see Jan de Vries, *The Economy of Europe in an Age of Crisis, 1600-1750* (Cambridge: Cambridge University Press 1976), and Aksel Christensen, *Dutch Trade to the Baltic about 1600* (Copenhagen: Munksgaard 1941).

13 Two thorough studies of the Hungarian cattle trade are Laszlo Makkai, "Der ungarische Viehhandel 1550-1650," pp. 483-506, and Gyula Ember, "Ungarns Aussenhandel mit dem Western um die Mitte des xvi Jahrhunderts," pp. 86-104; both articles appear in Bog, *Aussenhandel*. Another valuable collection of articles dealing with Hungary's trade relations with the West is Othmar Pickl, ed., *Die wirtschaftlichen Auswirkungen der Türkenkriegen* (Graz: Universität Graz 1971). The classic study of Moldavia's foreign trade during this period is Ion Nistor, *Die auswärtigen Handelsbeziehungen der Moldau im xiv-xvi Jhr* (Gotha: Andreas Perthes A.G. 1911).

14 See M. Rey, *Zwierciadło*, ed. J. Czubek and J. Los (Cracow 1914), p. 157. For a discussion of the Polish view on these developments see J. Górski, *Poglady merkantilystyczne w polskiej mysli ekonmicznej xvi i xvii wieku* (Wrocław: Ossolineum 1958), pp. 83-4.

15 This view is strongly argued by Zsigmond Pach, "The Shifting of International Trade Routes in the 15-17th Centuries," *Acta Historica* 41 (Budapest 1968): 187-311. A position similar to Pach's is taken by De Vries, *Economy of Europe*, pp. 119-20 and 161-2.

16 There exists a vast literature on this topic. Małowist discusses this issue at length in *Wschód a Zachód*, pp. 375-85. Other important studies are Zsigmond Pach, *Die ungarische Agrarentwicklung im 16-17 Jahrhundert: Abbiegung vom westeuropaischen Entwicklung* (Budapest: Akadémiai Kiadó 1964); Antoni Mączak, "Zusammenhänge zwischen Fernhandel und ungleichmässiger Entwicklung polnischer Wirtschaftsgebiete im 16 und 17 Jahrhunderts," *Jahrbücher für Wirtschaftsgeschichte* 3 (1971): 219-27; Jerzy Topolski, "Causes of Dualism in the Economic Development of Modern Europe," *Studia Historiae Oeconomicae* 3 (Poznan 1968): 3-12.

17 This is another topic on which much has been written. A ground-breaking
    study was Jan Rutkowski, "La genèse du régime de la corvée dans l'Europe
    Centrale depuis la fin du Moyen Age," *La Pologne au VI⁰ congrès international
    des sciences historiques* (Oslo 1928), pp. 2–28. Another important Polish con-
    tribution is Władysław Rusinski, "Hauptprobleme der Fronwirtschaft von 16
    bis 18 Jahrhunderts in Polen und den Nachbarnländern," *Papers of the First Inter-
    national Conference of Economic History in Stockholm* (The Hague: Mouton 1960),
    pp. 415–23. Also see Ferenc Maksay, "Gutwirtschaft und Bauerlegen in Ungarn
    im 16. Jahrhundert," *Vierteljahrschrift für Sozial- und Wirtschaftsgeschichte* 45 (1958):
    37–51. Developments in Moldavia are treated in P.V. Sovetov, *Issledovaniia po
    istorii feodalizma v Moldavii,* vol. 1 (Kishinev: Shtiintsa 1972), and in D.I. Dragner
    and P.V. Sovetov, "Perestroika struktury zemlevladeniia v Moldavii xv–xviii
    vv.," *Istoriia SSR* (1968), pp. 70–92; for Livonia see Arnold Soom, *Der Herrenhof in
    Estland im 17 Jahrhundert* (Lund: Eesti Rootsis 1954); and for Ukraine the basic
    work on this topic is Veniamin Miakotin, *Prikreplenie krestianstva levobrezhnoi
    Ukrainy v xvii–xviii vv.* (Sofia 1932); also see I.D. Boiko, "Prozvoditnelnye sily v
    selskom khoziastve Ukrainy v xvi–xvii v," *Ezhegodnik po agrarnoi istori vostochoi
    evropy* 3 (1961): 165–73. An overview of the problem and of the appearance of the
    so-called second edition of serfdom may be found in *Slavic Review* 34 (1975):
    225–79.
18 See V.V. Doroshenko, "Model agrarnogo stroia Rechi-Pospolitoi xvi–xvii,"
    Ezhegodnik po agrarnoi istorii vostochnoi evropy 7 (1965): 114–29.
19 There is some debate as to the effectiveness of these price regulations. See
    Witold Kula, *The Economic Theory of Feudalism* (Warsaw: PWN 1976), pp. 80–1.
20 The plight of the towns is discussed in Stanisław Herbst, "Miasta i mieszczans-
    two renesansu Polskiego," in Stanisław Arnold, ed., *Odrodzenie w Polsce* (Warsaw:
    PIW 1955), pp. 336–65. Also see Henryk Samsonowicz, "Das polnische Bürger-
    tum in der Renaissancezeit," and Jenö Szücs, "Das Städtewesen in Ungarn im
    15–17 Jahrhundert," in *La renaissance et la réformation en Pologne et en Hongrie*
    (Budapest: Adadémiai Kiadó 1963), pp. 97–179.
21 See Jerzy Topolski, "La régression économique en Pologne du xvi ⁰ au xviii⁰
    siècle," *Acta Poloniae Historica* 7 (1962): 39.

CHAPTER TWO: FIVE EAST EUROPEAN ELITES

1 For an interesting discussion of agrarian societies see Gerhard Lenski, *Power
   and Privilege* (Chapel Hill: University of North Carolina Press 1965), pp.
   189–295.
2 Ibid., p. 196.
3 See Quincy Wright, *A Study of War* (Chicago: University of Chicago Press
   1965), p. 653.
4 Lenski, *Power and Privilege*, p. 231.
5 On the *szlachta* in general see Jarema Maciszweski, *Szlachta Polska i jej panstwo*
   (Warsaw: Wiedza Powszechna 1969). A very good synthesis is Andrzej Wyczan-

ski, *Polska Rzecza Pospolita Szlachecka, 1454-1764* (Warsaw: PWN 1965). Also useful is Michał Sczaniecki, "Les origines et la formation de la noblesse polonaise au moyen age," *Acta Poloniae Historica* 36 (1977): 101-8. Also see the thorough study by Hans Roos, "Ständewesen und parlamentarische Verfassung in Polen (1505-1772)," in Dietrich Gerhard, ed., *Ständische Vertretungen in Europa 17 and 18 Jhd* (Göttingen: Vandenhoeck & Ruprecht 1970), pp. 331-67.

6 On clans see Kazimierz Tymieniecki, "Genetyzm (ustroj rodowy) czy feudalizm," in *Przegląd Historyczny* 52 (1961): 547-61. For a recent and differing view see Janusz Bieniak, "Rody rycerskie jako czynnik struktury spolecznej w Polsce XIII-XIV w.," in Henryk Lowmianski, ed., *Polska w okresie rozdrobnienia feudalnego* (Warsaw 1973), pp. 161-201. Also see Maria Koczerska, *Rodzina szlachecka w Polsce późnego średniowiecza* (Warsaw: PWN 1975).

7 For *szlachta* land holdings and allodialism see Sczaniecki, "Les origines," and Roman Grodecki, *Polska Piastowska* (Warsaw: PWN 1969), pp. 434-40.

8 See Sczaniecki, "Les origines," p. 104, and Maciszewski, *Szlachta polska*, p. 35.

9 None the less, access was still possible, as indicated by the work of a déclassé nobleman who indicated in that in the sixteenth century at least 2,300 families illegally called themselves *szlachta*. See W. Nekanda Terpka, *Liber generationis plebeanorum* ("Liber chamorum"), ed. Wlodzimierz Dworzaczek et al. (Wrocław: Ossolineum 1963).

10 The classic study of the *sejm* is Stanisław Kutrżeba, *Sejm walny dawnej Rzeczpospolitej polskiej* (Warsaw 1919). A popular survey of the *sejm* is Marek Borucki, *Sejmy i sejmiki szlacheckie* (Warsaw: Kiażkia Wiedza 1972).

11 On the cultural aspect of *szlachta* see Andrzej Zajączkowski, *Glowne elementy kultury szlacheckiej w Polsce. Ideologia i struktura spoleczna* (Wrocław:Ossolineum 1969), and, not always in agreement, Janusz Tazbir, "Proba okreslenia kultury szlacheckiej w Polsce przedrozbiorowej," in *Tradycje szlacheckie w kulturze*, pp. 7-34. See also, by same author, "Wzorce osobowe szlachty polskiej w XVII wieku," *Kwartalnik Historyczny* 4 (1976): 784-97. For Sarmatism see Tadeusz Mankowski, *Geneologia Sarmatizm* (Warsaw: PIW 1946).

12 For more recent studies of the magnates see Wlodzimierz Dworzaczek and Adam Kersten, "Magnateria polska jako warstwa spoleczna," *XI Congress of Polish Historians* (Torun 1974), pp. 1-12. Also see a condensed French version of Tazbir's views in "Les magnats - élite de la société nobiliare," *Acta Poloniae Historica* 36 (1977): 119-33. For a study of the magnates during the Saxon period see Teresa Zielinska, *Magnateria Polska epoki saskiej* (Wrocław: Ossolineum 1977). Also see Maciszewski, *Szlachta polska, pp.* 54-70; Zdzisław Kaczmar, "Oligarchia magnacka w Polsce jako forma panstwa," *VIII Congress of Polish Historians*, vol. I (Cracow 1958), pp. 223-41; Henryk Olszewski, *Sejm Rzeczypospolitej epoki oligarchii, 1652-1763* (Poznan: UAM 1966); Wladisław Czaplinski, *Życie codzienne magnaterii polskiej w XVII wieku* (Warsaw: PIW 1976).

13 The following statistics indicate what an exclusive social group the magnates became: in the early seventeenth century 70 per cent of the magnates married outside their social group; in the late seventeenth century 40 per cent did so;

and in the early eighteenth century only 18 per cent contracted marriages outside their own milieu. See Tazbir, "Les magnates," p. 132.

14 A wealth of statistical data concerning eighteenth-century Poland may be found in the following works: Tadeusz Kórzon, *Wewnętrzne dzieje Polski za Stanisława Augusta*, 5 vols., vol. 1 (Cracow: Akademija Umętnosći 1897), 78–152; Irena Gieysztorowa, "Research into the demographic history of Poland," *Acta Poloniae Historica* 18 (1968): 5–17; Hans Roos, "Ständewesen und parlamentarische Verfassung in Polen (1505–1772)," in Dietrich Gerhardt, ed., *Ständische Vertretungen in Europa*, pp. 310–67; and Jörg Hoensch, *Sozialverfassung und politische Reform: Polen in vorrevolutionären Zeitalter* (Cologne and Vienna: Böhlau Verlag 1973).

15 On Polish-Hungarian ties, see János Bak, *Königtum und Stände in Ungarn im 14–15 Jahrhundert* (Wiesbaden: Steiner 1973), p. 41, for the Hungarians' consciousness, dating from the mid-fifteenth century, of these similarities. Also see the extremely valuable but little-known study by Stefan Tomashivsky, "Uhorshchyna i Polshcha na pochatku XVIII v.," in *ZNTSh* 83 (1908): 97–133; 84 (1908): 33–87; 85 (1908): 43–80; 86 (1908): 31–58. Another useful study is Josef Leszczyński, "The Part Played by the Countries of the Crown of St. Wenceslaus and by Hungary in the Freedom Ideology of the Polish Gentry," *Otkázy dejin středni a východni Evropy* 2 (1975); 25–58. Most recently the topic has been studied by Lajos Hopp, *A Lengyel-Magyar Hagyományok újjászülétese* (Budapest: Akadémiai Kiadó 1972). For an interesting comparative study of the Polish and Hungarian as well as the Lithuanian and Czech political systems of the fifteenth and sixteenth centuries see Stanisław Russocki, "Monarchie stanowe środkowo-wschodniej Europy XV–XVI wieku," *Kwartalnik Historyczny* 84 (1977): 73–92.

16 On early Hungary see Antal Bartha, "Hungarian Society in the 10th Century and the Social Division of Labour," *Acta Historica* 9 (1963): 333–59. Also see Lajos Elekes, *A középkori magyar allam története magalaptásától mohácsi bukásáig* (Budapest: Kossuth Könyvkiadó 1964).

17 For a discussion of the magnates in the medieval period see Erwin Pamlényi et al., ed., *Die Geschichte Ungarns* (Budapest: Corvina 1971), pp. 63–8, 70–1. Also see Charles d'Eszlary, *Histoire des institutions publiques hongroises*, 3 vols., vol. 1 (Paris: Marcel Rivière 1963), 352–63; and György Szekely, "Évolution de la structure et de la culture de la classe dominante laïque dans la Hongrie des Arpads," *Acta Historica* 16 (Budapest 1970): 151–70.

18 On the early nobles see d'Eszlary, *Histoire des institutions* 1:363–7; Pamlényi, *Die Geschichte Ungarns*, pp. 55–7, 82–5; Gusztav Heckenast, *Fejedelmi (királyi) szolgálónépek a Korai Árpádkorban* (Budapest: Akadémiami Kiadó 1970). Also see Gyula Szekfü, "Die Servienten und Familiaren im ungarischen Mittlealter," *Ungarische Rundschau* 2 (1913): 524–57.

19 For a discussion of the Golden Bull see Heinrich Marczali, *Ungarische Verfassungsgeschichte* (Tübingen: Mohr Verlag 1910), pp. 17–27.

20 See Palmeny, *Die Geschchte Ungarns*, p. 95.

21 On strong monarchy in Hungary see ibid., pp. 71–5, 104–19. For the

prerogatives of the king see Marczali, *Ungarische Verfassungsgeschichte*, pp. 42–56;
Tibor Kardos, "Zentralisierung und Humanismus im Ungarn des 15. und 16.
Jahrhunderts," *Studia Historica* 53 (1963): 397–415.

22 On the nobility and *komitats* see d'Eszlary, *Histoire des institutions* 1:262–70; Bak,
König und Stände; Lajos Elekes, "Système diètal des ordres et centralisation dans
les états féodaux," *Studia Historica* 53 (1963): 331–95. For the seventeenth century
see Jean Berenger, *Les "Gravamina": Rémontrances des diètes de Hongrie de 1655 à 1681*
(Paris: Presses universitaires de France 1973), pp. 48–70.

23 An English-language introduction to Hungarian parliamentarism is György
Bónis, "The Hungarian Feudal Diet (XIII–XVIII centuries)," *Anciens pays et
assemblées d'états: Recueil de la Société Jean Bodin* 26 (Brussels 1965): 187–207. For in-
cisive reviews of the historiography of this question see the reprint of Rudolf
Steinacker's well-known article, "Über Stand und Aufgaben der ungarischen
Verfassungsgeschichte," in *Austro-Hungarica* 1 (Munich 1963): 1–74; and Marczali,
Ungarische Verfassungsgeschichte, pp. 34–42. An older but still useful work is Julius
Andrassy, *The Development of Hungarian Constitutional Liberty* (London: Kegan
Paul Trübner 1908).

24 Citation from C.A. Macartny, *Hungary: A Short History* (Edinburgh: Edinburgh
University Press 1962), p. 49. The entire problem of the *corona regni* is
thoroughly discussed by János Karpat in his article "Die Idee der Heiligen
Krone Ungarns in neue Beleuchtung," in Manfred Hellmann, ed., *Corona Regni*
(Weimar 1961), pp. 349–99. For an English-language treatment of the problem
see the dissertation of Laszlo Peter, "The Antecedents of the 19th c. Hungarian
State Concept: A Historical Analysis. The Background of the Creation of the
Doctrine of the Holy Crown" (Oxford University 1966).

25 The basic work on the *Tripartitum* is still Fraknói Vilmos, *Werböczi Istvan*
(Budapest: Magyar Törteneti Eletrajzok 1899). For the text and introduction to
Werböczi's work see György Bónis, "*Tripartitum*," in Alfred Wolf, ed., *Mit-
telalterliche Gesetzbücher in Faksimiliendruck*, vol. 2 (Glaschütten/Taunus, 1971).

26 On the impact of the Ottomans a good English overview is Kálmán Benda,
"Hungary in Turmoil, 1580–1620," *European Studies Review* 8 (1978): 281–304. Also
see Jósef Perenyi, "Wirtschaftliche und soziale Umgestaltung in Ungarn unter
der Türkenherrschaft im XVI und XVII Jahrhd.," *Otkázy dejin středni a východni
Evropy* 1 (Brno 1971): 85–104; I. Sinkovics, "Der Angriff der Osmanen im
Donautal im 16. Jahrhundert," *Études historiques hongroises* (Budapest 1975), pp.
349–80. A popular and well-illustrated work is Lengyel Balázs, *A
törökmagyaroszgágon* (Budapest: Móra Ferenc Könyvkiadó 1971).

27 On Hungary under the Ottomans see Ferenc Maksay, "Ungarn's Landwirt-
schaft zur Zeit der Türkenherrschaft," *Agratörteneti Szemle* 9, *Supplement* (1967):
10–37.

28 On Transylvania see Kálmán Benda, "Les bases sociales du pouvoir des princes
de Transylvanie," *Studia Historica* 53 (1963): 430–47; Tibor Wittmann,
"L'idéologie de centralisation de la principauté de Transylvanie et ses rapports
européens," *Studia Historica* 53 (1963): 431–7. For an overview of the ad-

ministrative structure see d'Eszlary, *Histoire des institutions* 2: 260–7; Ladislas Makkai, *Histoire de Transylvanie* (Paris: Presses universitaires de France 1946).

29 Henry Marczali, *Hungary in the Eighteenth Century* (Cambridge: Cambridge University Press 1910), p. 35.

30 For two good studies of magnates after the Ottoman conquest see Marczali, *Hungary in the Eighteenth Century*, and Király, *Hungary in the Late Eighteenth Century* (New York: Columbia University Press 1968). Also see Berenger, *Les "Gravamina,"* pp. 28–41.

31 On the post-Mohács nobility see Király, *Hungary in the Late Eighteenth Century*, pp. 32–42; Marczali, *Hungary in the Eighteenth Century*, pp. 102–48; Berenger, *Les "Gravamina,"* pp. 41–5. For a discussion of the *hayduks* see György Mody, ed., *A hajduk a magyar törtenelemben* (Debrecen 1969); and Kálmán Benda, "Der Haiduckenaufstand in Ungarn und das Erstarken der Stände in der Habsburgermonarchie," *Nouvelles études historiques* 1 (1965): 299–313.

32 Statistical information on Hungary is available in József Kovacsics, "The Population of Hungary in the Eighteenth Century," *Third International Conference of Economic History* (Munich: Mouton 1965), pp. 137–45; also useful is Kálmán Benda, "Hungary in Turmoil, 1580–1620," *European Studies Review* 8 (1978): 281–304; see also György Bónis, "Die ungarische Stände in der ersten Hälfte des 18. Jahrhunderts," in Gerhard, *Ständische Vertretungen*, pp. 286–309, and Berenger, *Les "Gravamina"*; also see *Istoriia Vengrii*, vol. 1 (Moscow: Nauka 1971), and Palményi, *Die Geschichte Ungarns*.

33 The best general work on German Livonia is Reinhard Wittram, *Baltische Geschichte* (Munich: Oldenbourg 1954). For an older version see Leonid Abrusow, *Grundriss der Geschichte Liv-Est-und Kurlands* (Riga: Jonck & Poliewsky 1908). Also useful is Arnolds Spekke, *History of Latvia* (Stockholm: Dauvaga 1951), and the Soviet work *Istoriia Latviiskoi SSR*, vol. 2 (Riga: Latiivskoe gosudarstvennoe izdatelstvo 1952). An especially exhaustive and valuable work dealing primarily with sixteenth-century Livonia is Edgars Dunsdorfs and Arnolds Spekke, *Latvijas Vēsture 1500–1600* (Stockholm: Dauvaga 1964). For a history of Estonia see *Istoriia Estonskoi SSR*, vol. I (Tallin: Estonskoe gosudarstvennoe izdatelstvo 1961).

34 On the competition of sovereigns see Gustav Rathlef, *Das Verhältnis des livländischen Ordens zu den Landesbischofen und zur Stadt Riga im 13. und in der ersten Hälfte des 14 Jahrhd.* (Dorpat 1875); and Otto Stavenhagen, "Der Kampf des Deutschen Ordens in Livland um den livländischen Einheitsstaat im 14. Jahrd.," *Baltische Monatsschrift* 53 (1908): 145–59, 20–225; and Wittram, *Baltische Geschichte*, pp. 28–41.

35 On the Livonian *ritterschaft* see Wittram, *Baltische Geschichte*, pp. 41–4. For a thorough discussion of the terms of vassalage see Arvid v. Transehe-Roseneck, "Zur Geschichte des Lehenwesens in Livland," *Mitteilungen aus dem Gebiete der Geschichte Liv-Est-und Kurlands* 18 (1908): 1–281. The evolution of the *ritterschaft* is also discussed in Ia. Zutis, *Ostzeiiskii vopros v XVIII veke* (Riga: Knigoizdatelstvo 1946), pp. 20–49.

36 On the nobility of Estland see H.V. Wedel, *Die Estländische Ritterschaft* (Berlin 1935); and *Istoriia Estonskoi ssr*. In 1241 land in Estland under Danish rule was distributed as follows: the *ritterschaft*, 75 per cent; the crown, 20 per cent; and the church, 5 per cent. The Danish crown's share quickly diminished over time: in 1241 it had 1,083 *haken*; by 1346 only 188 *haken* remained. The ethnic composition of the *ritterschaft* was about 100 German families, 10 Danish families, and 8 to 10 Estonian families. See *Istoriia Estonskoi ssr* 1: 187–8.

37 On the Livonian *landtag* and estates see Julius Eckhardt, "Der livlandische Landtag in seiner historischen Entwicklung," *Baltische Monatschrift* 3 (1861): 38–78, 116–59. For the evolution of Livonian institutions see also Alexander v. Tobien, *Die Livländische Ritterschaft* (Riga: Löffler 1925), pp. 1–15. Also see S. von Holstein, "Zur Geschichte der livländische Privilegien," *Baltische Monatschrift* 4–9 (1900): 236–48, 311–19.

38 The peasants of Livonia were among the most exploited in Eastern Europe. Their situation worsened notably as the grain boom began and more land passed into the hands of the nobility. For example, in the 1550s a common corvée in Livonia was two to three days per week all year round; by the 1600s the corvée had risen to five to six days a week, and between 50 and 80 per cent of the peasants' produce went to their lords. See *Istoriia Estonskoi ssr* 1: 290, and *Istoriia Latvskoi ssr* 2: 124. For a treatment of the peasant issue in later periods see Zutis, *Ostzeiskii vopros*. See also Arved v. Transehe-Roseneck, *Gutsherr und Bauer in Livland im 17. und 18. Jahrhundert* (Strassburg 1890).

39 The loss of the original of the *Privilegium Sigismundi Augusti* gave rise to a discussion about the authenticity of this document. However, recent research has shown that the documents authenticity is beyond question: see E. Tarvel, "Stosunek prawopanstwowy Inflant do Rzeczypospolitej oraz ich ustroj administracyjny w 1561–1612," *Zapiski Historyczne* (Cracow 1969), pp. 49–76. For the text of the negotiations between the Livonians and Sigismund II August see M. Dogiel, *Codex diplomaticus Regni Poloniae et Magni Ducatus Litvaniae*, vol. 5 (Vilnius 1750), pp. 223, 228. Also see E. Aidnik, "Zur Geschichte des 'Privilegiums Sigismundi Augusti' für die Livländische Ritterschaft," *Historische Zeitschrift* 157 (1937): 69–74; and J. Lossius, "Zur Geschichte des Originals des Privilegiums Sigismundi Augusti," *Baltische Monatsschrift* 22 (1873): 217–25. A list of the twenty-seven articles of the *Privilegium* may be found in Julius Eckhardt, *Livland im achtzehnten Jahrhundert* (Leipzig: Löffler 1876), pp. 35–8.

40 For a recent treatment of Polish rule in Livonia see Tarval, "Stosunek prawnopanstwowy," and E. Kuntze, "Organizacja Inflant w czasach polskich," in *Polska a Inflanty* (Gdansk 1939), pp. 7–43. Also see Wittram, *Baltische Geschichte*, pp. 77–88.

41 On the Swedish takeover of Livonia see Otto Greiffenhagen, "Begründung und Ausbau der schwedischen Herrschaft in Livland durch Gustav Adolf," *Baltische Monatsschrift* 22 (1920): 325–35; and Bjorn Liljedahl, *Svensk förtvaltning i Livland 1617–1634* (Uppsala: Almqvist & Wiksells 1933). For the most recent study see also Harry Thomson, *Schweden und seine Provinzen Estland un Livland in ihrem gegenseitigen Verhältnis 1561–1710* (Oldenburg 1975), pp. 100–6.

42 A description of the various institutions of the Livonian nobility may be found in Tobien, *Die Livländische Ritterschaft*, pp. 1–38. Also see Georg von Rauch, "Volks-und Staatsauffassung in Livland zur polnischen und schwedischen Zeit," *Deutsches Archiv für Landes-und Volksforschung* 4 (1940): 450–73; and Wittram, *Baltische Geschichte*, p. 87.

43 For statistical information about Livonia see Edgards Dundorfs, *Latvijas Vesture*, pp. 175–221.

44 The most authoritative history of Moldavia is L.V. Cherepnin, ed., *Istoriia Moldavskoi SSR*, 2 vols. (Kishinev: Kartia Moldoveniaske 1965). Also useful is N.A. Mokhov, *Moldavia ephokhi feodalizma* (Kishinev: Kartia Moldoveniaske 1964); and Andrei Oţetea, ed., *The History of the Romanian People* (Bucharest 1970). For a contemporary description of Moldavia see Dmitrii Kantemir, *Opisanie Moldavii* (Kishinev: Kartia Moldoveniaske 1973).

45 For a description of *hospodars'* prerogatives and other aspects of the political system see F.A. Grekul, *Sotsialnoekonomicheskii i politicheskii stroi Moldavii vtoroi pol. XV veka*, (Kishinev: Gosudarstvennoe izd. Moldavii 1950). Also see the French summary in N. Grigoras, *Instituţii feudale din Moldaova* (Bucharest: Editura Acadmiei RSR 1971). See *Istoriia Moldavskoi SSR* I: 117–20, and Mokhov, *Moldaviia*, pp. 163–4. For a description of the *hospodar's* office from one who held it see Kantemir, *Opisanie Moldavii*, pp. 47–93. Also see Constantin Şerban, "Problèmes de la centralisation de l'état dans les pays roumains au moyen age," *Nouvelles études d'histoire publiées à l'occasion du XIe congrès des sciences historiques, Stockholm, 1960* (Bucharest: Éditions de l'Académie de la RPR 1960), pp. 49–56.

46 For a discussion of the boyars see D. Ciurea, "Quelques considérations sur la noblesse féodale chez les roumains," *Nouvelles études d'histoire publiées à l'occasion du XIIe congrès des sciences historiques, Vienne, 1965* (Bucharest 1965), pp. 83–92. Also see *Istoriia Moldavskoi SSR* I: 95–107. An interesting description of the boyars' offices is Kantemir, *Opisanie Moldavii*; see also N. Stoicescu, *Sfatul domnesc şi marii dregători din Ţara Româneasca şi Moldava* (Bucharest: Academiei RSR 1968).

47 See *Istoriia Moldavskoi SSR* I: 95.

48 Ibid., p. 97.

49 Ibid., p. 129.

50 On the numbers of military servitors see P.V. Sovetov, *Issledovaniia po istorii feodalizma v Moldavii*, 2 vols., vol. 1 (Kishinev: Shtiintsa 1972), p. 493. Compare to Mokhov, *Moldaviia*, p. 219. Because of servitor weakness, the general assemblies, a favourite tool of servitors in Eastern Europe, were weakly developed.

51 Ottoman tribute: A thorough discussion of the issue of Moldavian tribute to the Porte is Mihail Berza, "Variatille exploatarii tarii romaneşti de catre Poarta Otomana in secolelel XVI–XVII," in *Studii şi materiale de istorie medie* (1958), pp. 59–71. Also see Mokhov, *Moldaviia*, p. 210.

52 For the impact of Ottoman tribute on landholdings see *Istoriia Moldavii* I: 199–204. Also see F.A. Grekul, *Agrarnye otonosheniia v Moldavii v XVI-pervoi polovine XVII vv.* (Kishinev: Shtiintsa 1961).

53 This is not to say that "new" boyars did not acquire land. They did. In the seventeenth century these five leading families owned about one-third of all villages in the land (*Istoriia Moldavii ssr* I: 192). But land was an *attribute* of power, not a way to power. See P.V. Sovetov, "Typologicheskie puti razvytogo feodalizma i turetskoi zavoevanie Moldavii i Valakhii i ee vliianie na istoricheskoe razvitie," in *Iugovostochnaia Evropa v epokhu feodalizma* (Kishinev: Shtiintsa 1973), pp. 84-93, who presents the socio-economic context for this phenomenon.

54 An incisive discussion of the economic downturn is D.M. Dragnev, "Progress, zamedlennoe razvitie ili ekonomicheskii upadok? ('Ob osobennostiakh ekonomicheskogo razvitiia Dunaiskikh kniazhestv v xvii–xviii vv')," in *Iugo-vostochnaia Evrope*, pp. 99-108. A detailed study of this development is Sovetov's *Issledovaniia.* Also see Mokhov, *Moldaviia*, pp. 317-87; and *Istoriia Moldavskoi ssr* I: 242-3.

55 On the boyar mentality see N.A. Mokhov, "Aspekty sotsialnoi psykhologii feodalnykh soslovii Moldavii (otonoshenie k narodam sosednykh stran)," in *Iugo-vostochnaia Evropa*, pp. 170-9. For boyar attitudes in a later period see Vlad Georgescu, "The Romanian Boyars in the 18th Century: Their Political Ideology," *East European Quarterly* 7 (1973): 31-40, see also E.M. Russev, "Vneshnepoliticheskaia kontseptsiia boiarskogo letopisaniia Moldavii," *Iugo-vostochnaia Evropa*, pp. 163-70.

56 For examples of the boyars' declarations of sympathy for Polish ways and system see Russev, ibid., p. 164. Also see Eugen Stănescu, "Unity and Diversity in the Political Thought of the Early Romanian Society," *Nouvelles études d'histoire* (Bucharest: Éditions de l'Académie de la RSD 1965), pp. 91-110. In 1684 Miron Costin attempted to come to an arrangement with the Polish king whereby the king would have sovereignty over Moldavia if the boyars received the same rights and privileges as did Poles. (Stănescu, p. 106).

57 For statistical data on Moldavia see P.V. Sovetov and D. Dragnev "Perestroika struktury zemlevladeniia v Moldavii xv–xvii vv," *Istoriia ssr* 2 (1968): 70-92. Mokhov (*Moldaviia*, pp. 219-23) estimates the population of the principality at 300,000.

58 The historical literature on Ukraine during the Khmelnytsky uprising is vast. Among the leading works on the topic are Mykhailo Hrushevsky, *Istoriia Ukrainy-Rusi*, 10 vols. (Kiev 1905-36; repr., New York: Knyhospilka 1954-8), vols. 8-9; Viacheslav Lypynsky, *Ukraina na perelomi* (Vienna: Dniprosoiuz 1920); Ivan Krypiakevych, *Bohdan Khemlnytsky* (Kiev: Naukova Dumka 1965); and Oleksander Ohloblyn, *Dumky pro Khmelnychynu* (New York: ODWU 1957). For an English-language treatment of this period see George Vernadsky, *Bohdan, Hetman of Ukraine* (New Haven: Yale University Press 1941).

59 For the rise of the Ukrainian Cossacks see Gunter Stöckl, *Die Entstehung des Kosakentums* (Munich: Isar Verlag 1953); Zbigniew Wójcik, *Dzikie Pola w Ogniu: O Kozaczyznie w dawnej Rzeczypospolitej* (Warsaw: Wiedza Powszechna 1968); and Hrushevsky, *Istoriia Ukrainy-Rusi*, vol. 8; also see Linda Gordon, *Cossack Rebel-*

lions: Social Turmoil in the Sixteenth-Century Ukraine (Albany: State University of New York Press 1983).

60 See Krypiakevych, *Khmelnytsky,* p. 16.

61 Khmelnytsky began his uprising in April 1648 with about 4,000 to 5,000 Cossacks from the Zaporozhian *sich*; in May the number rose to 15,000; in June it was close to 70,000 to 80,000 and consisted mostly of peasants; in September close to 150,000 peasants and Cossacks joined him, and in February 1649 Khmelnytsky boasted that he had 200,000 men. Most of Khmelnytsky's followers were peasants. The Cossack core of his forces consisted of about 40,000 men. See Krypiakevych, *Khmelnytsky,* pp. 207–8. For a careful study of the Cossack army see O.M. Apanovych, *Zbroini syly Ukrainy* (Kiev: Naukova Dumka 1969).

62 For a discussion of Ukrainian Cossack goals see Hrushevsky, *Istoriia Ukrainy-Rusi* 9: 1479–1508.

63 A thorough treatment of the Cossack administrative system is V.A. Diadychenko, *Narysy suspilno-politychnoho ustroiu livoberezhnoi Ukrainy* (Kiev: Akademiia Nauk Ukrainskoi RSR 1959). A concise English-language treatment of the subject is Zenon Kohut, "The Abolition of Ukrainian Autonomy (1763–1786)" (PHD dissertation, University of Pennsylvania 1975). Also see George Gajecky, *The Cossack Administration of the Hetmanate* (Cambridge: Harvard Ukrainian Research Institute 1978); and H. Schumann, "Der Hetmanstaat, 1654–1764," *Jahrbücher für Geschichte Osteuropas* 1 (1936): 499–548.

64 For an objective overview of the controversy surrounding the Pereiaslav Treaty see O.E. Gunther, "Der Vertrag von Pereiaslav im Widerstreit der Meinungen," *Jahrbücher für Geschichte Osteuropas* 2 (1954): 232–57. Also see the very thorough work by John Basarab, *Pereiaslav 1654: A Historiographical Study* (Edmonton: Canadian Institute of Ukrainian Studies 1982).

65 The formation of this new Cossack elite has been studied by Lev Okinshevych, *Znachne viiskove tovarystvo v Ukraini-Hetmanshchyni* (Munich: Zahrava 1948), and more recently by Zenon Kohut, "Problems in Studying the Post-Khmelnytsky Ukrainian Elite," in *Rethinking Ukrainian History,* ed. Ivan L. Rudnytsky (Edmonton: Canadian Institute of Ukrainian Studies 1981), pp. 103–19.

66 For the incorporation of the former *szlachta* into the Cossack elite see Lypynsky, *Ukraina na perelomi,* pp. 88–185.

67 When Bohdan Khmelnytsky's son Iuras was appointed *hetman* by the Ottomans, they referred to him as the "prince of Sarmatia."

68 See "Istochniki," p. 242.

69 Orlyk to Yusuf Paşa, 10 March 1712, in "Perepiska," p. 57.

70 Statistical data on Left Bank Ukraine may be found in O.S. Kompan, "Do pytannia pro zaselenist Ukrainy v XVII st.," *Ukrainskyi istorychnyi zhurnal* 1 (1960): 65–77: M.I. Slabchenko, *Hospodarstvo Hetmanshchyny v XVII–XVIII st.,* 3 vols. (Odessa: Derzhavne Vydavnytstvo Ukrainy 1924); *Istoriia Ukrainskoi RSR,* 8 vols. (Kiev: Naukova Dumka 1979), vol. 2; V.O. Holobutsky, *Ekonomichna istoriia Ukrainskoi RSR* (Kiev: Vyshcha Shkola 1970). Much relevant data can also be ex-

trapolated from I.K. Kirilov, *Tsvetushchee sostoianie vserossiiskogo gosudarstva* (Moscow: Nauka 1977).

71 Cited in Viacheslav Lypynsky, *Ukraina na perelomi* (Vienna: Dniprosoiuz 1920), p. 22. A recent discussion of proposed reforms in the Commonwealth is Maria Pryshlak, "'Forma Mixta' as a Political Ideal of a Polish Magnate: Lukasz Opalinski's 'Rozmowa Plebana z Ziemianinem'", *The Polish Review* 23 (1981): 26–42.

CHAPTER THREE: THE ABSOLUTIST OFFENSIVE

1 Halil Inalcik, *The Ottoman Empire; The Classical Age, 1300–1600* (New York and Washington: Praeger 1973), p. 86.

2 Ibid., p. 87.

3 Ibid., p. 80.

4 Stanford Shaw, *The Ottoman Empire*, 2 vols., vol. 1 (Cambridge: Cambridge University Press 1977), p. 226; and A.D. Novichev, *Istoriia Turtsii*, 4 vols., vol. 1 (Leningrad: Izdatelstvo Leningradskogo universiteta 1963), p. 55.

5 Inalcik, *Ottoman Empire*, p. 80.

6 See Donald Pitcher, *A Historical Geography of the Ottoman Empire From Earliest Times to the End of the Sixteenth Century* (Leiden: Brill 1972), pp. 124–35, for a concise discussion of the Ottoman imperial administration.

7 A useful if somewhat one-sided overview of Ottoman rule in Moldavia is provided by Mokhov, *Moldaviia*, pp. 206–363. The Ottoman point of view is presented by Halil Inalcik, "Ottoman Methods of Conquest," *Studia Islamica* 2 (1954): 103–30. A classic study of Moldavian relations with the Ottoman Porte is C. Giurescu, *Capitulatiile Moldavei cu Poarta Otomană* (Bucharest 1908). Also see P.P. Panaitescu, "De cen-au cucerit turcii tările romane," *Interpretari romanești* (Bucharest 1947), pp. 149–59. Recent studies on the topic are M. Neagoe, "Contributii la problema aservirii Moldovei fata de imperiul otoman," in *Studii* 17 (1954): 311–22; N. Beldiceanu, "La Moldavie ottomane à la fin du xve et au début du xvie siècle," *Revue des études islamiques* 37 (1969): 239–61; Ion Matei, "Quelques problèmes concernant le régime de la domination ottomane dans les pays roumains," *Revue des études sud-est européennes* 10 (1972): 56–81; Cristina Rotman, "Das Problem der Wiederherstellung der osmanischen Herrschaft über die rumanischen Länder zu Beginn des 17. Jahrhunderts," *Deutsch-Rumänisches Colloquium* (Munich: Südosteuropa Gesellschaft 1974), pp. 11–21; Tahsin Gemil, "Considérations sur les rapports politiques roumano-ottomans au xviie siècle," *Revue roumaine d'histoire* 15 (1976): 654–67. An excellent English-language survey of the problem is Keith Hitchens, "Ottoman Domination of Moldavia and Wallachia in the 16th Century," *Asian Studies* 1 (1966): 123–41. Also see the collection of articles in *Revue des études sud-est européennes* 13 (1975): 403–47; and Peter Sugar, *Southeastern Europe under Ottoman Rule, 1354–1804* (Seattle and London: University of Washington Press 1977).

8 B.N. Ermuratskii, *Obshchestvenno-politicheski vzgliady Dmitriia Kantemira* (Kishinev: Kartia Moldoveniaske 1956), p. 87.

9 Mihail Berza has written two detailed studies on the subject of Ottoman economic exploitation of the principalities. See his "Haraciul Moldovei şi Ţării Româneşti in sec. xv–xix," *Studii* 2 (1957): 7–48, and "Variaţile exploatării Tarii Romineşti de catre Poarta Otomanà în secolele xvi–xviii," *Studii* 4 (1958): 59–71. For the early period of the tributary relationship see Mihail Guboglu, "Le tribut payé par les principautés roumaines à la Porte jusqu'au début du xvie siècle," *Revue des études islamiques* 37 (1969): 49–75. The Ottoman monopoly on the purchase of foodstuffs in Moldavia has been treated by Walter Hahn, "Die Verpflegung Konstantinoples durch staatlich Zwangswirtschaft," *Vierteljahrschrift für Sozial- und Wirtschaftgeschichte* 9 (1926): 1–25; and N. Grigoras, "Obligaţiile în muncă faţă de stat şi turci ale populaţiei din Moldova," *Studii* 18 (1965): 895–1914.

10 Berza, "Variaţile exploatarii," pp. 60–1.

11 Ibid., p. 62.

12 Mokhov, *Moldaviia*, p. 213.

13 For Ottoman plans to impose a centralized form of government in the principalities see Metin Kunt, "17 Yüzyilda Osmanli Kuzey politikasi üzerine bir yorum," *Boğaziçi Üniversitesi Dergisi* 4–5 (1976–7): 111–16.

14 For statistical data see Ernest Werner, "Despotie, Absolutismus oder feudale Zersplitterung," *Jahrbuch für Wirtschaftsgeschichte* 3 (1972): 107–28; for estimates of the land area of the empire see Pitcher, *A Historial Geography of the Ottoman Empire*, pp. 134–5. Estimates of the population of the Ottoman empire may be found in Ferdinand Braudel, *The Mediterranean* (New York: Harper 1972), pp. 395–6. The most thorough analysis of Ottoman demography may be found in Omer Lutfi Barkan, "Essai sur les données statistiques des registres de recensement dans l'empire ottoman aux xve et xvie siècles," *Journal of the Economic and Social History of the Orient* 1 (1958): 30–3.

15 See A. Kan, *Istoriia Shvetsii* (Moscow: Nauka 1974), p. 219.

16 Ibid., p. 193.

17 A good overview of the topic of Swedish rule in Livonia may be found in Wittram, *Baltische Geschichte*, pp. 84–107. The most thorough study of Swedish policy in Livonia is Alvin Isberg, *Karl xi och den livländske adeln, 1684–1695* (Lund: Gleerup 1953). Also see his "Baltiska privilegiefràgor, 1697–1700," in *Svio-Estonica* 15 (1960): 103–15. A recent study of Swedish administrative practice in Livonia is Anna Meurling, *Svensk Domstolförvaltning i Livland, 1634–1700* (Lund: Gleerup 1967). An older but still useful study is Otto Grieffenhagen, "Begrundung und Ausbau der schwedischen Herrschaft in Estland und Livland durch Gustav Adolf," *Baltische Monatschrift* 5 (1929): 325–35. A very useful work which deals with Sweden's policy towards all of her overseas provinces is Sven Lundkvist, "The Experience of Empire: Sweden as a Great Power," in Michael Roberts, ed., *Sweden's Age of Greatness, 1632–1718* (New York 1973), pp. 20–57. A recent and very informative study on this topic is H. Thomson, *Schweden und seine Provinzen Estland und Livland in ihrem gegenseitigen Verhältnis, 1561–1710* (Oldenburg 1975).

18 For a discussion of the *Reduktion* as it applied to the entire empire see Kurt

Agren, "The *Reduktion*," in Roberts, *Sweden's Age of Greatness*, pp. 237–64. The classic study of the *Reduktion* as it applied to Livonia is Johan Vasar, *Die Grösse Livländische Güter-Reduktion* (Tartu 1931). A more recent and very detailed study is Edgars Dunsdorfs, *Der Grosse Schwedische Kataster in Livland 1681–1710* (Stockholm: Wahlström & Widstrand 1950). A very recent Soviet study which provides a detailed analysis of the Swedish income from the *Reduktion* in Livonia is H.I. Piirimäe, "Die reduzierten Güter in Livland als Einnahme-quelle des schwedischen Reiches," in *Problemy razvitie feodalizma v stranakh Baltiki* (Tartu 1972), pp. 47–73.

19 See Piirimäe, "Die reduzierten Güter," pp. 64–7.

20 Lundkvist, "The Experience of Empire," p. 23.

21 Ibid., p. 41.

22 Wittram, *Baltische Geschichte*, p. 92.

23 S.A. Carlsson, "Finlands ämbetmän och Sverige rike under 1700-talet; Grupper och gestalter," *Studier om individ och kolletiv i nordisk och europeisk historia* (Lund 1965), p. 71.

24 According to Wittram, *Baltische Geschichte*, p. 94, there were sixteen Livonian field marshals in the Swedish army.

25 For statistics relating to Sweden see Kan, *Istoriia Shvetsii*; Thomson, *Schweden und seine Provinzen*; Claude Nordmann, *Grandeur et Liberté de la Suede* (Paris and Louvain: Nauwelaerts 1971); Piirmae, "Die reduzierte Güter"; and Dunsdorfs, *Der grosse Schwedische Kataster*.

26 See Leopold v. Ranke, "Die Grossen Mächte," *Historisch-Politische Zeitschrift* (1833), p. 17.

27 The topic of Habsburg absolutism in Hungary is so broad that only the more basic and recent studies can be mentioned. An excellent survey of the subject may be found in Oscar Redlich, *Weltmacht des Barock: Österreich in der Zeit Kaiser Leopolds 1*, 4th edn. (Vienna 1961), pp. 196–235, 415–84. Studies of Habsburg administrative practice and theory during the absolutist period are Hermann Bidermann, *Geschichte der österreichischen Gesaamt-Staats-Idee, 1526–1804* (Innsbruck 1867); Theodor Mayer, *Verwaltungsreform in Ungarn nach der Türkenzeit* (Vienna and Leipzig 1911); and Fritz Walter, *Österreichische Verfassungs und Verwaltungs Geschichte von 1500 bis 1955* (Cologne and Vienna 1972). Recent Hungarian scholarship has provided several interesting studies on the subject: Gyözö Ember, "Die absolute Monarchie der Habsburger als Hindernis der ungari-shen nationalen Entwicklung," *Acta Historica Academiae Scientiarum Hungaricae* 4 (1955): 73–96; Lászlo Makkai, "Die Entstehung der gesellschaftlichen Basis des Absolutismus in den Ländern der österreichischen Habsburger," *Studia Historica* 43 (1960): 3–41, Ágnes Várkonyi, "Habsburg Absolutism and Serfdom in Hungary at the Turn of the 17th and 18th Centuries," *Nouvelles études historiques publiées a l'occasion du XIIe congrès international des sciences historiques par la commission nationale des historiens hongrois*, vol. 1 (Budapest: Akademiai Kiadó 1965), pp. 355–87; Kálmán Benda, "L'absolutisme et la résistance des ordres au xve siècle dans les états de la Maison d'Autriche, *Études historiques hongrois*, vol. 1

(Budapest: Akadémiai Kiadó 1975), pp. 381–98; Mathias Bernath, "Ständewesen und Absolutismus im Ungarn des 18. Jahrhunderts," *Südost Forschungen* 22 (1963): 347–55. The French historian Jean Bérenger has also examined the subject. See his "Les fondements théoriques de l'absolutisme dans la Hongrie du XVIIᵉ siècle," *Mélanges offerts a Aurélien Saugeot pour son soixantequinziéme anniversaire* (Budapest: Akadémiai Kiadó 1972), pp. 23–8; also see Karl Nehring, "Die Anfänge der habsburgischen Herrschaft in Ungarn," *Deutsch-Rumänisches Colloquium*, pp. 112–23.

28 Redlich, *Weltmacht*, p. 155.

29 Ibid.

30 V.P. Shusharin, et al., eds., *Istoriia Vengrii*, 3 vols., vol. 1 (Moscow: Nauka, 1971), p. 322.

31 Redlich, *Weltmacht*, p. 215.

32 See Makkai, "Basis des Absolutismus," p. 41; and Várkonyi, "Absolutism and Serfdom," p. 356.

33 An excellent example of the Habsburgs' approach to the liquidation of Transylvanian autonomy is the plan prepared by the Habsburg military governor of Transylvania, General A. Caraffa. See Andreas Gräser, ed., "Caraffa's Project: Wie Siebenbürgen unter k.k. österreichischer Devotion zu erhalten," *Archiv des Vereins für Siebenbürgische Landeskunde*, n.s., 1 (Kronstadt 1853): 162–88.

34 A rich source for statistical data pertaining to the Habsburg empire in the late seventeenth century is Jean Bérenger, *Finances et absolutisme autrichien* (Paris: Publications de la Sorbonne 1975). Also see H. Helczmanovski, ed., *Beiträge zur Bevölkerungs und sozialgeschichte Österreichs* (Vienna 1973), pp. 96–106.

35 In the early 1970s the nature of Russian absolutism became the subject of a heated controversy among Soviet historians. For an overview of this controversy see Thomas Esper, "Recent Soviet Views of Russian Absolutism," *Forschungen zur osteuropäischen Geschichte* 20 (1973): 113–33. Also see N.M. Druzhinin, ed., *Absoliutizm v Rossii XVII–XVIII vv.*) (Moscow: Nauka 1964); Richard Pipes, *Russia under the Old Regime* (New York: Scribners 1974); Hans-Joachim Torke, *Die staatsbedingte Gesellschaft im Moskauer Reich* (Leiden: Brill 1974); and B.I. Syromiatnikov, *"Regularnoe" Gosudarstvo Petra pervogo i ego ideologiia* (Moscow: Akademiia Nauk SSSR 1943).

36 For the growth of Russian control over Ukraine see Georg v. Rauch, *Russland: Staatliche Einheit und nationale Vielfalt* (Munich: Isar Verlag 1953), pp. 25–30; Boris Nolde, *La formation de l'empire russe*, vol. I (Paris: Institut d'Etudes Slaves 1952), pp. 37–53, 108–15, and his *L'Ukraine sous la protection russe* (Geneva 1915); Konstantyn Kononenko, *Ukraine and Russia: A History of Their Economic Relations, 1654–1917* (Milwaukee: Marquette University Press 1958); Hedwig Fleischhacker, "Aleksei Mikhailovich und Bogdan Chmelnickij," *Jahrbücher für Kultur and Geschichte der Slaven*, n.s. 9 (1935): 11–52; Ivan Dzhydzhora, *Ukraina v pershii polovynyi XVIII v.* (Kiev: Vseukrainska Akademiia Nauk 1930); C.B. O'Brien, *Muscovy and the Ukraine: From the Pereiaslavl Agreement to the Truce of Andrussovo, 1654–1667* (Berkeley: University of California Press 1963); and, most recently,

Orest Subtelny, "Russia and the Ukraine: The Difference That Peter I Made," *Russian Review* 39 (1980): 1–17.

37 For a thorough and non-partisan review of the many different opinions expressed about the nature of the Pereiaslav Treaty, see Oscar Gunther, "Der Vertrag von Pereiaslav im Widerstreit der Meinungen," *Jahrbücher für Geschichte Osteuropas* 2 (1954): 232–57. Also see Orest Subtelny, "Mazepa, Peter I and the Question of Treason," *Harvard Ukrainian Studies* 2 (1978): 158–83; and Basarab, *Pereiaslav 1654*.

38 See O'Brien, *Muscovy and Ukraine*, p. 113; and Andrii Iakovliv, *Ukrainsko-Moskovski dohovory v XVII–XVIII vikakh* (Warsaw: Pratsi Ukrainskoho Naukovoho Instytutu 1934), p. 125.

39 See K.A. Sofronenko, *Malorossiiskii prikaz russkkogo gosudarstva vtoroi poloviny XVII i nachala XVIII veka* (Moscow 1960); and Subtelny," Russia and the Ukraine," pp. 4–6.

40 Hrushevsky, *Istoriia Ukrainy-Rusi* 9:1417.

41 See Iakovliv, *Ukrainsko-Moskovski dohovory*, p. 76.

42 Ibid., p. 86.

43 See V.N. Romanovskii, *Perepis naseleniia levoberezhnoi Ukrainy 1660 goda* (Stavropol 1967), p. 45.

44 Iakovliv, *Ukrainsko-Moskovski dohovory*, p. 127.

45 Oleksander Ohloblyn, *Hetman Ivan Mazepa i ioho doba* (New York: ODFFU 1960), p. 261.

46 "The Letter of Orlyk to Iavorsky," in Orest Subtelny, *The Mazepists: Ukrainian Separatism in the Eighteenth Century* (Denver: East European Monographs 1981), p. 184.

47 Ibid., p. 183.

48 Ibid., p. 185.

49 For statistical data on early eighteenth-century Russia see V.M. Kabuzan, *Narodnaselenie Rossii v XVIII-per. polovine XIX v.* (Moscow: Akademiia Nauk SSR 1963). Also see his *Izmeneniia v razmeshchenii naseleniia Rossii* (Moscow: Akademiia Nauk SSR 1971); *Ocherk istorii SSR (XVIII)*, vol. I; Kirilov, *Tsvetiushchee sostoinieei*; Richard Hellie, *Enserfment and Military Change in Muscovy* (Chicago: University of Chicago Press 1971); and Ia.E. Vodarskii, *Naselenie Rossii v kontse XVII-nachale XVIII veka* (Moscow: Nauka 1977).

50 See Paul Haake, *August der Starke* (Berlin: Paeld 1926), p. 78.

51 Ibid., p. 79.

52 The best discussion of Wettin policy in the Commonwealth may be found in the collection of articles edited by Józef Gierowski and Johannes Kalisch, *Um die polnische Krone* (Berlin: Rütten & Loening, 1962). An older but still relevant exchange of ideas among Johannes Zierkusch, Otto Schmidt, and Paul Haake on the nature of Wettin policy is "Zur Geschichte August des Starken: Die polnische Politik der Wettiner im 18. Jahrhundert," in *Neues Archiv* 26 (1905): 107–29. Also see Albrecht Philipp, "Zur Geschichte der wettinischen Reformsversüche in Polen," *Neues Archiv* 24 (1913): 168–74. Among the older Polish works

are Kazimierz Jarochowski, *Dzieje panowania Augusta* II (Poznan: Merzbach 1874); and Marceli Handelsman's article "Zamach stanu Augusta II," in his *Studja historyczne* (Warsaw 1911), pp. 3–49. More recent literature on the subject includes two studies by Józef Gierowski, *Między saskim absolutyzmem a złotą wolnością* (Wrocław: Ossolineum 1953) and *W cieniu ligi północnej* (Wrocław: Ossolineum 1971). Also see Józef Gierowski, "La France et les tendances absolutistes du roi de Pologne, August II," *Acta Poloniae Historica* 17 (1968): 49–70. A study which tends to de-emphasize the absolutist nature of August II's plans is Henryk Olszewski, *Doktryny prawno-ustrojowe czasów saskich, 1697–1740* (Warsaw: PWN 1961). Also see Janusz Wojtasik, "Walka Augusta II z obozem kontystowsko-prymasowkim w pierszym roku panowania (1697–98)," *Przegląd historyczny* 60 (1969): 24–93. Among the latest contributions to this topic are Jacek Staszewski, "Pomysly reformatorskie czasow Augusta II," *Kwartalnik historyczny* (1975), pp. 736–65; and Józef Gierowski, "Centralization and Autonomy in the Polish-Saxon Union," *Harvard Ukrainian Studies* 3–4 (1979–80): 271–84.

53 See Karl Biedermann, *Deutschland im 18. Jhr.*, 2nd edn., 3 vols., vol. 1 (Leipzig: Scienta Verlag 1880), p. 102.

54 A socio-economic treatment of Saxony is Karlheinz Blaschke, "Soziale Gliederung und Entwicklung der sächsischen Landbevölkerung im 16. bis 18. Jahrhundert," *Zeitschrift für Agrargeschichte und Agrarsoziologie* 4 (1956): 144–55.

55 For a detailed list of August II's costs in winning the Polish crown see Johannes Kalisch, "Zur Polenpolitik Augusts des Starken 1697 bis 1700" (PHD dissertation, University of Leipzig 1957), app. 4. Also see Charles Sass, "The Election Campaign in Poland in 1696–7," *Journal of Central European Affairs* 12 (1952): 111–27.

56 The text of this project, which was entitled "Projekt jak Tron Polski dziedicznym uczynic ... ," may be found in Edward Raczynski, ed., *Obraz Polaków i Polski w XVIII wieku* (Wrocław: Schletter 1843), pp. 1–9. Gierowski, *W cieniu*, p. 107, believes that the document was written in 1699. He also does not exclude the possibility that it might be an apochryphal work.

57 A text of this interesting document may be found in Józef Gierowski, ed., *Rzeczpospolita w dobie upadku, 1700–1740* (Wrocław: Ossolineum 1955), pp. 194–7. For a discussion of this resolution see Olszewski, *Doktryny*, p. 50.

58 August II's plans for Moldavia and Wallachia are treated in V.D. Koroliuk, *Polska i Rosja a wojna północna* (Warsaw: Książka i Wiedza 1954), pp. 84–6. A thorough study of August II's diplomatic activity is Jacek Staszewski, *O miesce w Europie: stosunki Polski i Saksonii z Francją na przelomie XVII i XVIII wieku* (Warsaw: PWN 1973).

59 See Borys Krupnyckyj, "Zu den polnischen Teilungsprojekten, 1709–1711," *Zeitschrift für Osteuropàische Geschichte* 9 (1935): 388–402.

60 For statistical data on Saxony see Blaschke, "Soziale Gliederung und Entwicklung," pp. 144–55. Also see R.I. Kotzschke and H.H. Kretzschmer, *Sächsische Geschichte* (Frankfurt am Main 1965); and Albrecht Philipp, *August der Starke und die Pragmatische Sanktion* (Leipzig: Von Quelle & Meyer 1908).

CHAPTER FOUR: THE GENERAL CRISIS IN EASTERN EUROPE

1 Most of the contributions to this debate have been reprinted in Thomas Aston, ed., *Crisis in Europe, 1560–1660* (London: Routledge & Kegan Paul 1965). Also see the most recent and incisive discussion by Thomas Rabb, *The Struggle for Stability in Early Modern Europe* (Oxford: Oxford University Press 1975). An East European treatment of the topic is Miroslav Hroch and Josef Petran, "Europejska gospodarka i polityka xvi i xvii wieku: kryzys czy regres?" *Przegląd Historyczny* 55 (1964): 251–67.

2 See Ivo Schöffer, "Did Holland's Golden Age Coincide with a Period of Crisis?" *Acta Historiae Neerlandica* 1 (1966): 82–197. Other dissenting opinions may be found in E.H. Kossmann, "Trevor-Roper's 'General Crisis,'" *Past and Present* 18 (1960): 8–11; and A.D. Lublinskaia, *French Absolutism: The Crucial Phase, 1620–1629* (Cambridge: Cambridge University Press 1968).

3 See J.H. Elliott, "Revolution and Continuity in Early Modern Europe," *Past and Present* 42 (1969): 35–56. Also see A. Lloyd Moote, "The Preconditions of Revolution in Early Modern Europe: Did They Really Exist? in *Canadian Journal of History* 8 (1972): 207–34; and Robert Forster and Jack Greene, eds., *Preconditions of Revolution in Early Modern Europe* (Baltimore: Johns Hopkins Press 1970). For an East European view of the subject see Jerzy Topolski, "Rewolucje w dziejach nowożytnych i najnowszych (xvii–xx wiek)," *Kwartalnik Historyczny* 83 (1976): 251–67.

4 Perez Zagorin, *Rebels and Rulers, 1500–1660*, 2 vols. (Cambridge: Cambridge University Press 1982).

5 Ibid., 1:41.

6 Ibid., ii: 2.

7 See Reinhard Wittram, "Patkul und der Ausbruch des Nordischen Krieges," *Nachrichten der Akademie der Wissenschaften in Göttingen, Philo-Historische Klasse* 9 (1952): 201–32. Also see Alvin Isberg, "Johann Reinhold Patkul och Livland åren 1699–1701," *Karolinska Förbundets Årsbok* (1960), pp. 71–97; a recent study of Patkul is Yella Erdmann, *Der livländische Staatsmann Johann Reinhold von Patkul* (Berlin: Haude & Spenersche 1970).

8 This statement was part of a complaint which Patkul and others lodged with Charles XI in 1692. See Thomson, *Schweden und seine Provinzen*, p. 231. Also see Wittram, *Baltische Geschichte*, p. 92.

9 Thomson, *Schweden und seine Provinzen*, p. 246.

10 Erdmann, *Patkul*, p. 62.

11 Ibid., p. 65. For the full text of the proposal see E. Herrmann, "Atkenstücke aus dem Polnisch-Schwedischen Kriege, Livland betreffend," *Archiv für die Geschichte Liv-Esth- und Courland* 7 (Reval 1852): 1–10.

12 A summary of these documents may be found in Thomson, *Schweden und seine Provinzen*, p. 314.

13 The full text of this agreement may be found in Hermann, "Aktenstücke aus den Polnisch-Schwedischen Kriege," pp. 10–23.

14 Wittram, *Baltische Geschichte*, p. 92.

15 For Patkul's activity during this period see N.G. Ustrialov, *Istoriia tsarstvovaniia Petra Velikogo*, 6 vols., vol. 3 (St Petersburg 1858–63), pp. 294–383.

16 Thomson, *Schweden und seine Provinzen, p.* 308.

17 Ibid., p. 318.

18 Two classic studies of the Commonwealth during this period are Wladisław Konopczynski, *Polska a Szwecja* (Warsaw: Instytut Popierania Polskiej Twórczosci 1924); and Józef Feldman, *Polska w dobie wielkiej wojny pólnocnej, 1704–1709* (Cracow: Polska Akademja Umiejętności 1925). More recent studies of the period are Józef Gierowski, *W cieniu ligi pólnocnej* (Wrocław: Ossolineum 1971); and Andrżej Kaminski, *Konfederacja Sandomierska wobec Rosji w okresie poaltransztadzkim 1706–1709* (Wrocław, Warsaw, and Cracow: Ossolineum 1970).

19 For Charles XII's plans prior to the invasion of Poland see Ragnhild Hatton, *Charles XII of Sweden* (London: Weybright & Talley 1968), pp. 167–85. Also see Gustaf Jonasson, *Karl XII: S. Polskapolitik 1702–1703* (Stockholm: Svenska Bokförlaget 1968).

20 This election is described in detail by Konopczynski, *Polska a Swecja*, p. 47.

21 Charles XII's dislike of revolutions and his anti-Saxon propaganda is discussed by Hatton, *Charles XII* , pp. 168–79.

22 Konopczynski, *Polska a Szwecja*, p 51.

23 See Olszewski, *Doktryny prawno-ustrojowe*, p. 82.

24 See Julian Janczak, "Der Palej Aufstand," in *Um die polnische Krone*, pp. 95–129.

25 The number of Lesczynski's supporters is cited by Jadwiga Lechicka, *Rola dziejowa Stanisława Leszczyńskiego* (Torun: Towarżystwo Nauk 1951), p. 27.

26 For the text of this treaty and a commentary see Konopczynski, *Polska a Szwecja*, pp. 50, 355. Also see Feldman, *Polska w dobie*, pp. 116–32.

27 Konopczynski, *Polska a Szwecja*, p. 46.,

28 This issue is treated in detail by Józef Gierowski, *Między saskiem absolutyzmem a złotą wolnością* (Wrocław: Ossolineum 1953).

29 Ibid., p. 292.

30 Ibid.

31 See Józef Feldman, *Stanisław Leszczynski* (Warsaw: PWN 1959), p. 101.

32 Gierowski, *Między saskiem absolutyzmem*, p. 5.

33 Ibid., p. 305.

34 Feldman, *Stanisław Leszczynski*, p. 100.

35 Stefan Kieniewicz et al., *History of Poland* (Warsaw: PWN 1968), p. 273.

36 For Mazepa's contacts with Leszczynski see Mykola Andrusiak, "Zviazky Mazepy z Stanislavom Leshchynskym i Karlom XII," *ZNTSh* 152 (1933): 1–59. Also see Subtelny, *The Mazepists*, pp. 26–32.

37 "Letter of Orlyk to Iavorsky," in Subtelny, *The Mazepists*, p. 191.

38 See *Trudy Imperatorskago russkago voenno-istoricheskago obshchestva* (St Petersburg 1909), p. 276.

39 See "Letopisanoe povestvovanie o Maloi Rossi," pt. 3 in *Chteniia* I (Moscow 1847): 52.

40 "Dopros Apostola," December 1708, "Istochniki," p. 214.

41 Nikolai Kostomarov, *Mazepa i Mazepintsy*, 2nd. edn. (St Petersburg: Stasiulevich 1885), p. 435.

42 Peter I to F.A. Apraksin, 30 October 1708, *Pisma i bumagi*, vol. 8 (Moscow: Akademiia Nauk SSR 1960), p. 253.

43 Peter I to Menshikov, 27 October 1708, ibid., p. 237.

44 "Stati Gosudaria Petra I iavniia i tainiia blizhnemu stolniku Andreiu Izmailovu," 18, 27, 30 July 1709, "Istochniki," pp. 228–31.

45 Menshikov to Peter I, 26 October 1708, *Pisma i bumagi* 8: 947.

46 "Ukaz vsemu malorossiiskomu narodu," 6 November 1708, ibid., p. 276.

47 Skoropadsky's manifesto, 8 December 1708, "Istochniki," p. 198.

48 Charles XII's manifesto, 7 November 1708, ibid., p. 207.

49 General Rönne to Peter I, 30 March 1709, *Pisma i bumagi* 9: 748.

50 See N.I. Shutoi, *Borba narodnykh mass protiv nashestviia armii Karla XII 1700–1709* (Moscow: Sotsialno-ekonomicheskaia literatura 1958), p. 385.

51 For a discussion of these tribute payments see Mokhov, *Moldaviia*, pp. 348–9.

52 Miron Costin, *Opere Alese: Letopiseţul Ţǎrii Moldovei* (Bucharest: Ştiinţificǎ 1965), pp. 224–47.

53 For a general overview of Russo-Moldavian ties see N.A. Mokhov, *Ocherki istorii moldavsko-russko-ukrainskikh sviazei* (Kishinev: Shtiintsa 1961). Also see L.E. Semenova, "Iz istorii rumuno-russkikh sviazei kon. XVII–nach. XVIII vv.," *Vestnik Moskovskogo universiteta* 3 (1958): 159–80; H. Kirichenko, "O russko-moldavskhikh otonosheniakh v pervom desiatiletii XVIII v.," *Uchnenie zapiski Kishinevskogo gosudarstvennogo pedagogicheskogo instituta* 6 (1957): 21–9; I. Cheban, "O vzaimootnosheniiakh Moldavii s Moskovskim gosudarstvom v XV–XVIII vv.," *Voprosy istorii* 2 (1945): 59–71.

54 A thorough discussion of Brîncoveanu's ties with Peter I is L.E. Semenova, *Russko-Valashskie otnosheniia v kontse XVII–nachale XVIII v.* (Moscow: Nauka 1969).

55 See A.A. Kochubinskii, "Snosheniia Rumunov i Iugoslavian s Rossiei pri Petre velikom," *Zhurnal ministerstva narodnogo prosveshcheniia* 162 (1872): 52–140.

56 For Cantemir's ties with Russia see P.P. Panaitescu, *Dimitrie Cantemir Viata şi Opera* (Bucharest 1958), pp. 103–9; St Ciobanu, *Dimitrie Cantemir în Rusia* (Bucharest 1925); Andrei Pippidi, "Politicǎ şi istorie în proclamatia lui Dimitrie Cantemir din 1711," *Studii* 26 (1973): 923–46; Florin Constantiniu, "La politique étrangère de Dimitrie Cantemir: analyse d'une décision," *Revue roumaine d'études internationales* 7 (1973): 119–29; Demetrius Dvoichenko-Markov, "Demetrius Kantemir and Russia," *Balkan Studies* 12 (1971): 383–98.

57 The various versions of the text of the treaty are discussed in H. Kirichenko, "Tekst russko-moldavskogo dogovora 1711 g." According to Pippidi, "Politica şi istorie," *Studii*, p. 923, the treaty was preserved in nine copies: "seven in Latin, one in German, one in French." A text of the treaty may be found in *Istoricheskie sviazy narodov SSSR i Rumunii*, vol. 3 (Moscow: Nauka 1970), pp. 323–7.

58 Ion Neculce (1672–1745) was a boyar and close associate of Cantemir. For his political views see E. Russev, "Vneshnepoliticheskaia kontseptsia boiarskogo

letopisaniia Moldavii," in *Iugo-vostochnaia Evropa v epokhu feodalizma* (Kishinev: Shtiintsa 1973), pp. 167–9.

59 See Kantemir, *Opisanie Moldavii*, p. 139.

60 Cited in Pippidi, "Politica şi istorie," p. 924.

61 Ion Neculce, as cited in Russev, "Vneshnopoliticheskia," p. 168.

62 See Pippidi, "Politica şi istorie," p. 939.

63 Ibid., p. 939.

64 Ibid., p. 937.

65 A. Papiu-Ilarian, ed., *Descriera Moldovei* (Bucharest 1872), p. 109.

66 See *Istoricheskie sviazy narodov SSSR*, p. 332.

67 Ibid.

68 Neculce's estimate is cited by Mokhov, *Ocherki istorii*, p. 127. The *Istoriia Moldavskoi SSR* 1: 310 states that there were 200,000 Ottomans and 40,000 Russians at Prut.

69 See Semenova, *Russko-Valashskie otnosheniia*, pp. 117–42.

70 For an analysis of the Prut Treaty see Akdes Kurat, "Der Prutfeldzug und Prutfrieden von 1711," *Jahrbücher für Geschichte Osteuropas* 10 (1962): 55–7; and Svetlana Oreshkova, *Russko-turetskie otnosheniia v nachale XVIII v.* (Moscow: Nauka 1971).

71 See Kochubinskii, "Snosheniia Rumunov," pp. 118–21; and Mokhov, *Ocherki istorii*, pp. 131–3.

72 For the Phanariot influence in Moldavia in the pre-1711 period see C. Obedeanu, *Grecii in Tara-Romaneasca* (Bucharest 1900); and a recent study, Constantin Şerban, "Les préliminaires de l'époque phanariote," in *Symposium de l'époque phanariote* (Salonika 1974), pp. 29–41. Also see N. Berezniakov, "Turetskofanariotskii gnet v Moldavii," in *Feodalnie otnoshenie v Moldavii v period XIV–XVIII vekov* (Kishinev: Shtiintsa 1950), pp. 129–62.

73 The historical literature on Rákóczi is vast. In the pre-WW II period the most authoritative biography of the prince was Sándor Márki, *II Rákóczi Ferenc*, 3 vols. (Budapest: A Magyar Történelmi Társulat Kiadósa 1907–10). A recent biography is Béla Kopëczi and R. Ágnes Várkonyi, *II Rákóczi Ferenc* (Budapest: Gondolat 1976). For the prince's autobiography see Béla Köpeczi, ed., *L'autobiographie d'un prince rebelle: Confession et memoires de Francois II Rákóczi* (Budapest: Akadémiai Kiadó 1977). Other noteworthy works which appeared recently on the occasion of the 300th anniversary of Rákóczi's birth are Béla Kópeczi, Ágnes, Várkonyi, and Lajos Hopp, eds., *Rákóczi-tanulmányok* (Budapest: Akadémiai Kiadó 1980); and Kálmán Benda, ed., *Európa és a Rákóczi-szabadságharc* (Budapest: Akadémiai Kiadó 1980). A brief English-language overview is Béla Köpeczi, "Ferenc Rákóczi II," *The New Hungarian Quarterly* 61 (1976): 39–57. Also see the dated but still useful Louis Hengelmüller, *Franz Rákóczi und sein Kampf für Ungarns Freiheit* (Stuttgart and Berlin 1913).

74 For Rákóczi's landholdings see Béla Köpeczi, *La France et la Hongrie au début du XVIIIᵉ siècle* (Budapest: Akadémiai Kiadó 1971), p. 25.

75 Kálmán Thaly, an often uncritical historian of the Hungarian rebels, wrote a

study of the Bercsényi family, *A szekesi gróf Bercsény csalad 1470–1835* (Budapest 1887–92). For the correspondence between Rákóczi and Bercsényi see Kálmán Thaly, ed., *Gróf Berscényi Miklós levelei Rákóczi fejedelemhez* (Pest 1877).

76 A recent and thorough study of Hungarian-French relations during this period is Köpeczi, *La France et la Hongrie.*

77 A copy of this manifesto may be found in Kálmán Thaly, *A szekesi gróf Bercsényi csalad,* vol. 2, pp. 369–80.

78 Rákóczi's Polish period has been treated in the following works: Kazimierz Jarochowski, "Epizod Rakoczowy w dziejach panowanija Augusta II od roky 1703–1719," in his *Z czasow saskich* (Poznan: Piotrowski 1886), pp. 187–323; Stefan Tomashivsky, "Uhorshchyna i Polshcha na pochatku XVIII v.," in *ZNTSh* 86 (1908): 89–133; 87: 75–87; 88: 33–73; 89: 43–80; 90: 31–58. For the most recent treatment of Hungarian-Polish ties see Lajos Hopp, *A Lengyelmagyar hagyomanyok újjászületése* (Budapest: Akadémiai Kiadó 1973). Hopp has also written a study of Rákóczi's stay in Poland, *A Rákóczi-emigrácio Lengyelországban* (Budapest: Akadémiai Kiadó 1973).

79 The term *kuruc* is derived from the Latin *cruciatus,* "crusader," a name applied to Hungarian peasants who assembled for a crusade against the Turks in 1514 and then launched the great revolt, led by György Dosza, against the nobles.

80 Thomashivsky, "Uhorshchyna i Polshcha," p. 35.

81 *Istoriia Vengrii,* 3 vols., vol. 1 (Moscow: Nauka 1971), p. 430.

82 For a discussion of this question see Zsigmond Pach, "Le problème du rassemblement des forces nationales pendant la guerre d'indépendance de François II Rákóczi," *Acta Historica* 3 (Budapest 1954): 95–113.

83 *Istoriia Vengrii* 1:438. Also see Várkonyi, "Habsburg Absolutism and Serfdom in Hungary at the Turn of the XVII–XVIII Centuries," pp. 355–87.

84 The etomology of the term *labanc* is difficult to establish. It may derive from the German *lanzer* or *landsknecht.*

85 For the text of the document see Sándor László, *Magyarorszag törtenete,* vol. 1 (Pest 1857), pp. 135–6.

86 The well-organized production of munitions of the *kuruc* armies is discussed by Gusztav Heckenast, *Fegyver- és lószergyártás a Rákóczi-szabadságharcban* (Budapest: Akadémiai Kaidó 1959.

87 For a discussion of Rákóczi's absolutist tendencies see Ágnes Várkonyi, "Az abszolutizmus kérdéseiröl," *Történelmi Szemle* 5 (1962): 37–51. Also see Várkonyi's very interesting treatment of these absolutist tendencies in her article "Historical Personality, Crisis and Progress in 17th Century Hungary," *Studia Historica* 71 (Budapest 1970): 265–99.

88 See *Istoriia Vengrii* 1:439.

89 The debates of Ónod were widely reported in the European press. For a survey of the coverage see Köpeczi, *La France et la Hongrie,* pp. 417–22.

90 Ibid., pp. 338–9.

91 Ibid., pp. 335–52.

92 Rákóczi's ties with Peter I have been thoroughly studied. Sándor Márki, *Nagy*

Péter czár és II Rákóczi Ferenc szövetsége 1707-ben (Budapest 1913); József Perenyi, "II Rákóczi Ferenc es I Peter diplomáciai kapcsolatainak kezdetei," in Endre Kovács, ed., *Magyar-orosz történelmi kapcsolatok* (Budapest: Akadémiai Kiadó 1956); Ia. V. Shternberg, "Russko-vengerskie otnosheniia perioda poltavskoi pobedy," in M.B. Grekov and V.D. Koroliuk, eds., *Poltavskaia pobeda* (Moscow: Akademiia Nauk SSR 1959). Also see A.V. Florovsky, *Ot Poltavy do Pruta* (Prague 1971).

93 See Endre Kovács, *Magyarok és lengyelek a törtenelem sodrában* (Budapest 1973), pp. 193-4.

94 Zagorin, *Rebels and Rulers* 2 : 32.

95 Ibid., 2: 52-3.

CHAPTER FIVE: THE ÉMIGRÉ EPILOGUE

1 For an interesting discussion of earlier Czech and Slovak emigrations see Eduard Winter, *Die tschechische und slowakische Emigration in Deutschland im 17. und 18. Jahrhundert* (Berlin: Akademie Verlag 1955). Also see Otakar Odložilík, "Ze zápasů pobělohorské emigrace," *Časopis Matice Moravské* 56 (1932): 1-58, 369-88.

2 It appears that the only other Livonian was Otto Arnold von Paykul, a Livonian expatriate living in Saxony. See Martin Ottow, "Otto Arnold von Paykul," *Jahrbuch des baltischen Deutschtums* 5 (1975): 51-64.

3 The early phase of Patkul's exile is treated in Ustrialov, *Istoriia*, and most recently by Erdmann, *Patkul*, pp. 54-66.

4 See Ottow, "Paykul," p. 58.

5 For a discussion of Charles XII's stay in Bender see Hatton, *Charles XII*, pp. 309-65. The stay of the Ukrainians at Bender is treated in Subtelny, *The Mazepists*, pp. 53-104.

6 Mazepa's fortune became the object of a bitter dispute between Voinarovsky and the exiled *starshyna*. See Subtelny, *The Mazepists*, pp. 58-9.

7 A perceptive biography of Mazepa is Ohloblyn, *Hetman Ivan Mazepa*. Also see Nikolai Kostomarov's classic study *Mazepa i Mazepintsy*.

8 For the text of the document see "Perepiska," pp. 18-9.

9 The Latin original of this document was published in ibid., 1-17. A study of this document is Mykola Vasylenko, "The Constitution of Pylyp Orlyk," *The Annals of the Ukrainian Academy of Arts and Sciences in the U.S.* 6 (New York 1958): 1260-96. The most recent analysis of the document may be found in Subtelny, *The Mazepists*, pp. 65-70.

10 A study of Orlyk's career is Borys Krupnytsky, *Hetman Pylyp Orlyk (1672-1742): Ohliad ioho politychnoi diialnosti* (Warsaw: Pratsi Ukrainskoho Naukovoho Instytutu 1938). Also see Subtelny, *The Mazepists*.

11 See Subtelny, *The Mazepists*, pp. 71-89.

12 Ibid., p. 126.

13 The best source for the initial period of Leszczynski's exile is Józef Feldman, *Polska a sprawa wschodnia* (Cracow: Polska Akademia Umiejętnosci 1926). Also see Feldman's *Stanisław Leszczynski* and Hatton, *Charles XII*.

14 A discussion of the tensions between the Polish and Ukrainian émigrés may be found in Subtelny, *The Mazepists*, pp. 84–6.

15 See Hatton, *Charles XII*, p. 339.

16 Feldman, *Leszczynski*, p. 107.

17 For a full-length study of Cantemir's stay in Russia see Ştefan Ciobanu, *Dimitrie Cantemir în Rusia* (Bucharest: Academia Română 1925). Also see Panaitescu, *Dimitrie Cantemir*. Two English-language articles on the topic are Grigore Nandriş, "Rumanian Exiles in 18th Century Russia," *Revue des études roumaines* 1 (Paris 1953): 44–71, and Demetrius Dvoichenko-Markov, "Demetrius Kantemir and Russia," *Balkan Studies* 12 (1971): 338–98.

18 For estimates of the number of Moldavian émigrés in Russia see Nandris, "Rumanian Exiles," p. 386.

19 Russian sources provide the following information about the number of leading Moldavian émigrés: high officials of the court, 9; boyars, 13 (and 130 aides); officers (captains and colonels), 9 (33 aides); lower-ranking officers, 19 (51 aides); the *hospodar's* staff, 75. See *Pisma i bumagi* II : 389. For an enumeration of the thirty-five boyar families represented among the émigrés see Ciobanu, *Cantemir în Rusia*, p. 387.

20 Cantemir to Peter, 1 August 1711, *Pisma i bumagi*, II: 63.

21 On 13 October 1711 Charles Whitworth reported to his government that "all the confiscated lands of Mazepa, the late *hetman* of Ukraine, have been given to him [Cantemir] for his maintenance." An estate belonging to Dmytro Horlenko, a close associate of Mazepa, was given to one of Cantemir's men. See *Pisma i bumagi* II: 387. A large part of the land which Cantemir received in Ukraine belonged to General R. Shidlovsky, the commander of the Ukrainian Cossacks in the *slobodas* who had been arrested on the tsar's orders for crossing the Polish border without authorization. The Ukrainian *starshyna* resented the Moldavian émigrés and indicated to the tsar that they were not to be trusted. See *Pisma i bumagi* II: 389. Also see Panaitescu, *Dimitrie Cantemir*, pp. 126–8, who mistakenly considered Shidlovsky to have been an associate of Mazepa.

22 As cited by Panaitescu, *Dimitrie Cantemir*, p. 128.

23 See F.C. Weber, *Das veränderte Russland* (Frankfurt-Leipzig 1744), p. 217.

24 Panaitescu, *Dimitrie Cantemir*, p. 131.

25 Ibid., p. 132.

26 Ibid.

27 For Rákóczi's stay in Poland after 1711 see Hopp, *A Rákóczi-emigráció Lengyelországban*, and especially his Polish-language study "Pobyt Ferenca Rakoczego II w Gdansku," *Rocznik Gdanski* 25 (1966): 115–59. About 2,000 Szeklers who had been with Rákóczi moved from Transylvania to Moldavia.

28 During the rebellion Rákóczi's wife resided in Poland, mostly in Warsaw. His two sons, Józef and György, were under detention in Vienna. For a contem-

porary account of József's career see H.E.S., *Merckwürdiges Leben und Taten des Prätendenten von Ungarn und Siebenbürgen, Jóseph Ragoczy* (Frankfurt and Leipzig 1739).

29 See Hopp, "Pobyt," p. 133.

30 Ibid., p. 139.

31 Kópeczi, *La France et la Hongrie*, p. 139.

32 For a discussion of Rákóczi's financial troubles in France, and in particular of the Hotel de Transylvanie affair, see Emile Pillias, "Études sur François II Rákóczi, Prince de Transylvanie, pendant son séjour en France," *Revue des études hongroises* 3–4 (1934): 280–301.

33 See Köpeczi, *La France et la Hongrie*, pp. 316–19.

34 The details regarding Patkul's entry into Russian service may be found in Ustrialov, *Istoriia* 4: 154–7. Ustrialov also provides a very informative overview of all the documentary sources relating to Patkul.

35 Ibid., p. 163.

36 For a detailed description of Patkul's arrest and execution see Erdmann, *Patkul*, pp. 209–79.

37 Ciobanu (*Cantemir în Rusia*, p. 391) claims that by 1712, of the original 4,000 Moldavian refugees, only 2,000 remained in Russia. For the conflicts between Cantemir and his boyars see Ciobanu, p. 390.

38 See Panaitescu, *Dimitrie Cantemir*, p. 136.

39 For Cantemir's praise of Peter I as the ideal absolutist ruler see V. Potlog, "D. Kantemir o vnutrennei i vneshnei politike Rossii i Ukraini xvii–nachala xviii vv.," *Uchenie zapiski* 117 (Kishinev 1971): 420–45.

40 Gyula Szekfü, *A Számüzött Rákóczi* (Budapest: A Magyar Tudományos Akademia Kiadása 1913), p. 165.

41 See Kálmán Thaly, *De Saussure Czézarnak* (Budapest 1909), pp. 156–7, for the conditions of Rákóczi's stay in Rodosto. Also see Imre Karacson *A Rákóczi emigració török okmányai, 1717–1803* (Budapest 1911), p. 9, n. 2, for the Ottomans' use of the royal title when referring to Rákóczi.

42 Szekfü, *Rákóczi*, p. 297.

43 Ibid., p. 315.

44 Ibid., p. 208.

45 Ibid., p. 297.

46 Ibid., p. 320, for details of the Bohn episode.

47 During his stay in Salonika Orlyk kept a detailed dairy in which he also kept copies of his voluminous correspondence. For a discussion of this fascinating source see Orest Subtelny, "From the Diary of Pylyp Orlyk," *Ukrainskyi Istoryk* 12 (1971): 95–105. The original may be found in Diariusz. In his diary Orlyk notes that his subsidy from the Porte was 120 talers per month.

48 Diariusz 8: 66–7, 85–6, 106, 115, 121. Rákóczi and Orlyk also shared a common correspondent in the person of Father Cachod, a Jesuit based in Istanbul. The latter regularly reported whatever he learned from the two émigrés to Dirling, the Austrian ambassador at the Porte.

49 For Orlyk's correspondence with the duke of Holstein and General Sztenflicht see Diariusz 8: 121–3.

50 Feldman, *Stanisław Leszczysnki*, p. 116.

51 Leszczynski's entourage included his wife, his aged mother, and two daughters, plus several ladies-in-waiting. There were also five to six officers, Michal Tarlo, the former palatine of Lublin, Baron Stanisław Meszek, two to three servants, and two priests. Altogether his entourage consisted of about twelve to fifteen persons. See Pierre Boyé, *Stanislaus Leszczynski et le troisième traité de Vienne* (Paris: Berger Levrault 1898), p. 32. For funds Leszczynski depended on the 100,000 écus that Charles XII promised to give him with the conclusion of peace. But after the king's death the Swedish ministers were loath to provide this sum. Only in 1723 did Sweden provide him with a modest pension of 30,000 écus annually. France also provided some funds.

52 Feldman, *Stanisław Leszczynski*, p. 22.

53 Authors who stress this aspect are Feldman, *Leszczynski*, and Pierre Boyé, especially in his *Le marriage de Marie Leszczynski et l'Europe* (Nancy, Paris, and Strasburg: Berger-Levrault 1939).

54 For a recent study of this issue see Emanuel Rostworowski, *O polską koronę* (Wrocław and Cracow: Ossolineum 1958), pp. 9–49.

55 Panaitescu, *Dimitrie Cantemir*, p. 140.

56 For a discussion of Cantemir's role as a propagandist and for texts of his manifestos see E. Lozovan, "D. Cantemir et l'expansion russe au Caucase (1722–1724)," *Revue des études roumaines* 13–14 (1974): 91–107. Also see Panaitescu, *Dimitrie Cantemir*, pp. 134–40.

57 Panaitescu, *Dimitrie Cantemir*, p. 141. Maria eventually returned to Peter I's favour. However, after his death Empress Catherine excluded her from the court, and she died a spinster in Moscow in 1757.

58 For an interesting discussion of the activities of Cantemir's nephew see E. Shulman, *Russko-moldavskoe boevoe sodruzhestvo, 1735–1739* (Kishinev: Shtiintsa 1962), pp. 21–51.

59 Panaitescu, *Dimitrie Cantemir*, p. 141.

60 See Rostworowski, *O polską koronę*, for a detailed study of Leszczynski's efforts to regain his crown.

61 Ibid., p. 80.

62 See Orlyk's Diariusz 9: 53.

63 Leszczynski to Orlyk, 19 February 1726, Diariusz 9: 61. For a more detailed treatment of this subject see Orest Subtelny, "Mazepists and Stanislavists: The First Ukrainian and Polish Emigrés," in Peter Potichnyj, ed., *Poland and Ukraine: Past and Present* (Edmonton: Canadian Institute of Ukrainian Studies 1980), pp. 83–97.

64 Diariusz 9: 132.

65 Leszczynski to Orlyk, 7 March 1727, Diariusz 9: 238.

66 Orlyk to Leszczynski, 7 March 1727, Diariusz 9: 249. Referring to this epistle, Orlyk noted in his diary, "Let no one be scandalized by what I wrote, for

politics demanded that I write thus in order that with the aid of God I might find a way out of this land."

67 For Rákóczi's ties with Leszczynski see Szekfü, *A Szamüzött Rákóczi*, pp. 325. Also see A.A. Kochubinskii, *Graf A.I. Ostermann i razdel Turtsii* (Odessa 1899), p. 24.

68 Szekfü, *A Szamüzött Rákóczi*, p.330.

69 See Köpeczi, *Confession et mémoires de Francois II Rákóczi*, p. 33.

70 See Rostworowski, *O polską koronę*, p. 213.

71 Hryhor Orlyk (1702–59) had been granted a commission in August II's army with the backing of Flemming. In October of 1729 he was secretly contacted by Leszczynski's old supporter József Potocki and by Antoine Monti, France's ambassador to Poland. They succeeded in persuading Orlyk to work for Leszczynski and the French. A not always reliable biography of Hryhor is Ilko Borshchak, *Velykyi Mazepynets: Hyrhor Orlyk* (Lviv: Chervona Kalyna 1932). Also see Rostworowski, *O polską koronę*, and his "Orlik, Grzegorz," *Polski słownik biograficzny* 24 (Warsaw 1979): 202–5.

72 For Orlyk's correspondence with the Zaporozhians and his attempts to warn them about Russian sovereignty, see Appolon Skalkovskii, "Filip Orlik i Zaporozhtsy," *Kievskaia starina* 4 (1882): 106–24.

73 Although Rákóczi did not have the available troops, he offered to send "his men" to aid Leszczynski during the siege of Gdansk. See Szekfü, *A Szamüzött Rákóczi*, p. 320. For Rákóczi's final years see Ignác Kont "Les dernières années de F. Rákóczi II," *Revue de Hongrie* 5 (1910): 32–46.

74 Feldman, *Leszczynski*, p. 162.

75 Anna Ivanovna to A.I. Shakhovskoi, 25 April 1734, SRIO, 108: 134.

76 For a brief overview of József Rákóczi's activities see Köpeczi and Várkonyi, *II Rákóczi Ferenc*, pp. 422–4; and Albert Vandal, *Une ambassade française en Orient sous Louis XV* (Paris: Plon Nourrit 1887), pp. 318–19.

77 Orlyk sent a copy of his letter to the grand vizier to Hryhor on 30 October 1738 (Archives du ministère des affaires étrangères, Paris: Pologne, 180: 227, 260).

78 The young Rákóczi's sudden death cast suspicion on his personal physician, who was jailed by the Ottomans. See Kochubinskii, *Graf Osterman*, p. 420, n. 1.

79 Ibid., p. xxxvi.

80 Castellane to the French foreign ministry, 7 June 1742, cited in E. Hurmuzaki, *Documente privitore la istoria Romanilor*, suppl. 1, vol. 1 (Bucharest 1886), p. 569.

81 Rostworowski, *Polski słownik biograficzny* 24: 204.

82 Studies dealing with Cantemir's scholarly works are numerous, especially as the 300th anniversary of his birth was recently and widely celebrated. See K. Korbu and L. Chobanu, eds., *Nasledie Dmitriia Kantemira i sovremennost* (Kishinev: Kartia Moldoveniaske 1976); a special issue dedicated to Cantemir's scholarship is *Dimitrie Cantemir*, *Sitzungsberichte der Akademie der Wissenschaften der DDR* 13 (1974): 1–95; also see Panaitescu, *Dimitrie Cantemir*, and his "Le prince Démètre Cantemir et le mouvement intellectuelle russe sous Pierre le Grand," *Revue des études slaves* 6 (1926): 249–55. Also useful is V.N. Ermuratskii, *Dmitrii*

Kantemir: myslitel i gosudarstvennyi deiatel (Kishinev: Kartia Moldoveniaske 1973). For a brief English-language treatment of the subject see S. Callimachi, *Demetrius Cantemir* (Bucharest 1966). A bibliography of Cantemir's works may be found in Constantin Şerban, "Démètre Cantemir dans l'historiographie roumaine et étrangère," *Revue roumaine d'histoire* 12 (1973): 919–45.

83   For Leszczynski's reign in Lorraine and Bar see Boyé, *Stanislaus Leszczynski et le troisième traité de Vienne*. This French author is at times overly critical of the king-in-exile.

84   For Leszczynski's published works see *Oeuvres du philosophe bienfaisant*, 4 vols. (Paris 1764). An analysis of his political writings may be found in Jadwiga Lechicka, *Rola dziejowa Stanisława Leszczynskiego oraz wybor z jego pism* (Torun: Towarżystwo Naukowe 1951); Witold Zakrżewski, "Proba analizy porównawczej pogladow polityczno-spolecznych: Montesquieu a Leszczynski," *Kwartalnik historii nauki i techniki* (1956), pp. 685–714; Jean Fabre, "Stanislas Leszczynski et le mouvement philosophique en France au XVIIIe siècle," and Emanuel Rostworowski, "Stanislas Leszczynski et les lumières à la polonaise," both in P. Francastel, ed., *Utopie et institution au XVIIIe siècle* (Paris and The Hague 1963), pp. 2–15; K.M. Dziewanowski, "King Stanisław Leszczynski: Some Remarks and Question Marks," *Jahrbücher für Geschichte Osteuropas* 16 (1968): 104–16.

85   There has been some debate about Leszczynski's authorship of the *Głos wolny*. Boyé has argued that the king's French secretary, Solignac, composed most of the work. Modern Polish scholarship has disproved this view. See Emanuel Rostworowski, *Legendy i fakty XVIII w.* (Warsaw: PWN 1963), pp. 67–125. The text of the work is in Stanisław Leszczynski, *Głos wolny wolność ubezpieczający* (Cracow: Biblioteka Polska 1858).

86   For a discussion of this proposal see Emanuel Rostworowski, "Stanisław Leszczynski – Republikanin Pacyfista," *Kwartalnik Historyczny* 74 (1967): 1–19. See also Eleanor Schlimgen, "Stanisław Leszczynski, Reformer in Exile," *Bulletin of the Polish Institute of Arts and Sciences in America* 3 (1945): 621–47.

87   Köpeczi and Várkonyi, *II Rákóczi Ferenc*, p. 369.

88   Rákóczi's views, as expressed in his writings, may be found in Szekfü, *A Szamüzött Rákóczi*, pp. 369–77, and in Köpeczi and Várkonyi, *II Rákóczi Ferenc*, pp. 369–77.

89   Among Rákóczi's followers in exile was Klemen Mikes, who played an important role in the development of literary Hungarian. See Joseph Remenyi, "Klemen Mikes, Hungarian Exile (1690–1761)," *Symposium* II (1957): 123–6.

90   See Carl Schirren, "Patkul and Leibniz," *Mittheilungen aus der Livlandischen Geschichte* 13 (1884): 435–45.

91   The best-known of these pamphlets is the *Deduction der Unschuld* (Leipzig 1701). For a survey of Patkul's writings see Johann v. Recke and Karl Napiersky, eds., *Allgemeines Schriftsteller und Gelehrten Lexikon der Provinzen Livland, Esthland un Kurland*, vol. 3 (Mitau: Steffenhagen 1831), pp. 382–5.

92   For a discussion of Orlyk as a bibliophile see Ilko Borshchak, "Pylyp Orlyk – Knyzhnyk," *Bibliografichni visti* 2–3 (Kiev 1929): 48–54. The article also contains

a list of books in the *hetman*-in-exile's private library. Also see Ilko Borshchak, "V knyhozbirni hetmana Orlyka," *Literaturno-naukovyi zbirnyk* (1923), pp. 260–6. An English translation of Orlyk's letter to Iavorsky constitutes the appendix of my study *The Mazepists*, pp. 178–205. For a description of Orlyk's diary see my article "From the Diary of Pylyp Orlyk," pp. 95–104.

93 See n. 47.

94 See Rostworowski, "Orlik, Grzegorż," *Polski słownik biograficzny*. Also see Ilko Borshchak's interesting but often inaccurate *Hryhor Orlyk*. It is noteworthy that Voltaire was quite aware of the similarities in the position of the East European émigrés and compared the plight of Patkul, Cantemir, and Mazepa; see *Russia under Peter the Great*, trans. Michael Jenkins (Rutherford: Fairleigh Dickenson Press 1983), p. 161.

95 See Robert Williams, "European Political Emigrations: A Lost Subject," *Comparative Studies in Society and History* 12 (1970): 140.

96 Everett Stonequist, *The Marginal Man. A Study in Personality and Culture Conflict* (Chicago and Boston: Scribners 1937), p. xvii. In connection with this concept see Várkonyi, "Historical Personality, Crisis and Progress in 17th Century Hungary," *Studia Historica* 71 (1970): 265–99.

97 Stonequist, *Marginal Man*, p. 154.

Bibliographical and Historiographical Essay

This essay is not meant to be a comprehensive listing of all the works utilized in this study or an in-depth analysis of the relevant historiographical trends in East European history. Rather, its goal is to note some of the important issues related to this study, to sketch the approaches used in dealing with them, and to enumerate where possible the recent Western-language works that provide unique insights and informtion.

I

The perception of East European history as a distinct category of European history developed in the 1920s and 1930s. Elaborating on ideas which he had expressed earlier, the Czech historian Jaroslav Bidlo argued in his seminal article "Ce qu'est l'histoire de l'Orient européen" (*Bulletin d'information des sciences historiques en Europe orientale* 6 [1934]: 82–93) that the Eastern part of Europe was distinguished by its cultural features and specifically by the confrontation within the region of Roman Latin and Byzantine Orthodox cultural spheres. Responding to Bidlo, the Polish historian Oscar Halecki wrote "Der Begriff des osteuropäischen Geschichte" (*Zeitschrift für osteuropäische Geschichte*, n.s., 5 [1934]: 1–21) and later expanded his views in his well-known book *The Limits and Divisions of European History* (London and New York: Sheed & Ward 1950). Halecki's contention, based primarily on the study of intellectual history, was that while Eastern Europe had a frontier relationship with Europe, it was none the less an organic part of it. A useful survey of this scholarly discussion, and particularly of the contributions of German scholars to it, may be found in Klaus Zernack, *Osteuropa: Eine Einführung in seine Geschichte* (Munich: Beck 1977).

The issue of East European distinctiveness, especially in the early modern period, was revived in the 1960s and 1970s. Not surprisingly, the region's Marxist scholars focused their attention on Eastern Europe's economic history. Specifically, they concentrated on its economic detour into agrarianism, which evolved in the sixteenth century and characterized the region until modern times. The noted Polish economic historian Marian Małowist, a pioneer in this area of study, has written what is perhaps the most complete study of Eastern Europe's unique economic development, *Wschód a Zachód Evropy w XII–XVI wieku: Konfrontacja struktur spoleczno-gospodarczych* (Eastern and Western Europe in the XII–XVI centuries: The confrontation of socio-economic structures [Wrocław: Ossolineum 1973]). Many of the works of East European economic historians have been made available in Western languages. Some of the more important of these are Jerzy Topolski, "Causes of the Dualism in the Economic Development of Modern Europe" (*Studia Historiae Oeconomicae* 3 [1968]: 3–12); Zsigmond Pach, "The Shifting of International Trade Routes in the 15–17th Centuries" (*Acta Historica* 14 [Budapest 1968]: 287–321); Stanisław Hoszowski, "Central Europe and the Price Revolution" (in *Economy and Society in Early Modern Europe*, ed. Peter Burke [New York 1968], pp. 85–103). Also see Witold Kula, *Theorie économique du systeme féodal: pour un modèle de l'économie polonaise, 16ᵉ–18ᵉ siècles* (Paris: Mouton 1970). The peripheral and colonial nature of the East European economy as it related to the West European "core" has been discussed in the global context by Immanuel Wallerstein in his two-volume work *The Modern World System* (New York and London: Academic Press 1974, 1980). One of the major socio-economic consequences of Eastern Europe's economic detour was the renewed enserfment of the peasantry of the region. As might be expected, this topic has been studied exhaustively by Marxist scholars. A useful overview of their work may be found in *Slavic Review* 34 (1975): 225–79.

While East European scholars concentrated on their region's socio-economic peculiarities, several West European specialists have attempted to develop generalizations about its political characteristics. For example, Gordon East, in "The Concept and Political Status of the Shatter Zone" (in *Geographical Essays on Eastern Europe*, ed. Norman Pounds [Bloomington: University of Indiana Press 1961], pp. 1–23), and Hugh Seton-Watson, in *The "Sick-Heart" of Modern Europe* (Seattle and London: University of Washington Press 1975), stress the unusually high degree of instability and conflict that has typified the region in the twentieth century. The present study is also an attempt to underscore the common political features of Eastern European countries in the early modern period.

II

Among the many studies of elites Gerhard Lenski's *Power and Privilege* (Chapel Hill: University of North Carolina Press 1965) is one of the most enlightening. Some of Lenski's fruitful ideas regarding elites in pre-modern and agrarian societies have been recently elaborated by John Kautsky in *The Politics of Aristocratic Empires* (Chapel Hill: University of North Carolina Press 1982). Turning to the nobilities of Eastern Europe, one finds numerous studies of the well-established and powerful Polish and Hungarian nobilities. By way of introduction the somewhat dated essays on the Polish and Hungarian nobilities in A. Goodwin, *The European Nobility in the Eighteenth Century* (London: Black 1953), are still useful. A fascinating discussion of the Polish *szlachta* may be found in Norman Davies, *God's Playground: A History of Poland* ([Oxford: Oxford University Press 1982], vol. 1). An overview of the recent research on the Polish nobility is available in *Études sur la noblesse*, a French-language issue of *Acta Poloniae Historica*

36 (1977). Recent studies of the Hungarian nobility may be found in *Noblesse française, noblesse hongroise* XVIe-XIXe siècles (ed. Béla Köpeczi and Eva Balázs [Budapest: Akademiai Kiadó 1981]). Thorough surveys of these two elites are also provided in Dietrich Gerhard, *Ständische Vertretungen in Europa 17 und 18 Jahrhunderts* (Göttingen 1970). Although it concentrates on a somewhat later period, Béla Király's *Hungary in the Late Eighteenth Century* (New York: Columbia University Press 1969) provides a good description of the noble-dominated society. Also see Andrżej Kaminski, "The *Szlachta* of the Polish-Lithuanian Commonwealth and Their Government" (in *The Nobility in Russia and Eastern Europe*, ed. Ivo Banac and Paul Bushkovitch [New Haven: Yale Russian and East European Publications 1983], pp. 17–46).

Works on the Livonian *ritterschaft* are relatively few and seriously dated. This is because Estonian and Latvian scholars, since the expulsion of the Germans from the Baltic countries, have shown little interest in the topic. A brief, informative survey of the development of the Livonian elite may be found in the work of the noted Baltic German historian Reinhard Wittram, *Baltische Geschichte* (Munich: Oldenburg 1970). The classic study of the *ritterschaft* is Alexander v. Tobien's *Die Livländische Ritterschaft* (Riga: Löffler 1925).

Compared to the Polish, Hungarian, and Livonian nobilities, the elites of Moldavia and post-1648 Left Bank Ukraine have been little studied. On the one hand, the relative impact and influence of the latter two elites was relatively less than those of the former three; on the other, populist and socialist ideological influences among Ukrainian and Romanian historians dampened their interest in the study of native elites. Among the few Western-language studies of the Moldavian nobility are the following: D. Ciurea, "Quelques considerations sur la noblesse féodale chez les roumains" (*Nouvelles études d'histoire publiées à l'occasion du XIIe congrès des sciences historiques, Vienne, 1965* [Bucharest 1965], pp. 83–92), and Vlad Georgescu, "The Romanian Boyars in the 18th Century: Their Political Ideology" (*East European Quarterly* 7 [1973]: 31–40). In the Ukrainian case the study of the Cossack elite has been totally ignored in Soviet Ukraine for obvious political and ideological reasons. In recent decades the only serious studies on the post-1648 Ukrainian elite have been those of Zenon Kohut. The latter's unpublished PH D dissertation, "The Abolition of Ukrainian Autonomy (1763–1786)" (University of Pennsylvania 1975), provides a concise overview of the evolution of this elite, and his articles "Problems in Studying the Post-Khmelnytsky Ukrainian Elite (1650s to 1830s)" (in *Rethinking Ukrainian History*, ed. Ivan L. Rudnytsky [Edmonton: CIUS 1981], pp. 103–19) and "The Ukrainian Elite in the Eighteenth Century and Its Integration into the Russian Nobility" (in the above-mentioned *The Nobility in Russia and Eastern Europe*, pp. 65–98) are most enlightening.

III

Since the evolution of absolutism in Eastern Europe was essentially the evolution of modern state building, albeit by extraregional powers, literature on the state and its origins is of central concern in the present study. Much of the seminal work in tracing the origins and properties of the evolving state has been done by German scholars. Among their many important contributions to this central issue are the following three articles: Walther Näf, "Frühformen des 'modernen Staates' im Spätmittlealter" (*Historische Zeitschrift* 37 [1951]: 225–43); Otto Hintze, "Wesen und Wandlung des modernen Staates" (*Sitzungsberichte der preussische Akademie der Wissenschaften Philosophisch-historische Klasse* [1931], pp. 790–810); and Otto Brunner, *Land und Herrschaft* (Brünn; Munich, and Vienna 1943). A main thrust of these works is that the modern state is a product of early modern Europe. A good survey of the problem may be found in J.H. Shennan, *The Origins of the Modern European State* (London: Hutchinson University Library 1974). The issue of how the various models of the modern state may be applied to early modern Eastern Europe has been treated by Gunter Stökl with his usual depth and broadness of scope in "Die Wurzeln des modernen Staates in Osteuropa" (in *Jahrbücher für Geschichte Osteuropas* 3 [1953]: 255–69).

Two decades ago William McNeill wrote his stimulating essay *Europe's Steppe Frontier, 1500–1800* (Chicago and London: University of Chicago Press 1964). Although his primary focus was the closure of the East European frontier by the "bureaucratic empires," McNeill also touched upon the nature of absolutism in Eastern Europe. His work indicated that a broad, comparative approach could be fruitfully applied to the study of the region's history. A major drawback, however, was the author's inability to utilize the literature and sources written in East European languages. Absolutism in Eastern Europe has also been treated recently in Perry Anderson's *The Lineages of the Absolutist State* (London: NLB 1974). One of the strong points of this important work is that it draws the necessary distinction between absolutism in Western and in Eastern Europe. However, its dependence on Marxist analysis leads the author to identify the absolutist state solely with the socio-economic interests of the nobility and to ignore the conflict between the political values and system of the absolutist state on the one hand and that of the East European nobility on the other.

There is an adequate number of Western-language studies of the individual absolutist empires and states which moved into Eastern Europe. For a discussion of the political principles and practices upon which the Ottoman empire was founded and developed, Halil Inalcik's *The Ottoman Empire: The Classical Age, 1300–1600* (New York: Praeger 1973) is most useful. More detailed analyses of Ottoman expansion into the Balkans in general and Moldavia in particular may be found in Peter Sugar, *South Eastern Europe under Ottoman Rule, 1354–1804* (Seattle: University of Washington Press 1977), Halil Inalcik, "Ottoman Methods of Conquest" (*Studia Islamica* 2 [1954]: 1103–30), and Keith Hitchens, "Ottoman Domination of Moldavia and Wallachia in the 16th Century" (*Asian Studies* 1 [1966]: 123–41).

Sweden's empire building is not a popular topic with Swedish historians today. Among the relatively few modern studies in this field, especially noteworthy is Sven Lundkvist, "The Experience of Empire: Sweden as a Great Power," in the excellent collection *Sweden's Age of Greatness, 1632–1718*, edited by Michael Roberts (New York: Macmillan 1973). Among the several general histories of the Habsburg empire Victor-Lucien Tapie's *The Rise and Fall of the Habsburg Monarchy* (Paris: Praeger 1969) stands out for its felicitous combination of narrative and analysis. The classic work on the golden age of Habsburg absolutism is Oswald Redlich's *Weltmacht des Barock: Österreich in der Zeit Kaiser Leopolds I* (Vienna: Rohrer 1961). Recent Hungarian scholarship has produced several insightful socio-economic analyses of Habsburg absolutism's expansionism into Hungary. Among these are Laszlo Makkai, "Die Entstehung der gesellschaftlichen Basis des Absolutismus in den Ländern der österreichischen Habsburger" (*Studia Historica Academiae Scientiarum Hungaricae* 43 [1960]: 3–41), and Ágnes Várkonyi, "Habsburg Absolutism and Serfdom in Hungary at the Turn of the 17th and 18th Centuries" (*Nouvelles études historiques publiées à l'occasion du xiie congrès international des sciences historiques* I [Budapest 1965]: 335–87). The theoretical basis for the establishment of absolutism in Hungary is examined by the French historian Jean Berenger in "Les fondements théoriques de l'absolutisme dans la Hongrie du xviie siècle (*Mélanges offerts à Aurelien Sauageot pour son soixante-quinzième anniversaire* [Budapest 1973], pp. 23–8).

A most interesting and lively discussion of absolutism developed in the USSR in the late 1960s and early 1970s. Basically, the main issue of this discussion was to evaluate the relevance of the generalizations of Marx, Engels, and Lenin on the topic of absolutism to Russian historical reality. The debate was sparked by A. Ia. Averech's unusual challenge to Marxist orthodoxy. Specifically, the Soviet historian argued that Marx's contention that absolutism resulted from the balance of power between the entrenched nobility and the emerging bourgeoisie was not applicable to Russia because in the early modern period the Russian bourgeoisie was practically non-existent. Although this ideologically explosive issue was left unresolved after much debate, it did lead to an exceedingly fruitful discussion of the nature of Russian absolutism. For a summary of this controversy see Thomas Esper, "Recent Soviet Views on Russian Absolutism" (*Canadian-American Slavic Studies* 6 [1972]: 620–30). An exceptionally enlightening and persuasive treatment of the Russian political tradition is Richard Pipes, *Russia Under the Old Regime* (New York: Scribners 1974). Pipes is especially effective in tracing how old Muscovite autocracy, based on patrimonialism, adopted the new European absolutist forms during the reign of Peter I. The introduction of Russian absolutist reforms in Left Bank Ukraine is treated in my article "Russia and the Ukraine: The Difference that Peter I Made" (*Russian Review* 39 [1980]: 1–17).

Although studies of the Saxon attempts to introduce absolutism in Poland-Lithuania are relatively few, those which are available are of high quality. The leading specialist on this subject is the Polish historian Józef Gierowski. In addition to his numerous and thorough Polish-language studies, together with Johannes Kalisch he also edited *Um die polnische Krone* (Berlin: Bütten & Loening 1962), an excellent collection of studies of August II's absolutist plans and policies in the Commonwealth. An introduction to Gierowski's views on this topic may be found in his "Centralization and Autonomy in the Polish-Saxon Union" (*Harvard Ukrainian Studies* 3–4 [1979–80]: 271–84).

IV

There seems to be no end to books on revolution. Not only have historians and other scholars devoted much attention to the topic within the context of the twentieth century, but, primarily under the influence of English historiography, they have sought to find revolution in early modern Europe. The first major survey of the cluster of mid-seventeenth-century upheavals was R.B. Merriman's somewhat dated *Six Contemporaneous Revolutions* (Oxford: Oxford University Press 1938). In the 1960s and 1970s the discussion of widespread upheaval, formulated in terms of "the crisis of the seventeenth century," was stimulated by the work of H.R. Trevor-Roper and E.J. Hobsbawn. Their contributions, as well as other important studies on the topic, may be found in *Crisis in Europe, 1560–1660* (London: Routledge and Kegan Paul 1965). The most sophisticated, comprehensive, and systematic study of revolution and crisis in early modern Western Europe has appeared recently in the work of Perez Zagorin, *Rebels and Rulers, 1500–1660* (2 vols. [Cambridge: Cambridge University Press 1982]).

Eager to extend their generalizations about early modern revolution, Western historians since the 1960s have looked to Eastern Europe with unprecedented interest. They did find several major upheavals there in the seventeenth century, notably the Ukrainian uprising of 1648 and the Razin revolt of 1670 in Russia. However, these revolts, very different from each other, were both directed primarily against oppressive nobilities. As such they did not fit well into the pattern of anti-royalist uprisings in the West. For examples of this attempt to relate revolutions in Eastern and Western Europe to each other, see *Preconditions of Revolution in Early Modern Europe*, edited by Robert Forster and Jack Greene (Baltimore and London: Johns Hopkins Press 1970).

Modern East European scholars have been slow to view their region in terms of a general crisis. On the one hand the intense nationalism of the interwar period encouraged national compartmentalization, which dominated the work of East European historians longer than it did that of their Western colleagues. On the other hand ideological strictures imposed upon East European scholars discouraged the development of non-Marxist models, especially for the early modern period. One of the few works that does attempt to sketch the political features of Eastern Europe during this period is Józef Gierowski's brief article "L'Europe centrale au xviie siècle et ses principales tendances politiques" (in *xiii congrès international des sciences historiques* [Moscow 1970], pp. 1–15). But while they have ignored the region-wide crisis of the nobiliary political system and the widespread imposition of foreign absolutism, East European historians have studied and in some cases glorified the individual anti-absolutist conflicts. Often, quite anachronistically, they have viewed them as "progressive" national-liberation struggles rather than as noble insurrections and conspiracies.

Two excellent studies of Livonian resistance led by Johann Reinhold von Patkul against Swedish absolutism are available. They are Reinhard Wittram, "Patkul und der Ausbruch des Nordischen Krieges" (*Nachrichten der Akademie der Wissenschaften in Göttingen, Philo-Historische Klasse* 9 [1952]: 201–32), and Arvid von Taube, "Von ständischer Liberalität zu nationaler Selbstbehauptung. J.R.v. Patkul im baltisch-deutschen Geschichtsbild" (*Zeitschrift für Ostforschung* 4 [1957]: 481–510). The Western-language work which deals best with the conflict between Saxon absolutism and Polish republicanism is the aforementioned *Um die polnische Krone. Sachsen und Polen während des Nordischen Krieges*. Ukrainian resistance to Russian absolutism is treated in my work *The Mazepists: Ukrainian Separatism in the Early Eighteenth Century* (Boulder: East European Monographs 1981). A detailed examination of Mazepa's political values as opposed to those of Peter I may be found in my "Mazepa, Peter I and the Question of Treason" (*Harvard Ukrain-*

ian Studies 2 [1978]: 158–83). Among the few non-Romanian-language studies of Cantemir's uprising against the Ottomans are F. Constaniniu, "La politique étrangère de Dimitrie Cantemir: analyse d'une décision" (*Revue roumaine d'études internationales* VII [1973]: 110–29), and Demetrius Dvoichenko-Markov, "Demetrius Kantemir and Russia" (*Balkan Studies* 12 [1971]: 383–98).

Because the Hungarian war led by Rákóczi against the Habsurgs involved relatively large numbers of Hungarian peasants, it can be treated by Hungarian Marxist historians as a progressive liberation struggle. This consideration, as well as the historical importance of the conflict itself and the celebration of the three-hundredth anniversary of Rákóczi's birth, account for the recent spate of works about his struggle. Two modern Hungarian historians, R. Ágnes Várkonyi and Béla Köpeczi, have produced some of the most important recent studies of the Rákóczi revolt. The former has concentrated primarily on its internal aspects. Two of Várkonyi's thoughtful articles are "Habsurg Absolutism and Serfdom in Hungary at the Turn of the XVIIth and XVIIIth Centuries" (*Nouvelles études historiques* I [Budapest 1965]: 359–85) and "Evolution sociale et autonomie de l'état: L'absolutisme des Habsbourg et l'indépendance de la Hongrie" (*Acta Historica Academiae Scientiarum Hungaricae* 22 [1976]: 343–65). For a recent study of the military aspects of the war see the article by the American scholar Charles Ingrao, "Guerrilla Warfare in Early Modern Europe: The *Kuruc* War (1703–1711)" (in *War and Society in East Central Europe*, ed. Béla Király and Gunther Rothenberg, vol. 1 [New York: Brooklyn College Press 1979], pp. 47–66). Given the importance of foreign powers and diplomatic projects during the 1703–11 period, studies about Rákóczi's foreign relations are especially plentiful. The most noteworthy is Béla Köpeczi's *La France et la Hongrie au début du XVIIIᵉ siécle* (Budapest: Akademiai Kiadó 1971). Other recent studies of Rákóczi's far-ranging foreign relations are Linda Frey and Marsha Frey, "The Rákóczi Insurrection and the Disruption of the Grand Alliance" (in *Canadian-American Review of Hungarian Studies* 5 [1978]: 17–30); Béla Király and Peter Pastor, "The Sublime Porte and Ferencz II Rákóczi's Hungary" (in *The Mutual Effects of the Islamic and Judeo-Christian Worlds: The East European Pattern*, ed. Abraham Ascher et al. [New York: Brooklyn College Press 1979], pp. 129–48); Peter Pastor, "Hungarian-Russian Relations during the Rákóczi War of Independence" (in *War and Society in Eastern Central Europe*, ed. János Bak and Béla Király, vol. 2 [New York: Brooklyn College press 1982], pp. 467–92).

V

Historians generally lose interest in lost causes. Yet the rebel leaders whom we have discussed provide a striking exception to this rule. All of them occupy extremely important, even towering positions in their national historiographies. This is because, with the emergence of nationalism and heightened historical consciousness in the nineteenth century, they became symbols (with the exception of Leszczynski) of the struggle of their respective nations against foreign rule. Thus, in 1869, in his famous *Livländische Antwort*, the noted Livonian historian Carl Schirren summoned up a deified image of Patkul, calling him "Livonia's greatest son" and daringly citing his deeds as an example of what must be done if Livonia's traditional rights were threatened by Russia. In Hungary a demonstration of national self-confidence occurred after the Ausgleich of 1867 when, with great pomp and circumstance, the bones of Rákóczi were brought back from Rodosto. On the two-hundredth anniversary of Cantemir's birth a great flurry of publications reintroduced him to his countrymen. And in 1918, after the Russian empire had crumbled, the Ukrainians ceremoniously removed the anathema that had been placed upon Mazepa and made plans to bring his remains back to Kiev.

An overview of the vast literature which deals with the rebel leaders may be found in the following works: for Rákóczi, see Béla Köpeczi, "Jugements des historiens" (in his *La France et la Hongrie*, pp. 321–55); for Patkul, see Reinhard Wittram's abovementioned "Zur Beurteilung J.R.v. Patkul"; for Cantemir, see C. Şerban, "Demetrie Cantemir dans l'historiographie roumaine et étrangère" (*Revue roumaine d'histoire* XII [1973]: 919–45); for Mazepa, see Dmytro Doroshenko, *Mazepa* (vol. 1 of *Pratsi Ukrainskoho Naukovoho Instytutu* [Warsaw 1938], pp. 3–34); for Leszczynski, see J. Lechicka, *Rola dziejowa Stanisława Leszczynskiego oraz wybór z jego pism* ([Torun 1959], pp. 1–8). A most stimulating and perceptive discussion of émigré politics in general may be found in Hans Henning Hahn, "Möglichkeiten und Formen politischen Handelns in der Emigration" (*Archiv für Sozial Geschichte* 23 [1983]: 123–61).

Not only historians but poets, novelists, composers, and dramatists all over nineteenth-century Europe were fascinated by the real or alleged exploits of Mazepa, Patkul, Rákóczi, and Cantemir. The Ukrainian *hetman* was a special favourite. Byron, Hugo, Pushkin, Ryleev, Slowacki, Liszt, and Tchaikovsky made him the subject of their works. A detailed analysis of the dramatization of Mazepa may be found in Hubert Babinski, *The Mazeppa Legend in European Romanticism* (New York: Columbia University Press 1974). Patkul and Rákóczi were also the subjects of numerous poems, novels, and dramas. In our time the Soviet literary and film industries have churned out several productions glorifying Cantemir and emphasizing his ties with Russia.

For historians whose sympathies lay with the absolutist empires, the idealization of the rebel leaders was a challenge that could not be ignored. They responded by stressing in their works the rebels' personal failings, egotistical motives, and treasonous behaviour. In Russia, for example, pro-imperial writers made every effort to make Mazepa's name synonymous with treason. Even some nationalist historians took exception to the uncritical adulation which their countrymen showered on the nobiliary leaders. The most notable example was Gyula Szekfü's study of Rákóczi in exile, which appeared under the title *A Szamüzött Rákóczi* (Budapest: Magyar Tudományos Akademia Kiadása 1913). Instead of repeating the widely accepted descriptions of Rákóczi as "a prince of liberty," descriptions propagated by Kálmán Thaly and his disciples (Thaly proudly called himself the "court scribe" of the Rákóczi cult), Szekfü came out with a thoroughly documented, vividly written portrait of a dejected émigré. He argued that Rákóczi's exile was not martyrdom for the nation but merely an extension of his defeat: "The life of every exile is futile, useless for the interests of his country, since the reason for which he is exiled is precisely that the new order in this country cannot utilize the adherents of the previous regime and eases the situation by obliging them to leave" (p. 106). According to Szekfü, Hungarians were wrong to see Rákóczi as a beacon pointing to the future, for Rákóczi was nothing more than a "chunk of the petrified past." In the ensuing furor and attacks on Szekfü only the intervention of the universally respected statesman and scholar Count Julius Andrassy saved the career of the man who would go on to become one of modern Hungary's leading historians.

Romanian historians before the 1940s were similarly troubled by Cantemir. At the same time that they praised his efforts to cast off Ottoman rule and his contributions to Romanian culture, they criticized Cantemir for placing Moldavia under Russian overlordship. Nor, in the view of some Ukrainian historians, was Mazepa without fault; those who were populists found it difficult to accept as their national hero a man who was one of Ukraine's most acquisitive serf owners. In the case of Patkul, even as devoted an admirer as Schirren had second thoughts. Yet despite these reservations, the honoured place which had been accorded to the rebel leaders in their national historiographies remained secure. The reason for this was put most succinctly by Schirren. In explaining why he would not publish his less than laudatory findings about Patkul, Schirren stated that he "did not have the heart to take his countrymen's heroes from them."

After the Second World War the treatment of the noble leaders underwent a marked change. It was Rákóczi who fared best as the subject of historical research under the newly imposed Communist regimes. The ability of Hungarian historians to preserve this national symbol in a Communist system was facilitated by two "progressive" aspects of Rákóczi's career: his enlightened attitude towards the peasantry and his generally friendly relations with Russia. Cantemir too is looked upon with favour by Soviet, Romanian Communist, and émigré historians. In Soviet Moldavia much of this is because Soviet historians, since Moldavia's annexation to the USSR in 1940 have made Cantemir a symbol of the "eternal union" between the two lands. For Ukrainian émigré historians Mazepa continues to be a symbol of the struggle against Russia and for independent Ukrainian statehood. Soviet historians, meanwhile, denounce his "treachery" with monotonous regularity. They continuously emphasize the *hetman*'s two great sins – his anti-Russian and his elitist attitudes.

Only Leszczynski has been judged on the basis of his achievements rather than his symbolic stature. Many of Poland's leading historians, such as Kazimierz Jarochowski, Szymon Askenazy, Wadisław Konopczynski, Józef Feldman, Józef Gierowski, and Emanuel Rostworowski, have scrutinized his career. Few have been impressed with his achievements. Askenazy, for instance, considers him to be a "traditional *szlachta* romantic who could never grasp the concepts of modern statehood." But if they consider Leszczynski to have been such a mediocre figure, why have so many leading Polish historians devoted so much attention to him? No doubt, Leszczynski's important role in an era that marked the beginning of the end of Poland's sovereignty accounts for much of the interest. Furthermore, his biography is fascinating in itself. Finally, Leszczynski's policies and his reformist ideas emphasize a theme beloved of all Poles – the intimate ties of their homeland with Western Europe.

As is evident from this survey, it is not solely the needs of objective historical scholarship that explain the evolution of the study of the nobiliary leaders; it is also the demands of political ideology that have accounted for much of the attention and debate that have surrounded the study of the leaders of the East European nobilities in their struggle against foreign absolutism.

Index